STATUS *and* CULTURE

ALSO BY W. DAVID MARX

Ametora:
How Japan Saved American Style

STATUS
and
CULTURE

⊸✕⊸

How Our Desire for Social Rank
Creates Taste, Identity, Art, Fashion,
and Constant Change

⊸✕⊸

W. David Marx

VIKING

VIKING

An imprint of Penguin Random House LLC

penguinrandomhouse.com

LIBRARY OF CONGRESS CATALOGING-IN-PUBLICATION DATA

Names: Marx, W. David, author.
Title: Status and culture: how our desire for social rank creates taste,
identity, art, fashion, and constant change / W. David Marx.
Description: New York, NY: Viking, [2022] | Includes bibliographical references and index.
Identifiers: LCCN 2022006836 (print) | LCCN 2022006837 (ebook) |
ISBN 9780593296707 (hardcover) | ISBN 9780593296714 (ebook)
Subjects: LCSH: Social status. | Identity (Psychology) | Culture.
Classification: LCC HM821 .M379 2022 (print) | LCC HM821 (ebook) |
DDC 305—dc23/eng/20220216
LC record available at https://lccn.loc.gov/2022006836
LC ebook record available at https://lccn.loc.gov/2022006837

Printed in the United States of America
1st Printing

Book design by Daniel Lagin

For Geoffrey and Laura,
who gave me my first taste of taste

Contents

Part Four

STATUS AND CULTURE IN
THE TWENTY-FIRST CENTURY

THE GRAND MYSTERY OF CULTURE AND THE STATUS TABOO

Oh, how they laughed at Stu Sutcliffe's new haircut. Poor Stu had put aside his painting career in Liverpool to live in the most wretched corner of Hamburg, Germany, and play bass guitar in his mates' rock 'n' roll cover band with a silly pun-based name: the Beatles. And now those very Beatles—four Gene Vincent clones in pompadours held aloft with copious dollops of Brylcreem—were berating Stu for switching to a chic "Caesar cut" where the bangs fell straight down on his forehead.

The lads knew who to blame for Stu's sudden makeover: Astrid, his "existentialist" German girlfriend. She cut his hair to resemble the local art school boys, who were in turn imitating the latest French mode. Stu spent the next few days enduring constant japes for his coiffure, but then came an unexpected turn of events. The youngest Beatle, George, asked Astrid to cut his hair the same way. John and Paul capitulated several months later. While on vacation in Paris, they realized Stu's look would be necessary for picking up "Bohemian beauties on the Left Bank." But chasing tail was only an alibi: after time on the Continent, John and Paul had lost confidence in their British take on American swagger and now believed Stu's look would set them apart from the other English rock 'n' roll bands. Despite their initial mockery, the Beatles returned to Liverpool without Stu but wearing his distinctive "moptop."

With "near-baldness" being the hairstyling norm for men in England at the time, the Beatles' bangs loomed large in their legend. The *New York Times'* first-ever article about the group reported from the United Kingdom, "One shake of the bushy fringe of their identical, moplike haircuts is enough to start a riot in any theater where they are appearing." While young women loved the Beatles' hair, British adults found it "unsightly, unsafe, unruly, and unclean." Factories suspended young apprentices who dared to show up in a moptop.

As the Beatles planned their first visit to the United States in 1964, what had been mild British apprehension about shaggy hair escalated into full moral panic in America. University of Detroit students formed a Stamp Out the Beatles Society to protest the band's "un-American" haircuts. At the Beatles' first U.S. press conference, the media steered much of the conversation toward grooming. "Do you feel like Samson," asked one reporter, "[that] if you lost your hair, you'd lose what you have?" Another asked, "Are you going to get a haircut at all while you're here?" to which George Harrison offered the now famous rejoinder, "I had one yesterday." In the ensuing Beatlemania, companies pumped out fifteen thousand Beatles wigs a day, which TV hosts Ed Sullivan and Alfred Hitchcock plopped on their heads as a cheap gag.

At first young American men also scoffed at the "effeminate" moptop. But upon noticing the hairstyle's aphrodisiac effect on young American women, they decided it was time to grow out their crew cuts. As baby boomers brought moptops into their homes, the British invasion leaped from TV screens to suburbia. Parents hated it: a 1965 Gallup poll found that two-thirds of Americans opposed the Beatles cut. The eventual middle-class acceptance of longer hair on men came, argued LSD guru Timothy Leary, only with the prime-time television debut of *The Monkees*—an American clone of the Fab Four with "no controversy, no protest. No thinking strange, unique thoughts. No offending Mom and Dad and the advertisers." By 1968, parents calmed down, perhaps because such anguish over bushy fringes had become moot. A moptop looked eminently respectable compared with the Beatles' full-length hippie locks.

I was eight years old when I first encountered a photo of the Beatles' moptops, two full decades removed from the height of their infamy. At the time I lived in Oxford, Mississippi, an exceptionally tradition-minded town where parents still expected children to respond "Yes, sir" and "Yes, ma'am." When I saw the cassette cover for the compilation *The Beatles / 1962–1966*, I simply thought, *They look just like my brother and me.* Most young men in Oxford at the time wore their bangs down, not so different from Stu Sutcliffe in 1961. The

Beatles cut, which once divided nations and generations, had become profoundly ordinary even in the conservative South. As a kid I found it strange that such a conventional hairstyle could cause so much opprobrium. Today the outrage seems even more preposterous. The moptop has not just become normal but *classic*. In 2019, *GQ* noted it "looks just as good now as it did then."

Most of us know the story of the moptop and its backlash, but this familiarity may blind us to the odd human behaviors revealed therein. As with the moptop and thousands of the other micro social movements we call *trends*, humans hop en masse from one set of arbitrary practices to another, for elusive reasons. At first these minor stylistic differences engender terrible social friction—only to later win acceptance including the initial opponents. Later pundits herald the trends' originators as "icons" and "legends," and from there, formerly radical behaviors secure a place in our shared cultural heritage. Stu Sutcliffe decided to wear bangs one day and ended up creating a potent symbol of the era we call the early sixties.

These peculiarities of human behavior can be summarized in a broader enigma I like to call the Grand Mystery of Culture: *Why do humans collectively prefer certain practices, and then, years later, move on to alternatives for no practical reason?* As the undertaker Mr. Omer quips in *David Copperfield*, "Fashions are like human beings. They come in, nobody knows when, why, or how; and they go out, nobody knows when, why, or how."

By contrast technological change is very logical, as innovations provide greater efficiency and conveniences at lower costs. Our ancestors adopted the spinning wheel not as a "fad," but because it shortened the time required to twist fibers into yarn. From this perspective cultural change appears bizarre. What were Stu and his imitators hoping to accomplish with a moptop? What changed their taste? Neither evolutionary biology nor economics can explain this behavior—the moptop has no intrinsic value over other styles, nor offers more tactile pleasure. Was the moptop a form of self-expression? If so, how did everyone know what feeling this particular haircut expressed? And why would everyone seek to express the *same* emotions through the *same* haircut at the *same* time?

Unlike many other aspects of the human experience, there are still few authoritative answers on what alters our cultural preferences. A recent book trying to explain the mechanics of taste concluded by raising a white flag, dismissing changes over time as a "random walk" akin to the stock market's short-term fluctuations. For the last two decades, the most established theory of cultural change has cast it as "viral contagion," arguing that we succumb to fads like we contract the measles.

But cultural changes are never random, nor do they befall us as plagues. Trends happen because individuals choose to take up new behaviors. And when we examine the history of cultural change, there are clear *patterns* in how humans move from one practice to another. Sixty years before the moptop, social scientist William Graham Sumner seemingly predicted how it would rise and fall: "A new fashion of dress seems at first to be absurd, ungraceful, or indecent. After a time this first impression of it is so dulled that all conform to the fashion." In almost all instances, new behaviors begin as an exclusive practice of smaller social groups—whether elites or outsiders—and then eventually spread to the wider population. This is true for the diffusion of superficial hairstyles but also applies to things not considered "fashions": practical technologies like cars and hybrid seed corn, delicacies like chocolate and gin, political and spiritual beliefs, and the succession of artistic movements in modern art. The thing we call *culture* is always an aggregation of individual human behaviors, and if taste were the mere product of random idiosyncrasies and irrational psychologies, culture would display no patterns, only noise. The fact that preferences in these disparate fields follow a similar rhythm of change suggests there must be universal principles of human behavior at work—the presence of a "cultural gravity" nudging humans into the same collective behaviors at the same time.

For all the dismissal of cultural changes as superficial, they are central to our lived experience as humans. They define our identities and determine how others treat us. Every day we must make choices whether to follow social standards or "be ourselves." We come to find certain things "cool" without knowing why. We use markers of cultural change as touchstones for our past; embarrassing haircuts help us date old photos. The Beatles weren't just a band—they were *the band who wore moptops*. As we'll see by the end of this book, fashions explain behavioral change more than we've been willing to admit.

Ever since I discovered moptops as a child, I've been looking for answers to the Grand Mystery of Culture. During college, I made my first breakthroughs after examining how the Japanese street fashion brand A Bathing Ape amassed its cultlike fan base through a counterintuitive marketing strategy of hard-to-find stores, undersupplied products, and no advertising. Later, in graduate school, I focused my research on how economic systems affect the content of pop culture, looking specifically at whether monopolies in the music industry stymied artistic innovation. My first book, *Ametora*, followed the birth and growth of one particular cultural stream: how a single unorthodox business spread American style in postwar Japan, and decades later, Japanese clothing companies have come to influence Americans' sense of "traditional" apparel choices. And after working at a small independent magazine based in the Lower East Side and then overseeing Asia-wide communications for a multinational company in Tokyo, I have spent decades observing new trends in music, art, and fashion unfold in real time—all following the same classic pattern of rise and fall.

And yet, in all these long years of obsessively researching this topic, I never found a single book that explains the Grand Mystery of Culture. Over the centuries many wise scholars have uncovered critical insights about taste and cultural change, but they tend to be buried in turgid prose or minor corners of the academic literature. If I wanted this knowledge stitched together into a single coherent explanation, I would have to do it myself.

So as I began to synthesize all the significant theories and case studies to explain how culture works as a system and why culture changes over time, I realized that there was one key concept that links everything together—and that is *status*. The problem is: status itself has also long been a mystery.

What exactly do I mean by "status"? We use the word colloquially to describe an individual's position in an informal ranking of social importance. Every community has a status hierarchy, with the famous, powerful, and esteemed at the top; the majority of people in the middle; and the unfortunate, disadvantaged, and despised at the bottom. Our position in the hierarchy governs our daily experiences as individuals. If we have high status, things go well, people are nice to us, and we're relatively happier. If we lack status, we grow bitter and depressed. Sociological research demonstrates that our social position affects long-term well-being, motivates our behavior, and becomes a goal in its own right—and thus can be considered a fundamental human desire.

We seek status because it provides esteem and favors from others. But it's never easy to obtain. High status is a position within a hierarchy, so the more who seek to move up, the more difficult it becomes to reach the top. This inherent uncertainty puts many on a never-ending quest for higher position. Researchers recently concluded that the achievement of high status only makes people want more.

Despite the importance of status, there has been a conspicuous lack of discussion about its influence on human behavior. This stems, in part, from the fact that most people view stratification as a social ill. Philosophers beseech us to define ourselves without reference to others' judgments, while religious leaders implore us to contemplate a higher spiritual order. Advocates for democracy and socialism blame status hierarchies for societal dysfunction and struggle. The author Tom Wolfe concluded in the 1970s that status was the "fundamental taboo, more so than sexuality and everything of that sort. It's much easier for people to talk about their sex lives in this day and age than it is to talk about their status." Open discussion of social hierarchy is unpleasant and impolite. When the British novelist Nancy Mitford mused on the subtle differences between upper-class and middle-class speech in a 1955 essay, "unprintably violent" letters poured into her publisher's editorial office. This also explains why we dislike social climbers: they remind us there is a ladder to climb. In fact, the modern word "villain" derives from the status-related sin of lowly villein feudal tenants daring to seek a higher social position.

This collective unease with status has greatly impaired our ability to recognize its effects—and has held us back from solving the Grand Mystery of Culture. Once we understand status, cultural change is much less mysterious. Just as microeconomics posits that markets form as self-interested individuals maximize utility for their money, a similar "invisible-hand" mechanism exists between status and culture: in seeking to maximize and stabilize status, individuals end up clustering into patterns of behavior (customs, traditions, fashion, fads, taste) that we understand as *culture*.

This is not to say that culture exists only as a means to mark status. All status symbols rely on objects and behaviors with practical or aesthetic value that enrich our lives. Many bourgeois class-marking cultural standards promote rational behaviors with obvious health benefits—such as eating organic vegetables rather than prepackaged foods, and doing daily exercise rather than watching endless hours of television. The radical art used in elite distinction is emotionally rewarding and spiritually invigorating. Culture makes possible human self-understanding, complex thinking, and creative expression.

But as we'll see, status and culture are so intertwined that we can't understand how culture works without understanding status. And the best way to understand the status structures of society is to observe how they manifest in cultural patterns. The idea of their inexorable linkage dates back at least to the economist Thorstein Veblen's writings about conspicuous consumption in the Gilded Age, in which he posited that wealthy people buy expensive things to reveal they *can* buy expensive things. But the interactions go much deeper: Status shapes our aspirations and desires, sets standards for beauty and goodness, frames our identities, creates collective behaviors and morals, encourages the invention of new aesthetic sensibilities, and acts as an automated motor for permanent cultural change. Culture is embodied in the products, behaviors, styles, meanings, values, and sensibilities that make up the human experience—and it is status that guides their creation, production, and diffusion.

The principles of status and culture we'll uncover in this book provide us an invaluable toolbox for analyzing the world around us. We'll gain new clarity on old questions of taste, authenticity, identity, class, subcultures, art, fashion, fads, media influence, retro, and canons. And these lessons help us decode the latest trends, explain topical issues of "identity," and propose a common language for cultural critique. These principles aren't just important because culture plays a major role in our lives, but because the parts of life we believe transcend culture—technology, personal beliefs, and judgments of beauty—also get swept up in the vagaries of fashion.

These analytic tools are particularly helpful for addressing a pressing concern of the moment: Why does internet culture often feel *less valuable* than what we experienced in the analog world? Why does everything seem *less cool* than before?

The reasons are much clearer when viewed through the lens of how the internet has changed status signaling. Where we once pleaded for status in person (or through media reporting of real-life appearances at social events), there is now a twenty-four-hour, seven-day-a-week pageant of flexing on social media apps. Elites could once protect their status symbols behind information barriers and exclusive access to products; now nearly everything is available to nearly everyone. Meanwhile, the fragmentation of culture into the "long tail" has diluted the power of taste to serve as an effective means of social exclusion. And the inherent hyperspeed of the internet means fashion cycles pump out ephemeral fads rather than era-defining trends. Subcultures once provided society with a constant stream of cultural innovations, but the most notable outsider group of the twenty-first century has been the internet trolls rebelling against diversity, equity, and inclusion through revanchist slogans and memes.

Taken together, the changes to the status structure are conspiring against the widespread adoption of new cultural trends at the same frequency we experienced in the twentieth century. Many feel we've entered into a period of *cultural stasis*. On the internet, time moves so fast that it doesn't move at all. The transformation of idealistic hippies from the class of '68 into yuppie materialists fifteen years later provided the dramatic tension of the film *The Big Chill*; in 2022, culture from 2007 feels disappointingly familiar. Many bored with contemporary culture have fled into a "retromania" obsession with exhuming the past. Meanwhile, Gen Z appears to have abandoned previous generations' determination toward radical artistic innovation for laid-back amateurism.

Cultural stasis is not trivial: we measure the health of our civilization through the fecundity and profundity of cultural production. And we rely on stylistic changes to define our particular moment in time and space. Here too we will find answers from a deeper understanding of how status interacts with culture.

-◄❂►-

This book surely seems to tackle too many topics at once: social hierarchies, conventions, signaling, symbols, identity, class, subcultures, art, fashion, mass media, history, technology. But only in examining the intersection of these phenomena can we fully understand how status and culture function as a system. To demonstrate the universality of the principles behind status and culture, we'll examine a wide range of real-life historical examples, from hairstyles and clothing to pets, beverages, snacks, pop and classical music, celebrities and frauds, memes, novels, painting, and nightlife. (But by no means are they the *only* possible examples.) Likewise we must transcend the boundaries of academic disciplines to excavate and *synthesize* the wisdom of sociology, anthropology, economics, philosophy, linguistics, semiotics, cultural theory, literary theory, art history, media studies, and neuroscience. There are obvious disadvantages to working at this scale: the loss of nuance, the neglect of edge cases, the high potential for oversights. Such worries aside, we are in need of a basic conceptual framework around status and culture, and once this is in place, we can easily make further enrichments, expansions, and amendments.

Readers may already be familiar with many of the principles that guide culture, such as the "trickle-down" of fashion trends and the predictable return of outmoded styles as "retro." And some of the scholarly theories introduced, whether Pierre Bourdieu's deconstruction of "taste" or Everett Rogers's model for the diffusion of "innovations," have become well-known outside of academia. But the frequent discrepancies of these cultural laws with our personal lived experiences breeds an inherent skepticism about their predictive power. The challenge, then, is not just to catalog our collective knowledge about the mechanics of culture but to demonstrate why these social phenomena arise as a result of individuals' self-interested behavior. To do this carefully requires beginning with somewhat obvious observations and then building up to more remarkable conclusions. We'll eventually see how status seeking shapes our deepest personal desires, why profligate spending is logical, how status has been important in encouraging radical artistic invention, how fashion exists without a fashion industry, how elites influence what we remember, how postmodern politics have made us ashamed of taste, and how the moral duty to be "original" may be simply the democratization of aristocratic custom.

We'll reach these conclusions as part of working to solve the Grand Mystery of Culture, which we'll break into three parts:

PART ONE: Why do individuals cluster around arbitrary behaviors and take deep meaning from them?

We'll answer this by looking at the basics of status, how these principles push individuals into conventional behaviors, and how we use conventions to form our identities.

PART TWO: How do distinct styles, conventions, and sensibilities emerge?

Status struggles fuel cultural creativity in three important realms: competition between socioeconomic classes, the formation of subcultures and countercultures, and artists' internecine battles.

PART THREE: Why do we change behaviors over time, and why do some behaviors persist?

The internal mechanisms of status cause perpetual fashion cycles, and high-status groups tend to determine what becomes "history" and what is forgotten.

Once we understand how individuals' status seeking creates wider social movements, it'll be clear why the Beatles wore moptops, why so many people got angry about it, and why the look eventually caught on and became a "classic." In part 4, we'll then apply the principles of status and culture to the internet age to understand the alleged stasis of our present day.

Most explications of status, especially outlining the advanced rules of taste, sound like endorsement. This is not the intention. We come here to deconstruct status, not to praise it. The human propensity toward hierarchical order—especially in the form of racism, sexism, and other bigotries—has long acted as a pernicious barrier to realizing a truly democratic society. But if we seek to promote equality over hierarchy and encourage cultural creativity and experimentation, we must learn the full implications of how culture and status work together.

While status desire may be fundamental to humans, many readers may be tempted to conclude, "Yes, *other* people conform to these principles, but not me." The political scientist Russell Hardin once wrote that the "biggest thorn in all of social theory" is that readers "deny the relevance of our accounts to their behavior and motivations." This is especially true for status, which is not a "game" some choose to play but an invisible force undergirding the entirety of individual behavior and social organization. As individuals we regard our tastes and preferences as personal expressions—not mechanical reactions to a position in the social hierarchy. We believe in our own free will and seek to forge unique identities. We want great art and enduring beauty to derive from intrinsic value—not from elite associations. There will certainly be points in the course of reading this book when a particular principle may not apply to you. But it's important to remember that *culture*, as we live and breathe it, is never an objective measurement of every single individual's behavior—it's an abstracted and *interpreted* approximation. The best parallel may be chemistry: not every molecule moves the exact same way, yet we can still draw inferences about the properties of gases.

In all likelihood, status shapes your behavior in profound ways, just as it influenced the Beatles' switch from pompadours to moptops. And only when we become experts in status can we work to achieve the society and culture we desire.

Part One

STATUS AND THE
INDIVIDUAL

Chapter One

THE BASICS OF STATUS

--✕--

Understanding the logic of social stratification through farm-town collies and national champion look-alikes, James Baldwin and Lucky Strikes, the "queen" of fashion's modest origins, and Jack Kerouac's celebration of madness

--✕--

WHAT IS STATUS?

Whatever the ambiguities of the term "status," we can learn its basic principles from a single episode of the classic American television series *Lassie*.

In "Double Trouble," the young protagonist Timmy takes his farm-town collie, Lassie, to the annual dog show in Capital City. There Lassie is mistaken for the national champion collie King's Royal Lassie. As the dog-show staff takes official publicity photos of Lassie, they tell Timmy, "It means a lot to have an animal of her reputation and standing at a show like this one." The very generous dog-show chairman then provides VIP passes to the event and puts Timmy and his guardian up in the fanciest suite of the Country Club Hotel, complete with free room service. "People are sure being nice to us," muses Timmy. By the end of the episode, however, he realizes there's been a big mistake. He apologizes for partaking in rewards intended for a more distinguished animal. But thanks to Lassie's heroic acts at the dog show, the chairman forgives them. Timmy returns home to tell his mother, with his one-dollar allowance unspent in his pocket, "I had the best time of my whole life."

This episode reveals four crucial lessons about status. First, status denotes a position within a *social hierarchy* based on respect and perceived importance. The most esteemed individuals, such as King's Royal Lassie, reside at the top of the hierarchy; average members like Lassie are in the middle; and the least important and least valued are relegated to the bottom. In medieval societies, this hierarchy was explicit: the king and queen at the apex, then aristocrats, then the bourgeoisie, and, finally, the peasants. But as capitalism and democracy enabled individuals to make a name for themselves, status positions became less clearly defined. In the stylish sci-fi world of the animated series *Neo Yokio*, a "Bachelor Board" displays the official rank of the city's most desirable unmarried men in clear numerical terms. In real life, we lack a similar authoritative status scorecard for society that would tell us that Malik sits at #41,879 and Janette recently rose to #56,578.

Instead, status positions are best expressed as membership within *tiers* stacked up from high to low. We may not know King's Royal Lassie's exact position on the ladder, but her "dog-show winner" tier is higher than Lassie's "family-dog" tier. The tiers tend to reflect certain *categories* and *classifications*: high tiers for titled aristocrats, venture capitalists, and prize-winning show dogs, and low tiers for mendicants, criminals, and mangy mutts. As individuals, our status position is strongly tied to our membership in these categories, but within a tier, our ranking can go up or down based on further accomplishments and attributes. King's Royal Lassie sits at the upper echelons of canines, but she must compete each year on the circuit against other champion show dogs for the ultimate glories.

The second lesson from *Lassie* is that every status position comes with specific rights and duties, with the most desirable benefits accruing to those at the top. The vast majority of any population has *normal status*, for which they receive common courtesies and basic privileges—but no special treatment. When not mistaken for a prize-winning dog, Lassie had normal status: she would be allowed to attend the dog show but wouldn't receive VIP passes, nor be comped free hotel rooms. People with *low status* must do the most grueling work, for which they may be extended very few courtesies. Those who fall to *super-low status*, such as vagrants or members of hostile enemy groups, are treated as pariahs. If Lassie were rabid and violent, she would be ejected from the dog-show premises.

High status, in contrast, confers special treatment and exclusive benefits.

American air carriers honor the troops by allowing military personnel to board before other passengers. Meanwhile, VIPs with *super-high status*—celebrities, athletes, billionaires, King's Royal Lassie—receive outward expressions of respect, obtain superior services free of charge, enjoy special access to exclusive locations, and may be exempted from some social norms. In ancient times, a high status position often came with increased responsibilities, but in the more liberal twenty-first century, the famous and wealthy can reap fabulous benefits without many social commitments in return.

Social position and social benefits are inextricably linked, because perks such as superior hotel suites, first-class cabins, and front-row seats are finite in supply. If everyone can go to the VIP room, it's not a VIP room. Organizations motivate members by distributing the spoils in accordance with the hierarchy, which means for every benefit, there will be a cut-off point: those above the line receive it, and those below don't. In the heyday of the exclusive New York night-club Studio 54, super-high-status artists and movie stars entered without waiting, attractive people waited in line but eventually got in, and everyday people were denied entry. At New York's High School of Art and Design in the early 1980s, the pioneering graffiti writer Lady Pink had to compete with others to get a seat in the cafeteria: "We specifically had a Writer's Table. So for years and years whoever was the best automatically got the best table. Anyone who was worthy would sit, anyone else who wasn't worthy would just stand around." This link between hierarchy and benefits has two important effects: we care a lot about our ranking, because it determines the benefits we receive; at the same time, we can deduce our position in the hierarchy at any time by comparing our benefits with those of others.

The third lesson from *Lassie* is that status is *bestowed by others*. Status is a purely social phenomenon; it manifests in the interactions between individuals. Lassie takes on the superior status of King's Royal Lassie only when the dog-show organizers treat her with more respect. A castaway on a deserted island, like Robinson Crusoe, has no status. He gains a status position only when the escaped prisoner Friday appears on the island and becomes his servant. With Friday around, Crusoe can sit back and relax while his status inferior slaughters goats to make stew, buries the corpses of hostile intruders, and fends off wild bears. Now, if King George had washed up on Crusoe's island rather than Friday, we would expect that the monarch would keep his royal status, and

Crusoe would be on goat-cooking duty. A *macro* status position is, then, always reflected in our *micro* daily interactions with others.

This leads us to the final lesson. Our status position is always *contextual*, based on how we are treated in a particular time and place. Lassie may be a beloved dog in her hometown, but ignored in tonier parts of Capital City. Bob Dylan's "Ballad of a Thin Man" mocks the middle-class journalist Mr. Jones, who is outraged to be treated as a low-status "freak" when interloping in the demimonde. Our status position is always contingent and can change over time. Jack Nicholson, one of the most beloved actors in American cinema during the seventies, lost status during the Brat Pack teen-movie era of the eighties. After seeing the 1986 comedy *Ferris Bueller's Day Off,* he vented: "Well, that movie made me feel totally irrelevant to anything that any audience could want and 119 years old. . . . I literally walked out of there thinking my days are numbered. These people are trying to kill me."

In living among others, we always have a status position, and this position determines the quality of our daily life. This fact is not just true for contemporary individuals struggling to stay afloat in late capitalism, but has been the case for all humans throughout history. The pioneering sociologist Pitirim Sorokin declared, "Any organized social group is always a stratified social body. There has not been and does not exist any permanent social group which is 'flat,' and in which all members are equal. Unstratified society, with a real equality of its members, is a myth which has never been realized in the history of mankind."

Status structures develop, explains the sociologist Cecilia L. Ridgeway, because hierarchies "are a human invention to manage social situations." Every group has goals, and there are always members who can make greater contributions. Their rare and valuable gifts—the ability to kill a lion on the veldt or solve a difficult math problem during study group—will cause others to hold them in esteem. As an incentive for star performers to repeat their feats, groups provide a disproportionate share of the benefits as reward. This natural mechanism means a status hierarchy will form any time individuals work together toward a task. The anthropologist Victor Turner writes, "The moment a digging stick is set in the earth, a colt broken in, a pack of wolves defended against or a human enemy set by his heels, we have the germs of a social structure."

With status as a universal phenomenon, everyone on earth has a specific status position—both within their local community and as part of the "global village." Awareness of that position is integral to our lives. The anthropologist Edmund Leach writes, "All human beings have a deep psychological need for the sense of security which comes from knowing where you are. But 'knowing where you are' is a matter of recognising social as well as territorial position." And as we think about our place in the hierarchy, one thing becomes very clear: *higher* status is extremely desirable.

OUR FUNDAMENTAL DESIRE FOR STATUS

In the James Baldwin novel *Go Tell It on the Mountain*, the young Black protagonist, John Grimes, is "the smallest boy in his class . . . who had no friends." He dreams of becoming a "beautiful, tall, and popular" poet, college president, or movie star who drinks "expensive whisky" and smokes "Lucky Strike cigarettes in the green package." In an ideal future, "People [would fall] all over themselves to meet John Grimes." Faced with the hardships of racial discrimination and familial dysfunctions, the young Grimes yearns to take up a prestigious occupation that garners esteem and provides a comfortable, wealthy lifestyle. His salvation comes in the form of higher status.

Aspirations today may no longer be expressed in a particular brand of cigarettes, but for both the privileged and the underprivileged, there is a nearly universal desire to secure a comfortable social position. In status hierarchies where individuals can improve their position over time, most would prefer to be elevated. "Even if all actors received the same salary," writes the philosopher Bertrand Russell, "a man would rather act the part of Hamlet than that of the First Sailor." Status seeking is obvious among insufferable snobs, petty civil servants, and Porsche-driving hedge fund managers, but neither capitalism nor complex bureaucracies are necessary to stoke such ambitions. In the New Guinea highlands, where sea snail shells served as currency and men competed in the accumulation of livestock, powerful "Big Men" openly acknowledged that status symbols ruled everything around them. For one: "All I care for in my life are my pigs, my wives, my shell money and my sweet potatoes."

A growing body of empirical research concludes that status is a fundamental human desire. Normal status is nice, but long-term happiness requires a sense of higher status. Research subjects, for example, felt better "in a hierarchical group in which they alone would be afforded a high level of respect and deference, than in an egalitarian group in which all members would be afforded a high (and equal) level of respect and deference." This is why we care more about higher *relative* income than absolute income. A study found that 70 percent of research subjects would give up a silent raise in salary for a more impressive job title. And these findings don't just apply to postindustrial economies. Around the world "individuals experience elevated social well-being when they enjoy a higher income than others in their local geographic area." If economic success was just about achieving comfort, we would be satisfied with a specific level of income that secured our basic lifestyle needs. Instead we want more money to improve our status.

Why are we so hungry for status? Many point to an evolutionary "status instinct," echoing the power hierarchies we see in the animal kingdom. "In any organized group of mammals," writes the zoologist Desmond Morris, "no matter how co-operative, there is always a struggle for social dominance." As a potential proof point, status affects our brain chemistry and bodily functions. A higher status position results in the production of more serotonin, while being in the presence of a status superior raises our blood pressure. This thinking can go too far, however: the right-wing psychologist Jordan Peterson points to hierarchies in lobster communities as proof that humans evolved an "unspeakably primordial calculator, deep within you, at the very foundation of your brain, far below your thoughts and feelings" that "monitors exactly where you are positioned in society." These parallels between dominance hierarchies in the animal world and human status structures are far too simplistic. Grade-school bullying may resemble pecking orders, but status hierarchies tend to be based more on esteem rather than raw power. Status is more akin to language, argues Cecilia Ridgeway: "a social form that is deeply cultural and socially learned." We are not "status monkeys" any more than we are "song birds."

The entire debate around the status instinct may be moot. The benefits of higher status are so obvious that a hypothetical person born without an innate drive for status would still seek a higher position out of pure rational calculation. Normal status provides social approval, common courtesies and pleasantries, and relaxed communication with others. This is a major improvement from lower status, with its constant reminders of inherent inferiority, reprimands for the tiniest errors, marginalization, and potential social exile. High status further expands upon the benefits of normal status and offers protection against falling to low status. The *status benefits* of a higher position are plentiful, and the best way to understand the roots of status desire is to examine them in detail.

Esteem is the backbone of status hierarchies, and this form of social approval acts as a benefit in its own right. We like feeling liked. In his old age the U.S. President John Adams concluded, "The desire of the esteem of others is as real a want of nature as hunger; and the neglect and contempt of the world as severe a pain as the gout or stone." Social approval makes us feel that our talents are recognized, and this leads to increased self-esteem. "The familiar yearning to 'be someone' in life," writes Cecilia Ridgeway, "is not so much about money and power as about being publicly seen and acknowledged as worthy and valuable by the community." While we may be embarrassed by outright status seeking, most of us are comfortable with receiving recognition for significant achievements. Poets pursue their calling without the promise of clear financial rewards; surely they should at least be paid in honor and glory.

But as the economic philosophers Geoffrey Brennan and Philip Pettit write, esteem is only "an attitude, not an action," which "may or may not be expressed in praise or criticism." To discern that we are esteemed, we need concrete evidence in the form of kind words, pleasant facial expressions, careful body movements, and the granting of spontaneous favors. Imagine a twist to the *Lassie* episode where the real King's Royal Lassie makes a surprise appearance, and the dog-show chairman utters in a lifeless monotone, "We greatly respect you," yet grants no VIP passes nor hotel suites. King's Royal Lassie would hardly feel esteemed.

So, even if we are seeking esteem rather than superior treatment, we need some form of superior treatment to perceive the esteem. The demand for tangible status benefits thus can't be separated from a desire for respect. This is why bureaucratic institutions always provide more perks to employees who move up the hierarchy. At the Firestone Tire and Rubber Company in the 1950s, every rise to a higher position meant a larger office, with wood rather than glass enclosures, and increased proximity to the chairman.

Esteem can be expressed through a wide range of palpable benefits. People with above-average status experience *favorable interactions*—"salutations, invitations, compliments, and minor services." The champion golfer Lee Trevino noted, "When I was a rookie, I told jokes, and no one laughed. After I began winning tournaments, I told the same jokes, and all of a sudden, people thought they were funny." This positive attention doesn't just channel into greater self-esteem: life gets easier, especially during emergencies. "A man in a clean, well-pressed suit who falls down in a central London or Manhattan street," writes author Alison Lurie, "is likely to be helped up sooner than one in filthy tatters." People go out of their way to help a prince but not a pauper.

High status also means *more attention* and *rewards* for doing the same work as lower-status individuals. "The man of rank and distinction," notes the economist Adam Smith, "is observed by all the world. . . . Scarce a word, scarce a gesture, can fall from him that is altogether neglected." In his research, the economic sociologist Joel M. Polodny saw this very principle play out: "Higher-status actors obtain greater recognition and rewards for performing a given task at a given level of quality and lower-status actors receive correspondingly less." And so famous scientists secure research grants more easily than non-famous ones, and when collaborating on research papers, they receive the bulk of credit, even with minimal contributions. This attention also gives them more influence on group behavior.

Another favorable interaction is *deference*—the right to do as one pleases, at one's own pace, with few interventions or interruptions. In Roman society, elites reclined at dinner, while children sat and slaves stood. At very high levels, deference can translate into an exemption from regular rules and norms. Old Money American families kept long lines of credit with their grocers and handymen, paying their bills only after weeks of hat-in-hand beseeching. The literary critic Diana Trilling remarks that individuals want to be writers "not only because of the promise of celebrity but also because of what the life of the artist promises of freedom to make one's own rules." Pop culture celebrates the heavy metal singer Ozzy Osbourne for snorting copious amounts of unhealthy substances, including a line of live ants—hedonistic behavior that would surely stifle the career of a middle manager at an insurance company.

An additional status benefit is *access to scarce resources*. As we saw before, a disproportionate distribution of rewards goes to the top as an incentive for further contribution. Vice presidents get higher salaries than entry-level hires. Celebrities sit at restaurants' best tables, are served off-menu special dishes, and have it all on the house. Status enables exclusive access to events, clubs, and social functions where other high-status individuals meet and fraternize.

The final status benefit is *dominance*—the ability to make others do things against their wishes. In theory status provides influence primarily through esteem rather than through fear. But where necessary, status can be wielded as power. On his 1969 album *Electronic Sound*, the Beatles' George Harrison recorded the musician Bernie Krause playing the Moog synthesizer and released it as his own composition. When Krause complained, Harrison became indignant. "You're coming on like you're Jimi Hendrix. When Ravi Shankar comes to my house, he's humble." Krause never sued. Beatles-level status absolved wholesale filching.

Higher status is a reliable pathway to acquiring the power and the glory—but it also provides defense against the threat of status loss. Studies show that high status makes people happy and healthy, and that low status leads to anger, depression, anxiety, and sickness. In any organization, "low-status members are more likely to feel negative emotions like sadness and, when things go wrong for the group, self-blaming emotions like guilt or shame." The social epidemiologist Michael Marmot coined the term "status syndrome" to describe the poor health of people at the bottom of the status hierarchy. And as the psychologist Dale T. Miller has shown, disrespect is "widely recognized as a common, perhaps the most common, source of anger." If low status escalates to complete ostracization, it can result in "psychological death." This explains the common psychological malaise known as status panic, status tension, or status anxiety.

All of this demand for higher esteem, however, inherently engenders social conflict: Status is a relative ranking, so not everyone can simultaneously achieve a high position. Status *is* zero-sum. For every person who goes up, someone must go down. Outcomes can feel unfair when we fail to move up after achievements or fall down after others succeed. This umbrage is further amplified due to cognitive biases that make us overestimate our abilities. A company found that more than 40 percent of its engineers claimed to be in the top 5 percent of ability, and among college professors, 90 percent claimed to be "above average." These minor delusions of grandeur intensify our desire for higher status by making us feel we deserve it. But maybe we're right: only *we* know the full extent of our accomplishments and talents. Or maybe we're wrong: we suffer from endowment effects that make us overvalue the assets we happen to possess.

While status desire may be universal, there is always variation in how high on the ladder individuals want to go. The anti-individualism of Pueblo society resulted in men never seeking leadership positions but only taking them after protracted coercion. Higher status positions often come with an increase in bothersome responsibilities—having to make difficult decisions for the group and behave as a role model. Rewards may not always exceed the duties. For others, duties provide a sense of superiority; Goethe channeled the concept of noblesse oblige in his line "To live as one likes is plebeian; the noble man aspires to order and law." By contrast, twenty-first-century pop stars, superstar athletes, and billionaires, who often make their fortunes on what would have been considered child's play in earlier ages, face few social obligations and often enjoy carte blanche to commit manifold sins. Even the most malicious, spouse-abusing musicians receive hagiographic film treatments. With a spotlight on their privileges and little attention to their dwindling responsibilities, celebrities inspire normal people to dream of high status without arousing much thought to its potential burdens.

For all the reasons we have seen, the achievement of high status may not quench the thirst for more. There may be decreasing marginal utility for money and power, but achieving status makes us want more. When Andy Warhol finally snagged an invitation to Truman Capote's famed masked ball, he merely thought, "You get to the point in life where you're actually invited to the party of parties—the one people all over the world were trying desperately to get invited to—and it still didn't guarantee that you wouldn't feel like a complete dud!" As we glance up at our status betters, they, too, are glancing up toward their own heroes. Early in his career Michael Jordan swept the top NBA awards, from most valuable player to top scorer, and even had his own signature Nike sneaker. But he felt inferior to legends Larry Bird and Magic Johnson until securing his own national championship. Other elites seek status fearing they may crash down like Icarus. After selling twelve million copies of his album *Play*, the electronic musician Moby became only more status obsessed: "I had been a marginal musician and I was suddenly getting all this attention. Part of me wanted even more attention. So I started thinking in terms of fame and public figure status. I wasn't even trying to make more money—I wanted to keep being invited to parties." Status benefits are addictive.

We now understand the practical reasons for desiring higher status and fearing low status. So the next question is, how do we get it?

STATUS CRITERIA

To her employees the fashion designer Gabrielle "Coco" Chanel was a queen. By the time of World War I, Chanel lived like royalty in Paris, riding around in the back of a chauffeur-driven Rolls-Royce, defining "chic" for the ultrawealthy, and cavorting with the legendary artists Pablo Picasso and Igor Stravinsky. But unlike an actual queen, Chanel was born at the bottom of society. She grew up in the backwater Auvergne region of France as the abandoned daughter of a disreputable family, educated at a convent as a charity pupil, barely able to write proper French, even as an adult. So how did Chanel take on noble levels of status in the eyes of others? "It is through work that one achieves," Chanel later proclaimed to her biographer. "Manna didn't fall on me from heaven; I molded it with my own hands. . . . The secret of this success is that I have worked terribly hard." While Chanel was certainly no heroine, the high status she enjoyed during her life (and continues to enjoy today, through her namesake product line) was not inherited but *achieved*.

Status hierarchies rank individuals on esteem and perceived importance. But individuals receive that esteem and importance when others believe they possess rare and valuable talents. Coco Chanel attained her high status as a successful, barrier-shattering fashion designer who provided one-of-a-kind designs that wealthy women coveted. There must be, then, a formula for achieving high status—certain *status criteria* at which we must excel.

Before we can understand the roots of status in our contemporary world, however, we first must acknowledge that cases like Coco Chanel's became possible only in the modern age. For most of human history, writes the philosopher Charles Taylor, "People were often locked into a given place, a role and station that was properly theirs and from which it was almost unthinkable to deviate." Older societies built their hierarchies around *ascribed status*, where individuals received their social ranking based on predetermined criteria, such as age, ethnic group, occupation, and gender. Pueblo tribes established their status hierarchy on the basis of birth order; the eldest had higher status, the young lower status. In feudal England blood and occupation set rank: "The king, the peer, the knight, the yeoman, the villein [feudal tenant], the merchant, the laborer, the artisan, the various sorts of person in orders, all occupied definite and le-gally fixed places in the hierarchy of society." Furthermore, this system was understood to be God's plan and couldn't be altered.

Business tycoons in the feudal age would be stuck at lower status positions until they could petition royals to bestow them with titles of nobility (for which they paid large sums of money). And even in postrevolutionary nineteenth-century France, social rigidity persisted on a tacit level. Marcel Proust wrote, "Middle-class people in those days took what was almost a Hindu view of soci-ety, which they held to consist of sharply defined castes, so that everyone at his birth found himself called to that station in life which his parents already oc-cupied, and from which nothing, save the accident of an exceptional career or of a 'good' marriage, could extract you and translate you to a superior caste." In a society based on ascribed status, Coco Chanel would be fated to remain a nobody.

Ascribed status runs counter to the modern belief that individuals should forge their own way in life and reap the subsequent rewards. Despite demo-cratic ideals and "free" markets, ascribed status categories still linger in soci-ety. Heredity remains powerful: the children of high-status families, whether noble princes or pathetic failsons, emerge at the top of the ladder before they can crawl. Racism is a toxic form of ascribed status that fixes social position to skin color. In *Caste*, author Isabel Wilkerson argues that discrimination in the United States against people of African descent is so codified and punishing as to mirror the caste system of Indian society. From slavery to Jim Crow to interactions in daily life today, Black Americans in the "subordinate caste" have been denied "respect, status, honor, attention, privileges, resources, benefit of the doubt, and human kindness." Basketball player LeBron James, who polls year after year as one of America's most admired men, told reporters, "No matter how great you become in life, no matter how wealthy you become, how people worship you, what you do, if you are an African-American man or African-American woman, you will always be that."

These kinds of ascribed status beliefs exist across all major demographic categories, such as age, gender identification, and sexual orientation. Our mod-ern vocabulary is full of words that reference these biases: e.g., "male privilege" is the granting of higher status to men for being men; "white privilege" is the granting of higher status for light skin. Sociologists describe those born to higher ascribed status categories as *status advantaged*, and those born outside of those categories as *status disadvantaged*. The latter group must find supplemental or alternative sources of status to even reach parity with their advantaged peers. In the worst cases of discrimination, certain groups are denied all semblance of *dignity*—the basic right to be treated as a potential candidate for normal status.

Contemporary liberal societies view ascribed status systems like feudalism or racism as insidious. The modern ideal is to organize society as a system of *achieved status*, where a higher position is based on personal achievements rather than immutable characteristics. The first challenge to ascribed status arrived with capitalism, as businesspeople could earn esteem and status benefits through amassing fortunes alone. The concept of nobility shifted from a title received from the monarch to an honor created by oneself through virtuous effort. The subsequent destruction of the feudal caste system ultimately opened the door for individuals like Coco Chanel to leave their hometowns and class of birth and reinvent themselves. The promise of status rebirth was for many years a selling point for immigrating to the New World. "American ideology," writes the author Vance Packard, "strongly supported the notion that the United States is unique in the world as a place where a poor boy can start at the bottom and become a great captain of industry." (Alas, he mentions only boys—another vestige of ascribed status.)

This opens the question, however, of what actually qualifies as "achievement." Every group and society believes in certain status criteria—assets, attributes, talents, and possessions that place individuals in a higher position. These ostensibly match the capabilities required for society to best function. Criteria thus differ by era, geography, and situational challenges. But no matter the circumstances, the highest achievements must demonstrate rare and valuable talents. The French sociologist Gabriel Tarde notes that in primitive times, the criteria were "physical vigour and skill, physical bravery" but changed centuries later to "skill in war and eloquence in council" and, still later, to "aesthetic imagination, industrial ingenuity, scientific genius."

Today, achievements tend to be embodied in particular forms of *capital*. In the past, *political capital*—access to power—reigned supreme. This could take the form of tribal leadership, religious authority, or government position. In a more secular and democratic world, the value of such capital has decreased. As meritocracy becomes more of a shared ideal, new forms of capital have emerged. *Educational capital*—university degrees and certifications—has become an important way to measure potential talent for taking on important social positions. Strong academic performance at top universities is understood to predict an individual's knowledge and ability for critical thinking, and also, the potential for securing superior employment opportunities. *Occupational capital* is the subsequent prestige attached to important and well-respected jobs, such as doctor, lawyer, or professor. This respect is not always linked to salary. Card sharks sit at lower status tiers than academics despite larger incomes.

In capitalist society, *economic capital*—cash, wealth, and property—becomes the most obvious and potent ingredient for achieving high status. Stockpiling great quantities of money can be a notable achievement in its own right, but money can also function as a vibrant symbol for other virtues, such as intelligence and hard work. (Alternatively, money can be symbolic of the ascribed status honor of birth into a wealthy family.) Money is very flexible as an asset, converting easily into power over others through business ownership, political connections, donations, and bribes. The rich can also use their cash to secure top-status benefits that they may be otherwise denied. The art critic John Berger writes, "Money is life in the sense that money is the token of, and the key to, every human capacity. The power to spend money is the power to live. According to the legends of publicity, those who lack the power to spend money become literally faceless. Those who have the power become lovable." The actress and courtesan Carolina Otero put it more pithily: "No man who has an account at Cartier could ever be regarded as ugly."

Other forms of capital provide further paths to status. *Social capital*—expansive networks of collegial relationships with elites—signals that an individual is treated as an equal within high-status groups. Our relations determine our reputation. Coco Chanel leaped to higher status after high-status customers made her fledgling apparel shop a premier destination. And, of course, there is *fame*—being known to many individuals. Throughout part 1, we'll encounter additional status criteria generated within the internal logic of the status system itself: namely, cultural capital, detachment, originality, and authenticity.

Besides capital, we also have *personal virtues* that may improve our interactions with others. We can receive esteem in our communities through intelligence, physical attractiveness (good looks, excellent grooming), behavioral and conversational charms (outgoingness, pleasant personalities, kindness, a sense of humor, control over the body and emotions, poise, and savoir faire), and personal integrity (bravery, honesty, sincerity, modesty). At extremely high levels, physical attractiveness can serve as *bodily capital*; fashion models, for example, get free entry to clubs and invitations to VIP areas with bottle service on their looks alone. While personal virtues can open the door to building more reliable forms of capital (and, for the most part, originate in aristocratic mores), they aren't particularly rare or valuable in their own right. There are many attractive, charming people among all ranks of society. The global hierarchy never revolves around the cleverest quips and the freshest breath. Models may socialize with billionaires but rarely become billionaires themselves from this fraternization alone.

Capital determines our membership in groups, and these memberships determine our status. The sociologist Georg Simmel writes, "In order to know a man, we see him not in terms of his pure individuality, but carried, lifted up or lowered, by the general type under which we classify him." Personal virtues can be symbolic of capital—e.g., comport and charm as marks of "good" breeding—but to be a "celebrity" or "surgeon" or "professor" requires specific forms of capital. Coco Chanel used her beauty, charm, and musical talents to move up the ladder from charity pupil to light entertainer to high-class courtesan. But she reached "queen" levels only after achieving fame and security by running her own successful business.

To "be somebody" in today's world requires accumulating significant amounts of capital, often across multiple criteria. Graduates of the most exclusive universities (educational capital) become friends with future leaders (social capital), embark on impressive careers (occupational capital), and make a lot of money (economic capital). This clustering is called *status congruence*, and it works to stabilize the status rankings. An individual's minor achievement in one area may not lead to a significant jump up the ladder; a multifront effort is required to prove greater importance. Despite claims of achieved status, status congruence reveals exactly how inequity becomes entrenched over time. Yes, many inspiring individuals made impossible status leaps; funk music pioneer James Brown was orphaned, grew up in a brothel, and was sent to prison as a juvenile, only to achieve fame and financial success at a global scale. But lingering ascribed status structures and the existence of status congruence means the wealthy and their offspring will always have an easier time gaining and maintaining high status than those born into families without capital.

At the same time, social mobility always *appears* to be possible, making us feel responsible for our own status. Folk wisdom asserts we can improve our lot in life by cleaning up, going back to school, being nicer, getting a better job, putting in longer hours, and practice, practice, practice. We're told virtue leads to a greater accumulation of capital. And so we are unlikely to feel fated to the status level we have at any particular time. Even the highest-ranking individuals often seek to achieve more. Those with high educational capital want economic capital. Those with high economic capital want social capital and political capital. In the 1960s many young people from Old Money families, like Edie Sedgwick, who possessed "inherited wealth, inherited beauty, and inherited intelligence," rushed to New York City to obtain the one thing they lacked: fame.

There is one final ramification of achieved status we must also consider: we resent individuals who claim or receive high status without meeting the requisite status criteria. Bertrand Russell writes, "Success should, as far as possible, be the reward of some genuine merit, and not of sycophancy or cunning." The universal emotion *envy* arises from individuals believing that others of similar or lower status assets have unfairly received greater benefits. The legitimacy of any hierarchy hinges on *status integrity*—a collective belief that the ranking of individuals is fair, and that they receive greater benefits for legitimate reasons. Esteem should never be granted for free. Status-seeking individuals violate the principle of status integrity when they demand better treatment than they "deserve." As a result, we treat unjustified claims to status with social disapproval, and violators' social standing may go down as a result. The moment Timmy realizes that Lassie has been mistaken for the superior King's Royal Lassie, he frets, "We're in trouble. Real trouble." Taking status integrity into account leads us to a central axiom for status desire: *Individuals seek higher status—insofar as its pursuit doesn't risk their current status level.*

Status criteria explain how Coco Chanel could leap to a higher position. (And then lose much of it in her twilight years after collaborating with the Nazis.) While the commonality of the human experience may lead to broad similarities in global status criteria, each society and group faces different goals and celebrates different values. And when they disagree on the proper criteria for forming the status hierarchy, they splinter.

STATUS GROUPS

"The only people for me are the mad ones," writes Jack Kerouac in *On the Road.* "The ones who are mad to live, mad to talk, mad to be saved, desirous of everything at the same time, the ones who never yawn or say a commonplace thing, but burn, burn, burn, like fabulous yellow roman candles exploding like spiders across the stars." Living in a 1950s America that cherished conformity, occupational success, and material possessions, Kerouac and his friends instead celebrated artistic talent, unorthodox morality, and peripatetic lifestyles. A mutual appreciation of these uncommon values formed strong bonds within a small community of novelists and poets forever known as the Beats.

Kerouac and his Beat friends are an example of a *status group.* Members of these groups share *status beliefs* about the value of certain status criteria. The strength of these beliefs creates cohesion among a group's members and, where those beliefs differ from those of other groups, stokes tensions with outsiders. The Beats didn't ignore their members' "antisocial" behaviors, such as drug use and fluid sexuality—they lauded them as transcendent acts.

Mainstream society functions as a macro status group, with the core status beliefs centered on the varieties of capital outlined in the previous section. *Alternative status groups* believe in criteria outside of traditional capital. Goths, punk rockers, or Civil War reenactors grant status based on uncommon criteria, such as the most gloomy makeup, highest mohawks, and most Ambrose Burnside–like facial hair. Within teenage gangs, strength and bravery determine the social order. A delinquent British girl in the 1950s explained, "In a gang like ours, all the girls go for the big kid. We call him Big Jim. He's really tough and he could have any of the girls. . . . My boyfriend is tough all right, but he's not as tough as Big Jim."

While these small communities appear at first more equitable than mainstream society—a voluntary meeting of like minds—the specificity of the group's status beliefs often make hierarchical structures even more pronounced. For surfers there is only one criterion that is supposed to matter: the ability to surf. The very best surfers have the most status, and the worst surfers have the least—irrespective of their 401(k)s and fancy domiciles. In fact, rich weekend surfers are often disparaged as "kooks" when they show off expensive gear without the talent to justify it.

In groups where everyone is dedicated to the same status beliefs, there will be strong status integrity. Members see the hierarchy as natural and, thus, legitimate. Deference to elites is automatic, and lower-status members lend their time, energy, and support to superiors for the sake of the group. Bertrand Russell writes, "When men willingly follow a leader, they do so with a view to the acquisition of power by the group which he commands, and they feel that his triumphs are theirs." Members of a basketball team happily reward the MVP with additional status if she sinks a winning shot at the buzzer.

As much as we may identify most closely with a single status group, we are all members of many: family, school, workplace, clubs. And since the status criteria and beliefs may differ among them, we behave differently based on the context. Kerouac's status improved among his family when he married his live-in girlfriend, but he impressed his Beat friends and fans only by leaving home and going on the road. In extreme cases this *code switching* between groups' competing demands can split us into multiple personalities.

Social mobility of the modern age allows individuals more freedom to choose their primary status groups. So how do we decide which groups to join? We are all born into a status group, and many remain there forever. Jack Kerouac decided to leave the straitlaced world of varsity football to write experimental novels alongside a few anarchic poets. We prefer the company of people like ourselves—especially to be among those with the same convictions. But if we're after status, a rational strategy would be to join a status group that appreciates the virtues and assets we happen to possess. The journalist and novelist Tom Wolfe learned over the years that, "whether they're intellectuals or stock car racers, [most people] tend to emphasize values that, if they were absolute, would make them special people." Empirical scholarship also bears this out: "People are more attracted to relationships, groups, and communities in which they would have reasonably high status rather than those in which they would be low status." Delinquent and marginal subcultures make a good home for those lacking most forms of capital, as they reward members for a *rejection* of mainstream values. Fringe groups flip the script and value extreme negations of traditional virtues. In reaction to the Puritan work ethic of proper society, the Beats decided "all effort was uncool, a hassle."

From this perspective, membership in alternative status groups appears to be a clever strategy for oppressed and unprivileged individuals to maximize their status. But there is an obvious flaw in this approach: our most immediate community can only provide *local status*—the ranking inside the small group. Research has shown that local status is more important to personal happiness than global status, especially for self-esteem. And life is easier when living among sympathetic peers. But even if we hide in an alternative status group, we can't escape our *global status*—the general ranking within broader society. For most, a high local status won't translate into a high global status, which is required for access to the best benefits. A surfer can be a great hero among other surfers but just a "beach bum" up the shore. The wider the gap between the esteem we feel inside our status group and outside in the "real world," the more we may feel inferior. The rich, meanwhile, enjoy high local status in their high-income status group and *also* high global status.

To obtain more social benefits, marginalized status groups must find a way to move up the global hierarchy. This turns society into a battle among status groups. The anthropologist Daniel Miller explains, "Each group attempts to project its interests, its 'capital' as the proper source for social reputation and status." The Beat poets used their success with literary critics and resonance with younger readers to convince many Americans of the inherent superiority of "madness" to conformity. A decade after Kerouac wrote *On the Road*, millions of upper-middle-class college students adopted its ethos and flocked to the alternative status group later known as hippies. In the status war the Beats won ground for their beliefs, and Kerouac died an icon, not a heretic.

For every winner in status group battles, there must also be losers. The pioneering sociologist Max Weber found that dominant groups that tumble down the hierarchy develop particularly strong resentments: "The more they feel threatened, the greater is their bitterness." Status envy is a common source of conflict in multiethnic states. When the majority Buddhist Sinhalese lost their monopoly on political power in Sri Lanka and the government started to provide job opportunities for Tamils, the Sinhalese rioted. Recent political turmoil in the United States also appears to resemble status envy. The political scientists Pippa Norris and Ronald Inglehart write, "The interwar generation of non-college educated white men—until recently the politically and socially dominant group in Western cultures—has passed a tipping point at which their hegemonic status, power, and privilege are fading." The Trump voting bloc continues to embrace older status beliefs anchored in ascribed racial, gender, and religious hierarchies, which are losing influence in a more diverse society. As long-disadvantaged groups gain status, this bloc complains about a decrease in esteem for people like themselves. A pro-Trump store owner and nurse in Baldwin, Michigan, told pollsters, "There is no respect for anyone who is just average and trying to do the right things."

Status is thus not just personal but political. "Society," writes Daniel Miller, "is not to be understood in terms of a simple hierarchy, but as a continual struggle over the hierarchy of hierarchies." Status is an ordinal ranking, and so even if the economic pie expands and material benefits increase for much of society, this doesn't equalize status in society. In fact, an overall increase in wealth only *raises* the bar for the capital required to gain status. Alternative status groups enable the status-disadvantaged to find new sources of status, but members may still worry about their global ranking. The constant struggles among status groups play a major role in the human experience—and, as we'll see later, fuel the creation of new culture.

Status is a fundamental human desire. Quality of life improves with a higher status position. Although no society is perfectly meritocratic, modern individuals play a larger role in determining their own status than in the past. High status awaits those who can excel at the key status criteria—namely, wealth, connections, education, career, and fame. Meanwhile, excluded individuals can seek out alternative sources of esteem within smaller status groups that better value their particular contributions. But anyone who tries to claim more status than they deserve may be punished.

Four important principles emerge from the internal logic of status hierarchies:

1. *Status maximization*: We desire high status and fear low status.
2. *Status achievement*: We can modify our status through talents, contributions, possessions, and virtues.
3. *Status integrity*: We should not claim more status than we deserve.

4. *Status mobility*: We can choose to move ourselves to new social contexts that better value our talents, contributions, possessions, and virtues.

Status ultimately describes our specific placement as individuals within a network of others, and how we are treated in that position. When we impress others, our treatment improves. But until now, we've ignored an even more basic determinant of status. To be a good member in any group requires following certain rules. This is where status and culture first intersect.

Chapter Two

CONVENTIONS AND STATUS VALUE

⊷⊶

The quest for status pushes us toward certain arbitrary choices—as demonstrated by black tie at debutante balls, the ranking of General Motors brands, and the seeming hypocrisy of hipsters.

⊷⊶

THE POWER OF CONVENTIONS

Whit Stillman's 1990 film, *Metropolitan*, follows Tom Townsend, a Princeton student and utopian socialist too concerned about the plight of underprivileged people to spend time at fancy parties. But as he grows bored during the winter holidays, Tom rents a tuxedo to attend a debutante ball—to see firsthand what he opposes. Failing to return the tuxedo on time, he wears it to another ball, this time to remedy the "escort shortage." Tom eventually settles in with a new social group of "upper haute bourgeois" debutantes and escorts. And once he purchases his own evening clothes, Tom is granted entry to a week's worth of exclusive engagements, where he can mingle with high society, enjoy free entertainment, and receive hot nutritious meals.

In the previous chapter, we saw how groups award high status to certain individuals with rare talents, abundant capital, and personal virtues. But *Metropolitan* reminds us that there is a more elementary requirement to gain status: *conformity to group norms.* There are expectations for members within every status group and tier to follow specific behaviors. The simple act of donning formal attire allows Tom to expand his social network and gain access to greater material benefits. But black tie is an *arbitrary* standard. No activity at a debutante ball requires a tuxedo the same way that an hour-long underwater party would require scuba gear. This reveals the first major intersection between status and culture: earning social approval requires not just making concrete contributions to the group's goals but also following a particular set of arbitrary practices.

Why "arbitrary"? We often use the word as a synonym for random, unfair, or superficial, but in the study of language and culture, arbitrary denotes choices where an alternative could serve the same purpose. Within spoken language, words are based on an arbitrary relationship between the signifier (the sound we make) and the signified (the meaning). The movements of the lips, tongue, and vocal cords to make the sound /dɒg/ in English are arbitrary, because another sound could also signify "dog," the concept. To that point, the French communicate perfectly well about canines using the word *chien* instead.

All discussion of culture focuses on the arbitrary aspects of human behavior. To survive, humans need food, shelter, and clothing, but as the anthropologist Marshall Sahlins writes, "Men do not merely 'survive.' They survive in a definite way." Intoxicating beverages serve a universal function; "cultural" differences emerge when Russians pour shots of vodka, Mexicans toss back tequila, and Mongolians sip fermented mare's milk. While these choices may have developed under particular geographical and agricultural conditions, they are arbitrary in the sense that humans can imbibe any of them to achieve the same purpose of inebriation. Global supply chains have proven this to be true: Mongolians now drink rum, and Russians enjoy scotch.

Arbitrariness is a critical part of the human experience, because we can eat, drink, dress, sing, dance, play, and think in a nearly infinite number of ways. And yet, once we settle on a particular behavior, we no longer see our decisions as arbitrary. The economist Jon Elster notes, "Human beings have a very strong desire to have reasons for what they do and find indeterminacy hard to accept." Our brains provide us with post facto rationalizations for our arbitrary acts. We often assume there must be evolutionary instincts that best explain our customary behavior. Stop signs must be red, we infer, because the color of blood signifies danger. Two centuries of anthropological research and several millennia of history, however, provide ample evidence that human behaviors aren't necessarily the result of rational thinking or unfiltered biological responses. For all the underlying "danger" suggested by the color red, the same shade indicates unbridled joy for many cultures. During China's Cultural Revolution, rabid Maoist youth demanded traffic lights be reversed so that the patriotic Communist red could mean "go."

We become particularly stubborn about insisting on the nonarbitrariness of our own cultural practices. Economist Adam Smith wondered several centuries ago why our customs, "though no doubt extremely agreeable, should be the only forms which can suit those proportions, or that there should not be five hundred others, which, antecedent to established custom, would have fitted them equally well." Every Oktoberfest, Bavarian men don lederhosen and women put on dirndl dresses and drink gigantic steins of beer while listening to music with the oompah tuba. Couldn't they also enjoy the festivities in jeans? No, explains a dirndl-wearing young Bavarian woman: "When you're in the beer tent, standing on the benches and everyone sings the same songs, you really feel that you're part of something. In jeans you just don't get into it in the same way." To Bavarians, lederhosen and dirndl are not "arbitrary" costumes: they express the essence of being Bavarian.

What makes us so attached to the arbitrary practices of our community in times when other choices are available? The answer is *conventions*—well-known, regular, accepted social behaviors that individuals follow and expect others to follow. To illuminate the relationship between status and culture, we must become experts in conventions. They are the "molecules" in the chemistry of culture—the individual units of collective behavior that make up the cultural whole. The Beatles' moptop is a convention, as are black tie, dog shows, and reading Kerouac's *On the Road* as an angsty teenager. Arbitrariness is key to conventions. Humans don't need conventions to breathe, nor do desert dwellers need conventions to draw water from the only functioning well. Conventions assist humans in coordinating around certain choices. Wherever we see people repeating a particular practice and rejecting its equally plausible alternative, there is likely a convention compelling everyone into making the same choice.

Once we know how to identify conventions, we'll find them everywhere. They manifest as *customs*, the tacit rules of a community. Customs can be so invisible within a group that we notice them only upon encountering alternative ways of life. "There are probably young men from Nevada," writes the journalist Calvin Trillin, "who have to be drafted and sent to an out-of-state Army camp before they realize that all laundromats are not equipped with slot machines." We are more cognizant of conventions when they take the form of *norms* and *manners*, because we may be reluctant to follow them. Meanwhile, *traditions*, like lederhosen and dirndl, are conventions anchored in historical precedence that serve as explicit symbols of the community. *Beliefs* can also have conventional elements. This is clear for superstitions: Americans fear the number 13, while Italians believe it's lucky.

Conventions change over time. In the late nineteenth century, elite American men wore heavy beards. In the early 1960s, despite the same follicular endowments, nearly all Harvard Business School students were clean-shaven, with only 4 percent in mustaches. Modern life is full of short-term conventions we call *fads*, such as Hula-Hoops and the Atkins diet. *Fashions* are conventions that appear in ornamental areas of life that change on a regular basis. "Conventional" is often used as a synonym for "boring," but antisocial misfits, delinquents, and rogues have their own conventions. Thieves speak in argot, punks wear safety pins in their clothing, and the Hobo National Convention drafted an official ethical code in 1889. Even substance abuse can be conventional: alcoholism became the "American writer's disease" after luminaries like Ernest Hemingway and Jack Kerouac made heavy drinking core to their writing process.

All *styles*, in the form of distinctive modes of expression, are conventions. Nineties hip-hop fashion was a well-known, tacit agreement to wear "oversized fits and long silhouettes." *Art* relies on convention to create aesthetic experiences. There are accepted guidelines that shape the creation and consumption of an artwork—the three-act structure and happy endings of Hollywood films, repeating choruses in pop songs, the fact that fans can sing along at a rock concert but not at a classical performance, the use of "[Catchy Phrase]: [How *Something* Did *Something*]" in the subtitles of nonfiction books. Recent Hollywood films deploy the convention of a "yellow filter" in postproduction to make footage from Central America and India look more squalid and sinister. And as we'll learn later, artists play with conventions—respecting some to woo in audiences and breaking others to create surprise.

Conventions are not just floating molecules that make up culture but also wield remarkable powers over humans in three key ways: (1) they regulate our behavior; (2) they become internalized as habits; and (3) they change our perception of the world. And from whence do conventions draw their power? *Status*. We ultimately follow conventions to gain social approval and avoid social disapproval, and in doing so, they change our behaviors and organize the data we gather from our senses.

Before we examine this process, we must first understand how conventions arise. Many form as explicit solutions to communal problems. A classic example is the direction of road traffic. Cars can either drive on the left or drive on the right—it's an arbitrary choice—but there must be agreement on the direction that is chosen, in order to avoid head-on collisions. In this case governments issue a *decree* on left or right and, in response, a convention forms where everyone drives on that side, even when no other cars are on the road.

Conventions can also arise organically. The U.S. government never issued a Tuxedo Proclamation—"Rule One: Men must wear cummerbunds." High-status American men simply maintained standards of dress for formal engagements, because wearing similar, atypical attire marked these events as special occasions. For many years, they wore British white-tie tailcoats. But then in 1886, the rebellious scion of a tobacco magnate, Griswold Lorillard, wore a shorter black jacket to exclusive engagements at his father's Tuxedo Club. This more casual look was christened the "tuxedo" and made inroads throughout the twentieth century as American society became more relaxed. After World War II, tails more or less disappeared, and the tuxedo settled in as the new standard for evening attire. Once the tuxedo became conventional, attendees at debutante balls and other formal events adopted it to be dressed the same as others.

For a convention to take root within a community and become "regular" behavior, it must become part of *common knowledge*—where individuals know something, know that others know it, know that others know that they know it, and know that others know that they know that they know it, ad infinitum. Men show up in tuxedos to debutante balls whose invitations specify "black tie" thanks to widespread common knowledge about precisely what constitutes black tie and when to wear it. Moving the population to a new convention requires building new common knowledge. During the reversion of Okinawa from American control to Japanese rule, the island chain needed to coordinate a switch from American-style right-side driving to Japanese-style left-side driving. The government chose July 30, 1978, as the first day of left-hand driving and ran a multimillion-dollar "7-30" advertising campaign to raise awareness of the change in policy. The plan worked: other than a few bus accidents, drivers were confident that other vehicles would also be driving on the left from July 30 onward.

Avoiding death is an excellent incentive to follow the conventions of road traffic, but why do humans care so much about conforming to such superficial conventions as moptops and tuxedos? Conventions provide a "solution" when trying to coordinate behaviors with others: the Beatles all wanted to have a unified look that was distinct from others, so they embraced the moptop. Once established, conventions then draw an additional power from emotional responses to expectations. Our brains prefer when other people meet our expectations, because this means we don't have to expend extra mental energy on thinking through alternatives. When others fail to meet our expectations in a negative way, we become frustrated and angry—even in times when the underlying behavior has no material impact on us. We then convert these emotional responses, either positive or negative, into outward expressions of our feelings. Meeting expectations elicits smiles and cheers. When they aren't met, the sociologist George Homans writes, an individual "has in effect been deprived of a reward, and he repays deprivation with hostility." Before the Beatles chose to wear moptops themselves, they were livid at Stu Sutcliffe for abandoning their agreed-upon look of greasy pompadours.

Receiving social approval for upholding conventions and disapproval for violating them has clear effects on our status position. To maintain normal status, we must meet group expectations, and if we fail to do so, we may fall to lower status. Following conventions is, then, key to being a member of good standing. Tom Townsend may have loathed debutante balls, but to even gain entry, he knew he must uphold the convention of black tie.

With the passage of time, individuals in status groups develop mutual expectations on how they should look and behave. Max Weber concluded, "Status groups are specifically responsible for all 'conventions': all 'stylisation' of ways of life, however expressed, either originates with a status group or is preserved by one." As everyone follows these rules to some degree, they manifest as observable behavioral patterns associated with those groups. If high society all wears tuxedos, we know the tuxedo as a "fancy," high-society form of dress. And within status groups, the fact that individuals regulate their behavior to conform to conventions turns those conventions into *social norms*.

At first, conventions regulate our behavior at a conscious level, but over time, they take on their second power through *internalization*. In belonging to a community—especially as children—we absorb the dominant conventions of our groups. The anthropologist Ruth Benedict explains, "The life-history of the individual is first and foremost an accommodation to the patterns and standards traditionally handed down in his community." We learn conventions from our family and friends through the *chameleon effect*, where we unconsciously mimic our peers in body movements and speech. We learn that these behaviors are associated with certain meanings and values: what's right, what's wrong, what goes with what. This process converts conventions into *habits*. There are many ways to describe mysterious airborne disk-shaped objects, but English speakers today say "flying saucer" as an automated reflex without imagining airborne dishware.

This internalization means the origins of most conventions often get lost to the ages. We learn these rules as "the way things are done." In eighteenth-century France, carriages drove on the left, but the leaders of the French Revolution switched traffic to the right as a "democratic" rejection of the ancien régime. Today the French drive on the right out of habit, not out of antimonarchical sentiment. The more the backstory is forgotten, the more conventions seem to be the "natural" order of the world. Violations consequentially are "unnatural" and require sanctions.

Once conventions become internalized, should we still call them "conventions"? In these cases, we act out of habit rather than as an intentional coordination with others or as a way to avoid social disapproval. That being said, there is still a strong link between status and habits: specifically, the social hierarchy influences *which* conventions we internalize. We are more likely to imitate the "correct" conventions practiced by high-status members of our communities. We may copy some behaviors indiscriminately. Even the "haughtiest country gentleman," writes nineteenth-century French sociologist Gabriel Tarde, could not "keep his accent, his manners, and his point of view from being a little like those of his servants and tenants." But when we do take up low-status acts, others are likely to nudge us back to the proper high-status alternatives. The inverse is also true: the psychologist Bruce Hood notes, "We dislike individuals from outside of our social group more if they mimic us." The unwanted imitation of low-status outsiders makes us conscious of our internalized conventions, and as a result, we may move on to less "polluted" alternatives.

Our status needs also guide us toward particular environments, where we'll likely imitate our peers. *The Onion* TV segment "Thousands of Girls Match Description of Missing Sorority Sister" joked that Ohio police struggled to find a missing woman with "dyed blonde hair, Ugg boots, purple nail polish, and oversized sunglasses" because this description fit nearly every sorority member in the state. Many sorority sisters may unconsciously gravitate toward the same styles—but only after making a status-based decision to join the group in the first place. Furthermore, new members tend to imitate high-ranking seniors. When the writer Stephanie Talmadge pledged a sorority, she was impressed by the upper-level students who wore "more makeup more expertly applied, and paired more expensive-looking dresses with coordinating accessories." Not only did they set standards, they enforced them: "We would submit photos of ourselves in our dresses from several angles to the recruitment chairs for approval."

Internalization unlocks the final power of conventions: setting our perceptual framework for observing the world. Our senses may gather information, but that information is then interpreted through a screen of conventional habits, beliefs, and knowledge. Depending on our cultural background, we hear, see, remember, and pay attention to things differently. The perception of time, for example, is a convention. The Japanese understand an agreed-upon meeting time as the last possible moment of proper arrival, while Middle Easterners view it as a very rough guideline. Perception of color is also conventional. Even though humans without color blindness can distinguish between 7.5 to 10 million different colors, our conventions determine how we divide that spectrum into specific chromatic units. The Russian language divides the American color blue into two distinct shades: light blue (*goluboy*) and dark blue (*siniy*). Conventions also change how we hear music. The neuroscientist and music scholar Daniel Levitin explains that musical scales are "a subset of the theoretically infinite number of pitches, and every culture selects these based on historical tradition or somewhat arbitrarily." The idea that major chords sound "happy" and minor chords are "sad"? That's a convention. While encountering a piece of "solemn" Indian music, the author Aldous Huxley confessed, "Listen as I might, I was unable to hear anything particularly mournful or serious, anything specially suggestive of self-sacrifice in the piece. To my Western ears it sounded much more cheerful than the dance which followed it."

These internalized conventions are known in sociology as *habitus*, and they guide our talking, walking, dressing, and thinking, as well as how we judge what is good, correct, fun, and beautiful. The French sociologist Pierre Bourdieu, who is most associated with the term, writes, "The schemes of the habitus . . . owe their specific efficacy to the fact that they function below the level of consciousness and language, beyond the reach of introspective scrutiny or control by the will." Once the social repetition of a convention lodges into our habitus, the practice will feel instinctive rather than arbitrary. From here, culture shapes the expression of basic physical needs. The cultural anthropologist Clyde Kluckhohn notes, "Even such apparently biological processes as sneezing, walking, sleeping, and making love are stylized." Evolutionary biologists often claim health is critical for choosing potential sexual partners. And yet the dominant aesthetic conventions of an era can push men toward women with ostensibly "unhealthy" appearances. Fashion advertisements in the 1990s propagated "heroin chic" by using emaciated models. Today white teeth are a sign of health; many centuries ago, elites in Asia preferred women with blackened teeth. Most people gag at the smell of necrosis—bacteria eating the dead cells of the human body—but during the centuries of foot binding in China, high-status men found an erotic appeal in the rotten odor emanating from women's tightly bandaged feet.

Internalization explains our strong attachments to group behaviors. Humans become very susceptible to the *is-ought fallacy*—defined by political scientist Russell Hardin as "a very nearly universal tendency of people to move from what *is* to what *ought to be* in the strong sense of concluding that what is right or good." Conventions start as solutions to coordination problems but take on moral dimensions over time. Customs different from our own aren't just unnatural but immoral. When first offered a chocolate beverage in the New World, the Milanese adventurer Girolamo Benzoni thought it "more a drink for pigs than a drink for humanity." In Chinua Achebe's novel *Things Fall Apart*, Nigerian tribal members complain about the depravity of a rival village: "All their customs are upside-down. They do not decide bride-price as we do, with sticks. They haggle and bargain as if they were buying a goat or a cow in the market."

Culture, writes anthropologist Marshall Sahlins, consists of "meaningful orders of persons and things." Conventions explain not only why certain persons do certain *things*, but the origin of collective *meanings* and *orders*. To follow the same arbitrary rules as another individual is to be part of the same "collectivity." As groups share certain practices, those practices form social bonds. The convention of wearing lederhosen and dirndl defines Bavarians as a people. Debutante balls are a rite of passage for wealthy WASP women. Russians don't just drink vodka as a stiff tipple—it's the lifeblood of the nation.

Each status group contains a multitude of distinct conventions, which all interlock through a strong internal logic. The custom for brides to wear white offers a logical parallel to the custom for widows to wear black. As we examine micro-conventions, we can discover broader macro-conventions acting as a "horizon" to which they all conform. *Paradigm* describes these macro-conventions— the underlying beliefs of a group that set the overall rules for permissible actions, offer guideposts in times of uncertainty, and build the frameworks for understanding and explanation. In the European feudal paradigm, all individual customs and traditions ultimately served to uphold the idea that society centered around the monarch and the Church. In a modern paradigm, conventions are anchored in the belief that the individual is the basic unit of society. Popular music after 1964 has conformed to a "Beatles paradigm"; the critic Ian Mac-Donald writes, "The Beatles' way of doing things changed the way things were done and, in so doing, changed the way we expect things to be done." Paradigms can also be arbitrary in a universal sense—different societies revolve around different paradigms—but once they become foundational, most minor conventions flow from their overarching ideas.

Despite a basis in mutual expectations and collectivities, conventions are not necessarily fair or democratic. If normal status depends on adhering to tacit rules, there are always political dimensions to who starts a convention and who maintains it. "Norms of partiality" benefit one group over another. Majorities commonly promote social norms that advantage themselves over minorities, and in internalizing these biased conventions, even the disadvantaged parties may come to accept them. The feminist critique of women's beauty standards, writes the sociologist Karen Callaghan, posits that "the woman who strives to achieve an aesthetic idea does so not for self-actualization or accomplishment, but for masculine approval." These standards have not just been oppressive but deadly. In the nineteenth century, stiff crinoline petticoats puffed out skirts so far that the cheap materials often brushed against open flames and caught fire. This arbitrary convention of dress caused three thousand women to be burned alive. Meanwhile, men wore wool suits both flameproof and close to the body.

Even when conventions tend to be obviously unfair or clash against communal principles, challengers face social disapproval for choosing alternatives. While dining out one day, the radical activist Emma Goldman lit up a cigarette with her male companions in a minor act of gender equality, only to be thrown out on the street. When Goldman persisted in her promotion of unpopular anarchist ideas, the United States threw her out of the country. Goldman's pursuit of change, despite the obvious adversities, demonstrates the economist Anthony Heath's assertion: "The fact that there is a social norm does not . . . automatically entail that it will be obeyed. Everyone has his price: the benefits of conformity must be compared with the benefits to be obtained elsewhere, and there is bound to be some level of alternative benefits that will successfully tempt the individual into deviance."

This tight relationship between conventions, social approval, and status supports the anthropologist Clifford Geertz's description of culture as "best seen not as complexes of concrete behavior patterns—customs, usages, traditions, habit clusters" but instead as "a set of control mechanisms—plans, recipes, rules, instructions—for the governing of behavior." Conventions create habits and patterns of behavior through carrots of social approval and sticks of social disapproval. Since culture is based on arbitrary behaviors, individuals could always wander aimlessly from practice to practice. Conventions, whether conscious or internalized, explain why people instead cluster around the same patterns. And status is intertwined in the entire process.

The literary scholar Raymond Williams called culture "one of the two or three most complicated words in the English language." Indeed: the 1952 book *Culture: A Critical Review of Concepts and Definitions* alone offers 150 definitions. Even our colloquial usage remains ambiguous: Is culture a way of life, fine art, pop culture, or organizational norms? While we may be no closer here to settling on a singular definition, we at least know what culture is "made of": *conventions are the individual units of culture.* Everything we point to as "culture"—customs, traditions, fashions, and fads—exists as conventions.

And by looking at culture as conventions, we can already explain one part of the Grand Mystery of Culture: why humans repeatedly choose arbitrary practices over valid alternatives.

Just as there are no status-less societies, the anthropologist A. L. Kroeber notes, "We have no record of cultureless human societies." Every society has a status structure, and every society has a culture—and now, with conventions, we get our first sense of how status and culture are linked. Conventions reveal the process in which group members form specific practices that go on to define them. But not all status groups are equal, and this suggests that conventions, too, will possess differential values.

RANKED CONVENTIONS AND STATUS VALUE

In 1906, future U.S. president Woodrow Wilson warned from his bully pulpit at Princeton University, "Nothing has spread socialistic feeling in this country more than the automobile. To the countryman they are a picture of the arrogance of wealth, with all its independence and carelessness." The average American yearly income at the time was $450; the cheapest cars started at $600, and their cost could reach ten times higher. At these prices automobiles were exclusive to the rich, and to Wilson's point, the public associated reckless driving with the upper class. But the next fifty years would quell Wilson's fears of socialist revolution. No, the rich didn't learn to drive safely; car ownership just became more common. The independence and carelessness once exclusive to the top of society became a shared part of American life.

The expansion of car ownership did not, however, alleviate divisions in society. Instead, the simple convention that "wealthy people drive cars" expanded into multiple conventions where brand affiliations mapped to specific status tiers. By the 1950s, the lower middle class drove Fords, Chevrolets, and Plymouths, while the middle-middle class drove Pontiacs, Dodges, Mercurys, and Studebakers. Upper management preferred Buicks, Oldsmobiles, and Chryslers. Corporate CEOs owned Imperials, Lincolns, and Cadillacs. (The chairman of the board opted for a special "Fleetwood" Cadillac.) Marketing campaigns made these status associations explicit. The writer E. B. White noted at the time, "From reading the auto ads you would think that the primary function of the motor car in America was to carry its owner first into a higher social stratum."

Conventional differences by status tier are inevitable because there must be observable ways to mark differences in rank. A superiority of position should be reflected in the superiority of benefits. While organizations often contrive these differences, they can also occur naturally. Stratification determines the social space we inhabit, and our family and closest friends tend to be at similar status levels. After spending time in the same community, we come to share the same habitus and lifestyle conventions. These are expressed in the expense, quality, and design of possessions; speech patterns (use of polite language or slang); means of earning a living; self-presentation (dress, hair, makeup, fitness); location and quality of domiciles; and hired services (do we mow the lawn or do we pay someone else to do it?). Max Weber noted, "Social status is normally expressed above all in the imputation of a specifically regulated style of life to everyone who wishes to belong to the circle." Lifestyle, in other words, is both a requirement of social rank and an expression of it.

In past societies based on ascribed status, formal rules and proclamations regulated lifestyle conventions. Sumptuary laws codified which classes could wear which garments. Aztec warriors marked their status through embroidered cotton cloaks, lip plugs, turquoise and gold earrings, and bright feathers— all of which were forbidden to commoners. There were also different standards of justice by status tier. European aristocrats resolved disputes through duels with pistols. Whatever risks of fatality, bowing out of a duel was seen as dishonorable. Only the upper class, however, had the right to duel. When Voltaire—a commoner—challenged the nobleman Chevalier de Rohan to a duel, the Chevalier was so incensed that he hired roughnecks to pummel the writer while he watched from his carriage with glee.

Isolated communities can also develop distinct conventions. Living in proximity to sugar factories, the Galician Jews of Ukraine and southeastern Poland came to prefer sweeter foods. Meanwhile, Litvak Jews, without access to beet sugar, ate saltier dishes. Despite their having a common language and genetic origin, the culinary distinctions between them became conventional, habitual, and imbued with meanings and norms. Even today Galician descendants still prefer sweet gefilte fish, while American-born Litvak grandmothers complain about *those Galitzianers* who put sugar in everything.

With the development of achieved status, we've abandoned sumptuary laws and given Lady Justice a blindfold. But status-tier-based conventions are still ever present, albeit more ambiguous. Café lattes have become a cliché for an elitist beverage, despite millions of low-income Americans drinking them daily. As much as so-called luxury goods are sold as adornment reserved for the very rich, the major European brands reap great profits from middle-class customers.

Even with mass media minimizing the effects of geographical isolation, the social differences of stratification still lead to isolated pockets of conventions. At Los Angeles Airport, celebrities pay exorbitant amounts to embark through a special private terminal outside of the public eye named PS, where they are delivered onto the tarmac by a BMW 7 Series sedan. Between these terminals and the rise of private jet travel, the once universal practice of schlepping through public airports by foot has become a middle-class convention.

This leads to the most crucial point of this chapter: not all conventions are equal. The LAX private terminal is not *another* terminal—it's understood as the *better* one. Black tie is fancier than street clothes, and Cadillacs are more prestigious than Chevrolets. Every convention can be placed on two hierarchies: (1) the tier *within* a single status group; and (2) the position *between* groups on the global status ranking. At Los Angeles Airport wealth and status create separate check-in conventions, but on a global level, the very act of checking into an airport remains a high-status activity.

Every convention, then, has a differential *status value*, reflecting how much status can be gained through conforming to it. A convention exclusive to a higher status group has high status value, while a convention associated with a lower status group has negative status value. Widely held customs have neutral status value.

Status value is implicit—we can't measure it like we would the price of commodities. And we often sense it in conventions without seeing a direct connection to high-status groups. Due to the status taboo, we rarely directly verbalize the fact that status value exists, but it's far from imaginary. No one may be healed with divine magic when they are told "bless you," but the statement has a neutral status value. Saying that conventional phrase to neighbors provides social approval; saying nothing or suggesting the neighbor may have caught a contagious illness will be met with social disapproval. When we follow a convention with high status value, we improve our chances to secure normal status from a higher-status group and thus derive superior social benefits. If we

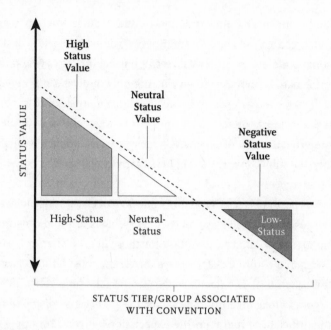

High
Status
Value

Neutral
Status
Value

Negative
Status
Value

STATUS VALUE

High-Status   Neutral-   Low-
                     Status   Status

STATUS TIER/GROUP ASSOCIATED
WITH CONVENTION

choose to take part in a convention with low status value, we risk losing those benefits.

To satisfy our fundamental desire for status, it is rational to consider status value when weighing an arbitrary practice against its alternatives. Perhaps an upper-middle-class New Yorker finds a Barcalounger more comfortable than an Eames chair, but only the Eames chair adheres to her high-status community's conventions of interior design. This changes the calculus of the purchase: Is the immediate comfort of a Barcalounger worth the long-term discomforts of status loss? An arbitrary practice may have no practical value over its alternatives, but once anchored in a convention, it offers status value and can improve our lives. This creates a constant trade-off between raw practicality and social approval. When useful Western goods such as radios and kerosene started to appear in Papua New Guinea, the local population still preferred to spend their money on ceremonial pigs to impress others through elaborate feasts.

But just as we internalize conventions, status value acts on our brains at a subconscious level. Conventions with high status value simply appear to us as beautiful ingredients for a dream life, whereas the conventions with low status value appear disturbing, toxic, or immoral. We often rationalize the allure of status value by attributing our attraction to other values, such as use value (practicality), exchange value (cost), sentimental value (memories), or idiosyncratic personal preferences. Empirical research is beginning to find proof that extrinsic information such as status value not only motivates our choices but even alters how we experience pleasure. A recent neuroscience experiment discovered that subjects preferred cheaper wines when unaware of the price, and then preferred the taste of expensive wines once prices were revealed. More interestingly, the subjects' pathways of brain activity changed along with their change in preference.

Since status position is relative, status value is also relative. Sociologist Pierre Bourdieu writes that, for each layer of society, "What is rare and constitutes an inaccessible luxury or an absurd fantasy for those at an earlier or lower level becomes banal and common." This plays out in the most famous passage of Tom Wolfe's 1987 novel *The Bonfire of the Vanities*; the protagonist, Sherman McCoy, is "going broke on a million dollars a year" because his bond-trading income is insufficient to maintain the expectations of New York upper-crust life. To keep up with his peers, he must shell out huge sums for club dues, luxury clothing, designer furniture, tuition at top-rank private schools, and children's birthday parties with carnival rides. Bourdieu explains predicaments like McCoy's: "Having a million does not in itself make one able to live like a millionaire, and parvenus generally take a long time to learn that what they see as culpable prodigality is, in their new condition, expenditure of basic necessity."

As we move up the status hierarchy, we must adopt conventions with higher status value. This mostly involves buying more expensive goods. The rich can spend more, and the expensive items they buy become standard within their status tier. "One does not move up in a one-class suburb," writes the cultural historian Russell Lynes about the standards of homeownership. "One moves out—to another suburb where the houses and the lawns are bigger, the trees older and taller, and the atmosphere is one of permanence not transience." Even without the experience of living among those with higher status, we can learn the proper conventions from glossy magazines, which exist for this purpose. *Harper's Bazaar* made sure readers in 1915 knew that "the woman who doesn't have at least one Chanel is hopelessly out of the running."

Knowing and participating in high-status lifestyle conventions—even certain greetings, subtle preferences, and nonverbal cues—is a critical part of gaining and maintaining high status. This particular knowledge is known as *cultural capital*, defined by the sociologists Michèle Lamont and Annette Lareau as "widely shared high status cultural signals (attitudes, preferences, formal knowledge, behaviors, goods and credentials) used for social and cultural exclusion." Cultural capital is most easily acquired through spending years absorbing the tastes, language, behaviors, and preferences of high-status people. For those born wealthy, cultural capital is embodied and unconscious. Upstarts must acquire this knowledge from scratch, and any awkwardness or mistakes may reveal their outsider origin. In some cases cultural capital can be useful in its own right—pairing the right wine with brie is delicious—but this knowledge takes its greatest value as a means to gain acceptance in the high-status world. In the 1950s, writer Vance Packard interviewed the head of a consulting company who concluded that "more important than belonging to the right club is ability to behave in the knowing manner once inside."

With an expansion in the paths to high status over the last century, there is no longer a single body of cultural capital. There is a Hollywood entertainment mogul way of being high status that is distinct from that of Texan oil magnates. But within each status group, members still must conform to particular conventions to maintain their standing. "The failure to consume in due quantity and quality," economist Thorstein Veblen writes, "becomes a mark of inferiority and demerit." Or as Sherman McCoy reasons in *The Bonfire of the Vanities*, "Once you had lived in a $2.6 million apartment on Park Avenue—it was impossible to live in a $1 million apartment!"

As an extension of status integrity, members of a status group tend to believe that individuals in each tier should consume *at their proper level*. The rich shouldn't live like the poor, and the poor shouldn't pretend to be rich. The Roman emperor Nero faced an assassination attempt—not for murdering his mother, kicking his pregnant wife to death, or burning Christians alive, but for daring to stoop to the low-status act of playing the stringed cithara in public concerts. Among the low-status groups, feelings of sour grapes or contempt for profligacy may breed resentment toward high-status-value conventions. In the 1852 book *Rural Architecture*, writer Lewis F. Allen advised farmers to ignore the principles of high design: "Leave all this vanity to town-folk, who have nothing better—or who, at least, think they have—to amuse themselves." Just as following the same conventions creates feelings of solidarity, conventional differences engender conflict. In *The Catcher in the Rye*, Holden Caulfield concludes, "It's really hard to be roommates with people if your suitcases are much better than theirs—if yours are really good ones and theirs aren't. You think if they're intelligent and all, the other person, and have a good sense of humor, that they don't give a damn whose suitcases are better, but they do. They really do."

During times of broad economic growth, lower status tiers can suddenly afford to take part in higher-status conventions. This raises the standards for all of society. Everyone feels they must also consume at a higher level to retain normal status—i.e., keeping up with the Joneses. Once the automobile became affordable by the middle class, being middle class required owning a car. Face-to-face interactions tend to be the most important reference for individuals to establish these norms of spending. This explains why the *neighbors* of lottery winners also end up buying fancier cars. But the mass media can trigger this on a national scale by resetting expectations of what constitutes a "normal" lifestyle. In 1956 President Sukarno of Indonesia blasted Hollywood executives, complaining that the middle class in his country suffered a new dissatisfaction with their lives after they watched American films in which average households owned luxuries such as automobiles and electric appliances.

So far we've seen how status requires conformity to certain arbitrary practices, and now we understand that the resulting conventions take on status value. Next we'll apply this knowledge to our own individual behavior—and how the specific pressures of our status position push us to be alike and also be different.

IMITATION AND DISTINCTION

The meme template for "Hipster Barista" shows a bearded, tattooed white man in a deep V-neck T-shirt, square glasses, and a black scarf—crossing his arms in disgust. According to Know Your Meme, typical captions on Hipster Barista play with "common 'hipster' stereotypes of being judgmental yet hypocritical." One example reads, "Serving these corporate capitalist pigs coffee makes me sick" with the punch line at the bottom: "—Tweeted from my iPad2."

In his essay "What Was the Hipster?" Mark Greif notes that the word "hipster" is "primarily a pejorative—an insult that belongs to the family of *poseur, faker, phony, scenester,* and *hanger-on.*" Everyone hates hipsters, even hipsters themselves. As the Hipster Barista meme illustrates, a primary source of perceived hipster villainy is their complaints about the imitative behavior of mainstream society *while* engaging in imitative behavior. When the mathematician and neuroscientist Jonathan Touboul published a research paper in 2014 about the behavior of neurons in the brain changing in order to be different from the ones around it, he called it the Hipster Effect: "Trying hard to be different often ends up in hipsters consistently taking the same decisions, in other words all looking alike."

But we should defend hipsters on this particular point. Simultaneous imitation and distinction aren't hypocrisy—they're universal human behaviors. As we learned earlier, normal status requires following certain conventions. This means *imitating* our peers, while *distinguishing* ourselves from the behaviors of lower-status groups and rivals. Meanwhile, achieving higher status requires *distinguishing* ourselves from our current status tier and *imitating* the practices of superiors. The end result is that imitation and distinction act as complementary magnetic forces on our lifestyle choices, pushing us toward our perceived superiors and away from our perceived inferiors. And the power behind those forces is status.

We seem to enjoy free will when making daily choices—what to eat and drink, how to dress, what to buy. We can select the flavor of kombucha or Powerade that best quenches our thirst at that particular moment. Whatever fundamental desires we have to be ourselves, however, must be aligned with our fundamental desire for status. Normal status requires an *imitation* of group norms. This can be very easy. Humans are hardwired for mimicry and absorb the behaviors of our community. In cases where we've internalized the expected norms, we make choices "for ourselves" that match external expectations. The award-winning Native American jewelry artist Keri Ataumbi crafts pieces that reference Indigenous motifs—an artistic choice, certainly, but one familiar to her after growing up on the Wind River Reservation and receiving instruction in tribal traditions from her mother.

Where imitation most commonly becomes a conscious act is when we join new groups later in life and seek other members' validation. Upon moving to Madrid from the countryside, the surrealist filmmaker Luis Buñuel was "paralyzed" by his "provincialism" and spent his days "trying to imitate the way people dressed and acted." Imitation is often the most rational solution to any dilemma. The economist Robert H. Frank writes, "Imitative behavior often occurs when someone who doesn't know exactly what to do identifies other persons who seem to know and are doing it."

Imitation is required for attaining normal status within a group, but there is an additional requirement: we must affirm our *differences* from rival groups. Anthropologist Ruth Benedict notes, "One of the earliest of human distinctions [is] the difference in kind between 'my own' closed group and the outsider." British upper-class terms of condemnation have included "NLU" (not like us) and "NLO" (not like one). Conventional differences are critical for group demarcation, and groups emphasize the distinct conventions that draw these clear lines. In the words of the anthropologist Mary Douglas, imitation creates "bridges" to compatriots, while distinction raises "fences" to keep out rivals. But where differences occur, every meaningful act of imitation also functions as distinction. Every bridge serves as a fence. In the musical *Grease* the girl gang the Pink Ladies wear matching pink satin jackets as a bridge to one another, but in doing so, raise a fence with other students.

Intentional distinction from rivals is best described as *counterimitation*. In the most obvious cases, counterimitation can feel mechanical and arbitrary: doing the opposite merely to do the opposite. A young musician who left the jazz scene in the early 1960s complained, "There's so much ritual and ceremony junk. They have to talk a special language, dress different, and wear a different kind of glasses. And it just doesn't mean a damn thing except 'we're different.'" With the is-ought fallacy and internalization, however, we tend to feel deep emotional umbrage toward our rivals' behavior. When a General Motors fan decorates his pickup truck with a decal of Calvin urinating on a Ford logo, he is expressing an honest belief about the inferior value of Ford trucks.

Normal status in a group requires both imitation and counterimitation. Higher status, on the other hand, requires standing above others through rare talents and valuable assets. By definition a higher position requires *individual distinction*. But personal difference also involves breaking norms, for which there may be sanctions. How do individuals negotiate these competing pressures? Many pursue the least controversial forms of individual distinction: namely, exceptional performance against the group's agreed-upon status criteria. Rank-and-file members of a basketball team never complain about an MVP's distinctively high number of points scored each game. As long as distinction fits within the collective beliefs of the group, individuals have more leeway to break from the norm.

Another low-risk form of individual distinction is *emulation*—the chasing of status value through the imitation of higher-status conventions. If everyone in a middle-class neighborhood owns a Toyota Camry, individual distinction can be as easy as buying a Mercedes-Benz, a car common among the rich. This isn't a particularly clever form of distinction, just a derivative imitation of well-known exceptional practices. And yet emulation is the wellspring for most individual aspirations and desires. American economist Thorstein Veblen writes, "Each class envies and emulates the class next above it in the social scale." Emulation is a safe bet, but not a sure one. It can fail where groups strictly enforce status integrity. Individuals taking part in higher-status conventions without the accepted levels of capital are castigated as impostors. But aspirants always have a built-in alibi for emulation: high-status people are successful, so their lifestyle choices, whether yoga, Gucci loafers, or paleo diets, must be *the right way to live*. Our superiors have more money and information, and better skills, and this positions their choices as exemplary references. When the robber barons emerged in the late nineteenth century as the first ultrarich Americans, they had no clear guide on how to build palatial homes, so they just copied the architecture of wealthy European families.

At its heart emulation is simply a form of imitation. True individual distinction requires eschewing convention to find new and unique behaviors. In Western society over the last few centuries, there has been not only more freedom to make lifestyle choices, but also a growing moral duty that we become self-actualized, distinctive humans. A "cult of the individual" has permeated culture, art, literature, media, and advertising. The philosopher Charles Taylor summarizes, "There is a certain way of being human that is *my* way. I am called upon to live my life in this way, and not in imitation of anyone else's." High status in modern society thus requires satisfying an additional status criterion: to be distinct. Mindless imitation becomes a low-status act. The philosopher René Girard notes, "We don't resign ourselves to the recognition that we are imitating people we admire and envy as the expression of our desires. We see it as something to be ashamed of." Fashion guides thus always recommend breaking the mold. In 1922 etiquette columnist Emily Post wrote, "The woman who is chic is always a little different," in contrast to "the dressed-to-the-minute women who, like sheep exactly, follow every turn of latest fashion blindly and without the slightest sense of distance or direction."

While there may be a philosophical origin to this obsession with individual distinction, these demands also match the internal logic of status structures. Emulation requires imitating the group above you, but for those at the top of the hierarchy, there should be no one to imitate. A good indication of having super-high status, then, is being able to get away with distinctive acts. The moral duty of self-actualization is actually a status duty: *individuals at the top of the hierarchy must pursue unique behaviors and distinctive choices.* The suits of former Egyptian leader Hosni Mubarak didn't just use custom wool but had pinstripes that spelled out his name in Arabic.

In theory, accomplishing this should be even easier than imitation. We can just follow our hearts and do whatever we want, no matter what others think. Or even better, we can do outrageous things, like wear Ziploc bags as shoes and a brown-paper grocery bag on our head that says, in purple Magic Marker, "Juxtaposed Pickle Exasperation." There are an infinite number of potential idiosyncrasies.

But alas, unconventional acts are tolerated only for those who already have high status. Sociologist George Homans explains, "To keep his high status a man must provide rare and valuable services to others, but so long as he does that, the other members may allow him some leeway in lesser things. He may even take the leeway. Mere slavish conformity to any old norm may put him back among the masses instead of keeping him set apart from them." And so the higher our status, the more distinctive we *can* be, and the more distinctive we *must* be. By this same logic, middle-status people tend to be conservative. "The living rooms of the lower middle class," writes the linguist Rudi Keller, "exhibit a higher degree of conformity than those of the upper middle class, while the living rooms of the upper middle class are less individual than the living rooms of the upper classes." Lower-status individuals, if already outside the realm of social approval, may also live more freely because they have nothing left to lose. But lower-status distinction is interpreted as mere rule breaking. Respected distinction is an elite privilege.

Individual distinction is risky—and often impossible to pull off when everyone is trying to achieve the same thing. We all face an additional challenge in *pluralistic ignorance*: the fact that we make our "different" choices without knowing everyone else's next actions. Ray Garcia, an old-school sneakerhead, confessed, "I didn't want to see one other person with the same sneakers as me. Not one," but achieving this requires not only choosing exclusive styles but guaranteeing they'll continue to be exclusive in the future as well. Distinction is difficult in modern society when we all share the same categories of self-definition: clothes, homes, cars, beverages. Pluralistic ignorance means even the boldest acts of individual distinction can end up looking like imitation.

The pressures of status give every individual a set of conflicting demands: imitate the group norms, counterimitate rivals, emulate superiors but not too obviously, and be unique but not too unique. In sum, we must distinguish ourselves to demonstrate individual difference for higher status, while concurrently imitating the conventions of our groups to retain normal status. There are no authoritative solutions to these contradictory requirements—only risk-management strategies. We must pick a position on a spectrum between pure individuality (breaking all known conventions at high risk, high reward) and total conformity (adhering closely to all established conventions at low risk, low reward). But from what we've learned, our position on the spectrum should be correlated with our status level. Those with high status dive into the deep end of distinction, while skittish members of normal-status tiers stick to the shallow end of imitation. Ascribed status categories also play a role in determining our place on the imitation-distinction spectrum. For the status-disadvantaged, the most efficient way to move up is clear and bold emulation. The status-advantaged, by contrast, can pursue subtler forms of individual distinction. This link between status position and distinction becomes important for a later discussion, as we'll see how status influences *innovativeness*—the propensity to take up new behaviors. Those who have either very high or very low status are more likely to try new things.

The social psychologist Marilynn Brewer posits that most people choose a strategy of "optimal distinctiveness" right in the middle of the spectrum, making distinctive micro-choices that conform to the group's macro-conventions. The writer John Seabrook explains this strategy in layman's terms: "You want to be perceived as original, but not so original that you are outside of the marketplace of popular opinion." In the 1990s TV drama *My So-Called Life*, Angela

Chase, the mousy protagonist, dyes her hair "crimson glow" to distinguish herself from her nerdy peers. She didn't invent the idea of bright red hair; it emulated a well-established convention among alternateens. But it allowed Angela to break away from her nerd peer group and take up with a higher-status crowd. Had she gone for true individual distinction—e.g., by partially shaving her head in homage to the *śikha* style of Hare Krishnas—she may have alienated everyone, even the rebellious outcasts.

Humans have an innate predisposition to imitate, but in modern times we must reconcile this with a moral duty to be distinct. To gain status, then, we must balance four specific requirements of imitation and distinction:

- To secure normal status, we must *imitate* group conventions.
- To avoid low status, we must *counterimitate* rival conventions.
- To gain higher status, we must *emulate* conventions with high status value.
- To achieve the highest status, we must strive for *individual distinction* through unique behavior.

No individual can pursue all four simultaneously. Instead we're likely to choose a specific risk-mitigation strategy that best matches our status position. This is not a trivial idea: our specific balance of imitations and distinctions determines our behavior and, as we'll see next, who we are.

When ice first became available in Sri Lanka, fishermen were finally able to sell their catch in urban markets. With rising incomes, many decided to emulate their middle-class superiors by buying televisions. They proudly placed the new TV sets in the very center of their huts—in villages that lacked electricity.

To solve the mysteries of human behavior, bioanthropologists point to instincts. Psychologists suggest manias, phobias, and disorders. Economists assume rationality. But the Sri Lankan fishermen's behavior is best explained through conventions—namely, actions taken in pursuit of status value. Linguist Rudi Keller argues that conventional thinking is arguably the "most fantastic and certainly most decisive of human abilities." The entire enterprises of language and culture exist only because we can so easily coordinate around arbitrary choices.

But this presents us with an uncomfortable truth. If status guides our be-havior, we make many choices for *nonrational* reasons. And this leads to skep-ticism about status value as a genuine value. Status value is fleeting and out of our personal control. It is always contingent upon where a convention sits within the social structure. Where we do choose for status value, our brains obfuscate the reasons and tell us we are desiring something more rational. But status value, despite how much we dislike and distrust it, *does* make a material impact on our lives. We must adopt practices with status value to gain higher status.

Conventions explain how status pushes us into following certain arbitrary behaviors. But to gain status for such acts, we can't follow conventions in pri-vate: we must perform them in front of others. Conventions are always more than the core action. They also act as *signs*.

Chapter Three

SIGNALING AND STATUS SYMBOLS

·)⊗(·

Status must be communicated, as illustrated by Beck's cryptic "Loser" years, the Cadillac of grain silos, Italian opera in *The Caine Mutiny*, and the Anna Delvey fraud.

·)⊗(·

STATUS CLAIMS AND STATUS APPRAISALS

At the very beginning of 1994, a goofy, long-haired singer-songwriter named Beck appeared out of nowhere and scored an overnight hit with the slacker rap anthem "Loser." No one seemed to know much about Beck, not even his last name. There were only the merest scraps of biographical information: he was from L.A., he worked part-time as a leaf blower, and before signing with major label DGC, he put out his music on a tiny indie label with the mischievous name Bong Load Records. "Loser" only added to the enigma, an unplaceable mix of preternatural pop instincts with absurd lyrics: "And my time is a piece of wax falling on a termite / That's choking on the splinters." Was Beck an idiot savant folkie pulled from the gutters of L.A., or a secret musical prodigy pretending to be an idiot savant folkie?

This question would be answered on February 20, 1994, the date of Beck's first appearance on MTV's alternative music show, *120 Minutes*. His DGC labelmate Thurston Moore, from the band Sonic Youth, would serve as the interviewer. Moore had heard "Loser" in a record store, and he, too, found Beck to be "a mystery." But upon their meeting in real life, Beck told Moore that his grandfather was the 1960s avant-garde Fluxus artist Al Hansen. The two then conspired to run the *120 Minutes* interview as a sixties-style happening in which Beck would evade Moore's questions in strange ways. How did it feel to have a hit song? Beck replied, "Surfing in an oil spillage." His real last name? Beck threw his Timberland boot behind the set. Beck "answered" a later question by pulling out a small Dictaphone and playing the dialogue back in reverse at chipmunk speed. To the audiences at home, the idiot savant folkie theory was looking strong.

On the fourth question, however, Beck gave the audiences the first clue into his true character. When asked, "What exactly is the first record you ever bought?" Beck responded without hesitation, "Probably a Haino record. Maybe *Xanadu*." "Wow," Moore deadpanned, "I'm sure all of our viewers are very familiar with those and can relate to you on it." To decode this cryptic answer: "Haino" meant the Japanese experimental noise guitarist Keiji Haino, and "*Xanadu*" referred to the Olivia Newton-John 1980 roller-skating disco box-office bomb, which by the time of the interview had become a relic of forgotten kitsch. Name-dropping impenetrable guitar noise and a widely loathed disco album—as his *first* record purchases—revealed that Beck knew an incredible variety of esoteric music. Beck was *signaling*: hinting at deep knowledge to suggest much greater mastery of his craft than the mere ability to pump out novelty singles.

The term "signaling" is used in both economics and zoology to describe when individuals communicate their high quality through specific clues in order to be selected by another party. In the wild, male birds signal their fitness for mating by flaunting gaudy plumage. In the job market, candidates signal their fitness for jobs by pointing to college degrees.

Signaling also works to explain the process of acquiring status. As the sociologist Hugh Dalziel Duncan reminds us, "Status enactment is always *a plea*, a petition, for status is *given*, never taken." We must ascertain the status level of strangers to treat them properly, and only when our own status is recognized do we receive social benefits. Signaling is a communication process. We make a *status claim* to others through communicating certain signals, and then others perform a *status appraisal* by interpreting those signals.

Of course, status claims and appraisals are not always conscious acts. We all implicitly signal every day through our behavior, possessions, speech, and knowledge, and we read everyone else's behavior as signals. This means that every action we take—in conforming to convention—transcends the action itself and becomes a *sign*. Beck's preference for Japanese noise music is not just the enjoyment of distorted dissonance, but when publicized, serves as a clue into understanding Beck as a musician. He won over the higher-status Thurston Moore through name-dropping Fluxus, Japanese noise, and kitsch disco. They became frequent musical collaborators, and in 2011 Beck produced Moore's solo album *Demolished Thoughts*.

The ubiquity of status claims and appraisals transforms humans—even small children—into very efficient calculators of social position. The psychologist Cameron Anderson and his colleagues write, "Symbols as seemingly insignificant as slight differences in the amount of orange juice given to siblings, the decor in a person's office, or negligible differences in clothing can become objects of concern because they are decoded as markers of status." Researchers at Princeton University found that we judge wealth levels through individuals' clothing in as little as 130 milliseconds, proving Coco Chanel's maxim "If you wish to do business, the first thing is to look prosperous."

We don't have to signal to everyone—only in times of information asymmetry. Our friends, family, and neighbors know us well and made conclusions about our status level long ago. Most public individuals have a *reputation* based on past actions and interactions. (Fame maximizes these reputations to extreme degrees, with the mass media educating millions on the high status of celebrities.) But in modernity—the epoch that the anthropologist Charles Lindholm defines as "the condition of living among strangers"—most of us need to constantly claim status upon interaction with unknown parties. And in a world of achieved status, we may also need to signal recent increases in status to our acquaintances.

Why is signaling the main expression of status claims? Surely we could be more honest and direct: "Excuse me, madam, I am a very important person with high status, and as such, I expect to be treated with great courtesy and receive ample material benefits." This, unfortunately, doesn't work in light of the status taboo. We cringe when we hear desperate celebrities screeching to inadequately deferential inferiors, "*Do you know who I am?*" More fundamentally, direct status claims are self-defeating. Economist Jon Elster notes, "Nothing is so unimpressive as behavior designed to impress." We tend to discount information where there are obvious motivations to exaggerate; there's no truth in advertising, as they say. This logic extends to status claims: the highest-status individuals should have strong enough reputations to reduce the need for aggressive signaling. Boasting and bragging thus become an implicit sign of low status. Here we land upon the *principle of detachment*: very high-status individuals should seem detached from active attempts to gain status. In fact, the most successful status claims should never appear to *be* status claims.

Detachment prevents us from outright exclamations like "Give me status!" So perhaps an alternative path could be the overt demonstration of our status assets. We could show off our wealth through opening a suitcase of gold bullion or flashing the top-line number of a cryptocurrency wallet. But this also is unlikely to work. There is little time in social interaction for elaborate performances or an extended audit of financial portfolios. Moreover, such overwrought and unnatural status claims would also violate the principle of detachment. There is something unsavory about someone who goes around flashing the contents of a suitcase filled with currency.

With these limitations in mind, signaling emerges as the most practical solution. Rather than make explicit status claims, we can deploy subtle signals. Our *demeanor*—"etiquette, dress, deportment, gesture, intonation, dialect, vocabulary, small bodily movements and automatically expressed evaluations concerning both the substance and the details of life"—can provide evidence or symbols of high status without making us look as if we're making a status claim. Economists define signals as the "observable characteristics attached to the individual that are subject to manipulation by him." Combining this knowledge with what we learned about our imitations and distinctions, our signals draw upon the conventions we *consciously* choose to follow or not. The 1970s basketball star Walt Frazier signaled his success by driving around Manhattan in a Rolls-Royce. To reveal his deep musical knowledge, Beck name-dropped obscure albums.

At the same time, our demeanor also contains *cues*—involuntary and difficult-to-conceal features, such as body size and shape, gait, way of speaking, and degree of calmness. Cues are observable manifestations of our habitus, upbringing, and community affiliations, and because they can't be easily controlled, they are much more effective for gauging status levels than signals. Anyone can enhance their status claims by acquiring luxury goods and other high-status signals. Cues, on the other hand, develop as the result of unconscious or long-term conditioning. As Jay Gatsby said about Daisy Buchanan in

The Great Gatsby, "Her voice is full of money"—a timbre, accent, and cadence possible only after a lifetime living among the upper classes. Cues that place individuals as members of certain classes are also known as *social shibboleths*. In the most archetypal example, working-class Brits dropped the *h* sound in words, a trait that became even more obvious as a marker when they put the *h* back in the wrong places during attempts to sound proper. (Thus Eliza Doolittle of *My Fair Lady*'s famous line: "In 'ertford, 'ereford and 'ampshire, 'urricanes 'ardly hever 'appen!")

Cues can either bolster or betray signals, making them valuable to appraisers looking for a glimpse into the "real" individual. Beck took up a weirdo slacker persona for his debut album but, over time, cues from his behavior and musical prowess cast further doubts on the authenticity of his sui generis leaf-blower origin story. Beck makes more sense as not just the grandson of an avant-garde artist, but as the son of David Campbell, a legendary music producer and arranger who worked on 450 gold and platinum albums. The interplay between signals and cues has critical implications for our behavior. The status-advantaged can often signal status with their cues alone, lessening the need to signal. The status-disadvantaged need more valuable signals to override their low-status cues. The philosopher Simone de Beauvoir believed women dressed up more than men because a man could rely on his profession for status claims, while "the woman who is deprived of *doing* anything feels that she expresses what she *is*" through adornment.

Besides signals and cues, there is an important third category of information used in status appraisals: *significant absences*. Appraisers also look for what is missing. An absence can be a refusal to participate in a convention, or participation in a different one from what is expected. In societies where businessmen wear neckties, *not* wearing a necktie offers useful information to suss out an individual's occupation. This may lead to ambiguities: tielessness is customary among blue-collar workers but also employees in the creative industries. But the fact that *not* doing things plays a role in status appraisals means no one can ever opt out of making status claims. Everything we do, say, and own—or choose not to do, say, or own—becomes a sign. Knowing this, we hide parts of ourselves that may get in the way of our status claims. In the early 1990s Beck decided that having no last name was more suitable to his slacker folkie persona than using that of his father or maternal grandfather.

Overall, signaling reveals that status must be earned from strangers through a subtle act of communication. We play an active role in status claims by choosing which signals to present and which to hide. Logically, then, to gain higher status, we adopt specific objects and behaviors with higher status value.

STATUS SYMBOLS

Twice the price of normal concrete grain silos, the navy-blue glass and steel Harvestore was the grain silo of choice for wealthy American farmers in the 1970s—the "Cadillac" of grain silos. "The one thing [Harvestores] were good for was a landmark," recalled a farmer. "When someone would ask where we lived, we would just say look for the three blue silos." Mere interest in purchasing a Harvestore drew farmers into a country-club-like social scene: salesmen wined and dined customers on seminar cruises and treated them to Las Vegas weekends. By the early 1980s these "Wisconsin skyscrapers" towered over the most prosperous farms in the American heartland. Harvestores weren't the most cost-efficient silos, nor even the most practical ones (farmers claimed problems with mold, and there were instances of spontaneous combustion), but they functioned very well as *status symbols*—observable objects and behaviors that aid individuals in status claims. Farmers who owned a Harvestore or two could communicate a higher status position than those who owned standard-issue silos.

As we just learned, status appraisers look for clues in our demeanor and possessions to estimate status, and so the most obvious way to signal a high social position is to show off certain goods or engage in certain behaviors with high status value. This begins inside the home. Simone de Beauvoir writes, "The home is not merely an interior within which the couple is shut away; it is also the expression of that couple's standard of life, its financial status, its taste, and thus the home must need be on view to other people." Farmers, likewise, show off their financial successes through farm equipment such as Harvestore silos. But now with modern society requiring constant signaling to strangers, the most effective status symbols are portable or transportable: luxurious cars, clothing, jewelry, accessories, and fragrances. To impress "transient observers," economist Thorstein Veblen advises, "the signature of one's pecuniary strength should be written in characters which he who runs may read." An Hermès handbag can broadcast status on the go.

In semiotics, "symbol" is a technical term for a sign that requires preexisting knowledge to be interpreted. Early-twentieth-century European women used camellias as a symbol to communicate their desire to be seduced. Suitors had to know the code to read this flower as an invitation. But a flower is also a flower—something used as adornment. The underlying object or behavior "transporting" the symbolic meanings is known as the *sign-vehicle*. Since we should avoid bragging about social position, successful status symbols rely on sign-vehicles that play a natural role in our daily lives. A million-dollar hunk of iron could be evidence of wealth, but it wouldn't work as a status symbol because normal people don't own raw industrial materials. The Harvestore, on the other hand, functions as a grain silo, and so it makes an ideal status symbol. Beyoncé and JAY-Z's daughter Blue Ivy Carter carried a Louis Vuitton Alma BB, because she needed a bag to schlep around her books and toys.

The principle of detachment means all status symbols require *alibis*— reasons for adoption other than status seeking. Beck listened to avant-garde noise for its aesthetic charms, not just to show off indie cred. Fancy cars always tout desirable features. The ultrapremium Eldorado Brougham Cadillacs of the late 1950s came with "anti-dive control, outriggers, pillarless styling, projectile-shaped gull-wing bumpers, [and] outboard exhaust ports." Status symbols that lack credible alibis tend to fail: ankle watches were popular at the beginning of the twentieth century, but they're not a practical way to tell time. Companies that produce luxury goods, from Louis Vuitton to Tiffany, Rolex, and Dom Perignon, understand the need for alibis, and their marketing provides detailed explanations of great craftsmanship, rare materials, unsurpassed comfort, and the highest levels of quality control. And yet, luxury goods never work as luxury goods based purely on functionality. They also must have status value. The philosopher Jean Baudrillard writes, "The functionality of goods comes afterward, adjusting itself to, rationalizing and at the same time repressing these fundamental structural mechanisms." The best proof of this can be found in the fact that luxury goods that are initially exclusive to a small segment of the population, such as nutmeg or air-conditioning, cease to be luxuries once they're widely available—despite their quality improving over time.

Even when armed with alibis, some status symbols are more conspicuous than others. Within wealthy communities, the most effective status symbols can be so discreet as to look like unconscious cues. In the past, only expensive tailored suit jackets came with working buttons on the sleeves, and so rich men would leave a button undone "accidentally" to show off this detail. Tom Wolfe explains, "There are just two classes of men in the world, men with suits whose buttons are just sewn onto the sleeve, just some kind of cheapie decoration, or—yes!—men who can unbutton the sleeve at the wrist because they have real buttonholes and the sleeve really buttons up." Well-to-do men who were familiar with this convention could read the signal of open cuff buttons and appraise the wearer as having high status.

How do we choose which status symbols to use? The social psychologists Dale T. Miller and Deborah A. Prentice have found in their research that "individuals generally try to present themselves in the most favorable possible light." In signaling, this translates into brandishing symbols associated with the highest possible status groups and tiers. As we saw in chapter 2, individuals know the positions of certain conventions within a social hierarchy and thus can interpret certain objects and practices as markers of status position. In the eighteenth century, economist Adam Smith noted the *principle of associativity*: "When two objects have frequently been seen together, the imagination requires a habit of passing easily from one to the other. If the first is to appear, we lay our account that the second is to follow." Status symbols rely on these associations. Harvestores became symbols of farming success, because the most successful farmers owned them. Playing squash suggests relations with the high-status people who play it.

Status symbols, therefore, must have clear associations with high-status groups. Poorer farmers paid double for Harvestore silos because they promised a means to be appraised as wealthy. Beck name-dropped noise artist Keiji Haino because the most erudite indie music fans loved his music. We use a specific word to indicate these high-status associations: *cachet*. The term comes from *lettres de cachet*, royal communications in medieval France that carried the official seal of the king. The monarch was a "fountain of honor," endowing prestige to anything associated with him. Cachet thus came not from the contents of the letter, but from the fact that the letter was sent by the king. Cachet explains why a Jaguar might at times be less mechanically reliable than a Toyota or Nissan, and yet more prestigious. High-status associations can change anything into a premium item. In the late 1970s the little-known Hong Kong clothing manufacturer Murjani transformed normal five-pocket denim pants into high-priced "designer jeans" by putting socialite Gloria Vanderbilt's name on the tag. Cachet powers the often elusive concept "cool"; nothing can be cool without associations to particular groups of high-status individuals, namely, musicians, celebrities, and popular teens.

The fact that cachet arises through associations with certain individuals and groups means that it can travel across "chains" of associations. When European elites fell in love with Russian ballet at the turn of the twentieth century, everything Russian took on cachet, including the borzoi breed of dogs. Status symbols gain value when associated with elites, but may also lose that value once associated with lower-status groups instead. Too much usage among non-elites, writes Adam Smith, means a status symbol "loses all the grace which it had appeared to possess before, and being now used only by the inferior ranks of people, seems to have something of their meanness and awkwardness." In the late 1950s the British rock 'n' roll singer Cliff Richard made black shirts with white ties stylish for a brief moment; then their quick uptake by mobsters and demimonde touts turned them into an obvious mark of lower social position.

To maintain cachet a convention must be exclusive to a high-status group. Rich people drink water, but the act of drinking water carries no cachet, because everyone drinks water. There must be a marked difference protected through barriers to imitation. In economics, these are called *signaling costs*— the cost it takes for an individual to acquire a certain signal. A lapel badge that says "I am extremely rich" isn't convincing because its creation and possession incur no significant costs. A Ferrari 812 Superfast, on the other hand, is more convincing because its $350,000 price tag makes imitation difficult. Successfully claiming high status requires not just demonstrating the ability to pay the signaling costs but to *easily* pay those costs.

Cachet and signaling costs are distinct qualities, but they're connected. Signaling costs are required to create and maintain the exclusion required for cachet. This tends to happen naturally: elites prefer conventions with high signaling costs, which gives their costly choices cachet. The favorite fruit of aristocrats in the eighteenth century was the pineapple, not just because of its delicious taste but because reproducing a warm growing climate in Europe made each pineapple cost the modern equivalent of around $10,000. But signaling costs alone don't create status symbols. A garbage truck is more expensive to purchase than most Lamborghinis, but no one considers a garbage truck to be a luxury automobile, because rich people don't drive them.

There are five common signaling costs. The first and most obvious is *money*. Since wealth correlates to status position in capitalist society, most status symbols are expensive. English-style horseback riding has status value because it's an expensive skill to learn. The second cost is *time*. A PhD signals experience because it takes years and years of education and validation from established professors. This is why traditional societies treat older people with high status: their valuable wisdom can only be accrued from decades of living.

The third cost is *exclusive access*. High-status people are granted access to restricted locations where they attend special events. There they acquire things unavailable to others. In the world of rowing, the Cambridge University Boat Club's mint-blue Beefeater T-shirt is very prestigious, since the only legitimate ways to acquire one are rowing for Cambridge or trading jerseys with them after a race. The fourth cost is *cultural capital*—knowledge of conventions acquired through spending time among high-status people. For example, espousing credible and detailed opinions about the relative merits of Harvard College's freshman dorms Thayer and Holworthy is limited to the school's former and current undergraduates.

The final cost is *norm breaking*. As we learned in the last chapter, breaking a convention leads to social disapproval. Using their leeway to be different, elites can more easily pay the costs of social disapproval. Arthur Capel, Coco Chanel's wealthy lover, dined in elegant restaurants wearing a casual sports jacket rather than a formal dinner jacket "because it pleased him to give an impression of strength and rudeness."

The rise and fall of signaling costs have an effect on status value. Pineapples can no longer signal status when they are available at every supermarket for a few dollars. Elites sometimes choose goods with low signaling costs, but the cachet tends to dilute very quickly. Absinthe became a high-status drink in the early nineteenth century thanks to associations with victorious French soldiers from the African campaigns. But anyone could order an absinthe. Within a few years, "absinthe had become a proletarian vice associated with epilepsy, epileptic offspring, tuberculosis, neglected children, and spending the food money on drink."

Each status group believes in the supremacy of its preferred status criteria, and this influences which signaling costs the members of the group care most about. New Money focuses on financial costs. Subcultures thrive on exclusive access and knowledge. This means *anything* can be a status symbol if it has cachet and high signaling costs. Coco Chanel made fake costume jewelry more chic than precious stones. For the economist Gary Becker, Stephen Hawking's *A Brief History of Time* was not just a difficult book on theoretical physics but something displayed "on coffee tables and as a source of pride in conversations at parties."

Money may be the most common signaling cost, but in a world with millions and millions of wealthy people, the most credible status symbols need to erect barriers beyond price. The Hermès Birkin has long been considered the most covetable handbag, not just because it is expensive, but because the brand's staff are instructed to only sell them to established patrons. Few people can afford them, and even fewer can build up the long-standing relationship to buy one. Receiving a Birkin hand-me-down from a parent may trump new models by adding the time-signaling cost: "Oh, my mother has owned a handful of these for ages."

In needing to signal high status, we deploy exclusive goods or behaviors that suggest associations with elite groups. The reliance on these status symbols, however, opens up a loophole in the signaling process: if we claim status through symbols rather than revealing the actual state of affairs, there can always be misinterpretations and intentional deceptions.

SIGNALING PROBLEMS AND CHEATING

In Herman Wouk's 1951 novel *The Caine Mutiny*, Ivy League graduate Willie Keith catches a glimpse of nightclub singer May Wynn flawlessly belting out Italian-language opera. Willie interprets May's ability to "carol a Mozart aria with understanding" as a clear "mark of high breeding." He's instantly lovestruck—and relieved. After years of searching, Willie has finally found a beautiful, talented, and cultured woman whom his strict WASP mother will like. But he soon learns that May is the daughter of Italian immigrants. This additional information turns her exceptional abilities into "a mere racial quirk of a lower social group" rather than a symbol of years spent in higher education. Bound by his own ethnic prejudices, Willie found that May's operatic singing in Italian "lost its cachet."

In using symbols, status claims and appraisals potentially face the problems inherent in all communication—namely, that status appraisers may not *perceive* the signals nor *interpret* them as proper classifications of status ranking. Willie Keith misinterpreted May Wynn's Italian abilities as a symbol of high breeding rather than native fluency, setting himself up for later disappointment.

Because signals must be subtle, our appraisers may fail to notice them. This is the problem of *perceptibility*. In the 1980s the graffiti artist Jazzy Art joined the "secret society" of hard-core sneakerheads by buying rare Bata sneakers. But the shoes weren't well-known, and strangers laughed at him on the basketball court for wearing "rejects." Elites and cults often use imperceptibility to their advantage, embracing symbols so inconspicuous that only other members will notice. But most people want credit for their hard-earned status symbols. This is why suburban families park their new cars on the street despite owning a garage. No one can appraise an automobile they can't see.

Even if appraisers can perceive a symbol, they must also know how to read it the intended way. This is the problem of *interpretability*. Symbols may have many meanings, but for status purposes, appraisers must know a very specific meaning: the associations to a specific position on the status hierarchy. The problem is that no symbols ever have stable, permanent meanings, especially across different countries, cultures, and eras. This fact powers a recurring joke in the film *Back to the Future*, where everyone keeps reading Marty McFly's preppy red goose-down vest as a marine life preserver: "Hey, kid! What did you do, jump ship?" A key problem with time travel to the past, we learn, is that we can't signal using style conventions that don't yet exist. Another issue is that appraisers always have their own personal associations with our status symbols. An elegant high-priced scent may have also been the favorite of a regrettable ex.

Linguists speak of *semantic drift*: the slow change in words' meanings over time. This principle also applies to cultural symbols, which can often come to mean the very opposite. Many Americans dress baby boys in blue and baby girls in pink; before World War II, it was the reverse. The cachet of symbols changes based on the status of associated individuals and groups. When hip-hop pioneer Kool Herc moved from Jamaica to New York in the 1970s, his new neighbors ridiculed his home island as a Caribbean backwater. Herc was warned, "Don't walk down that way cause they throwing Jamaicans in garbage cans." But after reggae musician Bob Marley became a global celebrity, everything Jamaican took on a new cachet, and Herc could celebrate his country of origin. Cachet can just as easily plummet. In the 2010s celebrities such as the rapper Macklemore wore their hair long on top and closely shaved on the sides. But then fascist-sympathizing alt-right figures such as Richard Spencer adopted the same style, likely in homage to Hitler Youth. The haircut came to be known as the "fashy," leading left-leaning hipsters to abandon it.

In an age of mass media, people work hard to actively shape symbols' meanings for their own purposes. Companies rely on advertising and marketing campaigns to imbue products with cachet. Luxury brands associate the abstract smell of their perfumes with specific celebrities: Keira Knightley for Chanel's Coco Mademoiselle Eau de Parfum Intense, Natalie Portman for Miss Dior. The Adidas Superstar began as a premium basketball sneaker, but once the rap unit Run-DMC made it part of their uniform, Adidas signed the group in an endorsement deal, forever transforming its image into a powerful and lasting symbol of the New York hip-hop scene.

When different groups use the same symbol, multiple meanings may emerge. In the 1980s, conservative, pro-business French youth wore stodgy tassel loafers as a subtle protest against the Socialist government. But French leftist youth also started to wear those same shoes to get better tables at upscale restaurants. This diminished the loafer's political valences. With the need for interpretability, symbols tend to weaken when meanings become ambiguous. And in most cases, rivals don't like sharing the same symbols anyway. When the conservative blogger Mike Cernovich tweeted, "Get a pair of Clark's [sic] desert boots, you can't lose," the style writer Derek Guy proclaimed within minutes, "RIP Clarks Desert Boots."

In order to get ahead of failures in perceptibility, interpretability, and ambiguity, we adopt certain techniques to ensure semiotic success. The first is *choosing the most suitable status symbols for our appraisers*. We put on our best clothes for a fancy restaurant or a dinner with our significant other's parents, knowing this will meet their expectations. The second is *adjusting based on feedback*. Nike founder Phil Knight wore a black bowler hat early in his career to look more mature but realized quickly that "it made me look mad. Stark, staring mad. As if I'd escaped from a Victorian insane asylum inside a painting by Magritte."

The final and most important technique is *redundancy*, ensuring our signals and cues work together to tell a unified story of high status. A parvenu won't just drive a Porsche but will also live in a luxury condo and enroll her children in the top private schools. The motorcyclist hoping to gain status for his rebellious motorcyclist life can own a motorcycle, wear a motorcycle jacket, always carry a motorcycle helmet, have a tattoo of a Harley-Davidson, and put a sticker on his laptop that says "My other machine is a Harley-Davidson." But as we see here, overredundant signals may look too intentional—and boring. We must also engage in *redundancy management*, striking the perfect balance between clarity and overeagerness.

These communications problems are all minor, however, compared with an even bigger loophole in the entire status-signaling process: *cheating*. As the famed semiotician Umberto Eco explains, "Every time there is signification there is the possibility of using it in order to lie." Consider the grifter Anna Sorokin—aka Anna Delvey—who convinced New York's elites that she was an heiress to a German solar power fortune, as a result of her wearing expensive outfits from Celine, Alexander Wang, and Balenciaga, and showering hotel staff and taxi drivers in a daily confetti bomb of hundred-dollar bills. By using all the right signals of wealth, Sorokin could enjoy the status of an actual heiress. The journalist Jessica Pressler writes, "Anna looked at the soul of New York and recognized that if you distract people with shiny objects, with large wads of cash, with the indicia of wealth, if you show them the money, they will be virtually unable to see anything else." Until law enforcement intervened, Sorokin's cheating worked wonders.

In a feudal world of rigid castes and sweeping poverty, there were insurmountable limits on the degree to which the low-born could pretend to be high-born. Today relative prosperity and easy access to consumer credit enables middle-class individuals to stretch their salaries toward the purchase of onetime upper-class status symbols, such as designer handbags and European sports cars. Bernard Arnault, chairman and CEO of the LVMH luxury conglomerate, would not be one of the world's wealthiest people if the company stuck to selling Louis Vuitton trunks and Moët & Chandon champagne only to the top 1 percent. LVMH invested in the DFS network of duty-free stores in airports and shopping malls around the world, which make luxury goods more accessible and affordable. A significant portion of the modern economy is based on committing light symbolic deceit.

We all emulate, but the principle of status integrity requires us to seek out, dislike, and even punish the most flagrant cheaters. The handwringing over Anna Sorokin goes beyond her alleged criminality. "To lay false claim to war honors was a paramount sin among the Crow [tribe]," writes anthropologist Ruth Benedict, "and by the general opinion, constantly reiterated, [the cheater] was regarded as irresponsible and incompetent." Within a status group, rank-and-file members don't want to see equal comrades rise up on false pretenses, and those at the top don't want fakers drifting into their midst. Groups thus banish cheaters to the lowest levels of status.

That being said, cheating comes in degrees, the same way fudging a few numbers on tax returns isn't the same as large-scale financial fraud. Some forms of trickery have become conventional. In a world where "gentlemen prefer blondes," brunettes are able to dye their hair without being considered Delvey-level grifters. Besides, we can always hide our emulations behind solid alibis: e.g., the reliable German engineering of luxury sedans, the durable and supple leather of opulent handbags. Our fear of being seen as cheaters makes us more likely to borrow status symbols from one status tier up and not higher. And in considering how much we can pay in signaling costs, we can usually hop a step but not an entire flight of stairs. Anna Sorokin may have remained Anna Delvey had she not aimed so high.

Since most of us believe we deserve more status, is there any reason to feel guilty about engaging in small deceptions? Where we are confident of future success, why not go ahead and reap the benefits today? Kim Ki-woo, the young protagonist of the Korean film *Parasite*, self-justifies the use of fake university documents to get a tutoring job: "I don't think of this as forgery or crime. I'll go to university next year. I've just printed out the document a bit early." In fact, this kind of bluffing—fake it till you make it—is now an accepted and celebrated way to get ahead in life. Signaling fraud can even boost the status claimer's confidence levels. Economist Robert H. Frank explains, "The wearer of an elegant suit of clothing may not really fool anyone at all, in a cognitive sense, into thinking he has higher ability than he actually has. Yet the suit may still influence important judgments and behaviors in very subtle, noncognitive ways." Cheating, then, can lead us to a higher status tier, at which point we can prove ourselves worthy of staying there. And for those incapable or unwilling to advance through education, training, or hard work, cheating may be the sole means of improving one's status level. (And research shows that lower-income individuals believe "the game is rigged" and may be already skeptical that hard work is the key to life success.)

Through our own temptations to cheat through symbols, we also recognize that everyone may be cheating through symbols. This makes us even more vigilant in status appraisals. The best method to detect fakery is *triangulation*— considering all signals, cues, and significant absences together. Triangulation forces us to look beyond single status symbols and toward the entire package of symbols. The sociologists Yiannis Gabriel and Tim Lang note, "Objects don't make individual statements, but rather they communicate together with other objects, just like individual items on a menu or on a plate acquire their significance in the light of the other items." In 1970s Japan, ownership of a Louis Vuitton bag worked well as a status symbol because they could be acquired only while vacationing in Paris. With the massive expansion of the brand's retail network in the 1990s, Vuitton bags were suddenly everywhere, carried by both young women from upper-middle-class families and working-class "cabaret hostesses." Anyone appraising a woman's status could no longer judge position through the bag alone, but only within the context of the woman's makeup, hairstyle, clothing choices, and use of language. In these cases, cues become particularly effective for revealing fakers, because they're so hard to manipulate. Negative social shibboleths can overshadow even the best status symbol.

In the last chapter, we saw how individuals gain or lose status depending on which conventions they follow and ignore. Now we see how the need to claim status to strangers makes these conventional behaviors into symbols that will be interpreted. Culture, therefore, is a fundamentally *communicative* activity, and everything we do becomes a symbol of our social position.

But cheating will always be inevitable as long as we rely on symbols, and this shifts appraisals beyond individual status symbols to an entire package of signals, cues, and significant absences. We then decide which signals to wield and which to avoid, all while trying to appear detached from the entire process. Where we become aware of our damaging cues, we hide them. Over time these choices made on behalf of our status goals form not just our signaling strategies but our tastes and identities.

Chapter Four

TASTE, AUTHENTICITY, AND IDENTITY

‹❈›

Our choices become us, from John Waters's good bad taste to the meltdown of Vanilla Ice and the invention of Billie Holiday.

‹❈›

TASTE

In 2018 the French government bestowed the Order of Arts and Letters on American filmmaker John Waters, "one of the most important figures in cinema," for pushing artistic boundaries, promoting French film, and daring to confront "complex issues of gender, sexuality and class." Back in Waters's hometown of Baltimore, Maryland, the local art museum named a rotunda in its European art galleries after him, and the city's tourist website offers an itinerary for a "John Waters Baltimore tour." In October 2021, Waters graced the cover of *Town & Country*, one of America's oldest lifestyle magazines for upper-income households. These accolades from hallowed institutions are an unexpected outcome for the "Prince of Puke," a director notorious for filming some of the most revolting moments in movie history. Waters wrote in the early eighties, "If someone vomits watching one of my films, it's like getting a standing ovation." Yet his explorations into the depraved depths of bad taste have won Waters acclaim from the high priests of good taste. Maybe this was the plan all along. "One must remember," writes Waters, "that there is such a thing as good bad taste and bad bad taste."

Like "status" and "culture," "taste" is yet another contentious term of frustrating ambiguity, only made more confusing by Waters's achievements in "good" bad taste. What exactly do we mean by "good taste" and "bad taste"? For many centuries, Western elites followed the philosopher Immanuel Kant's clear and authoritative definition: taste was "the faculty of estimating the beautiful." Someone with good taste could properly and virtuously identify beautiful things as beautiful things. And in those years, beauty was found in complex pieces of classical music, venerated artworks in museums, and the intricate craftwork of skilled artisans. A person with bad taste, on the other hand, found allure in the vulgar, ersatz, and wretched. Bad taste, thought Voltaire, was a "sickness of the spirit."

This use of taste is essentially a metaphor—equating our capacity to make proper aesthetic judgments with the deeply ingrained ability to detect flavor. A healthy palate finds coffee bitter and candy sweet, and, likewise, the well-adjusted person perceives the most elegant art, style, and fashion as "good" and inferior versions as "bad." For all his transgressions, John Waters upholds this older, elitist idea of taste; he knows that rancid aesthetics can be just as stomach turning as rancid meats.

The modern age of cultural pluralism, however, precludes a single, authoritative standard for good taste. In Roman times, the Latin dictum *de gustibus non est disputandum* ("in matters of taste, there can be no disputes") meant that there should be no disputes because good taste was so self-evident. Today the phrase has flipped to become a mantra of liberal openness: don't bother fighting about aesthetics because beauty is in the eye of the beholder. With this, the definition of taste has shifted from "the proper identification of beauty" to a more neutral "propensity toward certain lifestyle choices." The former Apple industrial designer Jony Ive wears Clarks Wallabees, listens to loud techno, and drives a white Bentley. John Waters adores 1950s B movies, trailer parks, and memorabilia from serial killers and leftist terrorist groups. We can conclude they have "different" tastes without judging one set better than the other.

With John Waters vaulted into the highest echelons of good taste through celebrations of bad taste, we can fully dispose of any previous notions that taste is an innate biological preference or a universal aesthetic criterion. Standards of taste are always relative to the dominant conventions of the era and the society, and so the only way to make sense of taste is to analyze it as a social mechanism. This is not to dismiss the entire concept of taste as a relic of European ethnocentrism. The philosopher Hannah Arendt called taste "the chief cultural activity," because the individual propensity toward certain aesthetic choices over others works to form the patterns we know as culture. Choice defines us as individuals. As the critic Roger Scruton writes, "Taste, like style, is the man himself."

For our purposes, taste is a crucial concept in providing a direct link between status seeking and the formation of individual identities. Taste involves choice, and from what we've learned so far, we make our aesthetic choices within the context of status. Our particular tastes may have genetic and psychological elements, but they manifest only in social activity. Our habitus provides the unconscious conventions that decide what we find pleasurable. Our group membership nudges us to make the right imitations, counterimitations, and emulations, which manifest as signals, cues, and significant absences. At any moment, status value distorts our preferences, making certain objects and conventions more attractive than others. Taste, then, does serve as a useful measure for who we are: our past, present, and future.

There is a reason taste focuses on "superficial" aesthetics rather than practical actions. People from very different backgrounds use the same screwdrivers, automotive lubricants, and kitty litter. Nonfunctional choices like ceramics, photographs, and rugs better reveal one's internal preferences, because we can assume people's choices reflect their deepest predilections. In the 1970s, John Waters adored the tabloid cult of celebrity murderer Charles Manson, so he spent much of his time attending the Manson Family trials. If he hadn't been interested, he would have taken up a different hobby.

In status appraisals, taste first assists in the simple task of screening whether a stranger is "one of us." Sociologist Pierre Bourdieu writes that taste is a "match-maker"—a force that "brings together things" and also "people that go together." In the *Simpsons* episode "Two Bad Neighbors," Homer goes to war against patrician former president George H. W. Bush, and yet immediately bonds with former president Gerald Ford over a mutual love of football, nachos, and beer. Common interests inspire reciprocal judgments of "good taste" and bestowing of social approval; mismatched preferences engender disapproval and social distancing. As the British philosopher David Hume writes, "We are apt to call barbarous whatever departs widely from our own taste and apprehension: But soon find the epithet of reproach retorted on us."

For all the talk of individual signals in the last chapter, taste is much more important in status appraisals than the consideration of a single status symbol. By triangulating all the signals, cues, and absences, we understand someone's taste as a gestalt. We can call this a *sensibility*—the underlying "feel" that choices express. Specific groups have specific sensibilities, but compared with an infinite number of signals, sensibilities are relatively more finite: e.g., basic, classy, WASPy, boho. Waters's personal aesthetic, for example, derives from the camp sensibility; his own ideas on taste echo Susan Sontag's famed line "Camp asserts that good taste is not simply good taste; that there exists, indeed, a good taste of bad taste." The punk sensibility of destruction, rebellion, and outrage manifests in a taste for mohawks, ripped clothes, aggressive music, and anarchist sloganeering. The vanilla "mainstream" sensibility opts for blockbuster action films, Top 40 radio, reality television, famous athletes and celebrities, casual clothing, and sensible automobiles. We use the term "eccentric" to describe individuals whose manifold choices go in wayward directions, such as the nineteenth-century French playwright Alfred Jarry, with his pink turban over dyed green hair, robotic staccato voice, an apartment decorated with bloody handprints, and pistols at the ready for shooting crickets.

The alignment of sensibilities to certain social groups results in a defined number of *taste worlds* within each society. Individuals occupying a particular taste world share the same broad aesthetic and make similar choices in cars, clothing, music, beverages, etc. Up until the 1950s, American culture contained three taste worlds: the highbrow of wealthy elites and intellectuals (classical music, abstract art, serious literature), the middlebrow of the upper middle classes (urbane popular culture with intellectual undercurrents), and the lowbrow of the lower middle classes (schmaltzy songs, popular cinema). In the 1970s middlebrow readers of *The New Yorker* played tennis and dined out at healthy gourmet restaurants, while lowbrow *Reader's Digest* readers went bowling and ate homestyle cooking. Even religious teachings conformed to these taste worlds: upper-class Episcopalians preferred more "literate" sermons than adherents of other denominations. Over the last fifty years the number of American taste worlds has greatly expanded, especially as minority and immigrant communities formed their own status groups with unique conventions.

This clear relation between taste worlds and social position makes taste a very useful classifier in status appraisals. But if we return to Kant's definition—the *faculty* of estimating the beautiful—taste also involves skill. To have good taste means making better choices than others. Oleg Cassini designed First Lady Jacqueline Kennedy's elegant clothing, but he valued her ability to choose the right pieces: "Jackie played a very active role in the selection of her clothes. Her sense of style was very precise; she would make editorial comments on the sketches I sent her. She always knew exactly what she wanted; her taste was excellent." Judgments on taste don't just classify but gauge personal virtues and talents. When someone can't distinguish between an expensive, high-grade, artisanally made guitar and a cheap, mass-produced model, the scholar David Berger writes, "We don't say that they have 'different tastes' in musical instruments. We say that they are 'poor judges' of musical instruments." The skill aspect of taste means it never just expresses our unconscious habitus, but can be shaped through conscious choices. Good taste can be a reflection of noble birth—or the result of self-improvement.

While having good taste qualifies us for normal status, we can aim for higher status by developing *great* taste. We can "cultivate" ourselves over time to make more advanced choices that will garner more respect. To develop a sophisticated taste for wine, the oenophile Allan Sichel says, the student should first "trust his own palate." But after that point, there must be a conscious desire to learn more. Then, "as experience grows and perception becomes keener, his taste is certain to change and wines which at first pleased may now bore or actively displease." To gain status from great taste involves progress across three attributes: deep knowledge, congruence, and bounded originality.

Great taste first requires a deep knowledge of potential choices. For John Waters, "To understand bad taste one must have very good taste." Familiarity with Chippendale furniture—or even better, knowing the differences between cabriole legs and fluted legs—is a clear demonstration of cultural capital. Deep knowledge also opens up new aesthetic experiences that are fundamental to improving taste. In fact, cultural capital is best exhibited through not just knowing "higher" forms of art but *appreciating* them. Two people who enjoy the same art must have similar exposure to the same conventions, and therefore, belong to the same collectivity.

For Kant, understanding the beautiful meant transcending immediate sensual pleasures and relishing refined forms of "contemplative" aesthetics. The "Kantian aesthetic," as anthropologist Daniel Miller writes, is "one of refusal, a foregoing of the immediate pleasure of the sensual and the evident in favour of a cultivated and abstracted appropriation through an achieved understanding." There is also an anti-Kantian aesthetic, which we could label "immediate": no special knowledge of conventions is required to enjoy the thrills of roller coasters, catchy Top 40 songs, and ice cream sundaes. Kantian taste requires us to find pleasure in things that take time and effort to appreciate: classical music, avant-garde art, postmodern novels, and gourmet cuisine. Enjoying Philip Glass's five-hour opera *Einstein on the Beach* is easier if the viewer has the knowledge to properly contemplate long periods of repetitive music and jerky dance movements without much plot or dialogue. Since deep knowledge opens up a wider range of appreciation, we see how elite taste engages with more difficult art forms—and why educational capital often correlates with cultural capital.

Expanded knowledge, however, is not enough to move up the taste hierarchy. Lifestyle choices also must reveal *congruence*—an internal consistency with the target sensibility. Every day we choose goods, styles, and actions across a long list of categories, from clothes to food to automobiles to houses to furniture. Things "go" with one another. Congruence means all personal choices work together in harmony. This requires knowing the proper relations and associations between objects and behaviors, and therefore, congruence itself also reflects deep knowledge. We learn taste congruence through expert combinations: the interior design suggestions found in furniture stores, the kitchen arrangements in appliance ads, and the styling recommended in fashion magazines. These established groupings of products are called *constellations*, and each taste world contains distinct sets. Congruence in taste means replicating these constellations or making well-balanced adjustments to the predetermined formulas. To assemble a praiseworthy home bar in a Brooklyn apartment requires owning the right glassware, shaker, jigger, ice bucket, a bottled-in-bond rye, a craft gin, and a single-village mezcal. A University of Alabama sorority may achieve congruence in stocking strawberry vodka, peach schnapps, and Malibu coconut rum.

Incongruence indicates bad taste—e.g., parking a pink Cadillac in front of a nineteenth-century English manor, layering a Chanel jacket over a Juicy Couture tracksuit, pouring Tabasco sauce on the main course at a Michelin-starred restaurant. Status symbols live and die by their context: an antique Chippendale cabinet can make the study in a heritage home, but will look absurd in a concrete dorm room strewn with plastic Solo cups and dirty laundry. There is no successful emulation without congruence. If we plunk a single high-status status symbol, like distinctive glasses or a flashy car, into our otherwise humdrum demeanor, it can seem out of place and fail to impress our appraisers. Good taste requires knowing *not* to overdo a single signal if it doesn't match everything else.

Deep knowledge opens the door to better taste, and congruence reveals our commitment to a high-status sensibility. But the truest marker of excellent taste is *bounded originality*. As we learned before, the highest-status individuals can't imitate anyone lower on the hierarchy and, therefore, must make distinctive choices. Great taste requires uniqueness. Moreover, there is no *skill* in copying others' choices. Scholar of Kantian aesthetics David Berger writes, "To like what one 'ought' to like is *not* to exercise taste." This idea holds across most taste worlds. For the sneakerhead Will Strickland, "Outright biting [copying] someone's kicks and then rocking them the same exact way is wack." Great taste needs to be more than a regurgitation of high-status clichés. Choices should express the individual's exceptional character. They must surprise and delight. This requirement for originality explains the elite disdain for fashion, which is often dismissed as following the opinions of others. Kant fumed, "Fashion belongs under the title of *vanity*, because there is no inner worth in its intention; and also of *foolishness*, because in fashion there is still a compulsion to let ourselves be led slavishly by the mere example that many in society give us." If taste is a mirror into our soul, it shouldn't appear to be copied wholesale from the pages of Condé Nast publications.

The reason for a *bounded* originality is that all choices must still conform to a certain sensibility and ensure congruence. "The faculty of taste," writes the philosopher Ludwig Wittgenstein, "cannot create a new structure, it can only make adjustments to one that already exists. Taste loosens and tightens screws, it does not build a new piece of machinery." Originality works best when the individual has already established mastery of a high-status sensibility and enjoys high-status privilege. Mass media disparages the invented baby names of disadvantaged communities, warning they harm children's future prospects, while disregarding the life successes of the uniquely named Gore Vidal and McGeorge Bundy.

Originality is much easier with granular knowledge and expertise, because knowing what is distinctive requires knowing what is common. Those looking to improve their taste can always learn more about the full range of choices, each choice's meaning, and their former and current status value. This provides individuals with the confidence to go beyond the well-known and into exciting new directions, perhaps even unearthing unforeseen pleasures in commonplace items. The famed food critic Anthony Bourdain arguably reached the foodie pantheon not by celebrating haute cuisine but by championing overlooked delicacies such as the Japanese convenience store egg-salad sandwich. Successful artists forge unique sensibilities by combining preexisting artifacts and conventions in new ways. The movies of director Quentin Tarantino pay direct homage to older films, and yet in 2018 the Oxford English Dictionary recognized "Tarantinoesque" as a term describing a distinct cinematic style.

A critical point about originality, however, is that choices never need to be original on an absolute, universal scale. They must merely be surprising within the community. A shortcut for great taste is *arbitrage*, finding easily procured things in one location and then deploying them elsewhere where they're rare. Stylish teenagers from the Bronx in the 1970s would avoid shopping on nearby Fordham Road where everyone bought clothes, and instead take the subway down to Delancey Street in Lower Manhattan to buy "nice and fresh" clothes unavailable uptown.

Since taste reveals our personal feelings, communicates our cues and signals, and offers a canvas for self-improvement, it inevitably plays a role in status claims and appraisals. As John Waters's work has shown, taste is visceral: we are attracted to or repulsed by people based on their choices and appreciations. Shared tastes create social bonds and secure normal status; oppositional tastes engender conflict.

Perfect taste, however, doesn't just require making choices that satisfy certain standards. We also have to prove that our choices are appropriate and natural for our particular life stories.

AUTHENTICITY

From everything we've learned so far, we can imagine the high status of some-one who tops the Billboard pop charts in a new genre, has his debut album go multiplatinum, is named "pop's reigning sex symbol," dates Madonna, inks a lucrative endorsement deal with Coca-Cola, and stars in his own Hollywood film. Yes, in early 1991, Vanilla Ice truly had it all.

But then came meltdown. "Everyone seems to hate Vanilla Ice," declared the very first sentence of his *New York Times* profile from early in 1991. He first faced accusations of musical thievery from critics: "Ice Ice Baby" stole the bassline from Queen and David Bowie's "Under Pressure" and the "Ice ice baby / too cold" chant from the African American fraternity Alpha Phi Alpha. The real trouble began after inconsistencies emerged in Ice's public biography. In the early days when his birth name remained a "closely guarded secret," Ice boasted to the *Times* about a Miami ghetto background dabbling in "gangs and stuff," where he survived five stabbings and won multiple motorcycle champi-onships. In reality Ice was Robert Matthew Van Winkle, from a well-to-do Dal-las suburb. He brushed these criticisms aside with an Eric B. & Rakim lyric: "It ain't where you're from; it's where you're at." But by that point Vanilla Ice was nowhere: his follow-up album and film *Cool as Ice* flopped, and he became one of America's long-standing national jokes.

In terms of status criteria, Vanilla Ice had a strong claim for high status: money, fame, good looks, sex appeal, talent, drive, and even the ascribed status advantages of white male privilege. And unlike other reviled musicians of his time, such as Milli Vanilli and New Kids on the Block, Ice wrote his own music and choreographed his own dance moves. He may have even been sincere about his desire to make good music. (In retrospect, the critic Jeff Weiss ad-mits, "'Ice Ice Baby' remains a perfect debut rap single.") But none of this was enough. Vanilla Ice failed at a crucial meta-category required to tie his status claims together: *authenticity*. All of his signals, however valuable, were incon-gruent with who he really was.

Authenticity is an obvious virtue in the realm of material goods. Things should be what they are supposed to be. "A pine table is a proper thing," stated a nineteenth-century interior design guide, "but a pine table that pretends to be black walnut is an abomination." Authentic things are true things. Truth conforms to our expectations; fakery disappoints. A strange birdsong, notes Immanuel Kant, is beautiful when we believe it's "nature's handiwork" and less so when we realize it's a wooden birdcall. Authenticity has become particularly important in the modern era, where manufacturers can easily pump out ersatz copies of desirable goods. The art critic Dan Fox writes, "[Authenticity] promises a ticket to the truth. Shops, restaurants, real estate, and a range of leisure activities all promise the bona fide, the genuine, the real McCoy." Coca-Cola sells itself as "the real thing." Meanwhile, the high-end chocolate brand NōKA went out of business after investigative reports revealed its $854 per pound chocolate was just repackaged French bonbons.

These standards for authentic goods now apply to human beings as well. To be authentic, explains philosopher Charles Taylor, requires discovering and realizing one's "originality." An authentic self embodies positive virtues, such as honesty and self-confidence. Self-actualizing personalities, according to the psychologist Abraham Maslow, are "marked by simplicity and naturalness, and by lack of artificiality or straining for effect." Genuine people are also more reliable, as we can expect them to be consistent over time. The measure of authenticity applies to not only actions but also desires. Theorist René Girard writes, "The 'inauthentic' person is the one who follows directives from others, whereas the 'authentic' is the person who desires autonomously." Those who behave for the approval of others are "phonies," to quote Holden Caulfield. There is universal disdain for poseurs—individuals who are caught fielding an overly crafted persona. To hip-hop critics, Vanilla Ice was always a "white poseur," and most Americans eventually came to agree with this assessment. Inauthenticity is not just an act of cunning deception but implies a lack of self-confidence to resist external forces—those who end up always jumping on the bandwagon. Pretension is another manifestation of this personal deficiency: the sin of acting more erudite than one's education and social position justify.

If appraisers are willing to provide high status based on our taste, they want to be careful that those tastes have been legitimately acquired. Authentic taste should be anchored in an individual's specific life journey. To the philosopher Walter Benjamin, the authenticity of a thing requires a "testimony to the history which it has experienced." In a world where everything is available for purchase, individuals can always develop tastes for the express purpose of gaining status. Impostors abound. Ideally all signals should be *behavioral residue*—reflections of how we live rather than items acquired for the purpose of claiming status. Authentic tastes are "natural" tastes—an effortless extension of the inner self and origin story rather than a calculated set of borrowings and acquisitions. Like musicians say about the blues, "You either have it, or you don't."

To be judged as authentic, we must provide information validating the provenance of our taste. Signals, cues, and significant absences are compared with our immutable characteristics and demographic details, such as age, gender, race, sexual orientation, and native language. The whole package should tell a congruent story. As the sociologist Erving Goffman writes, "An individual who implicitly or explicitly signifies that he has certain social characteristics ought in fact to be what he claims he is." The ideal taste should be "true to one's roots." Vanilla Ice's talents and tastes were grounded in art forms created in the Black community. To avoid incongruence between these hip-hop conventions and his WASPy background, he invented a fictitious Miami gangbanging persona. Unlike Anna Sorokin/Delvey, Robert Matthew Van Winkle perpetrated no crimes in creating the character named Vanilla Ice, but he did commit the cultural sin of being inauthentic in a world where keepin' it real is the supreme virtue.

A precursor to authenticity was the past emphasis on *suitability*—i.e., making the choices that best match our particular lifestyle and sensibility. Elsie de Wolfe, perhaps the most famous arbiter of taste for home decor in the early twentieth century, was not subtle: "My business," she wrote, "is to preach to you the beauty of suitability. Suitability! *Suitability*! SUITABILITY!!" Before debuting as a novelist, Edith Wharton published a volume on home design in which she recommended Americans avoid the "superficial application of ornament totally independent of structure" and instead choose design where "the architecture of the room became its decoration."

Suitability means conformity to certain standards, and here we get a hint of how authenticity can become a prison. For all the infinite choices in life, we are "allowed" to associate publicly only with ones "suitable" to our immutable characteristics and background. Tastes should be the product of long-held habits. This makes time an important factor in gauging authenticity, and tastes look more "natural" when their origins lie far in the past. When Coco Chanel put No. 5 perfume on the market, she dishonestly claimed to have stumbled upon the scent at some forgotten place long ago rather than admitting that it was made from scratch.

By extension, personas appear more authentic when they include a few "mistakes"—i.e., sloppy behaviors, low-status habits. Perfect taste suggests an overexertion of effort. Great taste should appear natural. In men's fashion the ultimate style move is *sprezzatura*, embracing intentional errors such as undone buttons and misaligned neckties. Gianni Agnelli, the head of Fiat, wore watches *over* his shirtsleeves. The courtier Baldassare Castiglione best explicated the idea of sprezzatura, believing it an important counterbalance to times when "achieved grace and charm" becomes "a frivolity and a vanity, even an unmanliness." Intentional amateurism can be attractive for those who already have high status. The hip Misshapes parties in early-twenty-first-century New York prohibited beat matching, the professional DJ skill of seamlessly moving from one song to another. Clunkier transitions were more authentic and, therefore, cooler.

All of this leads us to the central paradox of authenticity: we are supposed to listen to the voice in our hearts, to "discover and articulate our own identity"— and yet, only *others* can judge whether we are authentic. Appraisers compare our taste with our demographic profile, and where there is a suspicious mismatch, they deny us status.

This stems from the fact that following a convention doesn't make us automatic members of its collectivity. The Pink Ladies in *Grease* don't have to accept someone as a Pink Lady even if she shows up in the same satin jacket. This makes authenticity also function as a tool for exclusion. Old Money families long used cultural capital to banish New Money from their social milieu. And in the last century authenticity has become a powerful bulwark for status-disadvantaged communities who create desirable cultural styles and artifacts. "Marginalized groups seeking to control valuable artistic production," writes anthropologist Charles Lindholm, "now often claim that only those people proven to be genealogical members of the group (defined variously as a tribe, nation, race, or ethnicity) have the right and the innate capacity to produce its characteristic art forms." *Cultural appropriation* describes illegitimate majority use of minority conventions, especially as status symbols. Elvis Presley appropriated Black rhythm 'n' blues and became the so-called king of rock 'n' roll. The hip-hop community mounted stronger defenses; by emphasizing authentic storytelling from the Black experience as a core virtue of the music, the economic rewards have been better channeled to Black rappers and producers, such as JAY-Z and Dr. Dre.

The most powerful form of authenticity thus remains *authenticity by origin*: the principle that groups who formulate a convention are the best at replicating it. Scotch must be made in Scotland, and bourbon whiskey must be made in Kentucky. Globalization, however, has made this standard more difficult to enforce. In 2010 a Taiwanese whiskey, Kavalan, bested three homegrown scotches at the Burns Night competition in Leith, Scotland. Within contemporary pop culture, conventions change so frequently over time that their origin points are unclear. Pizza may be from Italy but rose to prominence in the United States. Our standards are shifting toward *authenticity by content*: the principle that the best things are those made by the original methods (i.e., "It ain't where you're from; it's where you're at"). Blue jeans may be an "American" garment, but Japanese textile mills have better preserved earlier American production techniques, such as natural indigo-dyed, slubby fabric woven on narrow looms. The independent American denim brand Prps, which proclaims "Authenticity is our first priority," gained its global prestige through a pioneering embrace of Japanese denim.

This shift from authenticity by origin to authenticity by content is proof that we remain obsessed with keeping it real, even in an increasingly inauthentic world. Authentic goods are still more valuable than exclusive goods. And an individual's taste must match their backstory. Fakers and poseurs will be punished. This has an overall effect of keeping us conservative when choosing signals. Our best tactic is to choose signals close to our immutable characteristics and in line with our origin stories. This has obvious political implications: as much as marginalized communities can better protect their creations through regulating authenticity, the overall focus on naturalness works much better for the manor born. The high-status individual, writes sociologist George Homans, "can afford to relax and be a natural man." Strivers at the bottom must acquire status symbols and build on top of their origin stories. Authenticity can be yet another privilege of the elite.

Perhaps the most significant lesson from authenticity is that our status appraisers never judge us on a single signal, cue, or significant absence: they compare our tastes against our demographics to understand *who we are*.

PERSONA, IDENTITY, AND SELF

In understanding the effects of status on individual behavior, we have arrived at a paramount concern of modern life: *Who am I?* We now understand the myriad difficulties of landing upon clear answers. Which "I" are we talking about? There appear to be three: persona, identity, and self. In signaling, we build *personas*—observable packages of signals, taste, sensibility, immutable characteristics, and cues absorbed from our upbringing and background. Others use this persona to determine our *identity*. At the same time, we have a *self* within our minds, known only to us. Persona, identity, and self are never quite the same. All of the additions, subtractions, and redactions made for status can cause our persona to feel like an ersatz, sanitized, cardboard cut-out version of the self. And if others classify us based on this highly edited persona, our public identity may drift far from "the real me."

At a cosmic level, we all enjoy an *absolute identity*—a grand totality of distinguishing differences, including unique DNA sequences and an unrepeatable series of life experiences. Every single person on earth *is* different. When we ask "Who am I?" then, the question is simply whether others effectively acknowledge the distinctiveness of our existence. Before modern times, personal identity was simply a role and status: membership in a clan, tribe, and caste, as well as the specific position within that community. We now seek an individual identity that transcends demographic categories and classifiers. If we can be easily summarized through stereotype, category, and class alone, we're failures. For whatever solidarity we feel with those who share the same immutable characteristics and lifestyles, we still seek to be more than our ethnicity, gender, sexual orientation, disabilities, age, hometown, and occupation.

Popular culture often presents these existential questions as a battle between the individual and society. From what we've learned so far, it's not society that is the issue as much as the specific concerns of status—our ranking and valuation, and how it improves or hinders our daily lives. Every individual's conscious and unconscious conventions, level of demand for upward mobility, and degree of distinctiveness correlates to status group, tier, position, and assets. Identity, then, can't exist outside of the social hierarchy, as status influences each part of our self-definition, whether persona, identity, or self.

The effects of status are most obvious in the persona—the public expression we craft in our social interactions. We have little choice in how we first appear in society: we have immutable characteristics and give off cues unconsciously absorbed from our community. But we're never condemned to our origin story. Jean-Paul Sartre concluded, "Man is nothing else but what he makes of himself," to which the philosopher Michel Foucault raised the stakes: "We have to create ourselves as a work of art." Eleanora Fagan was a five-foot-five African American woman born in 1915, the product of a teenage pregnancy and the survivor of a traumatic childhood. After living in a series of relatives' homes, she eventually settled as a teenager with her mother in a Harlem brothel, where they were both arrested for prostitution. But Fagan demonstrated great talent as a jazz singer, and after taking a stage name and crafting a new persona, she became legendary in America as Billie Holiday. Eleanora Fagan created Holiday, for which she is still remembered today.

While celebrities such as Billie Holiday, David Bowie, and Lady Gaga offer extreme examples of how individuals create larger-than-life personas, the pressures of status mean that every individual crafts their public image to some degree. Whatever our internal preferences, we imitate the arbitrary practices of our community and ignore equally valid alternatives in order to gain approval and avoid disapproval. To move up the status ladder, we gravitate toward common goals, such as amassing capital, refining talent, improving personal virtues, and acquiring more impressive status symbols. When we need to stand out, we are quick to emulate, imitating established conventions from higher status tiers. For most, self-expression takes the form of attempting to classify oneself in aspirational communities: e.g., "I'm goth" or "I'm an entrepreneur." When we do tiptoe into more distinct choices, we make sure they conform to the standards of detachment, congruence, and authenticity. For whatever freedom we have to craft personas, status value makes some options more attractive than others. We can always make idiosyncratic choices, break conventions, or stubbornly ignore social pressures, but the social punishments may be strong enough to bring us back to the norm.

After negotiating all of the demands of status, the resulting persona is almost like *cultural DNA*—a sequence of choices, behaviors, and experiences acquired over the course of our lives. Perhaps it would resemble something like this:

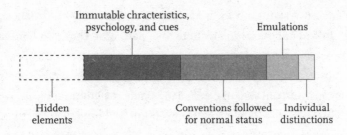

Unlike physical DNA, every individual is able to edit the contours of this sequence: the proportions of constituent elements, as well as what is displayed and what is hidden. Yet a large portion of the cultural DNA sequence is out of our control. Individual distinctiveness applies only to the very margins. Certain people are skilled at making choices so bold that their entire persona emerges as "original," but status pressures make *complete* difference nearly impossible. Status determines most of our persona, compelling us to make the same choices as others in our communities.

In reality the influence of status goes even further than simply providing the content for identities. As we saw in chapter 2, position within the hierarchy determines the degree of difference an individual seeks—and is *allowed* to seek. The very top elites must pursue extreme distinction, and they enjoy enough deference to break conventions. Individual distinctions thus play a larger part in their personas. Middle-status individuals, on the other hand, tend to be conservative and follow conventions more closely. Those at the bottom may also make distinctive choices out of disregard for social protocols, but their distinctions are seen as regrettable transgressions.

Originality is thus an aristocratic privilege. In *Beyond Good and Evil*, Friedrich Nietzsche explains, "The ordinary man . . . *waits* for an opinion about himself and then instinctively submits to it," while "it is the *intrinsic right of masters* to create values." In our modern world this piece of status logic has transformed into a widely held virtue: *everyone should maximize individual difference*. From the Romantic era onward there has been a fundamental social belief, writes philosopher Charles Taylor, that "each individual is different and original, and that this originality determines how he or she ought to live." Whether this ethos emerged from philosophical conviction or raw status logic, it's firmly embedded in modern life—from the taglines of pickup truck commercials to the lyrics of Avril Lavigne's "Sk8er Boi." We should all "follow our heart," no matter the repercussions, and always avoid becoming a sheep, clone, or poseur. Modernity has democratized the aristocratic propensity toward individual distinction. But uniqueness remains an easier action for those at the top, which means that the easiest way to resolve the fundamental tension between being original and getting along in society is to acquire high status.

The freedom gained at high-status levels isn't the only effect of the status hierarchy on our persona crafting: the inherent biases of ascribed status structures force discriminated individuals to more intensely craft their personas to achieve normal status. The status-advantaged gain high-status cues without conscious effort and can thus make successful status claims *without* acquiring status symbols or hiding shibboleths. The nonchalance, speech patterns, and bodily movements of Old Money *are* status symbols. The French poet Théophile Gautier wrote that the novelist Gustave Flaubert "was smarter than us. . . . He had the wit to come into the world with money."

Advising everyone to "be yourself" is therefore unfair as a broad mandate in a world still marked by bias: not everyone is born into a set of privileged attributes and behaviors. The requirement to stay "detached" from the status process rewards elites and punishes non-elites. Before status-disadvantaged individuals can be themselves, they must band together to open a path toward upward mobility. This is the logic behind *identity politics*, where individuals sharing demographic characteristics unite to raise the status levels associated with their defining trait. But until there is dignity for every immutable characteristic, persona crafting remains an important tool for status equalization. Was it Billie Holiday's moral duty to stay "authentic" to Eleanora Fagan and not create a new persona? Fellow singer and friend Carmen McRae explained about Holiday, "The only time she's at ease and at rest with herself is when she sings." Holiday appeared much happier being her crafted stage persona than having to maintain "Eleanora Fagan." To stigmatize persona crafting is, then, to support the status ladder as it exists today.

Moreover, the emphasis on being yourself overlooks the fact that self-definition is a continual process. We are writing a novel of identity for others, and the persona is simply the latest draft. Whoever we are, there is always an unstated opportunity for future revisions. And in a world of permanently shifting symbolic meanings, we'll surely have to make changes, regardless of whether we want to or not.

For all these concerns, the persona is a mere "application." Receiving an identity requires being identified by others. *Why* are others identifying us? The most immediate reason for their attention is status appraisal. To properly inter-act with strangers, we must know their status. All identifications involve clas-sifications of individuals into groups and tiers based on taste and immutable characteristics. Everything is fair game in these identifications. From social science research we know that even the paltriest personal trivia—stances, ac-cents, clothing choices, furniture arrangements—can offer clues to status. At the same time, appraisers identify us through the signals, cues, and significant absences *they* find important. We may have control over what others observe, but we have no control over how they classify us. Nor do they: their means of perceiving and identifying us is based on their habitus. So, for all practical purposes, questions of identity are bound up with status. Personas are vehicles for status claims, and identities are results of status appraisals.

Every identification, thus, becomes an *evaluation*. The high-status show dog King's Royal Lassie has a more valuable identity than mid-status farm-town Lassie. When KRL interacts with others, she receives benefits others do not. This principle emerges in the phenomenon of celebrity impersonation. After the success of the film *Jaws* in 1975, two schlubs went around the United States pretending to be director Steven Spielberg and lead actor Richard Dreyfuss. Their mere physical resemblance to the celebrities alone provided very little; to *be* them, on the other hand, afforded a wide array of social benefits. In most cases, then, our anxieties about identity are worries about valuation. We don't just want a distinct identity—but a *high-status* distinct identity.

A valuable identity can feel good even when we're alone. Self-esteem is more credible when it corresponds to social esteem. Moral philosophers have long believed we should never rely on others to determine our value. Jean-Jacques Rousseau complained about the dreaded "social man" who "knows how to live only in the opinion of others, it is, so to speak, from their judgment alone that he derives the sense of his own existence." We modern humans are thus faced with two competing ideals of individual distinction: the aristocratic principle of *esteemed* difference, and the moral ideal of authentic self-expression, esteem be damned. As long as we desire status, however, the former is a better goal, as it allows us to live with freedom *and* social approval. In discussing his desire to found a shoe company, Nike's Phil Knight writes, "I wanted what everyone wants. To be me, full-time." Knight could have been himself full-time as an impoverished nobody. His course of self-actualization instead was building a globally admired, $200-billion-plus shoe company. As long as the desire for status is fundamental, uniqueness works best only when it is part of a larger status strategy.

Any pursuit of social approval, however, may lead to conflict with the wayward desires of our inner self. These choices and desires always feel more authentic to us because they emerge directly from our consciousness. Charles Taylor writes that we "tend to think that we have selves the way we have hearts and livers," with "our thoughts, ideas, or feelings as being 'within' us." Yet we now understand that these desires, at least in part, derive from community conventions so internalized they become indistinguishable from instinct. Our convictions develop from social norms, and our aspirations borrow from high-status lifestyles. John Grimes in *Go Tell It on the Mountain* hopes to one day smoke Lucky Strike cigarettes because he lives in a world where they already exist as a brand with cachet.

The demands of the self usually conform so closely to societal norms that we feel no tension in acting upon our desires. The self emerges most clearly at times when our passions clash with social protocol. Their very inconvenience makes them feel "true." Over the last 150 years, however, psychologists and neuroscientists have warned us against attributing too much authenticity to our thoughts. Our brains are always engaged in *rationalization*: framing raw demands from our subconscious as well-grounded, logical requests. Psychologist Bruce Hood elaborates, "Even if you deliberate over an idea, turning it over in your conscious mind, you are simply delaying the final decision that has, to all intents and purposes, already been made." Later, "having been presented with a decision, we then make sense of it as if it were our own." The overwhelming number of truth-cloaking mechanisms in our brains has convinced Hood that the self is an "illusion." Whether or not this is the best framing, we should certainly abandon the idea that the self is a "real me" cordoned off from any social influence.

In hoping to deny the influence of status, however, our brains rationalize the attraction to status value using palatable alibis, such as the pursuit of high quality and beauty. In doing so we interpret inauthentic external desires as authentic demands from our heart. We then voice these alibis with pride as our deepest thoughts. As everyone obscures their status desire, it results in a lack of public discussion around status seeking, which in turn further propagates the status taboo and makes us ashamed of wanting status.

Sociologist Everett Rogers, who spent a lifetime researching how innovations are diffused through society, found that "respondents may be reluctant to admit that they adopted a new idea for status conferral." To his point, when researchers asked iPod owners in the early 2000s why they bought the device, most buyers cited "utilitarian reasons, such as small size or large memory capacity, as well as appreciation for the sleekness of the design." According to its owners, the iPod succeeded for reasons unrelated to its use as a status symbol. But if functionality was so critical, why did Microsoft's comparable Zune music player end up as the most mocked product of that decade? The famed gadget reviewer David Pogue called it "more practical" than the iPod—a larger screen, better battery life for video, and wi-fi connectivity to other devices. Yet few wanted one—or would dare buy one.

So, with respect to persona, identity, or self, status determines much of who we are. Our personas conform to the requirements for normal and high status, and our status position determines our demand for status symbols and our desired degree of distinctiveness. Identity appears to be the outcome of status appraisal. And the self absorbs status-related desires at an unconscious level and rationalizes them as authentic personal thoughts. This isn't to say that humans are *victims* of status—just that we are inherently social creatures who, as sociologist Georg Simmel writes, "*consist* of interactions with others" (emphasis added). Modern questions of personal identity are best considered in the context of status.

We should therefore abandon the fantasy of pursuing identities that transcend status. Even those who drop out of society to pursue an ascetic, solitary life end up with a status. And thanks to the principle of detachment, withdrawal often becomes an effective path toward higher social position. The sociologist Thomas Frank writes, "Today there are few things more beloved of our mass media than the figure of the cultural rebel, the defiant individualist resisting the mandates of the machine civilization." There is also great esteem for dedicated and disciplined individuals who devote themselves to rectitude, salvation, and harmony with the universe. Beatitude begets glory, and glory begets status.

Knowing all of this, we should temper our severe self-expectations regarding the achievement of pure originality. Even the most unique individuals will have a lot in common with others. The best we can hope for is a *relative* originality created in the margins of our persona. At the same time, not everyone needs to be different for difference's sake. For those at the top, the pursuit of distinctiveness is important for receiving higher status. But to foist the requirement of uniqueness on everyone is unnecessary, unnatural, and often cruel. If we allow everyone to be themselves, this should also provide the freedom to be identical to others.

At least we can thank liberal society for expanding the number of strategies toward valuable identities. Compared with our ancestors, we enjoy greater flexibility in choosing the most suitable lifestyles and face minimal punishments for deviating from custom. There is broad tolerance for membership in alternative status groups, whether naturist/nudist communities or the BTS Army. In a cosmopolitan world, we are free to craft our personas as much as we please. At the same time, this makes crafting personas more competitive, and there will always be elements of individual competence in determining success of those personas. But admitting that persona crafting is universal—and the role status plays in that process—would begin to better equalize that competition. Everyone should know how to win: how to gain esteem, how taste can be refined, how personas are judged, and how to balance detachment, congruence, originality, and authenticity. We all compete for status, whether we like it or not. We can at least better explain the rules to make it a fairer fight.

In learning the basics of status, conventions, signaling, and taste through part 1, we now know enough to solve the first part of the Grand Mystery of Culture: *Why do individuals cluster around arbitrary behaviors and take deep meaning from them?* This phenomenon arises because individuals, in seeking status, must publicly communicate certain conventions as proof of membership in particular groups. Every person who donned a moptop, dressed in Chanel's designs, or bought a Harvestore did so because these collective choices offered higher status value than alternatives. And no matter how distinct these individuals are on a micro level, the participation in the same conventions forms patterns when aggregated on a macro level. In the end, individuals' self-interested pursuit of status leads to the mysterious commonalities of behaviors we interpret as culture.

These principles now lead us to the next part of the Grand Mystery: *How do distinct styles, conventions, and sensibilities emerge?* The answer, to be explored in part 2, is related to individuals' and groups' struggles for status. While not everyone seeks the same status levels or will pursue the same assets, we now see that there are a finite number of strategies:

Status Strategy #1: Perform better against the status criteria— and reveal it in signals.

Study hard, go to a prestigious college, get a good job, make money, hone talents, conform to high-status conventions—and signal every improvement along the way. This is easier said than done, especially for those from disadvantaged backgrounds. "When people say that their relative standing is important," writes economist Robert H. Frank, "what most of them really mean is that it would be nice to have high relative standing, but not at the expense of changing their behavior significantly." Status seeking is like weight loss: we'd love to be slimmer without having to eat right and go to the gym. Also, status through achievement is useful only for an accomplished few. If all achieve the same exceptional feat, it's no longer exceptional.

Status Strategy #2: Pretend to be high status.

Mastery of the signaling process—emulating high-status taste without being a member of an elite—can fool many status appraisers and lead to high-status treatment in a particular setting or moment. Pretenders can then use their temporary status boost as a launchpad to get more credit for future achievements, which in turn may create actual high status. This strategy works well for those with more ambition than talent. But as Vanilla Ice and

Anna Delvey learned, there is a spiked pit of low status waiting for those who get caught.

Status Strategy #3: Change the status criteria in your favor.

We can gain status by persuading society to value *our* particular status criteria and beliefs. Artists, prophets, and philosophers have succeeded in expanding society's natural focus on money and power toward more intellectual attributes like creativity. New criteria can also be deployed as a defense. As economist Jon Elster writes, "The hard way of doing better than others is to improve one's own performance. The easy way is to trip up the competition." Changing the status criteria is never easy, however, and this strategy tends to be most successful for those who already have standing.

Status Strategy #4: Form a new status group.

Those fated to low status can leave the main status group to seek comfort in smaller splinter groups. A banjo player facing disrespect in a punk music world can move over to the Dixieland jazz circuit. This strategy works well for providing local status—the main source of self-esteem—but forgoes the most desirable material benefits that come with global status. This is why alternative status groups tend to combine this approach with Status Strategy #3. The Dixieland jazz circuit will attempt to convince the world that Dixieland jazz is the most important American musical tradition. In the twentieth century, we saw this play out when individuals fled into subcultures and countercultures that ended up influencing the mainstream status criteria.

To seek higher status we choose one or more of these four strategies, and by doing so, we enter into social competition. Individuals attempt to stand out against their peers, inferiors steal the status symbols of superiors, elites fight off upstarts and cheaters, and alternative status groups challenge established status beliefs. The resulting friction in jockeying for position, as we'll see next, serves as a critical engine of creativity and invention.

Part Two

STATUS AND CREATIVITY

Chapter Five

CLASSES AND SENSIBILITIES

⊰❈⊱

Jacob the Jeweler's bling, the faux patina of a blackened Cartier Tank watch, the yuppie cliché of Beaujolais nouveau, and Super PRO-Keds— all examples of how collective signaling strategies create aesthetics and artifacts

⊰❈⊱

NEW MONEY

"Whenever I need something incredible," explained the rapper Nas to the *New York Post* in 2003, "I go to Jacob." He was referring to Jacob Arabo, aka Jacob the Jeweler, the New York–based Uzbek American who served as the de facto minister of jewelry for the hip-hop nation. Nas was an early customer, and he then introduced the jeweler to the next generation of upcoming rappers. When Kanye West secured his first record advance in 2002, he bought his mother a Rolex, then, as immortalized in his song "Touch the Sky," he "went to Jacob" an hour after getting his advance, because he "just wanted to shine." Since then West has bought a treasure chest worth of pieces from Jacob, including a jewel-encrusted "Jesus piece" using aquamarines for blue eyes and rubies for blood.

Aside from the lottery, record industry advances on royalties have been one of the few legal ways in which people from modest backgrounds get rich quick. These financial windfalls transform status nobodies into somebodies overnight. The lucky recipients become members of an unofficial group that best embodies capitalism's promises of personal transformation—New Money, also known as nouveau riche, parvenus, and arrivistes. What does the fundamental human desire for status predict for them? The most rational way to move up the social hierarchy is to convert raw wealth into status symbols associated with higher-status lifestyles. This is the aim of *conspicuous consumption*—the intentional purchase of expensive goods to demonstrate an abundance of wealth. The simplicity of this approach has made conspicuous consumption nearly universal among New Money, no matter the era, language, or geography. When the Chicago gangster Al Capone bought a palatial Miami home in the late 1920s, his wife, Mae, decorated it in grand style: replicas of Louis XIV furniture, gold-trimmed dinner services, miniatures made from real ivory, and four metal elephants.

New Money's love for ostentation leads us to the main topic of this chapter: the sensibilities underlying taste are never random, independent results of idiosyncratic and irrational minds. Members of socioeconomic classes possess similar status assets, which lead to similar signaling strategies. As these individuals signal the same ways, their behavior becomes conventional to the community, and over time businesses offer specific goods—i.e., cultural artifacts—that cater to their taste. In this process a taste world is formed. New Money pours their ample funds into luxury goods for a quick status boost. Their public lifestyles and all the related accoutrements not only embody their sensibilities but, as we see with Jacob the Jeweler, provide popular culture with many of its most prominent and aspirational elements.

Socioeconomic classes are only one source for artifacts, styles, values, and sensibilities. To solve the second part of the Grand Mystery of Culture—*How do distinct styles, conventions, and sensibilities form?*—we'll examine the creativity that emerges from three categories of status groups: classes, subcultures, and avant-garde artists. Humans may be born with a creative instinct, but the need for status-related differentiation motivates individuals to pursue counterintuitive, idiosyncratic, and outrageous inventions. These new ideas form as the shared culture of small communities, and then those groups' global status determines the degree to which they influence the taste of broader society.

By this measure, socioeconomic classes provide the clearest example of how status influences taste. What do we mean by *class*? Putting aside the long academic debate on the topic, classes are groups of individuals with common levels of capital who share similar values and convictions. The economist Joseph

Schumpeter writes that members of a class "look out into the same segment of the world, with the same eyes, from the same viewpoint, in the same direction." Individuals born into a certain socioeconomic class share a foundational set of unconscious conventions—i.e., the same habitus. This manifests in communal beliefs, concrete lifestyle differences, and distinct taste worlds. The historian Paul Fussell notes that, for Americans, class determines "the place you live, the way you look, the shape and surface of your driveway, the items on your front porch and in your living room, the sweetness of your drinks, the time you eat dinner, the stuff you buy from mail-order catalogs, the place you went to school and your reverence for it, and the materials you read."

Members of each class adhere to similar conventions and oppose rivals' alternatives. That doesn't mean, however, that classes work as coordinated advocacy groups. Max Weber warns, "A class itself is not a community." Individual members of classes pursue the same goals for *themselves*, not necessarily for the group. Taste arises within a class because individuals with the same status assets agree on shared values that emphasize the importance of those assets.

The most common class definitions divide society into upper (capital owners), middle (salaried white-collar workers), and lower (blue-collar laborers) segments, but to better understand the relationship between status and culture, we'll look at individuals in four groups based on the *quantity* and *variety* of status assets. In chapter 1, we saw that sources of capital tend to cluster, so we can make useful divisions through just two particular types: economic and cultural. Economic capital consists of money, property, and wealth, whereas cultural capital is the knowledge of high-status conventions required to gain normal status from those in established high-status groups.

Class Name	Economic Capital	Cultural Capital
New Money	Extremely high	Low
Old Money	High	High
The Professional Class	Moderate	Moderate
Those without Capital	Low	Low

Individuals signal with the assets they have and believe to be the most valuable, and this forms the sensibility behind their tastes. New Money signals
through sheer wealth, which turns into an extravagant sensibility based on
conspicuous consumption. Old Money signals through quieter codes that emphasize cultural capital. When these classes choose certain material goods that
match those tastes, the resulting artifacts and conventions become the culture
of that group. Jacob the Jeweler and his creations (and even films about that
world, such as *Uncut Gems*) have taken a prominent place in American pop
culture, thanks to New Money demanding these goods as part of their signaling strategies.

If we return to our status strategies, nouveau riche individuals have suc-
ceeded at Status Strategy #1—performing better against the status criteria.
Through luck or skill, they've amassed great economic capital, and they demand a higher status in line with their achievements. This requires converting
their raw wealth into public status symbols to let others know they have arrived.
The titular character of F. Scott Fitzgerald's *The Great Gatsby* was born in North
Dakota as the nobody James Gatz but is reincarnated as the legendary Jay
Gatsby through a profitable career in bootlegging. He could have used his fortune to buy understated material comforts for a hidden mansion or stashed his
money into the bond market to guarantee a stable income stream for dozens of
potential Gatsby grandchildren. But in his fundamental desire for status (and to
win back his lost love), Gatsby uses his money to tell the world he is somebody,
putting together an infinite wardrobe of silk shirts, living in a giant mansion, and
hosting legendary bacchanals for all of New York.

Today there are many legitimate ways to become a multimillionaire: finance,
law, medicine, sports, entertainment, and startups, to name a few. The resulting
large fortunes enable large expenditures. The British industrialist Sir Bernard
Docker and his wife became legendary in staid postwar England for their
"Golden Zebra"—a luxury Daimler coupe with real gold instead of chrome, an
ivory dashboard, and zebra-skin seats (because "mink was too hot to sit on").
In more recent years the Canadian entertainer Drake built a 50,000-square-
foot home in Toronto called the Embassy, featuring a two-ton black marble bath-
tub, a chandelier composed of twenty thousand pieces of hand-cut Swarovski
crystal, and a regulation-size basketball court under a pyramidal skylight. His
two-story closet houses a vast collection of Hermès Birkin bags for a future

wife, including the Himalaya Birkin, which has gone for $382,000 at auction. The house concept, as Drake explained to *Architectural Digest*, is "overwhelming high luxury."

"Overwhelming" is the key term here. Conspicuous consumption is a universal language: it's obvious *evidence* of wealth. No cultural capital is needed to read its codes. Any uninformed, impoverished child from any region on earth would be able to assess the scale of Drake's fortune. (Or as John Waters film star Divine quipped, "You can always tell how rich people are by the amount of garbage they have.") New Money status symbols thus have very low symbolic complexity: they make sense as signals to everyone, including members of a parvenu's low-status community of birth.

The inherent usefulness of low symbolic complexity explains why conspicuous consumption is so common in highly stratified, poorly educated societies, where a small number of elites rule over an impoverished population. The dictators and oligarchs of economically underdeveloped autocracies and gilded petrostates can demonstrate status simply by owning material goods their subjects never could. Zimbabwean dictator Robert Mugabe maintained a fleet of luxury autos, including one of the only eighteen Rolls-Royce Phantom IVs ever made. His wife was known as Gucci Grace for her love of European luxury goods. In these countries most come to desire the same obvious luxury goods, because possession would put them on the "right side" of society. Western aesthetes often berate "third-world dictator" tastes, but the United States experienced its own version of this pattern in the robber baron years of the late nineteenth century. Historian Russell Lynes writes, "The rich were becoming fabulously rich, so rich that their taste was divided by a towering wall of wealth from the taste of the rest of the people. They might, almost, have lived in different worlds."

Before consumer society, the main method of overwhelming others with wealth was what Thorstein Veblen calls *conspicuous waste*—flamboyant expenditure to demonstrate the possession of unlimited resources. The thirteenth-century Italian nobleman Giacomo da Sant'Andrea once burned down his own villa just to thrill guests. In potlatch ceremonies, Indigenous Pacific Northwest tribes gained status by gifting incredible riches to adversaries; the purpose, as analyzed by the French philosopher and novelist Georges Bataille, was "humiliating, challenging and obligating" rivals who would have trouble reciprocating. Today spectacular financial profligacy is still common among the ultrarich. In addressing rumors of excessive monthly wine consumption, the actor Johnny Depp told *Rolling Stone*, "It's insulting to say that I spent $30,000 on wine, because it was far more."

The rich in industrial societies can also signal wealth through *conspicuous leisure*—playing in public while everyone else is hard at work. Middle-class students pursue higher education to acquire useful skills for a professional career, but scions of the rich can spend that same time learning ancient Greek and Latin. Conspicuous leisure, however, has been a less effective signal in modern times. "Leisure works as a way of attaining honor in small societies where everyone knows everyone else," writes the sociologist Peter Corrigan, but ceases to mean much in "large societies of strangers." Moreover, time is money; in late capitalism the ultrarich work even longer hours than the poor.

In the rapidly growing and anonymizing economy of the modern age, conspicuous consumption emerged as the most efficient means of signaling. When Veblen analyzed the phenomenon in the late nineteenth century, extravagant purchases focused on luxury "carpets and tapestries, silver table service, waiter's services, silk hats, starched linen, many articles of jewelry and of dress." Today New Money has moved on to ski lodges, supercars, and Gulfstream planes—luxurious expenditures that have become standard items within their closed communities. This creates conventions among higher income bands to buy goods of a certain price. Veblen called these "pecuniary canons of taste." Most conspicuous consumption, then, is simply emulation of these canons. Kanye West knew to go to Jacob, because his heroes Nas and JAY-Z had already made Jacob's jewelry a standard purchase for the hip-hop elite.

But rich individuals can always burst through the canon by spending even *more*: the cars rarer, the houses larger, the summer houses more numerous. Birkin bags are very expensive, but Drake shells out for the Himalaya Birkin. Mega-yachts, racing stables, and manor estates perform poorly as investments but function well as distinction. Upon exhausting ideas on how to further gild one's own life, the rich can always indulge in *vicarious consumption*—outfitting family and servants in high-end clothing and accessories. Once Gatsby had enough silk shirts, he spent his surpluses on entertaining all of New York.

In their willingness to accept expensive new products for signaling wealth, parvenus are often attracted to *novelties*—the latest and greatest styles, gadgets, and fashions. In the 1950s, Old Money women still dressed according to stuffy

British traditions, while New Money followed the quicker pulse of Paris run-ways. A drug dealer's pad in Marin County in the late 1960s offered color TVs and stereos in every room, laser light show displays, and revolving beds. For the nouveau riche, the disposability of fashion is a feature, not a bug: the con-stant replacement of goods to obtain the newest fashionable item provides an-other avenue for conspicuous waste. Moreover, novelties align with the core New Money belief that contemporary luxuries are credible status symbols. Japanese ecommerce entrepreneur Yusaku Maezawa may not be able to fill European manors with galleries of Thomas Gainsborough and Pierre-Auguste Renoir paintings, but he can pay $6.9 million for a Jeff Koons sculpture.

Conspicuous consumption doesn't always work as an effective signaling strategy. During the Great Depression and World War II, lavish lifestyles clashed with the emphasis on communal sacrifice. And even in ordinary times, conspicuous consumption violates the principle of detachment. New Money signals lack plausible deniability; they're too on the nose. Conspicuous pur-chases also feel inauthentic when they transcend credible lifestyle needs: Is there any *practical* reason to own a closet of unused luxury bags for a nonexis-tent life partner?

The ultimate flaw with conspicuous consumption is that the artifacts (such as yachts, mansions, and luxury brand goods) themselves inevitably become associated with New Money—a group lower in status than Old Money. "Nou-veau riche" is a pejorative term; few want to be famous for their *recent* acquisi-tion of wealth. In the 1980s, the music executive Allen Grubman purchased a Rolls-Royce to celebrate his successes in the music industry but sold the car when he realized it "was like a blinking neon sign on my forehead: NOUVEAU RICHE." Many New Money tastes can often also be judged as incongruent hyperextensions of the lower-class habitus—e.g., SUV limos, cinema-sized TVs, and diamond dog collars.

But the strategy that underlies conspicuous consumption is so logical that we should expect future cohorts of New Money to continue buying expensive things simply *because* they are expensive. Economists call this the "Veblen ef-fect": goods become more desirable with a higher price tag. A gargantuan luxury industry has emerged over the last century to serve these needs, producing ex-clusive clothes, jewelry, accessories, and beverages while simultaneously build-ing common knowledge about their cachet through advertising and marketing.

These companies not only provide "higher-quality" versions of everything imaginable but continually make even rarer and pricier versions to fuel the last mile of the status race. When Johnnie Walker Black became too popular to attract the new business elite in the early 1990s, the distillery offered Johnnie Walker Blue; when Blue became too common among the wealthy, there was Blue Label King George. There are Rolls-Royce sedans for the merely rich, while the Swiss company Eurocash AG built a "gold-plated, fully armored, and astronomically expensive" Rolls-Royce Phantom EWB for an elite Middle Eastern businessman.

On the whole, New Money has left a significant mark on global culture. The pioneering economist Werner Sombart believed capitalism itself arose from the insatiable hunger for imported luxury goods among European aristocrats. And he traces the particular aesthetic sensibilities gothic, Renaissance, baroque, and rococo directly to "styles expressing the will of ruling groups." Today the unwavering need for wealth-based status symbols among New Money continues to propagate specific aesthetics, namely, an over-the-top sensibility of extravagance. Jacob the Jeweler is known to more people than can ever buy his wares. Today's dynamic capitalist economy ensures that there will always be New Money, who will convert their wealth into status symbols made for that very purpose. And in less complex economies, the resulting "vulgar" luxury sets the standard for good taste. In advanced economies, however, New Money status claims face serious opposition from other classes—starting with a powerful counteroffensive from the established rich.

OLD MONEY

H. Jeremy Chisholm attended Le Rosey, the expensive Swiss boarding school that counts among its alumni members of the Rockefeller and Rothschild families, as well as multiple European monarchs. His father was heir to a New England paper industry fortune, and his mother, a surrealist painter, was the daughter of socialite Vera Bate Lombardi of the Baring banking family. Chisholm's great-grandmother Rosa Frederica Baring was so Old Money that after divorcing his great-grandfather, she married into the British royal family.

In the late 1970s, the very Old Money Chisholm became annoyed that New Money types began to wear Cartier Tank watches. Previously Cartier had limited sales of the distinctive square wristwatch to a more exclusive clientele:

luminaries like designer Yves Saint Laurent and Jackie Kennedy. Before 1960 no more than one hundred were made a year. But as Cartier ramped up production, rich bankers, lawyers, and entrepreneurs snapped them up as status symbols. Wanting to make a statement about this vulgarization, Chisholm paid full price for a new Tank watch and asked metallurgists to turn the gold casing into a tarnished black. While his New Money acquaintances in Palm Beach bragged about their new shiny Cartiers, Chisholm sought to prance around with a seemingly long-worn Tank watch in a vile dark patina. But alas, the jeweler never discovered the right antialchemy to ruin the casing, so Chisholm foisted the shiny gold timepiece on his stepson, who promptly lost it.

Chisholm's scheme was a mere prank, but it reveals a key distinction between New and Old Money tastes. Where New Money desires the latest, biggest, and brightest, Old Money seeks to be modest, antiquated, and muted. And just as conspicuous consumption is universal among New Money, the Old Money sensibility of being "casual, careless, nonchalant, insouciant, easy, unstudied, natural, effortless" is shared among hereditary wealth in the United States, the United Kingdom, France, and Japan. Charles, the Prince of Wales, wears old jackets and shoes with visible patches. New England heiresses drive beat-up station wagons. Wealthy Tokyo merchants of the early nineteenth century strived to be *iki*—a word meaning "detached," "refined," and "urbane"—and therefore preferred subdued kimonos over flashy ones. This quiet shabbiness among the very richest can appear illogical to the uninitiated, especially New Money individuals. But as we'll learn, musty Old Money aesthetics are an equally rational signaling strategy as New Money's money-drenched boasting.

In his 1899 work *The Theory of the Leisure Class*, Thorstein Veblen predicted an eventual split in sensibilities among New and Old Money: once there was a need for differentiation within the leisure class, "loud dress" would be deemed "offensive" and replaced with "subtler signs of expenditure." This is an obvious outcome when individuals claim status with their most exclusive assets. New Money signals with economic capital. Old Money, on the other hand, has an advantage in the *longevity* of their status superiority, which can be demonstrated through social capital (strong relationships with other rich families) and cultural capital (knowing how to behave at the very top of society). H. Jeremy Chisholm's family network extended from British royals and banking families to Coco Chanel and the modern-art world. He was comfortable in any high-society setting, from Miami country clubs to St. Paul's alumni lunches. His lived experience in the upper-class milieu provided the cues and signals that made up his good taste and valuable identity.

For most of history, especially in feudal societies, hereditary wealth has garnered more esteem than new wealth. To be granted an audience with the French king in 1760, applicants had to prove a noble family pedigree extending back three centuries. Even in nineteenth-century France, in the wake of a series of revolutions and republics, sociologist Gabriel Tarde wrote, "ancestral prestige still immensely outweighs the prestige of . . . recent innovations" and, therefore, "the classes or persons who have real prestige are those classes that have had power and wealth up to a still recent period." There may be chimerical properties behind our lingering obsession with nobility; philosopher Bertrand Russell draws a line from the "magic properties of chiefs, through the divinity of kings, to knightly chivalry and the blue-blooded aristocrat." But from the perspective of status integrity, Old Money's multigenerational wealth is a more reliable predictor of future position. New Money may be a one-generation fluke. Old Money Tom Buchanan is alive at the end of *The Great Gatsby*; the titular bootlegger lies dead in a swimming pool.

As reflected in that novel's particular rivalry, Old Money loathes New Money. There is an unconscious revulsion at the low-status habitus embodied in New Money taste. Old Money also resents any challenges to the existing social hierarchy. It believes that New Money is cheating by attempting to quickly buy its way into a high-status lifestyle without having built up prestige over the course of generations. Moreover, established families worry that New Money's aggressive conspicuous consumption may reset the standards for what constitutes an affluent lifestyle. With assets locked up in trusts to sustain their intergenerational wealth, Old Money doesn't have the same cash flow as newly minted millionaires and billionaires.

In a world where wealth alone determines status, New Money would rise to the very top of the hierarchy. Fears of this outcome push Old Money to erect new fences based on taste. Old Money thus pursues Status Strategy #3: *Change the status criteria in your favor*. As sociologist Cecilia Ridgeway explains, "High-status group members may use their influence and esteem to steer the group in directions that help maintain their own high status, which further maintains the hierarchy." To neutralize the signaling power of New Money, Old

Money refuses to engage in demonstrating their raw wealth. They emphasize modesty and detachment and, when needing to signal, deploy status symbols that emphasize time being rich over sheer wealth. From this perspective, Old Money taste may be more oblique than New Money taste, but it's no less mechanical.

These differences in taste offer an easy way for Old Money to disparage New Money. French aristocrats called parvenu taste *petit goût*—"trivial taste." Since the boldest acts of conspicuous consumption become associated with New Money, Old Money can simply refuse such extravagances to further isolate themselves from the practice. In the place of profligacy, they pursue "Spartan wealth"—austere choices that may seem nonluxurious at first glance. In economics, this technique is called *countersignaling*. This is not *non*signaling, just "countering" any signals based on raw wealth. By eschewing grand luxury purchases like Porsches and new Cartier Tank watches, Old Money effectively makes New Money excesses stand out as desperate attempts to signal—placing a spotlight on their violation of the detachment principle.

But doesn't countersignaling restrain Old Money from using their own vast fortunes in signaling? Yes, but Old Money often doesn't need to signal in the first place. The hereditary rich enjoy a strong reputation in their communities. Moreover, they care about receiving status only from their Old Money peers, who will pick up on their subtle cues. Sociologist Peter Corrigan writes, "The growth of wealthy classes in the nineteenth century led to the existence of a large enough number of the wealthy, and a sufficient rate of meeting with each other, to justify no longer paying attention to what the lower class thought." This is how the Earl of Lonsdale defended his shabby appearance: "In London, nobody knows who I am, so it doesn't matter. In Cumberland, everyone knows who I am, so it doesn't matter."

Just as the logic of signaling attracts New Money to luxury, countersignaling directs the Old Money sensibility toward *modesty*. If a fancy new Mercedes-Benz in the seventies was "a sign of high vulgarity, a car of the kind owned by Beverly Hills dentists," then American Old Money preferred "slightly dirty" Chevys, Fords, Plymouths, or Dodges, or perhaps an "old and beat-up" Jaguar or BMW.

This impulse also drives the Old Money ethos of *reduction*. The fashion designer Paul Poiret believed that "it is what a woman leaves off, not what she puts on, that gives her cachet." Beau Brummell, the godfather of modern men's style, aimed for invisibility: "If John Bull turns round to look after you, you are not well dressed; but either too stiff, too tight, or too fashionable." This is why the classic suits made on Savile Row—long considered to be the most luxurious in the world—feature no obvious frills. The fashion scholar Quentin Bell explains, "The good Savile Row tailor . . . achieves an effect of great expense by his very lack of flamboyance; the perfection of his cut is made manifest in its extreme discretion."

Concurrent with modesty is a pursuit of *functionality* over display. *The Official Preppy Handbook*, the popular 1980s guide to American Old Money taste, notes that "the ultimate accolade for a piece of clothing is 'useful.'" And so when Marshal Tito of Yugoslavia complimented Prince Philip of the United Kingdom on gold plates at a state dinner, Philip explained, "My wife"—that is, Queen Elizabeth II—"finds that it saves on breakages."

While modesty and functionality explain product choices, their presentation as signals should also have an air of *nonchalance*. This links to the aristocratic belief that hard work is for inferior classes. Old Money individuals have not achieved good taste—they *embody* good taste. Old Money virtues, according to *Old Money* author Nelson Aldrich Jr., are "a thing beyond learning, far beyond purchase. It is a secret of nature, like the grain in the wood." Nonchalance makes taste appear to be an inevitable product of the habitus—absorbed through an Old Money upbringing rather than learned in conscious imitation. This technique also helps Old Money battle the most cunning New Money type, the one who studiously educates themselves in high-status taste. The famed interior designer Mark Hampton made fun of New Money clients for their pedagogy: "One can almost hear the poor creature flipping the pages of *Architectural Digest* and *House and Garden* in her mind."

Modesty itself is not nonsignaling, however. As Jean Baudrillard notes, underconsumption "merely represent[s] a further degree of luxury, an added element of ostentation which goes over into its opposite and, hence, a *more subtle difference*." But only Old Money can achieve these reputational advantages, because appraisers are unlikely to read understatement as a true lack of resources.

After devaluing conspicuous consumption, Old Money can then introduce more subtle signals based on a rival signaling cost—time. Old Money taste focuses on what the anthropologist Grant McCracken calls "patina," visual proof of age in possessions. A dulled silver plate, for example, implies that the object has been owned for generations. The menswear writer G. Bruce Boyer once asked a Philadelphia patriarch where he purchased his tuxedo and was scolded, "I don't *buy* evening clothes. I *have* evening clothes." Crumbling old country estates and castles, collections of old painting masters, cellars of vintage wine, and slightly dented furniture from famed craftsmen all suggest a family that has amassed a formidable set of possessions through the centuries.

Patina also explains the rustic nature of Old Money aesthetics. Their rooms are often said to look "lived in," full of mismatched bric-a-brac and with hardwood floors covered in "Orientals so old as to be almost threadbare, suggesting inheritance from a primeval past." The Earl of Winchester, who at one point was the world's richest man, avoided any clothes that appeared to be recently purchased. At Yale in the 1950s the word "shoe" became slang for the upper crust, in reference to their white suede shoes worn to the state of dilapidation. Scholarship students could buy white bucks pre-dirtied in New York "to save [them] the embarrassment of looking as though you hadn't had them all your life."

Compared with New Money's love of fashion, Old Money seeks items of permanent value and rejects novelties. In the United States, Old Money flocked to stable "traditional styles" in the finest natural materials—such as wool, cotton, and linen—rather than synthetic polyester. Such choices were fundamental to the artifacts and conventions known as the "preppy wardrobe," as Nelson Aldrich Jr. lists out:

> LL Bean boots, Top-Sider moccasins, tasseled loafers; pure wool socks, black silk socks, no socks; baggy chinos, baggy brick-red or lime or yellow or pink or Pulitzer trousers, baggy Brooks Brothers trousers, baggy boxer underpants; shirts of blue, pink, yellow, or striped Oxford, sometimes buttoned down, some made for a collar pin, usually from Brooks or J. Press or The [name of town or college] Shop; jackets of tweed, corduroy, poplin, seersucker with padless shoulders, a loose fit around the waist, and (if tweed) a muddy pattern; a shapeless muddy-patterned tweed overcoat, its collar lopsidedly rolled up under one ear, a shapeless beige raincoat bleached by years of use and irresistant to rain; no hat, a cross country ski cap, a very old snap-brimmed felt hat, a very old tennis hat.

Rather than European designer brands, most of the items are practical responses to the weather conditions of a New England lifestyle—snowy in winter, muggy in summer. But after taking on the cachet of Old Money, these functional items ascend into a canon of permanent good taste.

Patina also encourages *archaism*, the preferences for antiquated styles over contemporary alternatives. Old Money disdains gadgets, from televisions to jewel-encrusted smartphones. Critic Stephen Bayley writes, "Most Englishmen of a certain class would prefer to live in a shoddily built, thermally inefficient, insecure travesty of classical architecture than commission a new house in a city." On Boston's tony Beacon Hill, shops have long cherished defective purple glass "Lavenders" in their windows, because these date their establishment to the mid-nineteenth century.

Obscure signals work well in the Old Money community, because it's a closed-off world of exclusive neighborhoods, boarding schools, and social clubs. Few have the chance to learn the inside jokes, secret handshakes, and correct cadence of banal chatter. Learning these conventions is, in Nelson Aldrich Jr.'s words, an Old Money "curriculum." In academic settings, nouveau riche children may be able to "acquire the social, linguistic, and cultural competencies which characterize the upper-middle and middle class," write sociologists Michèle Lamont and Annette Lareau, but "they can never achieve the natural familiarity of those born to these classes and are . . . penalized on this basis." In early-twentieth-century Britain, to say "cheers" before drinking was distinctly non-upper-class ("non-U")—something knowable only after much time spent socializing in a high-status milieu.

The emphasis on subtle codes rather than possessions centers Old Money status appraisals on tiny details rather than grand gestalts. As *The Official Preppy Handbook* advises, "A small percentage of polyester in an oxford cloth shirt or a lapel that's a quarter of an inch too wide can make all the difference." Codes not only measure the depth and length of an individual's time living in the high-status milieu but offer subtle distinctions invisible to outsiders. The British linguist Alan S. C. Ross writes, "In these matters, U-speakers have ears to hear, so that one single pronunciation, word, or phrase will suffice to brand an apparent U-speaker as originally non-U."

Until recently an appreciation for high culture was also an important part of Old Money distinction, because deep appreciation of classical music, opera, modern art, and literature was possible only after a long period of formal education and casual exposure. The rich had more leisure time to acquire this knowledge, which enabled them to enjoy more difficult art. In *Distinction* the sociologist Pierre Bourdieu accused contemplative Kantian aesthetics of being a scheme to emphasize exclusionary cultural capital. "A work of art," writes Bourdieu, "has meaning and interest only for someone who possesses the cultural competence, that is, the code, into which it is encoded." This means there is an "unequal class distribution of the capacity for inspired encounters with works of art and high culture in general." In previous eras Old Money became subscription audiences of symphonies and ballets, and the most illustrious served on the boards of museums. The knowledge of high culture never constitutes the entirety of cultural capital, but here we see how arts and entertainment take on status value beyond their aesthetic value.

So, in needing to best New Money in status claims, Old Money creates a distinct muted sensibility and supports particular sectors of social activity, such as the art world and high-end, independent clothing boutiques. The Old Money desire for patina also keeps older goods in cultural circulation: inherited artifacts are prized, and antiquated homes are renovated rather than razed. But this class is also responsible for many of the behaviors and norms we come to know as "virtues." This, in turn, justifies their belief in the superiority of their own choices. From these lofty heights, Nelson Aldrich Jr. writes, "They model things for everyone else, and thereby, or so they hope, influence national taste." Old Money aesthetics, then, don't just operate at the top of society but spur imitation among a much larger audience—specifically, educated middle-class individuals who are also hungry for alternatives to New Money vulgarity.

THE PROFESSIONAL CLASS

"I can't buy imported cheese in good conscience anymore, or state-of-the-art booties. I can't even buy a feisty little Beaujolais." So complained a thirtysomething corporate communications flack in 1985. Just a year before, *The Yuppie Handbook* appeared on bookstore shelves, both spoofing and canonizing the consumer habits of America's "young urban professionals." In the wake of the yuppie trend, actual young urban professionals distanced themselves from the stereotype. As the aforementioned yuppie concluded, "There's something vaguely nauseating now about being a yuppie."

For all its satire *The Yuppie Handbook* did identify a legitimate change to the American social structure. From the 1970s onward, ambitious and highly educated professionals in finance, law, medicine, and big business had begun earning much more than their parents. And in contrast to the rigid conformity of earlier corporate culture—e.g., IBM once required male employees to wear sock garters—yuppies pursued a colorful and cosmopolitan life of sophistication. They poured their earnings into American jogging shoes, imported French sparkling water, British Burberry coats, Japanese Walkmans, and Italian Gucci briefcases and loafers.

Just as we saw in the case of New Money and Old Money, the sensibility embodied in yuppie taste follows the logic of the professional class's signaling needs. The American upper middle classes attend elite universities and take well-paid jobs in big cities. A few years into their careers, they have built up a balanced mix of economic, social, and cultural capital. They are not as rich as New Money, and their cultural capital is *learned* rather than embodied. But after success in education and corporate life, they have honed their critical thinking and stockpiled an impressive degree of worldly knowledge. To succeed in the postmodern information economy requires ingesting, retrieving, and processing vast amounts of information, and the professional class considers their competence in these areas as justified criteria for higher status. Their most valuable signals, then, are not based on money or time being rich, but the exclusive possession of *privileged information*. The resulting professional class sensibility thus focuses on intelligent, high-quality, and unusual choices—a strong belief in taste itself. As *The Bluffer's Guide to British Class* jokes, "Taste is entirely a Middle Class concern. The Lower Class don't have it and the Upper Class don't need it." The professional classes compete through consumer choice because cultural capital—the knowledge of specific conventions—can get them further ahead in the world than any future chance at giant fortunes. By competing on taste, they can best rivals in their own ranks, impress Old Money, and embarrass New Money.

In this effort to accumulate cultural capital, professionals often start by emulating Old Money aesthetics. Born into the upper middle class in 1943, the

American cultural critic George W. S. Trow writes, "I was taught by my parents to believe that the traditional manners of the high bourgeoisie, properly acquired, would give me a certain dignity, which would protect me from embarrassment." Over the last century, once exclusive institutions such as Ivy League universities opened up to meritocratic achievers. There students learned the conventions required to appreciate "difficult" art, literature, films, and music. But they also adopted the leisure culture of elites. *The Official Preppy Handbook* jokes that Ivy League students from humble backgrounds in the 1980s forgot "all about Corvettes, *real* college football (Michigan vs. Ohio State), and sober moderation when enjoying a good time" and learned to "favor BMW's, fake college football (Williams vs. Amherst), and drowning in a whitecapped sea of Molson, Becks, and Heineken (light or dark)." So even if aspiring members of the professional class can't pass for true Old Money, they go out into the world with the analytical abilities to read cultural codes well enough to blend into high society.

With the number of college students expanding in the mid-twentieth century, this sensibility seeped into middlebrow culture. In 1980 Americans with no firsthand knowledge of Phillips Andover or Phillips Exeter made *The Official Preppy Handbook* a *New York Times* bestseller. In the ensuing preppy craze, Old Money–inspired brands like Polo Ralph Lauren, L.L.Bean, and Sperry became household names. The preppy look, in the eyes of Nelson Aldrich Jr., was an Old Money taste "package" marketed to young professionals: "Nonchalance sold along with 'naturally tailored' suits, magnanimity arriving in the mail with every L.L.Bean catalog, a sense of fair play included in the warranty of each Volvo station wagon." Old Money taste also better matched professional-class salaries. Most white-collar middle managers would blanch at leasing a Ferrari or flying first class to Bora Bora with Louis Vuitton luggage trunks, but would find it sensible to buy high-quality, long-lasting products that confidently disparage conspicuous consumption.

As an exemplar of this sensibility, the Volvo automotive brand became one of the American professional class's favorite cars. The Volvo allowed the emulation of Old Money aesthetics: a functional and modest foreign import that enabled consumers to leapfrog the entire automobile-status hierarchy of American New Money and the lower middle classes. The Swedish import was boxy and promoted as an ultrasafe, utilitarian car for people who wanted to reject the entire enterprise of planned obsolescence. One late-sixties ad boasted that Volvos "don't change much," and not being "new and exciting for 1968" meant not being "old and funny-looking for 1969."

With the economic boom of the 1980s, faux preppies grew up and became worldly yuppies. And at the end of the twentieth century, this group transformed again, into what the columnist David Brooks named Bobos (bourgeois bohemian), a group with taste that merged cosmopolitan yuppie consumerism and modest hippie sensibilities. He summarized Bobo tastes in these mock rules:

> **RULE 1:** Only vulgarians spend lavish amounts of money on luxuries. Cultivated people restrict their lavish spending to necessities.
>
> **RULE 2:** It is perfectly acceptable to spend lots of money on anything that is of "professional quality," even if it has nothing to do with your profession.
>
> **RULE 3:** You must practice the perfectionism of small things.
>
> **RULE 4:** You can never have too much texture.
>
> **RULE 5:** The educated elites are expected to practice one-downmanship.
>
> **RULE 6:** Educated elites are expected to spend huge amounts of money on things that used to be cheap.
>
> **RULE 7:** Members of the educated elite prefer stores that give them more product choices than they could ever want but which don't dwell on anything so vulgar as prices.

The sociologist Douglas Holt's academic research on "high cultural capital" Americans found proof of these tongue-in-cheek rules in the real world: "[They] are at least as willing to make material acquisitions, often spending large amounts of money in so doing, as long as these acquisitions can be rationalized as instrumental to desired experiences." The vast majority of Whole Foods customers have college degrees and, on average, a graduate degree.

In globalization and its promotion of multicultural diversity, the professional classes have been able to move beyond junior varsity Old Money aesthetics and build their own body of information-rich cultural capital. To maintain normal status among the upper middle classes, professionals must keep up with the latest trends in music, art, fashion, design, and entertainment, all understood within the context of deep historical knowledge. In the 1980s, while the lower class was curling up with *Reader's Digest*, *TV Guide*, and the *National Enquirer*, the upper middle class delved into serious articles in *The New Yorker*, *Harper's*, and *The Atlantic* for the latest cultural critique. In the more artistic fringes of the professional class, there has been a strong consumption of high culture, with a social life rich in opera and symphony performances, art gallery openings, and museum exhibits.

Media companies catering to this class create middlebrow entertainment: high-minded yet easily digestible content looking to reward an educated audience through winking references to their acquired knowledge. The greatest example may be *The Simpsons*, which mixes cartoonish ultraviolence with piquant social satire and passing allusions to Ludwig Wittgenstein. The professional classes are the most likely of all Americans to find humor in Homer lashing out at his Ivy League–aspiring daughter, Lisa, "I've had just about enough of your Vassar-bashing, young lady."

The professional class relies on the media and upscale retailers to learn what to buy and how to combine products to achieve maximum taste congruence. Instruction arrives under the guise of practical advice for maximizing the joys of life: film reviews, instruction at yoga retreats, photo books of classic style. The Condé Nast magazine empire—from *Vogue* and *GQ* to *The New Yorker*—was built upon teaching the latest high-status conventions to the professional classes, many of whom didn't live in New York to observe the trends themselves. This constant input of new information, preference for critically reviewed culture, and willingness to experiment with unknown or obscure forms shaped the professional class's taste—moving its identity away from mass culture, which was considered too obvious or direct. For a long time, any indulgence in mass culture had to be explained away as a "guilty pleasure." (As we'll see in chapter 10, this has been replaced by "I don't believe in the idea of guilty pleasures.")

In the last three decades, the professional class has splintered into two distinct factions. Those who work in investment banking, private equity, management consulting, and specialized forms of medicine and law often achieve fortunes on par with the lower ranks of New Money. Once they have the resources to signal through raw wealth, their tastes veer closer to conspicuous consumption. The other faction is the *creative class*, a term coined by the sociologist Richard Florida to describe those who find stable middle-class incomes through "creative" occupations such as writer, journalist, magazine editor, graphic designer, photographer, fashion buyer, and interior decorator. In their proximity to celebrity and the high-status milieu, creative-class jobs offer more in the way of status than in financial rewards. Being an obscure novelist doesn't provide enough income to thrive but can lead to esteem and other material benefits. The playwright Lillian Hellman noted, "[Horace] Liveright was possibly the first publisher to understand that writers care less for dollars than for attention." Not only do these individuals prefer cutting-edge culture and use it to signal, but their professional careers depend upon keeping up with the latest trends. The clerks at the indie music store Championship Vinyl in Nick Hornby's novel *High Fidelity* spend their days in pedantic discussions about the best albums and the ethics of music collection; however tedious, these debates are arguably core to the job.

At the bottom rungs of the creative class, lower incomes mean partaking in an ersatz version of sophisticated lifestyles. Instead of saving up to buy garments from high-end avant-garde designers, young creatives shop at thrift stores. At the same time, the creative class, as we'll see in subsequent chapters, is the first to embrace new styles from nominally lower-status groups and, in doing so, takes the lead in promulgating cultural change.

As with Old Money, the professional class encourages cultural invention by focusing social competition on information, innovations, and codes rather than obvious demonstrations of wealth. For the rich, culture becomes a realm to communicate symbols of their monetary advantages; members of the professional class, on the other hand, communicate superiority in their *manipulation* of culture. And since information is free, professionals see this form of high-status signaling as the most meritocratic means of status competition. Anyone can have good taste if they work at it. But the advanced aesthetic choices of the professional class never come to fully dominate the culture—because those at the bottom of the status ladder aspire to much simpler, bolder statements.

SIGNALING WITHOUT CAPITAL

"I had Super PRO-Keds in blue canvas. I'll never forget what that felt like. It was a coming of age." Thus began Bobbito Garcia's lifelong obsession with sneakers. The son of Puerto Rican immigrants, growing up in a rough neighborhood in Upper Manhattan, Garcia and his friends lacked the money to show off cars, luxury handbags, or antique furniture. But they could earn, scrounge up, or beg their parents for the funds to buy new pairs of sneakers. At first, athletes sought out the shoes as an advantage on the basketball court, but soon the rarest pairs of sneakers became powerful status symbols in their own right. When Garcia got his hands on Super PRO-Keds, he felt "glory." But glory fades: "I saw my boy with PRO-Ked 69ers that I'd never seen before. I was taken aback. Thought I was cool, but he was cool. He was a step ahead."

Thorstein Veblen understood that "no class of society, not even the most abjectly poor, forgoes all customary conspicuous consumption"—a principle that plays out in sneaker consumption and other semiluxury industries. In Russia there are "long lines of Range Rovers and BMW Gran Turismos" parked outside of decaying Soviet apartment blocks. Conspicuous consumption can be *more* useful for gaining status within poorer communities. In their 2007 paper "Conspicuous Consumption and Race," the economist Kerwin Kofi Charles and his colleagues note that African American and Hispanic people spend 30 percent more than whites from the same economic background on "visible goods" like cars and apparel. They conclude that this derives from two factors: (1) minorities look to their own ethnic bloc as their primary reference group; and (2) the costs are lower to signal higher status within less affluent reference groups than in wealthier racial groups. This means conspicuous consumption offers better cost-performance for members of poorer communities.

But what does signaling look like when individuals lack large amounts of economic, social, educational, or elite cultural capital? The professional classes advise the poor to channel their energy and money into education and career rather than into the purchase of status symbols. But not everyone has the patience to postpone status claims, nor does everyone have the potential to be a high achiever. For many the quickest path to higher social position is Status

Strategy #2: *Pretend to be high status.* When pretending, whom do they copy? New Money makes for the best idols, because extravagance is a universal language. A Gucci handbag is a Gucci handbag, a Ferrari is a Ferrari. And as philosopher René Girard notes, "There are no longer class differences in terms of desire—meaning that any external mediation in modern society has collapsed. People at the lowest social level desire what people at the highest level have."

For those who lack capital, signaling tends to adapt the logic of New Money conspicuous consumption to smaller-scale purchases. When most teenagers in the 1970s wore cut-rate, generic "skippy" sneakers, expensive brand-name sneakers became status symbols. There are canons of taste in both rich and poor communities. Bobbito Garcia bought PRO-Keds because, as his friend Lincoln Parker recalled, "even back then there was the notion of being accepted if you had certain products. PRO-Keds were one of those products." Every neighborhood had its own sneaker conventions: Nike was popular in uptown Manhattan, Adidas in Queens, FILA in Brooklyn. But as with any group, living up to the basic convention affords only normal status. Originality and authenticity are required to rise above others. Garcia explains, "Biting was frowned upon. Whether it was coming up with a new boogie move on the court or a new freeze on the linoleum, ballplayers and hip hop heads alike were pushing the creative envelope at all times."

But even if the status logic of taste holds across classes, the lack of capital results in differences between signaling at the bottom of the ladder and at the top. These limitations create two unique sensibilities: *kitsch* and *flash*.

Due to the inherent elitism in most cultural criticism, "kitsch" is a pejorative term. But we should think about kitsch in a value-neutral way—as a specific type of commercial product that copies the format of high culture (books, music, films, clothing, interior goods) but removes its artistic aspirations. Kitsch is low in symbolic complexity: little irony, few ambiguous emotions, and muted political gestures. Using stock emotions, kitsch meets consumers' expectations, thus requiring no specialized knowledge to understand. Kitsch may be ersatz art, but it delivers the experience of art to everyone. It entertains, reassures, and connects the audiences with others. Among the best-known examples of kitsch are Muzak, schmaltzy songs, paintings of Elvis on velvet, pink lawn flamingos, plastic miniature copies of marble busts, Soviet realist art, and the entirety of Las Vegas. But most pop culture adheres to the principles of kitsch. Popular Hollywood films employ stimulating scenes of sex and violence and then wrap everything up in a happy ending that doesn't challenge conventional beliefs.

To understand the appeal of kitsch, we must return again to Pierre Bourdieu's idea that the potential appreciation of high art is unequally distributed in society. Even with university graduation rates increasing over time, those at the bottom of society continue to have fewer educational opportunities. This can make high culture an alienating experience. Bourdieu writes, "If formal explorations, in avant-garde theatre or non-figurative painting, or simply classical music, are disconcerting to working-class people, this is partly because they feel incapable of understanding what these things must signify, insofar as they are signs." Everyone (other than the most self-punishing snobs) can enjoy basic sensual pleasures, but so-called Kantian "contemplative" aesthetics make better sense to those with ample educational capital. Kitsch feels good immediately, whereas avant-garde art intentionally breaks the very conventions responsible for delivering pleasurable experiences. To someone who hasn't learned the right conventions, Arnold Schoenberg's jarring twelve-tone compositions just sound like dissonant noise.

For those with the right knowledge, such as Old Money and the professional class, kitsch is loathsome. These groups complain about its lack of artistry (while likely fretting about its low status value at a subconscious level). Many creators and manufacturers—from Bauhaus to Sweden's IKEA and Japan's Muji—have attempted to fight kitsch by providing low-priced, mass-manufactured items in minimalist "good taste." But these goods can be insulting to those without capital. "Consumers of kitsch," writes the philosopher of art Tomáš Kulka, "do not buy kitsch because it is kitsch; they buy it because they take it for art." This often creates an inverse relationship between professional-class taste and mass popularity. After the invention of the phonograph, Thomas Edison was asked to approve records for sale: "After hearing them I would mark 'good,' 'fair' or 'rotten' to classify them for the trade. The 'rotten' records always made a hit with the public. Now all I have to do is condemn a bit of music and the factory works overtime to meet the demand."

Kitsch may be pleasurable, but its ubiquity means it doesn't provide any status boost. An advantage in signaling requires standing out. This encourages a *flash* sensibility—bright and showy aesthetics, usually achieved through the purchase of low-level luxury goods. Standing out through personal appearance is important for those who have fewer opportunities to signal educational attainment, career progression, and home ownership. And without hope of true upward mobility, there is a "culture of transience"—"easy come, easy go"—a propensity to live it up while you can.

Flash manifests in the consumption of bold goods in a bold style. Here we find the source of common aesthetic differences by wealth. In the 1950s the Color Research Institute of Chicago found that the highest income and education segments preferred "muted and delicate colors" while lower classes liked "brilliant hues and large doses." Early Jamaican immigrants to the United Kingdom wore "rainbow mohair suits and picture ties" as well as "neatly printed frocks and patent-leather shoes" that were "too loud and jazzy" for white Brits. The wealthy creative classes can play in musty and decaying garments as a means of detachment, but these goods just reinforce the stigma of poverty for those lacking capital. Minimalism is always a privilege; in signaling, the poor can't afford to look generic. The goal instead is maximal ornamentation on even the cheapest objects. Russians today pay thousands to have images of lemurs, reclining polar bears, Minions, and Chuck Norris airbrushed on their cars.

In providing the best cost-performance for signaling, flashy items, such as large logos and brand names on clothing, make sense for those with limited resources. The demonized "chav" working-class subculture in the United Kingdom flocked to the easily recognizable Burberry tartan pattern. In a media-saturated world, almost everyone is familiar with the big-box luxury brands. JAY-Z doesn't have to explain to his fans why he owns Porsches, Ferraris, and multiple Maybachs. Counterfeiters, who target poorer consumers, copy the luxury brands' most famous, logo-driven styles rather than subtler models. There is thus an important overlap between New Money extravagance and lower-status flash: both groups want big logos. But only New Money can easily buy the real thing.

The lower-status aspiration toward luxury goods manifests clearly in the behavior of lottery winners, who do not typically mimic Old Money lifestyles, place money into trusts, or patronize avant-garde artists. In 1961 factory worker Vivian Nicholson of Castleford, United Kingdom, won the equivalent of £3 million on football pools. She became famous nationwide for her "spend, spend, spend" lifestyle of jewelry, dresses from Harrods, intercontinental travel, and a pink Cadillac. Although this spree ended in financial ruin, Nicholson's life remains a well-known standard for glamorous living in working-class England. When a woman named Jennifer Southall won £8.4 million in the National Lottery forty-five years later, she announced her plans to do "a Viv Nicholson."

A significant portion of the modern consumer marketplace involves selling kitsch and flash at a mass scale. The creators and consumers of mainstream pop culture would never call these products "kitsch," but as we'll see in chapter 8, there is an implicit agreement to meet existing audience expectations with conventional formulas, obvious emotions, and safe political valences. Luxury brands, meanwhile, market themselves as purveyors of premium goods for the wealthy, but in practice, they make billions each year through entry-level goods intended for low-level conspicuous consumption. Sneaker brands develop new technologies for better athletic performance and then spend millions on marketing to imbue their goods with status value in poorer communities. This doesn't mean there is no innovation without capital: mass-culture creators can and do play with radical artistic conventions. (And in the next chapter, we'll see how subcultures are particularly important for cultural change.) But kitsch and flash are a better means for companies to profit, because most people in the marketplace have conservative, emulative tastes that correspond to people low to middle in the status ladder. There is always demand for obvious status symbols and immediate pleasures.

When signaling, individuals show off their most exclusive and most powerful status assets. These signaling needs then create a communal sensibility among people with the same capital. Companies respond by manufacturing specific goods that serve as status symbols for those classes' positional strategies. The end result is that a majority of society's cultural artifacts and stylistic conventions—at least the most conspicuous ones used in signaling—exist in large part to serve the distinction needs of classes. Specifically,

- New Money's use of economic capital in signaling spurs the creation of expensive luxury goods such as sports cars, limousines, mansions, yachts, summer homes, designer clothes, and furniture.

- Old Money's countersignaling and focus on patina and cultural capital incentivize companies to make classic, modest goods with a functional appeal.
- The professional class's signaling through information creates a market for middlebrow mass media/consumer guides, functional goods, artisanal goods, and copies of Old Money lifestyles.
- Underprivileged individuals' desire to take part in culture and outdo peers pushes companies to offer kitsch and flashy entry-level luxury goods.

Class also plays a major role in determining which artifacts stay in circulation. New Money buys the latest novelties and upgrades after a few years. Most kitsch is intended to be disposable, and the cultural industry continually pumps out new kitsch to replace it. Old Money, however, needs goods with patina for signaling, and thus these families tend to value and preserve older objects and aesthetics. By sticking with classic styles, they help keep their conventions valuable as "traditions." Critic Russell Lynes, in discussing the antiques boom in the United States, noted that "pewter that the family had put away when they could afford china, and luster candlesticks that had been forgotten when they could buy brass or silver[,] came out of the attic or the cold-cupboard to be proudly displayed and sold for gratifying prices to avid collectors." There is no functional need to revive these goods, but antiques stick around because they offer status value in signaling. In following the logic of Old Money aesthetics, the professional classes are often the most active participants in these trends, and as we'll see in chapter 9, the creative classes also revive older kitsch styles as retro in their constant search for novel forms of pop culture.

These effects of class on consumer choice challenge the idea that taste could be based on universal standards of beauty. In particular, the oft celebrated "elegance of simplicity" isn't an innate human preference but arises from a countersignaling strategy. In communities where a united and permanent class of elites rules over the population, good taste gravitates more toward obvious conspicuous consumption than modesty.

So much of what we celebrate in pop culture is created to satisfy classes' need for taste distinction. But as we'll now learn, *escaping* the class system is also a creative engine for new aesthetic sensibilities.

Chapter Six

SUBCULTURES AND COUNTERCULTURES

-)⊖(-

Alternative status groups—from drape-coated delinquents to Japanese mountain witches and anti-imperialist Jamaican communes—create radical styles that go on to influence mass culture.

-)⊖(-

FORMING ALTERNATIVE STATUS GROUPS

At the end of 1954, the George Hotel ballroom in Luton, England, posted a sign in its window stating: YOUTHS WEARING EDWARDIAN DRESS WILL NOT BE ADMITTED TO THE HOTEL DANCES. This was a devastating reversal of fortune for the Edwardian look. Six years prior, high-end tailors on London's Savile Row revived the early-twentieth-century style of long drape jackets, elegant patterned waistcoats, and slim trousers—both to evoke the British Empire's golden years and to celebrate the end of wartime frugality. But perhaps the style was too ornate. Shunned by serious businessmen, the Edwardian look attracted few outside of elite military officers and Oxbridge dandies.

Edwardian style did eventually go on to find a large and fervent fan base—among juvenile delinquents. Teenagers in London's working-class neighborhoods asked their local tailors to replicate the Savile Row look, while extending the long jackets to dramatic zoot-suit length and slimming the trousers into an extreme drainpipe shape. The teens hit the town in these audacious suits, with a greasy duck's-ass quiff hairstyle on their heads and thick rubber-soled brothel-creeper shoes on their feet.

British authorities had feared a rise in juvenile crime and social disorder in the aftermath of World War II, and now youth gangs were indeed roving around the country committing sensational crimes in fancy Edwardian suits. A moral panic ensued. Newspapers breathlessly reported the litany of Edwardian villainy: gang brawls, property destruction, arson, animal torture. But it was the teenage murder trials that solidified the associations between Edwardian dress and lawlessness—and gave the youth gangs their name. At the trial of twenty-year-old Edwardian Michael Davies, charged with stabbing a teen to death, a reporter from the tabloid the *Daily Express* heard young women call their well-dressed hooligan boyfriends "teddy boys," a play on the diminutive form of Edward. From this point forward, Christian ministers railed against the teddy boy look as "Devil's garb," while social workers proclaimed it "an ugly badge of violence." This prompted the first wave of posh Edwardians to abandon their suit collections; a Guards officer complained to the *Daily Mirror* that the emergence of the teddy boys meant "the whole of one's wardrobe *immediately* becomes *unwearable.*"

The United Kingdom survived the onslaught of the teddy boys, but the group lives on in our collective memory as a vivid example of a postwar *subculture.* The word first indicated smaller offshoots of the "main culture," but 1970s sociology focused the analysis of subcultures on loosely organized groups of young working-class outcasts who adopted unconventional styles and behaviors. Subcultures are a clear example of the alternative status groups introduced in chapter 1: collections of individuals lacking global status who form new hierarchies around status beliefs other than capital and mainstream virtues. In teddy boy circles, a slick style and "daring" garnered more esteem than proper manners and graduate degrees. Rising up the ranks in Birmingham teddy circles meant, for example, not being "custard." When all the kids were merely breaking milk bottles, a true teddy girl heroine would step up and smash out a shop window with her shoe.

Wanton destruction provided teddy boys and girls with more than weekend kicks. Communities such as gangs and cults offer the disrespected a chance to be reborn as beloved and welcomed comrades. Infamy is often preferable to anonymity. For those already at the bottom of the status ladder—and cynical about their prospects for upward mobility—the most attractive path forward is to adopt Status Strategy #4: *Form a new status group.* Sociologist George Homans writes, "Members of established low status in a group are particularly apt not to conform to its norms. Since they get little reward from the group, they are also particularly apt to leave the group altogether—if there is anywhere they can go." Subcultures make exits easier by providing a destination.

But as we learned in chapter 1, this status strategy has a major flaw: individuals in subcultures gain only local status. And if the group's foundational status criteria diverge too greatly from the mainstream, joining a subculture results in a major loss of global status. Even before the nationwide moral panic, the teds endured verbal slights for their clothing on the streets; teddy boy historian Michael Macilwee explains, "It took courage for the first pioneers to strut through their working-class neighbourhoods dressed like upper-class dandies, while most other youths wore their dads' uniform of 'demob' suits or baggy flannel trousers." The media hype further raised the social costs. Teds lost job opportunities and were denied entry at their favorite dance halls, cinemas, and bars. This calculus—enduring massive global status losses for gains in local status—made sense only for particularly disadvantaged teens who desired new sources of esteem *and* had little to lose.

From hobos to pickpocket gangs, subcultures have long existed. The big change came with consumerism, which elevated subcultural life beyond petty crime and cryptic argot and into extreme clothing styles, wild musical genres, strange social rituals, and recreational drug use. Writer Tom Wolfe explains, "For the first time in the history of man, young people had the money, the personal freedom and the free time to build monuments and pleasure palaces to their own tastes." The teds made the most of rising blue-collar wages to peacock each weekend in pseudo-aristocratic suits and immaculate pompadours, while their straitlaced peers trudged through the grind of school and work in drab clothing. Consumerism enabled subcultures to indulge in open hedonism as a counterimitation of mainstream society. Teds never gained global high status from conspicuous consumption and conspicuous leisure, but flashy clothes, wild behavior, weekly parties, and ceaseless dancing let them playact elite status every Saturday night.

As material conditions improved in advanced economies, postwar prosperity spawned a constant stream of subcultures around the world. In the United Kingdom, after the teddy boys came cosmopolitan mods on Vespa scooters, a cult that then morphed into laborer-chic skinheads. Similar outcast groups appeared elsewhere: hipsters, greasers, and outlaw bikers in the United States; bodgies and widgies in Australia; ducktails in South Africa; *zazous* and *blou-sons noirs* in France; *skinnknuttar* and *raggare* in Sweden; and *bosozoku* biker gangs in Japan. As soon as living standards pass a certain threshold, spectacu-lar subcultures can appear anywhere: e.g., the pink- and yellow-suited dandies La Sape in Congo and the gold-chained and Kappa sweat-suited Dizelaši in Serbia.

Disadvantaged ethnic minorities also form their own alternative status groups—crafting cultural oases of music, fashion, and leisure to escape struc-tural discrimination. The sociologist Dick Hebdidge writes, "Black culture, and especially Black music, has provided one of the strongest means of survival— a secret language of solidarity, a way of articulating oppression, a means of cultural resistance, a cry of hope." Young Jamaican immigrants to England in the 1960s, known as rude boys, wore flashy mohair suits and porkpie hats. In California, Chicanos created their own culture of low-rider automobiles. And in the apocalyptic ruins of the South Bronx in the 1970s, African American teens bonded over rapping, break dancing, deejaying, and graffiti, which co-alesced into the broader movement known as hip-hop.

In the 1960s, middle-class youth felt their own spirit of rebellion and aban-doned their parents' staid customs to form alternative status groups known as *countercultures*. Compared with subcultures, countercultures tend to embrace explicit ideologies, which members uphold as superior to traditional norms. While the teds were just out for a good time, countercultural Beats espoused ex-treme spontaneity, sexual freedom, and consciousness expansion as a spiritual antidote to the stifling "gray flannel" conformity of fifties America. A decade later hippies embraced psychedelic drugs and rejected technocratic thinking to turn on, tune in, and drop out. By the early seventies, numerous communes and New Age cults sought alternative ways of living to replace capitalist think-ing and bourgeois morality.

A less extreme middle-class version of the alternative status group is the *hobbyist group*: pods of individuals building mutual respect networks based on common interests. From Trekkies and hackers to Civil War reenactors and fur-ries, hobbyists are often derided in mainstream society for being nerds. And just as in the case of teens joining a subculture, open membership in certain hobbyist groups can result in low global status. But once inside the group, members enjoy the social approval of their peers. In Colin MacInnes's 1959 British novel *Absolute Beginners*, the teenage narrator explains the outsider appeal of jazz: "No one, not a soul, cares what your class is, or what your race is, or what your income is, or if you're a boy or girl or bent or versatile or what you are—so long as you dig the scene and can behave yourself and have left all that crap behind you when you come in the jazz club door." Joining a hobbyist group is easier than abandoning postindustrial society for life on a commune. Part-time members can hide their fandom at work and school. Colleagues need not know any details of Phil from Accounting's My Little Pony obsession.

But if subcultures form as a solution to compensate for status disadvantages, why do prosperous middle-class kids create their own alternative status groups? The best long-term status strategy for most suburban teens would be to study hard and follow the rules—not dress in weird ways that alienate authorities. First and foremost, hobbyist groups are always effective solutions to teenage boredom. But even the most privileged teenagers can benefit from extra esteem when they feel marginalized and oppressed, their freedom constricted by curfews, groundings, and financial dependency. And whatever their potential future status, they may suffer bullying and low status on the schoolyard. Writing about his enthusiasm for music, the critic Carl Wilson explains, "As a former bullied kid, I always figured it started from rejection. If respect or simple fairness were denied you, you'd build a great life (the best revenge) from what you could scrounge outside [bullies'] orbit, freed from the thirst for majority approbation." Many middle-class youth also adopted countercultural groups' radical beliefs in good faith. Hippie culture promised a purer and more peaceful form of liberal democracy. And in times of prosperity, the artificiality of consumer culture can arouse a desire for more primitive forms of living and folk traditions—i.e., "nostalgia for the mud."

In theory there is no age limit on membership to alternative status groups. And yet the most famous subcultures and countercultures have been *youth cultures*. From the 1950s onward, with the advent of automobiles, an expansive consumer market, and youth-focused mass media, teenagers have resolved their status anxiety by burrowing inside their own distinct communities. Teens use odd clothing styles, trendy dances, and slang ("groovy," "doobie," "cheugy") to erect clear fences between young and old. "For the first time, kids didn't want to look like their fathers," writes the journalist Nik Cohn about British postwar youth culture. "In fact, whatever their fathers looked like, they wanted to look exactly opposite." Youth culture enabled teens to flip the script and create criteria that made them superior to their prim parents. And as the newest members of society, they saw their parents' norms as arbitrary anyway.

While alternative status groups suggest a way to escape the class structure, individual members' tastes are still moored to their habitus. Teddy boys retained the patriarchal gender values, territoriality, and xenophobia of their working-class community. (Most notably, they were core instigators of the 1958 Notting Hill race riot against West Indian immigrants.) In a similar vein, working-class subcultures very rarely channel their social defiance into articulated political or spiritual beliefs. Japanese blue-collar bikers of the 1970s frightened authorities with right-wing paramilitary uniforms festooned with imperialist slogans, despite having little serious interest in actual right-wing ideology. Upper-middle-class hippies on college campuses, by contrast, laid out their antiestablishment attitudes with pseudo-philosophy and bookish rhetoric.

Over time, however, the distinctions between subcultures and countercultures blur, especially as countercultures find inspiration in the "authenticity" of subcultures. The Ivy League–educated Beat poets cribbed their deviant lifestyles from working-class white hipsters, and Beat books then inspired a middle-class hippie movement on college campuses. Countercultures can also trickle down into subcultures. As the mass media reported on the cerebral San Francisco psychedelic movement, runaways across America appeared in California to form a street urchin lumpenproletariat. In 1967 George Harrison of the Beatles visited the Haight-Ashbury area of San Francisco and recoiled at its deterioration: "I went there expecting it to be a brilliant place, with groovy gypsy people making works of art and painting and carvings in little workshops. But it was filled with horrible spotty drop-out kids on drugs."

Not surprisingly, mainstream society reacts with outrage upon the appearance of alternative status groups, as these groups' very existence is an affront to the dominant status beliefs. Blessing or even tolerating subcultural transgressions is a dangerous acknowledgment of the arbitrariness of mainstream norms. Thus subcultures and countercultures are often cast as modern folk devils. The media spins lurid yarns of criminal destruction, drug abuse, and sexual immorality—frequently embellishing with sensational half-truths. To discourage drug use in the 1970s, educators and publishers relied on a fictional diary called *Go Ask Alice*, in which a girl takes an accidental dose of LSD and falls into a tragic life of addiction, sex work, and homelessness. The truth of subcultural life is often more pedestrian. As an early teddy boy explained in hindsight, "We called ourselves Teddy Boys and we wanted to be as smart as possible. We lived for a good time, and all the rest was propaganda."

Of course the hostile feelings between mainstream society and alternative status groups are mutual. Subcultures invent pejorative terms to describe the majority culture: "normies," "trendies," "Sharons," "smoothies," "casuals," "basics." And every alternative status group creates binaries that highlight its own special criteria. "One is Hip or one is Square," famously wrote Norman Mailer of American subculture in his controversial essay "The White Negro"; "one is a rebel or one conforms, one is a frontiersman in the Wild West of American nightlife, or else a Square cell, trapped in the totalitarian tissues of American society, doomed willy-nilly to conform if one is to succeed."

For all the pop culture successes of subcultures and countercultures, however, they never overthrew the status system. Alternative status groups are mostly temporary solutions. Wearing Edwardian suits could not address structural problems including "unemployment, educational disadvantage, compulsory miseducation, dead-end jobs, the routinisation and specialisation of labour, low pay and the loss of skills." As teens in subcultures reach adulthood, the social costs of subculture membership begin to outweigh its benefits. At a certain age "selling out" is the better means to secure higher status. The original teddy boys hung up their drape coats upon marriage or military conscription. Many hippies hoping to escape the status ladder through joining a counterculture became disappointed to find power hierarchies and chauvinism in their new communities. If the 1970s communes had worked, their numbers would not have so dwindled.

On their good days, subcultures and countercultures function well as collective efforts to create alternative sources of status. And as with all status groups, members must live up to certain conventions to gain normal status. The difference is that with subcultures and countercultures, the conventions to follow are not just unique and distinctive—but shocking.

EXTREME STYLES

Bihaku ("beautiful whiteness") long reigned as the ideal for female beauty in Japan. But in the early 1990s girls from elite Tokyo high schools started to tan their skin golden brown and dye their hair a subtle shade of chestnut. This was not an ideological rebellion against *bihaku*: the tans approximated the post-vacation glow of expensive Hawaiian beach holidays. The darker skin also helped girls look older for sneaking into nightclubs. Bouncers came to call these girls *kogyaru* ("little gals") and, after the similarly styled Okinawan singer Namie Amuro became the biggest pop star in the country, millions of middle-class middle schoolers lightened their hair and bronzed their skin in tanning salons. By the mid-1990s most young Japanese women were more *kogyaru* than *bihaku*.

The *kogyaru* style eventually became so popular that high school delinquents from the provinces, the type who once joined all-girl biker gangs, also started to sport tans and hang out in Tokyo. But to adapt the style to their own social needs, they transformed the slightly risqué bronzed look into a radical makeup style called *ganguro* ("black face")—extremely dark skin tones, globs of white eye makeup, eyebrows drawn with Magic Markers, and big-eye contact lenses. Men's tabloids lusted after the *kogyaru* but hated the *ganguro*, casting the adherents as street urchins who slept in garbage-filled alleyways, refused to shower or change undergarments, and engaged in sex work for living expenses. By the end of the 1990s, *ganguro* took over the *kogyaru* movement, and their fashion magazines celebrated the most radical women, nicknamed *yamamba*—"mountain witches"—who intensified the look into full-scale tribal makeup, rainbow-colored hair extensions, demonic-colored contact lenses, and facial piercings. The *kogyaru* look began as a slight deviation in mainstream beauty trends among young wealthy women, but once it had been adopted by a working-class subculture, the conventions escalated into a style closer to the monsters of Japanese folklore than even the weirdest examples of the country's famed avant-garde fashion.

The development of *ganguro* style illustrates an important principle of alternative status groups: subcultures and countercultures don't form around minor stylistic divergences but around conventions of *extreme* difference.

Wealthy *kogyaru* tanned their skin and dyed their hair in admiration for the appearance of women in sunnier climes. *Ganguro* exaggerated these stylistic directions into a society-alienating costume. As we learned in chapter 2, status groups rely on distinct practices for self-definition. Subcultures and counter-cultures need particularly high fences that demonstrate their intentional sepa-ration from the standard class hierarchy of straight society. This requires going beyond the realm of acceptable difference. Teddy boys needed to exaggerate Edwardian style and add a greasy duck's-ass haircut to avoid any overlaps with similarly dressed Cambridge students. And the social dynamics of these groups, as we'll see, tend to push their styles into even wilder dimensions over time. In forging new conventions, subcultures and countercultures act as an important source of creativity.

The easiest method for subcultural distinction is the *negation* of standard conventions: intentionally doing the opposite of the mainstream. If conserva-tive businessmen have short hair, hippies have long hair. If middle-class hip-pies have long hair, working-class skinheads have buzz cuts. These negations can take the form of rejecting, reversing, exaggerating, or distorting existing looks. The darkened skin and white makeup marked *ganguro* not just from normal women but also from the first wave of wealthy *kogyaru*. Sixties mod style—slimmed suits with superfluous details such as extra buttons, flaps on pockets, and extra-deep vents—was "overtly close to the straight world" and yet "incomprehensible to it."

How do subcultures and countercultures settle on a particular direction for rebellion? Why did teds go Edwardian and *ganguro* darken their faces? Unoffi-cial groups seldom have formal councils to deliberate on their eccentricities. Instead conventions form over time in an organic process. Members casually propose radical ideas, and the most impressive ones stick around. The mods' slim suits and Lambretta scooters spread because they spoke directly to the aspirations of working-class teens at the time. Upon spying an early mod in the 1960s in London, a later follower of the style recalled, "In the distance I heard the distinct piston pop of an Italian scooter. . . . He looked brilliant, with cropped hair parted in the middle like he was French. I just stood and stared in disbelief at the sight of this 'cos in all honesty the scooter resembled a Roman chariot. . . . I would have given anything to have looked as good as that bloke did that night." He went out the next day and became a mod himself.

Youth subcultures are rarely artistic or design collectives, which means their stylistic innovations tend to adapt, warp, and blend preexisting looks and commodities rather than create new looks from scratch. The teddy boys pilfered their signature look from Savile Row. Most subcultural and countercultural innovation thus begins as *bricolage*—the mixing and matching of preexisting styles and objects to imbue them with new meanings. Since teenagers are confined to a distinct geographical space with limited pocket money, they must repurpose common objects to construct a unique look. The first British subcultures focused on tailored suits, because tailoring was standard at the time. Mods rode scooters because they couldn't afford cars. Early *bosozoku* bikers in Japan wore their *dokajan* cold-weather jackets from construction and janitorial jobs.

Bricolage pulls from here and there—emulations and counterimitations, bad taste and good taste. Anything can go into the mix as long as the end result, in the words of sociologist Dick Hebdidge, is *"obviously* fabricated." Bad taste serves as a rejection of mainstream styles, while emulations help impress mates. Teddy boys embraced Edwardian suits, and working-class Brits of the 1990s wrapped themselves in the Burberry tartan. In most cases the easiest form of distinction is to look intimidating, dangerous, and domineering. The Sex Pistols' Sid Vicious wore the leather jacket and jackboots of outlaw bikers and, for further self-alienation, a Nazi swastika T-shirt. Notably, this most taboo of all symbols was a favorite of late-twentieth-century subcultures, from the Hells Angels and Japanese bikers to the minority youth in Bronx gangs.

Unambiguous distinction requires tall fences, and there must be high signaling costs to keep out normies. Subcultural and countercultural styles require significant expenditures of time, money, and reputation. The tailored teddy boy suit was extremely expensive for a young blue-collar laborer in the 1950s, and the teds' elaborate, time-consuming quiffs were a form of conspicuous waste. Both dissuaded halfhearted teds. When groups have anticommercialist tendencies, like punks and hippies, the requirements may instead focus on extravagant changes to appearance, such as body piercings and mohawks.

Members themselves don't see their lifestyles as mere counterimitations, but perceive them as direct expressions of personal feelings. The Beats lived "subterranean values" in defiance of stifling fifties conformity: drug use, sex-

ual freedom, itinerant lifestyles, fistfights, and experimental writing techniques expressed "hedonism, disdain for work, aggressive and violent notions
of masculinity." Punks often insist, "Punk's not a fashion—it's an attitude."
Certainly, there is a punk "feeling" of combative disobedience, but there are
many potential ways to express this emotion. In theory, punk's deep suspicion
of fashion and commercialism could lead punks to dress as blandly as possible.
Safety pins and leather jackets, on the other hand, express their ideology while
conveniently also creating clear points of distinction from mainstream society.

Over time rebellious styles eventually become conventional within alternative status groups and, at that point, members must adhere to them to receive
normal status. To be a Juggalo—a fan of the music group Insane Clown
Posse—members are expected to dress in oversized red and black garments,
drink large quantities of low-priced Faygo soda, tattoo the band's Hatchetman
logo on their bodies, and greet fellow Juggalos with the salute "whoop whoop."
Just as the wealthy have cultural capital, subcultures develop *subcultural capital*. There is a correct way of being a Juggalo just as there's a correct way of
being Old Money. Upon visiting the Gathering of the Juggalos music festival,
the non-Juggalo writer Kent Russell noted the ubiquity of the Hatchetman
logo: "I saw the Hatchetman stitched onto shirts, pants, cheer shorts, bikini
tops, beanies, caps, and shoes; shaved into heads and chests; and tattooed on
so many pounds of lacquered flesh—on arms, shoulders, forearms, over the
avian bones on the backs of hands, across necks and asses, in the lee of breasts,
on calves, clavicles, and feet." Russell, by contrast, lacked this subcultural capital: no Hatchetman tattoo and no familiarity with the right way to say "whoop
whoop." He quickly fell to the lowest status within the Juggalo micro-society
and spent his days under "showers of refuse" as festivalgoers constantly threw
garbage at him.

Alternative status groups may represent an escape from the primary social
hierarchy, but they're not an escape from status structures in general. Just like
any other tribe or society, these groups demand conformity to conventions and
reward some members more than others. This fuels the common complaint
that joining a subculture is simply trading one uniform for another. John
Lydon (aka Johnny Rotten) of the Sex Pistols denounced the second generation
of punks: "They became clone-like. Now they totally missed the whole point,
that this was all about individual expression and personality. . . . *The* leather

jacket; *the* safety pin; *the* torn jeans; *the* bovver boots; *the* spiky hair." Few members perceive subcultural norm-following as mindless imitation, however. The sociologist David Muggleton interviewed a young punk who claimed that "punk is basically being yourself, freedom, doing what you wanna do, looking like you wanna, like, look like"—all while sporting a stereotypical punk mohawk.

The requirements on members can get more extreme when subcultures start to shrink in size. As *ganguro* scared away normal girls from the *kogyaru* style, the remaining members developed their own unique looks on the streets of Tokyo, incomprehensible to outsiders. This phenomenon echoes a principle seen in linguistics: languages of small Indigenous populations develop more complicated grammars and more difficult sounds than widely spoken tongues. When subcultures are small cults, the most dedicated members receive more status than hangers-on, which incentivizes the core members to indulge in even more extreme practices with higher signaling costs.

This often spirals into further extremity. If the subcultural looks are too outrageous, members take a large hit in global status. Fewer individuals will want to join, and the remaining members will become more reliant on the subculture for esteem. The weirder *ganguro* girls looked, the more they needed the respect of other *ganguro* girls to have any status at all. This often leads to high-status "total" members waging war on "partial" members. Hard-core ravers hated "Techno Traceys," and the LSD cult the Merry Pranksters detested no one more than the "weekend hipster." "Plastic"—inauthentic, protean—has long been one of the worst insults across the entire subcultural and countercultural realm. Punks hurled the "preppy punk" epithet at those who failed to get a visible tattoo or wear a tall mohawk. Groups may exile these apostates and compromisers.

Of course all subcultures and countercultures are collections of individuals, and few members ever live up to the full stereotype. Many of the original teddy boys never owned an Edwardian suit and just wore their fathers' hand-me-down jackets. And the boundaries between subcultures are often less explicit than portrayed in the media. But groups become defined by the most extreme elements, and the most *novel* conventions are the ones that become definitional. The most elaborate Edwardian suits came to represent "teddy boy" style rather than the median member's toned-down version.

Subcultures, then, become more and more extreme in their looks over time—and yet, it is often their most radical inventions that go on to influence mainstream society.

FROM THE FRINGES TO THE MAINSTREAM

Founded in 1940, Pinnacle was a rural Jamaican commune providing its Black residents a "socialistic life" removed from the oppression of British colonialism. Its founder, Leonard Howell, preached an unorthodox mix of Christianity and Eastern spiritualism: Ethiopia's Emperor Haile Selassie was considered divine, the Pope was the devil, and marijuana was a holy plant. Taking instructions from Leviticus 21:5, the men grew out their hair in a matted style that caused apprehension among outsiders, which was later called "dreadlocks."

Jamaican authorities frowned upon the sect, frequently raiding Pinnacle and eventually locking up Howell in a psychiatric hospital. The crackdown drove Howell's followers—who became known as Rastafarians—all throughout Jamaica, where they became regarded as folk devils. Parents told children that the Rastafarians lived in drainage ditches and carried around hacked-off human limbs. In 1960 the Jamaican prime minister warned the nation, "These people—and I am glad that it is only a small number of them—are the wicked enemies of our country."

If Rastafarianism had disappeared at this particular juncture, we would remember it no more than other obscure modern spiritual sects, such as theosophy, the Church of Light, and Huna. But the tenets of Rastafarianism lived on, thanks to one extremely important believer: the Jamaican musician Bob Marley. He first absorbed the group's teachings from the session players and marijuana dealers in his orbit. But when his wife, Rita, saw Emperor Haile Selassie in the flesh—and a stigmatalike "nail-print" on his hand—she became a true believer. Marley eventually took up its credo, and as his music spread around the world in the 1970s, so did the conventions of Rastafarianism—from dreadlocks, now known as "locs," as a fashionable hairstyle to calling marijuana "ganja." Using pop music as a vehicle, the tenets of a belittled religious subculture on a small island in the Caribbean became a part of Western commercial culture, manifesting in thousands of famed musicians taking up reggae influences, suburban kids wearing knitted "rastacaps" at music festivals, and countless red, yellow, and green posters of marijuana leaves plastering the walls of Amsterdam coffeehouses and American dorm rooms. Locs today are nearly as common as the Beatles cut, as seen on Justin Bieber, American football players, Juggalos, and at least one member of the Ku Klux Klan.

Rastafarianism is not an exception: the radical conventions of teddy boys, mods, rude boys, hippies, punks, bikers, and surfers have all been woven into the mainstream. That was certainly not the groups' intention. Individuals joined subcultures and countercultures to *reject* mainstream society and its values. They constructed identities through an open disregard for social norms. Yet in rejecting basic conventions, these iconoclasts became legendary as distinct, original, and authentic. Surfing is no longer an "outsider" niche: Boardriders, the parent company of surf brand Quiksilver, has seen its annual sales surpass $2 billion. Country Life English Butter hired punk legend John Lydon to appear in television commercials. One of America's most beloved ice cream flavors is Cherry Garcia, named after the bearded leader of a psychedelic rock band who long epitomized the "turn on, tune in, drop out" spirit of 1960s countercultural rebellion. As the subcultural scholars Stuart Hall and Tony Jefferson note, oppositional youth cultures became a "pure, simple, raging, commercial success." So why, exactly, does straight society come to champion extreme negations of its own conventions?

Subcultures and countercultures manage to achieve a level of influence that belies their raw numbers. Most teens of the 1950s and 1960s never joined a subculture. There were never more than an estimated thirty thousand British teddy boys in a country of fifty million people. However alienated teens felt, most didn't want to risk their normal status by engaging in strange dress and delinquent behaviors. Because alternative status groups can never actually *replace* the masses, they can achieve influence only through being imitated. But how do their radical inventions take on cachet? There are two key pathways: the creative class and the youth consumer market.

In the basic logic of signaling, subcultural conventions offer little status value, as they are associated with disadvantaged communities. The major social change of the twentieth century, however, was the integration of minority and working-class conventions into mainstream social norms. This process has been under way at least since the jazz era, when rich whites used the subcultural capital of Black communities to signal and compensate for their own lack of authenticity. The idolization of status inferiors can also be traced to nineteenth-century Romanticism; philosopher Charles Taylor writes that many came to find that "the life of simple, rustic people is closer to wholesome virtue and lasting satisfactions than the corrupt existence of city-dwellers." By the late 1960s, New York high society threw upscale cocktail parties for Marxist radicals like the Black Panthers—a predilection Tom Wolfe mocked as "radical chic."

For most cases in the twentieth century, however, the creative class became the primary means by which conventions from alternative status groups nestled into the mainstream. This was a natural process, since many creatives were members of countercultures or at least were sympathetic to their ideals. In *The Conquest of Cool*, historian Thomas Frank notes that psychedelic art appeared in commercial imagery not as a means of pandering to hippie youth but rather as the work of proto-hippie creative directors who foisted their lysergic aesthetics on the public. Hippie ads thus preceded—and arguably created—hippie youth.

This creative-class/counterculture link, however, doesn't explain the spread of subcultural conventions from working-class communities like the mods or Rastafarians. Few from working-class subcultures go into publishing and advertising. The primary sites for subculture/creative-class cross-pollination have been art schools and underground music scenes. The punk community, in particular, arose as an alliance between the British working class and students in art and fashion schools. Once this network was formed, punk's embrace of reggae elevated Jamaican music into the British mainstream as well. Similarly, New York's downtown art scene supported Bronx hip-hop before many African American radio stations took rap seriously.

Subcultural style often fits well within the creative-class sensibility. With a premium placed on authenticity, creative-class taste celebrates defiant groups like hipsters, surfers, bikers, and punks as sincere rejections of the straight society's "plastic fantastic" kitsch. The working classes have a "natural" essence untarnished by the demands of bourgeois society. "What makes Hip a special language," writes Norman Mailer, "is that it cannot really be taught." This perspective can be patronizing, but to many middle-class youth, subcultural style is a powerful expression of earnest antagonism against common enemies. Reggae, writes scholar Dick Hebdidge, "carried the necessary conviction, the political bite, so obviously missing in most contemporary white music."

From the jazz era onward, knowledge of underground culture served as an important criterion for upper-middle-class status—a pressure to be hip, to be in the know about subcultural activity. Hipness could be valuable, because the obscurity and difficulty of penetrating into the subcultural world came with high signaling costs. Once subcultural capital became standard in creative-class signaling, minority and working-class slang, music, dances, and styles functioned as valuable signals—with or without their underlying beliefs. Art school students could listen to reggae without believing in the divinity of Haile Selassie. For many burgeoning creative-class members, subcultures and counter-cultures offered vehicles for daydreaming about an exciting life far from conformist boredom. Art critic Dan Fox, who grew up in the London suburbs, explains, "[Music-related tribe] identities gave shelter, a sense of belonging; being someone else was a way to fantasize your exit from small-town small-mindedness."

Middle-class radical chic, however, tends to denature the most prickly styles. This makes "radical" new ideas less socially disruptive, which opens a second route of subcultural influence: the *youth consumer market*. The culture industry—fashion brands, record companies, film producers—is highly attuned to the tastes of the creative class, and once the creative class blesses a subculture or counter-culture, companies manufacture and sell wares to tap into this new source of cachet. At first mods tailored their suits, but the group's growing stature encouraged ready-to-wear brands to manufacture off-the-rack mod garments for mass consumption. As the punk trend flared in England, the staid record label EMI signed the Sex Pistols (and then promptly dropped them). With so many cultural trends starting among the creative classes and ethnic subcultures, companies may not understand these innovations but gamble that they will be profitable in their appeal to middle-class youth.

Before radical styles can diffuse as products, they are defused—i.e., the most transgressive qualities are surgically removed. Experimental and rebellious genres come to national attention by means of softer second-wave compromises. In the early 1990s, hip-hop finally reached the top of the charts with the "pop rap" of MC Hammer and Vanilla Ice. Defusing not only dilutes the impact of the original inventions but also freezes far-out ideas into set conventions. The vague "oppositional attitude" of a subculture becomes petrified in a strictly defined set of goods. The hippie counterculture became a ready-made package of tie-dye shirts, Baja hoodies, small round glasses, and peace pins. Mass media, in needing to explain subcultures to readers, defines the undefined—and exaggerates where necessary. Velvet cuffs became a hallmark of teddy boy style, despite being a late-stage development dating from a single 1957 photo in *Teen Life* magazine.

This simplification inherent in the marketing process lowers fences and signaling costs, allowing anyone to be a punk or hip-hopper through a few commercial transactions. John Waters took interest in beatniks not for any "deep social conviction" but "in homage" to his favorite TV character, Maynard G. Krebbs, on *The Many Loves of Dobie Gillis*. And as more members rush into these groups, further simplification occurs. Younger members have less money to invest in clothing, vehicles, and conspicuous hedonism. The second generation of teds maintained surly attitudes and duck's-ass quiffs but replaced the Edwardian suits with jeans. Creative classes may embrace subcultures and countercultures on pseudo-spiritual grounds, but many youth simply deploy rebellious styles as a blunt invective against adults. N.W.A's song "Fuck tha Police" gave voice to Black resentment against Los Angeles law enforcement; white suburban teens blasted it from home cassette decks to anger their parents.

As subcultural/countercultural conventions become popular within the basic class system, however, they lose value as subcultural norms. Most alternative status groups can't survive the parasitism of the consumer market; some fight back before it's too late. In October 1967, a group of longtime countercultural figures held a "Death of the Hippie" mock funeral on the streets of San Francisco to persuade the media to stop covering their movement. Looking back at the sixties, journalist Nik Cohn noted that these groups' rise and fall always followed a similar pattern:

> One by one, they would form underground and lay down their basic premises, to be followed with near-millennial fervor by a very small number; then they would emerge into daylight and begin to spread from district to district; then they would catch fire suddenly and produce a

national explosion; then they would attract regiments of hangers-on and they would be milked by industry and paraded endlessly by media; and then, robbed of all novelty and impact, they would die.

By the late 1960s the mods' favorite hangout, Carnaby Street, had become "a tourist trap, a joke in bad taste" for "middle-aged tourists from Kansas and Wisconsin." Japanese biker gangs in the early 1970s dressed in 1950s Americana—Hawaiian shirts, leather jackets, jeans, pompadours—but once the mainstream Japanese fashion scene began to play with a similar fifties retro, the bikers switched to right-wing paramilitary uniforms festooned with imperialist slogans.

The commercialization of outsider styles raises political questions, especially as companies squeeze cash out of cachet and force status-advantaged groups to seek out new oppositional styles. There is something obviously untoward about majority entrepreneurs profiting off the inventions of groups they otherwise oppress. Black artists invented jazz, rhythm 'n' blues, and funk, only to see white majorities imitate, defuse, and profit from them. Elvis prospered as the so-called king of rock 'n' roll through conventions he did not invent. On one hand the ensuing Black flight from the burden of white fandom has been a creative engine; jazz musicians, in one example, pursued experimentation to alienate their doting professional-class fans. One musician noted in the early 1960s about his square audience, "If you're working on a commercial band, they like it and so you have to play more corn. If you're working on a good band, then they don't like it, and that's a drag. If you're working on a good band and they like it, then that's a drag, too." But the organized pilfering of minority conventions is an unsustainable and unfair way to promote creativity in the system.

The rise of liberation ideology in the late 1960s helped curb the wholesale thievery of Black culture. Making authentic reggae and hip-hop requires firsthand accounts of racial oppression and close knowledge of life in Black neighborhoods. White rappers have remained marginal figures, gaining legitimacy at first only through jester/prankster personas (e.g., the Beastie Boys, Third Bass, Eminem). Vanilla Ice's failed career demonstrates the perils of unironic mimicry. In an age where cultural appropriation is taboo, authenticity has been a powerful tool for enabling subcultures to keep control of their conventions.

However, what complicates any analysis of subcultural influence on mainstream style is that the most famous 1960s groups often reappear as revival movements. Every year a new crop of idealistic young mods watches the 1979 film *Quadrophenia* and rushes out to order their first tailored mohair suit. We shouldn't confuse these later adherents, however, as an organic extension of the original configuration. New mods are seeking comfort in a presanctioned rebellion rather than spearheading new shocking styles at the risk of social disapproval. The neo-teddy boys of the 1970s adopted the old styles as a matter of pure taste: namely, a combination of fifties rock nostalgia and hippie backlash. Many didn't even know from where the term "Edwardian" originated.

Were the original groups truly "subcultural" if they could be so seamlessly absorbed into the commercial marketplace? In the language of contemporary marketing, "subculture" has come to mean little more than "niche consumer segment." A large portion of contemporary consumerism is built on countercultural and subcultural aesthetics. Formerly antisocial looks like punk, hippie, surfer, and biker are now sold as mainstream styles in every American shopping mall. Corporate executives brag about surfing on custom longboards, road tripping on Harley-Davidsons, and logging off for weeks while on silent meditation retreats. The high-end fashion label Saint Laurent did a teddy-boy-themed collection in 2014, and Dior took inspiration from teddy girls for the autumn of 2019. There would be no Bobo yuppies in Silicon Valley without bohemianism, nor would the Police's "Roxanne" play as dental-clinic Muzak without Jamaican reggae.

But not all subcultures and countercultures have ended up as part of the public marketplace. Most subcultures remain marginalized: e.g., survivalists, furries, UFO abductees, and pickup artists. Just like teddy boys, the Juggalos pose as outlaws with their own shocking music, styles, and dubious behaviors—and yet the music magazine *Blender* named the foundational Juggalo musical act Insane Clown Posse as the worst artist in music history. The movement around Christian rock has suffered a similar fate; despite staggering popularity, the fashion brand Extreme Christian Clothes has never made it into the pages of *GQ*. Since these particular groups are formed from elements of the (white) majority culture—rather than formed in opposition to it—they offer left-leaning creatives no inspiration. Lower-middle-class white subcultures can also epitomize the depths of conservative sentiment rather than suggest a means of escape. Early skinhead culture influenced high fashion, but the Nazi-affiliated epigones didn't. Without the blessing of the creative class, major manufacturers won't make new goods based on such subcultures' conventions, preventing their spread to wider audiences. Subcultural transgressions, then, best find influence when they become signals within the primary status structure of society.

⇥⟨≡⟩⇤

The renowned scholarship on subcultures produced at Birmingham's Centre for Contemporary Cultural Studies casts youth groups as forces of "resistance," trying to navigate the "contradictions" of class society. Looking back, few teds or mods saw their actions in such openly political terms. "Studies carried out in Britain, America, Canada and Australia," writes sociologist David Muggleton, "have, in fact, found subcultural belief-systems to be complex and uneven." While we may take inspiration from the groups' sense of "vague opposition," we're much more enchanted by their specific garments, albums, dances, behaviors, slang, and drugs. In other words, each subculture and counterculture tends to be reduced to a set of cultural artifacts, all of which are added to the pile of contemporary culture.

The most important contribution of subcultures, however, has been giving birth to new sensibilities—additional perceptual frames for us to revalue existing goods and behaviors. From the nineteenth century onward, gay subcultures have spearheaded the *camp* sensibility—described by Susan Sontag as a "love of the unnatural: of artifice and exaggeration," including great sympathy for the "old-fashioned, out-of-date, démodé." This "supplementary" set of standards expanded cultural capital beyond high culture and into an ironic appreciation of low culture. As camp diffused through twentieth-century society via pop art and pop music, elite members of affluent societies came to appreciate the world in new ways. Without the proliferation of camp, John Waters would not grace the cover of *Town & Country*.

As much as subcultural members may join their groups as an escape from status woes, they inevitably replicate status logic in new forms—different status criteria, different hierarchies, different conventions, and different tastes. Members adopt their own arbitrary negations of arbitrary mainstream conventions, but believe in them as authentic emotions. If punk were truly a genuine expression of individuality, as John Lydon claims it should be, there could never have been a punk "uniform."

The fact that subcultural rebellion manifests as a simple distinction in taste is why the cultural industry can so easily co-opt its style. If consumers are always on the prowl for more sensational and more shocking new products, record companies and clothing labels can use alternative status groups as R&D labs for the wildest new ideas. Yet we shouldn't downplay the potential social costs of subcultural rebellion. The anti-Mexican pogrom of Los Angeles in 1943 is known as the Zoot Suit Riots, because whites attacked minorities for daring to wear exaggerated suits. But as society has become more tolerant, there is reduced friction between subcultural rebellion and capitalism. Defiant symbols generated in outsider groups provide business with an invigorating "renewal" of styles to sell in the commercial marketplace.

Alternative status groups in the twentieth century did, however, succeed in changing the direction of cultural flows. In strict class-based societies of the past, economic capital and power set rigid status hierarchies; conventions trickled down from the rich to the middle classes to the poor. In a world where subcultural capital takes on cachet, the rich consciously borrow ideas from poorer groups. Furthermore, bricolage is no longer a junkyard approach to personal style—everyone now mixes and matches. In the end, subcultural groups were perhaps an avant-garde of persona crafting, the earliest adopters of the now common practice of inventing and performing strange characters as an effective means of status distinction.

For both classes and alternative status groups, individuals pursuing status end up forming new conventions without setting out to do so. Innovation, in these cases, is often a by-product of status struggle. But individuals also *intentionally* attempt to propose alternatives to established conventions. Artists are the most well-known example of this more calculated creativity—and they, too, are motivated by status.

Chapter Seven

ART

⊢⋈⊣

Edna Hibel didn't receive artist status for skillful paintings and draw-
ings; Henri Rousseau, Trisha Brown, and John Cage became legendary for their radical convention-breaking.

⊢⋈⊣

ARTIST STATUS

One day in 1908 Pablo Picasso was scrounging through a pile of canvases in
the Parisian junk shop Père Soulier, when he spotted a halting portrait of a
woman. The shopkeeper offered a bargain: "Five francs. You can paint on the
back." Upon closer inspection Picasso realized the abandoned painting was an
1895 work by Henri Rousseau, known as Le Douanier ("the customs officer").
Rousseau was a sixty-four-year-old former municipal toll collector who took up
painting full-time at the age of forty-nine only to have his childlike canvases
become the most celebrated joke of the French art world. In 1885 the Salon des
Champs-Élysées threw away his entries after spectators slashed them with
knives. A critic viewing his works at the Salon des Indépendants a few years
later concluded, "Monsieur Rousseau paints with his feet with his eyes closed."
Despite being subjected to constant rejections, aspersions, and pranks, Rousseau continued at his craft, a painter's beret worn proudly on his head. But even
his closest supporters believed the old man harbored pathetic delusions about
ever having his work be treated with respect.

Picasso had gone along with his peers' dismissal of Rousseau, but upon
seeing the painting at Père Soulier, he became a true believer. He promptly

organized a party at his studio to honor its creator. There Rousseau experienced a life-changing reversal of fortune. He entered Picasso's studio to find banners strung up with his name and guests that included the poet Guillaume Apollinaire, the painter Georges Braque, and the art collectors Gertrude and Leo Stein, who all feted him with original songs. From this point forward, Picasso and his contemporaries across Europe openly championed Rousseau's work. This was partly self-serving: boundary-pushing avant-garde artists hoped the legitimization of Rousseau's colorful and childish style would help persuade audiences to accept their radical works as well. Nevertheless, the "customs officer" Rousseau spent the last two years of his life having accomplished his ultimate goal: he was considered an *artist*. And his reputation has only grown since that time. Today his work hangs in museums around the world, including in New York's Museum of Modern Art, a few meters away from Picasso's most legendary masterpieces.

"Artist" is not an occupation—it's an honorific title. All humans are *creators* in some capacity, whether whistling during housework, doodling in classroom notebooks, or making memes about the day's celebrity foibles. This urge may even arise from a so-called creative gene in our DNA. But only a gifted few will combine their creativity with enough expertise to ever produce anything that earns admiration from others. When the unnamed narrator of *Breakfast at Tiffany's* meets his charismatic neighbor Holly Golightly, she asks, "Tell me, are you a real writer? . . . Well, darling, does anyone *buy* what you write?" Even commercial demand, however, leads creators only to the next status tier up—*craftspeople*. To become an artist, at the very top of the hierarchy, requires something much more transcendent. As various writers have expressed, the social position of the artist in contemporary society is akin to that of a "priest or a sorcerer"—a "visionary genius" with "extravagant individualism" who reaches "epiphanies" through a "magical process" of creation. Prophetic artists possess an "imagination to anticipate the actual experience of men in a certain period." Works of true genius don't just decorate rooms but put "humanity face-to-face with a new event, a new marvel."

Artists play an important social role. In the words of the philosopher Henri Bergson, their function is "to see and to make us see what we do not naturally perceive"—to show "things which did not explicitly strike our senses and our consciousness." Artists achieve these effects by tinkering with the deepest conventions in our brains—exposing our cultural assumptions, pointing out contradictions in our customs, creating new symbols, and expanding the meaning of old symbols. In their day, impressionist painting, minimalistic music, mobile sculptures, and absurdist drama all proposed new ways to perceive the world. And since conventions provide us with our meaning, values, and perceptual frameworks, forcing us to adopt new ones, even temporarily, literally *alters our minds*. As we absorb and accept these aesthetic experiences, our perception is forever changed. Apollinaire went as far to say that "the order which we find in nature" is "only an effect of art." As Oscar Wilde complained, sunsets just looked like Jean-Baptiste-Camille Corot paintings.

We esteem creators who entertain us and provide emotional experiences. We love the writers, composers, entertainers, and auteurs who both send us into personal ecstasy and connect us with others in solidarity. But the reason popular artists receive higher status in contemporary society than surgeons, sushi chefs, and charity workers is that they engage in mental sorcery: proposing radical ideas that go on to change the world.

In the eighteenth century, philosopher Immanuel Kant asserted three still authoritative criteria for artistic genius: (1) the creation of fiercely original works, (2) which over time become imitated as exemplars, and (3) are created through mysterious and seemingly inimitable methods. Henri Rousseau satisfied all three criteria, creating unique, inspirational paintings that seemed to arise from his bizarre subconscious. These Kantian requirements also match the most advanced status criteria of our era—namely, originality, influence, authenticity, and detachment. Original artworks are the highest expression of individualism; Hannah Arendt believed that an artist was the "last individual left in a mass society." As we've seen, to be imitated as an exemplar suggests a high status position. And a mysterious creation process suggests authentic self-expression detached from worldly concerns. Artists who create their works as a form of violent, uncontrolled catharsis have no time for signaling strategies. The gallery owner Betty Parsons praised painter Jackson Pollock as such: "He was completely unmotivated—he was absolutely *pure*." In combining these personal virtues with audience esteem and the fruits of commercial success (wealth, fame, and celebrity connections), successful and recognized artists are obvious candidates for super-high status.

Kant's criteria also explain why most creators never make it past lower tiers.

Hacks only copy. Folk art closely follows custom. Other than exceptions like Rousseau, naive artists and outsider artists tend to be uninfluential. Commercial artists work in well-known methods for a paycheck. Most who pick up a paintbrush, even the supremely talented, will never transcend the epithet "picture painter."

As with any status hierarchy, artists at the top receive exceptional status benefits. Recognized geniuses and virtuosos enjoy great fanfare wherever they go. Executives in the creative industry hire and fire rank-and-file creators on a whim but tolerate the idiosyncrasies of geniuses. Producers would surely sack a session piano player loudly humming contrapuntal harmonies during a recording session, but Glenn Gould got away with it whenever he recorded Bach. Artists reaping the benefits of their unbridled creativity can eschew manners, dress in strange ways, indulge in self-destructive behaviors, and mistreat their loved ones. Artists are permitted to miss deadlines, because no one can schedule divine epiphanies. Sigmund Freud believed artists were motivated by a hope to "attain honour, power, riches, fame, and the love of women." In the 1970s, famed producer David Geffen echoed this exact point about the musicians in his orbit: "Most of the artists were trying to make a living, trying to get laid, trying to figure out who they were. They weren't trying to change the world."

Whatever its potential benefits, art remains a high-risk path toward status. The most original artworks violate norms, and if they fail to attract critical notice, artists can fall to very low status. Rousseau spent years as a laughingstock, having to retrieve his own canvases from the garbage. This is why most creators take a less risky, entrepreneurial attitude toward art: harmonizing others' radical inventions with more established conventions to expand the potential market. In the 1980s, "hair metal" bands like Mötley Crüe, Poison, and Whitesnake secured big advances, fistfuls of drugs, and thousands of willing sexual partners through performing, but not altering, the conventions of a popular genre that recycled once dangerous musical ideas. Hedging, however, is taboo for the true artist, who must stay detached from any status concerns. Only hacks make art for money and power. This explains why artists so often deny any conscious motivations for their work—including the desire to make art in the first place. Jackson Pollock claimed, "When I am in my painting, I am not aware of what I'm doing."

But nearly every artist pursues a specific kind of status: *artist status.* Unless society considers a creator to be an "artist," his or her artworks won't receive serious consideration, interpretation, or evaluation. Anyone can make things, but as philosopher Ludwig Wittgenstein writes, "Only an artist can so represent an individual thing as to make it appear to us like a work of art." The visual artist behind Banksy is anonymous and may receive no status benefits when walking down the street, but his artworks require artist status to be experienced as something beyond childish prankery. Banksy's 2018 self-shredding painting at Sotheby's auction house was possible only because Sotheby's believed Banksy pieces worthy of auction in the first place.

Many creators pursue art as a transactional means of achieving specific status benefits, but even those with the purest of motive still must aim for artist status. The bumbling Henri Rousseau was "primitive in performance but not in intention." As the scholar Roger Shattuck writes, "His *intention* was really his *ambition*—the desire to show in official Salons. It was the only reward he could imagine after a life of obscurity and hardship."

The existence of artist status, then, allows two ways of looking at the creative process: (1) how status logic manifests in the art world; and (2) how the particular status structure of a society changes the way art is made and diffused. Art may appear to be the freest and most imaginative realm of human life, but the specific status needs of creators, audiences, and critics in the social configuration of modern times has had a profound effect on what kind of art is produced, recognized, and valued.

ARTISTIC VALUE AND RADICAL INNOVATIONS

During her lifetime (1917–2014), the American artist Edna Hibel received constant accolades for her painting and lithographs. A pupil raved, "There was nothing she could not draw. . . . She was really like an artist who came out of the Renaissance." In 1940 the twenty-three-year-old Hibel sold a Renoiresque painting to the Boston Museum of Fine Art, becoming the youngest American painter to have work acquired by a major institution. Later in her life Hibel's prints and paintings toured the world, even crossing the Iron Curtain to tour Soviet Russia and Communist China. Her works were presented to the Queen of England, and she was awarded a medal of honor by Pope John Paul II. When

Hibel turned sixty, two collectors founded an entire museum in Florida dedicated solely to her oeuvre.

But at the moment of this writing, there is no Wikipedia page for Edna Hibel, nor does her name appear in the standard volumes on art history. In 2015 the Edna Hibel Museum closed, with many of her canvases sent off to a little-known college museum in Wisconsin. Despite great prowess at her craft and the esteem of international luminaries, Hibel never attained the artist status of her predecessors Georgia O'Keeffe and Frida Kahlo nor of her contemporary Leonora Carrington. In fact, the well-trained, long-celebrated Edna Hibel ended up much lower in the artist rankings than the "primitive" Henri Rousseau. How exactly, then, does a talented creator go beyond having "nice paintings" and "pleasant poems" to win acceptance as a "true artist"?

The answer is very simple. To become artists, creators must create *art*. But this only leads to perhaps the most parodied rhetorical question of modern times: *What is art?* There is no authoritative answer, and there may never be one. The philosopher Noël Carroll examined the primary definitions of art—art as representation, art as expression, art as form, etc.—and found that most collapse once the category "art" must include twentieth-century avant-garde works such as Marcel Duchamp's ready-made urinal sculpture, *Fountain*. A single, inclusive definition of art is especially difficult because artists push beyond the boundaries every time a definition is proposed.

To understand the effects of status on creativity, however, we don't have to answer this question on an ontological or metaphysical level. We need only to think about why people consider certain works to be art and, based on those judgments, provide the creators with artist status. There are two definitions of art that work quite well for this narrower mission: the *institutional* definition and the *narrative* definition. In the institutional definition, art is whatever the art world deems to be art. An old Eljer porcelain urinal isn't art when sitting in a landfill, but Duchamp's *Fountain* is art because the Tate Modern displays it (well, a replica). In the *narrative* definition, art is whatever makes it into the story of art. Grecian urns, Edith Wharton novels, and Christo and Jeanne-Claude's fabric wrappings of islands are all art, because they function as tentpole moments in the long-running story of human civilization.

In both the institutional and narrative definitions, creators are granted artist status from prestigious individuals and institutions—namely, gallery owners, critics, established artists, and art historians. This art world decides which creators are geniuses and grants the commensurate privileges. Artists are invited to participate in shows and exhibits, receive serious reviews in the mass media, and, for a lucky few, appear in history books. The clearest short-term strategy toward achieving artist status, then, is to win acclaim from art world institutions. The narrative definition of art offers an additional, long-term path: posthumous recognition of works as important moments in the story of art. This has enabled creators rejected in their lifetime—for example, Vincent van Gogh, Franz Kafka, and Emily Dickinson—to be anointed as respected artists after death. The most ambitious creators attempt to bend the arc of history toward themselves, but since no one can predict the direction of art, no technique guarantees future success.

For most of his life, Henri Rousseau received no artist status, but he later satisfied both the institutional and narrative definitions. For his role in inspiring Picasso and his contemporaries, Rousseau achieved historical significance. The famed curator Roger Fry included him in a 1912 exhibition of postimpressionist painters and, as the twentieth century unfolded, art texts increasingly cited Rousseau's work as a key step in the development of the European avant-garde.

Edna Hibel experienced the opposite trajectory. She gained early and broad support from well-established institutions. But her most important champions were a Christian Scientist couple living in Boston with few connections to the New York art world. However pleasant her paintings, historians and highbrow critics showed little interest in her figurative work—especially at a time when her more radical contemporaries were overturning the basic tenets of representative art. *The Boston Globe* praised Hibel as "a sound draftsman and a vivid colorist" in 1940—but the art community of her era no longer prioritized these particular talents.

In her lifetime Hibel's work may have even brought more pleasure to more people than Rousseau's. But the institutional and narrative definitions of art imply that the quality of execution and responses from mass audiences are less important in assigning artist status. To understand this, we must identify two key values in each artwork. Philosopher of art Tomáš Kulka explains that there is *aesthetic value*—the ability to provide audiences with aesthetic experiences—and *artistic value*—the artwork's solutions to specific art world problems of the era. Artist status requires achieving artistic value, rather than aesthetic value, and others can assign this value to artworks whether the artist intended these solutions or not. Rousseau received recognition for his artistic value in proposing fantastical, dreamlike paintings that rejected the tenets of academic art, thus securing his legacy. Edna Hibel confined herself to the skilled execution of the reigning artistic conventions, and this lack of artistic value would be her downfall.

The difference between aesthetic and artistic value can be further explained through the concept of conventions. The aesthetic value of an artwork measures how masterfully an artist can use and abuse existing conventions to elicit emotional experiences from the audience. The sociologist Howard Becker writes, "Composers can create and manipulate listeners' expectations as to what sounds will follow. They can then delay and frustrate the satisfaction of those expectations, generating tension and release as the expectation is ultimately satisfied." These aesthetics and their related emotional effects are the way most people judge art: *Am I experiencing something? And am I gaining something from this experience?*

Artistic value, on the other hand, measures the originality of the artist's inventions—i.e., how much the proposed ideas break existing conventions and suggest new ones. As we saw with the institutional and historical definitions, the appraisers of artistic status tend to be highly educated denizens of the art world, and they are very knowledgeable about existing artistic conventions. To impress them, creators can't just make superficial changes to the dominant styles but must challenge the established notions of art at a fundamental level. In the French poet Charles Baudelaire's famous line, "The chief task of genius is precisely to *invent* a stereotype" (emphasis added). To create within the framework of someone else's stereotype makes the creator an epigone, and their work is mere "taste."

At first glance, artistic value seems like a better measure of imagination, but convention-breaking is a highly structured activity. Invention requires "answering" the works of previous artists. As the painter-theorist John D. Graham wrote in the 1920s, "A work of art is a problem posed and solved," and at any given time, the art world focuses on a limited set of communal problems artists attempt to solve. For centuries a long-standing problem in painting was how certain techniques and conventions could create lifelike representations of the world. When photography "solved" this problem, late-nineteenth-century painters moved on to new concerns. In their cubist years Pablo Picasso and Georges Braque explored how to paint all three dimensions on a flat canvas, and by trying to depict motion, the Italian futurists Umberto Boccioni and Giacomo Balla attempted to add the fourth dimension as well. All four men gained artistic status for these novel approaches, both in their lifetimes and in posterity.

The need to solve problems of an era means that artistic value is always contextual—a set of parameters that bind the creative process. There are perhaps an infinite number of potential problems in art, but to gain artist status, artists must solve the agreed-upon problems of the current moment. Henri Rousseau, for all of his technical and intellectual shortcomings, ended up creating works that answered problems on the minds of his peers. Edna Hibel, for all of her technical excellence, never spoke to her contemporaries' particular concerns. Deep knowledge of art history can be useful in the pursuit of innovation, as it reveals not only previous attempts at solutions but remaining issues to tackle. This idea powers the strange logic behind Spanish surrealist director Luis Buñuel's beloved maxim "What doesn't grow out of tradition is plagiarism." Poetry, to the literary critic Harold Bloom, is fundamentally a battle of younger poets against their predecessors: "Not the dialectic between art and society, but the dialectic between art and art." Genius inventions must, thus, fit into the "unbroken chain" of problems and solutions across art history.

When planning artworks, creators enjoy a wide range of choices: Which conventions should be followed and which should be challenged? Embarking on her career in the 1970s, the choreographer Trisha Brown forged artistic value for herself by defying some of the most fundamental conventions of dance. In classical ballet, dancers tend to stand upright in formal poses, and the staging allows audiences to view all of the action while seated. In Brown's *Floor of the Forest*, dancers slink along ropes in a horizontal structure erected at eye level, on which they try to slip into strung-up pieces of clothing. Spectators must crouch down or peer down from above to see the dancers in action. In *Man Walking Down the Side of a Building*, a man slowly descends on the side of a seven-story building at a ninety-degree angle, and in *Walking on the Wall*, dancers attached to harnesses and cables walk around the audience—on the walls. These negations of the basic assumptions in dance helped Brown win recognition as one of the most celebrated choreographers of the twentieth century. As long as artist status derives from historically grounded notions of artistic value, creativity in art becomes a highly structured activity.

Some may counter that the importance of *serendipity* to the creative process offers an escape from the binding requirements outlined above. Harold Bloom suggests "misreading" poems serves as an important source of creativity. The composer John Cage obsessed over scribbles on Erik Satie scores he believed were innovative calculations of new rhythmic systems; they were just shopping lists. Artists, however, never blindly accept the fruits of serendipity. Happy accidents go through the same filter as all other artistic choices; random discoveries must align with particular strategies or they'll be eliminated. As much as the painter Robert Rauschenberg loved random occurrences, the critic Calvin Tomkins found that "one of the few accidents in a painting that he will not accept, in fact, is an unplanned resemblance to some thing that he (or some other artist) has done before; when this happens he paints it out."

The twentieth century's successful artists often pursued artistic value to the detriment of their work's aesthetic value. Pablo Picasso's radical cubist painting *Les Demoiselles d'Avignon* is a signature piece at New York's Museum of Modern Art—but arguably for its artistic importance, not its aesthetic achievement. Picasso's art dealer believed this painting of Barcelona prostitutes to be "unfinished," and many of Picasso's peers found it in bad taste. When the Russian art collector Sergei Shchukin got an early peek at the canvas, he teared up and muttered, "What a loss for French painting."

The pursuit of artistic value leads artists far away from comfortable conventions, and this is the point. But this expertise, writes the literary critic Barbara H. Smith, often causes its own "provincialism" where "we become less and less *like* anyone else, and thus less able to predict anyone else's responses on the basis of our own." This engenders a clear split between artists and critics focused on artistic value, and wider audiences demanding aesthetic value (who may equate the experience with entertainment). General audiences complain that critics fail to appreciate the fun of big hits, from earnest Billy Joel songs to CGI-powered superhero films. Most audiences delight in minor innovations, not major challenges to their preferred art forms. The most broadly accepted form of artistry is *virtuosity*—"possessing an ability to perform brilliantly the creation of others." Artistic value has less appeal to mainstream audiences, which explains the long-running dismissal of abstract painting: "My three-year-old could do that." But if abstract artists' work is intended to answer a "relevant question," no, your three-year-old *can't* do that. Kindergarten finger paintings aren't clever commentary on the abstract works of Harlem Renaissance painter Beauford Delaney.

When artists cut too deep into standard conventions in pursuit of artistic value, audiences often renounce the changes. Music listeners are happy with small surprises but expect conformity to familiar notions of melody, harmony, and rhythm. Yet deep cuts are required to achieve artistic value. This is why Gertrude Stein noted that all important art is "irritating" and Marcel Duchamp quipped, "A painting that doesn't shock isn't worth painting." In the early days of modern art, indignation became a clear sign of artistic success. With the appearance of Duchamp's *Nude Descending a Staircase* at the 1913 Armory Show in New York, the painting "baffled and outraged so many visitors" that it became "the most famous painting of the modern era."

This poses a logistical problem for creators: until they are accepted as high-status artists, transgressive behavior may be met with social disapproval and low status. "Matisse and Picasso in 1900," theorist René Girard reminds us, "were considered incompetent by 99 per cent of their contemporaries." This helped form the stereotype of the struggling and misunderstood artist, sacrificing all immediate human relationships in pursuit of deeper universal truths. Aspiring artists must have a high tolerance for societal rejection—enough self-confidence, perspicacity, faith, or insanity to continue working against the backlash. Defiance is easy for self-centered narcissists; George Orwell listed "sheer egoism" as a primary motivation for writers. Mental disorders that numb the fear of punishment also improve the calculus of risk taking.

The most natural candidates for radical invention, then, are creators who see themselves as having low status. At the bottom of the pyramid, there is little to lose and much to gain. This explains why youth tend to be more radical than adults. Andy Warhol believed that "it's easy for a young person to support new ideas. He comes onto the scene fresh. He doesn't have any positions to defend or modify, no big time or money invested. He can be a brat, say whatever he pleases, support whatever and whoever he wants to without having to think, 'Will they ever invite me to dinner again?'" Poor treatment and inadequate respect also give young creators an easy way to justify their rebellion. Other sources of ire include oppressive traditions, rigid pedagogy, capitalist logic, bourgeois value systems, the public's bad taste, and the timidity of the former generation.

The arbitrariness of all artistic styles and standards means anyone can rip them up and start again. The human potential for artistic appreciation is so broad that no single method can monopolize aesthetic experience, nor solve every art world problem. Every established convention suffers from flaws and excesses. Academic rules and traditions become stagnant and limiting. Over-intellectual art can become detached from human emotion. Pop art blends too easily into commercialism. Dada nihilism is often indistinguishable from mindless pranksterism. At any time, rebellious artists always have an opening: either offer new solutions to these issues in good faith or cynically exploit the flaws of the established order to justify a new position.

The battle for artist status in the pursuit of artistic value turns the art world into a battlefield between aspiring and established artists. Upstarts propose radical oppositions to the reigning styles, and once they succeed, a new genera-tion of upstarts propose radical oppositions to the previous radical oppositions. This is why the story of art tends to be *dialectical*. Instead of slow, incremental changes to methods and concepts, art movements quickly swing from one extreme position to another. The social realist school of painting promoted the idea that art should work to support revolutionary politics. The next generation, the abstract expressionists, demolished the social realist approach by refusing to use representational forms that could be used for propaganda. Then the pop artists rejected the abstract expressionists' purism by adding elements of commercial kitsch to the canvas. A decade later, minimalists renounced pop's colorful media references to make the most reductionist art possible.

In this section we've landed on what seems like a ridiculous tautology: cre-ators gain artistic status by making art with artistic value. What this actually means is that individuals seeking high status for creative acts must propose innovative solutions to the particular concerns of the art world at that moment. This explains why an ingenious choreographer would experiment with danc-ers walking on the walls or down the side of a building. The more interesting question, however, may be why the public comes to accept these radical ideas. What smooths the path for "irritating" art to win the approval of larger audi-ences? Again, the answer is status.

THE ACCEPTANCE OF RADICAL ART

To write the orchestral piece *Atlas Eclipticalis,* John Cage consulted a star map from the Czech astronomer Antonín Bečvář and converted the arrangement of constellations into clusters of acoustic and electronic sounds. The resulting work lacks obvious melodies, harmonies, and rhythms, and there are empty moments reflecting the wide dark expanses of the night sky. In 1964 the conductor Leonard Bernstein chose *Atlas Eclipticalis* as part of a four-day New York Philharmonic showcase of contemporary music at Lincoln Center. Eager listeners, however, had difficulty concentrating on its performance, as the subscription audiences in black tie soon began to stand up and leave the hall in a huff. They found the music too strange—a sentiment shared by the musicians. The orchestra hissed Cage as he took his bow, and during the last performance, many whistled into their microphones and noodled random scales rather than follow the score. A few musicians even smashed Cage's electronic sound systems with their feet.

For both high-society patrons and classically trained musicians, *Atlas Eclipticalis* broke too many musical conventions, and this displeasure manifested as conspicuous acts of social disapproval. Like any good avant-garde artist, Cage showed detachment toward this public shaming: "Even when *Atlas* is performed badly, it still sounds interesting." Moreover, such public conflicts only added to his legend. A 2020 *BBC Music Magazine* survey asked 174 living composers to rank the greatest of their field: John Cage came out at number 31 of 50, higher than Pyotr Ilyich Tchaikovsky, Stephen Sondheim, and Erik Satie. Today there are multiple recordings of *Atlas Eclipticalis* available for purchase or streaming, on which the musicians reverently play the score—no hissing, humming, or destroying the equipment.

Subcultures demonstrated how convention-breakers can end up celebrated as cultural icons; artists are even greater examples of this phenomenon. "I threw the urinal into their faces," said Marcel Duchamp about his provocative piece *Fountain,* "and now they come and admire it for its beauty." In 1964 wealthy symphony patrons not only disliked *Atlas Eclipticalis* but believed walking out midperformance would better conform to social etiquette than listening respectfully. For classical audiences and musicians alike, open contempt for John Cage was an act of good taste. Not everyone today has come to love *Atlas Eclipticalis* as a musical composition, but few would be outraged by its sounds. And it would be considered boorish to walk out. In this sense, the status value associated with John Cage and his work has increased over time. And this transition from social disapproval to approval happened in tandem with audiences coming to appreciate his work. To understand how radical artistic ideas catch on with wider society, we should look to status as a potential catalyst.

As we saw in the last section, creators gain artist status from original solutions to the pressing concerns of the art world. But going back to Kant's definition of genius, creators must also become "exemplars," which is borne out in imitation by other artists and esteem from nonartists. Anyone can propose shocking ideas; only geniuses gain prestige and legitimacy for them. "The work of art," writes the art historian Herbert Read, "has its immediate origin in the consciousness of an individual; it only acquires its full significance, however, to the extent that it is integrated with the general culture of a people or period." Artists don't anticipate future conventions so much as they create them through the influence process. John Cage faced resistance in the world of classical music, but his ideas inspired a wide range of younger artists in other fields, including Trisha Brown and Yoko Ono. With these disciples' own successes, Cage's artistic ideas nestled into the basic contemporary approach to how art is created, experienced, interpreted, and valued.

Avant-garde ideas, however, can break escape velocity from the avant-garde community only if broader audiences no longer believe their appreciation will lead to negative social consequences. The neuroscientist and music scholar Daniel Levitin writes, "We surrender to music when we listen to it—we allow ourselves to trust the composers and musicians with a part of our hearts and our spirits." Status plays a role here: we "surrender" only when we "trust" the artistic integrity of the source. Audiences who walked out of *Atlas Eclipticalis* had literally refused to surrender to Cage. Had they respected his artist status, they may have tried harder to *hear* the piece. Cachet, thus, opens minds to radical propositions of what art can be and how we should perceive it.

The influence process for radical art is always an uphill struggle: works begin as an esoteric *idiolect*—symbols and ideas spoken and understood by a single person. Where established conventions are rejected, creators may be treated with low status. The first esteem that artists receive tends to be from contemporaries as a pure admiration of craft and creativity, especially as they work on solving the same problems. While futurism and dada are examples of organized schools, most movements, such as punk or grunge, develop organically as young artists converge on the same techniques. "One of the phenomenal things about the Pop painters," recalled Andy Warhol, "is that they were already painting alike when they met." Young artists often form their own alternative status groups for mutual esteem. David Byrne of the band Talking Heads discovered like-minded compatriots at the Lower Manhattan dive bar CBGB: "Some of us eventually came to realize that we wouldn't feel as comfortable anywhere else, and that the music in other places would probably be terrible. The hangout, then, is the place for the alienated to share their misanthropic feelings about the prevailing musical culture."

Further influence requires broad comprehension of an artist's idiolect. The poet William Wordsworth believed that "every author, as far as he is great and at the same time original, has had the task of creating the taste by which he is to be enjoyed." In the early twentieth century, artists often attempted to improve comprehension by laying out their ideas in manifestos and journals. At the same time, artistic geniuses must also be mysterious, which means their work contains ambiguities. Umberto Eco saw this as core to art's power: "A work of art *communicates too much* and therefore *does not communicate at all*, simply existing as a magic spell that is radically impermeable to all semiotic approach." Is John Cage's music a celebration of silence, an exploration into the potentialities of using environmental sound in composition, an assertion of the composer through a removal of the composer, or an extreme case of formalist experimentation? Yes. These ambiguities assist in the influence process by prodding critics and audiences to posit competing interpretations. The ensuing dialogue raises awareness and provides gravitas.

As we saw in the previous section, the fastest way for creators to gain artist status is to win over gatekeepers in the art world. For most artists, initial supporters are drawn from established artists, critics, gallery owners, and daring collectors. Since these people are high status, their favorite new radical artworks take on cachet among the creative and professional classes. Radical conventions work well as status symbols due to their high signaling costs around taste. The philosopher José Ortega y Gasset explains, "The characteristic of new art from a social viewpoint consists of dividing the public into two classes of men: those who understand it and those who do not." The painters Claude Monet and Paul Gauguin collected Paul Cézanne's bold postimpressionist work, while the stodgy U.S. president Calvin Coolidge refused to accept six Cézanne canvases that were gifted to the White House. In this logic, shock and confusion make artistic status symbols more valuable. As Tom Wolfe jokes about modern art, "If a work of art or a new style disturbed you, it was probably good work. If you *hated* it—it was probably great." Over time, more and more come to appreciate the work—and use appreciation in signaling—so that once-radical ideas become social norms. "The aficionado," writes the art historian Renato Poggioli, "often fears to be taken for a bourgeois if he expresses doubts or even justifiable reservations about this or that work, this or that movement."

John Cage found his most avid supporters among visual and performance artists, and these connections encouraged historians and museum curators to embrace him as a crucial figure in the development of postmodern art. With his reliable inclusion in museum exhibits, classroom lectures, and more daring musical festivals, Cage became embedded in the cultural knowledge required to be an educated person. There was a virtuous cycle for Cage: his originality, mystery, and influence provided him artist status; this encouraged serious institutions to explore his work; the frequent engagement with his work imbued Cage with cachet among the public, who then received a status boost for taking his work seriously.

Once most audiences *expect* new art to conform to esoteric ideas, such as silence as music, the ideas are no longer radical but simply conventional. In more commercial fields like popular music, this stage of conventionality entices less ambitious creators to turn formerly dangerous innovations into audience-friendly works. The pop critic Dan Ozzi notes, "Whenever a truly innovative artist defines a new sound, it gets carbon copied for at least a decade until what's left is an embarrassing abomination bearing almost no resemblance to the spirit of the original." Nirvana topped the charts with stylistic innovations borrowed from the cult act the Pixies; once grunge hit big, Nirvana copycats Bush and Stone Temple Pilots collectively sold fourteen million albums for their work in obvious grunge idioms.

Conventionality makes certain art styles pleasant and comfortable with audiences, but this kills their usefulness as "art." The literary critic Jonathan Culler writes, "Aesthetic expression aims to communicate notions, subtleties, complexities which have not yet been formulated, and therefore, as soon as an aesthetic code comes to be generally perceived as a code . . . then works of art tend to move beyond this code." Radical artists are often uneasy about their particular idiolect becoming too well understood. Jean Baudrillard notes that the successful artist is "condemned" to repetition, as audiences will ask for more and more of the same. The music group the KLF warned that most hit artists "spend the rest of their lives as a travelling freak show, peddling a nostalgia for those now far off, carefree days." Andy Warhol "retired" in 1965, feeling that "the basic Pop statements had already been made." He soon returned to make more of his coveted celebrity screenprints—as a baldly commercial undertaking.

The most ambitious artists never abandon their rebellious spirit and attempt to negate their *own* conventions on a constant basis. To prevent a "School of Satie," Erik Satie altered his own style for each new series of compositions. In the 1960s John Cage pledged, "Whenever I've found that what I'm doing has become pleasing, even to one person, I have redoubled my efforts to find the next step." This ceaseless search for innovation tends to work very well for already established artists. In the case of the Beatles, writes critic Ian MacDonald, "They kept [their music] from becoming stale by continually investigating new methods and concepts: beginning and ending songs in the wrong key, employing modal, pentatonic, and Indian scales, incorporating studio-effects and exotic instruments, and shuffling rhythms and idioms with a unique versatility."

John Cage never attracted the same mainstream admiration as the Beatles, but his ideas—music as conceptual art, silence as music, composition through chance—have greatly influenced the wider culture, whether postmodern performance or pop songs. We *hear* music differently now. The American conductor Robert Spano writes, "He called us to question our own perception before too quickly classifying a sound as beautiful or ugly, and to find beauty in the meeting of perceiver and perceived." The secret ingredient to getting non-artists to find beauty in avant-garde work, however, is status value. When creators achieve artist status, they kick off a process where the appreciation of their most daring work becomes a form of cultural capital. The structures that encourage distinction can, thus, play a direct role in expanding the population's capability for complex aesthetic comprehension.

-〈≡〉-

Throughout part 2 we've seen how status struggles within and between classes, subcultures, and artistic movements create new conventions, sensibilities, and artifacts—and how the resulting cachet helps these ideas influence broader society. Here we find our answer for the second part of the Grand Mystery of Culture: *How do distinct styles, conventions, and sensibilities emerge?* Classes' specific status assets end up as aesthetic sensibilities, giving us nouveau riche extravagance, Old Money modesty, professional-class sophistication, and low-income flash and kitsch. In bonding together to create alternative sources of status, subcultures and countercultures indulge in shocking behaviors that negate and exaggerate mainstream conventions. Avant-garde artists, hoping to gain esteem for themselves and their work, propose radical solutions to art world problems. The poet and critic T. S. Eliot believed in the "vital importance for a society of *friction* between its parts," and the previous three chapters reveal the exact mechanisms for how status struggles become "highly creative."

Not all conventions created for social distinction are equally beneficial to the cultural ecosystem, however. Conspicuous consumption relies on signs so simple that they serve as obvious evidence of wealth rather than symbols. Very little knowledge is required to read the status meanings of a giant mansion, a stretch limousine, or an oversized gold watch. The avant-garde, at the other extreme, relies on ideas of great symbolic complexity to erect fences between erudite allies and hopeless philistines. Full understanding of these inventions may require access to education, money, and leisure time, but the distinction emerges in the realm of symbols referencing other symbols, not simply in the direct display of acquisition costs.

There emerges, then, a clear connection between signaling costs and the symbolic complexity of the resulting convention. This relationship can be mapped on a spectrum, from pure economic costs to pure cultural costs, with "semieconomic" costs in the middle (where wealth is not the direct signaling cost, but assists in acquiring the knowledge to decode the symbol).

New Money deploys easily interpretable signals. Groups with limited economic capital, in contrast, must rely on symbolically complex conventions for

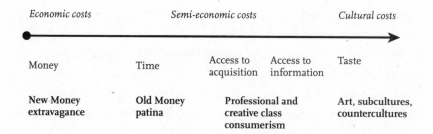

Economic costs	Semi-economic costs			Cultural costs
Money	Time	Access to acquisition	Access to information	Taste
New Money extravagance	**Old Money patina**	**Professional and creative class consumerism**		**Art, subcultures, countercultures**

effective barriers. With no money at their disposal, punks raise fences through radical fashions and behaviors. This means status motivation spurs more cultural creativity on the right end of this spectrum, as these groups' need for distinction produces new ideas, sensibilities, styles, and artifacts—not just more expensive things. This may explain why ultrastratified countries, with vast inequalities in incomes and limited internecine struggle inside the upper and professional classes, produce fewer complex inventions. In these cultural systems, status struggle focuses on conspicuous consumption, which reduces the incentive for individuals to pursue distinction within complex symbolic realms.

This is not to say that all status seekers make important contributions to the expansion of human consciousness. Most aspiring artists secure their desired level of status through repeating others' inventions. But in societies that value originality, influence, and mystery, many people will attempt to attain high status through the creation of subversive ideas. In past ages, where artists received relatively high standing as part of a guild or caste, these occupational groups enforced certain artistic standards, and virtuosity was the ideal. Creators in such environments tend to innovate through small incremental changes after embracing the core conventions over a lifetime. In Japan, traditional crafts allow a slow-moving, conservative form of change called *shu ha ri*—protecting the convention (*shu*), breaking the convention (*ha*), and then separating into a new convention (*ri*). But once Western society began to value radically distinct individuals, status rewards went to fierce artistic originality instead.

The role of status in spurring creativity doesn't mean humans make art *only for* status purposes. Artists can create for altruism, for God, for "the people," for the sheer joy of creation. The novelist Franz Kafka felt he had no choice but to pursue his craft: "I am made of literature, and cannot be anything else." Whatever the reason for their creation, however, radical proposals require some manner of high-status recognition to influence others. "Outsider art" is art outside the status system.

The fruits of status struggles expand the cultural ecosystem, but do they *change* society? For all of their dreams of dynamiting museums, the futurists' work now resides at the Museum of Modern Art like holy relics. Jean Baudrillard complained that avant-garde art can "parody this world, illustrate it, simulate it, alter it" but it "never disturbs the order, which is also its own." Status-driven cultural invention tends to be *rebellious* but not *revolutionary*. Truly radical art forms would not just provide established elites with new status symbols but change which groups are considered elite in the first place.

At least in the realm of human perception and symbolic communication, there have been palpable benefits of radical convention-breaking. Avant-garde art's disgust with cliché and kitsch created a norm for the constant production of new and differentiated cultural forms. André Breton, one of the founders of surrealism, saluted Marcel Duchamp as the model for the twentieth century: "Never has a more profound originality appeared more clearly to derive from a being charged with a more determined intention of negation." Within the field of electronic music, the status struggle between musicians produced hundreds of micro-genres, from minimal techno to digital maximalism. Beyond more creations and more styles, status struggle also proposes additional sensibilities to appreciate and value existing things in new ways. The successes of dada and surrealism as art movements allow us to enjoy the absurd comedy troupe Monty Python as "dadaesque" and "surrealist comedy." Andy Warhol believed that "once you thought Pop, you could never see America the same way again."

Societies that value radical invention end up with more diverse cultural ecosystems, a great abundance of artifacts, and a multiplicity of sensibilities. But there are two downsides. First, radical negation tends to "exhaust" itself by eventually doubling back to the starting point. The modernist poet Octavio Paz stated in the early 1970s, "Rebellion has turned into procedure, criticism into rhetoric, transgression into ceremony. Negation is no longer creative." This led to much confusion about next steps in the "postmodern" era, and one approach was to return to pre-modern ideas. At the 1981 A New Spirit in Painting exhibition at the Royal Academy of Arts in London, the critic Peter Fuller was shocked to find that the youngest painters had embraced traditional painterly goals: "apparent conservatism" was now the "progressive" option.

Second, the demands for originality pushed many artists to disturb conventions so deeply embedded in our brains that the artworks never found large audiences. Art that rejects aesthetic value in pursuit of artistic value often stagnates as "meta-art"—intellectual exercises with little emotional resonance. Without inclusive aesthetic experiences, art becomes trapped within elite circles. Few enjoy Schoenberg's twelve-tone composition as they do Beethoven's classical harmonies.

For most of the twentieth century, status struggles provided us with the incredible cultural diversity we enjoy in the present. And our gratitude for the artists and creators has, in turn, created more tolerance toward a wide range of "deviants" who may provide our future cultural enrichment. This direct connection between status competition and creativity has also revealed a few clues to solving the final part of the Grand Mystery of Culture: *Why do we change behaviors over time, and why do some behaviors persist?* For both art and subcultures, cachet from elite groups brought more individuals into new styles and persuaded initial detractors to accept irritating and norm-breaking ideas. Next, in part 3, we'll better understand exactly why populations move from one convention to another: the internal mechanisms inherent in the status hierarchy work as a motor for perpetual cultural change.

Part Three

STATUS AND
CULTURAL CHANGE

Chapter Eight

FASHION CYCLES

-)ex(-

Shortboards, purple cloth, Glenn O'Brien, cupcakes, "Doctorin' the Tardis," chocolate, and other tales from the endless racetrack of status-based cultural change

-)ex(-

WHAT DRIVES MODERN CULTURAL CHANGE?

The journalist William Finnegan learned to surf as a teenager in the 1960s on nine-foot boards—the traditional tool of the sport, similar in form to what Polynesians used when they first dared to ride the waves centuries ago. Finnegan spent months mowing lawns and pulling weeds to buy more of these towering boards: a Harbor Cheater, a custom slate-blue Larry Felker with a white fin. But everything changed one day in 1968 when Finnegan spotted an Australian professional surfer off the coast of Rincon Beach in Ventura County hitting heretofore impossible moves with unprecedented speed—all atop a *short* V-shaped board. The so-called shortboard revolution had begun, and within a year California's legions of young surfers "eagerly converted en masse to the new faith."

Overnight, Finnegan's precious surfboards were derided as inferior "longboards." And even though he considered them "beautiful" as objects, they were "embarrassing, no longer presentable at any self-respecting surf spot." Finnegan threw his immaculate Harbor Cheater up into the garage rafters and never touched it again. A friend who had poured his savings into a Steve Bigler signature model hurled it off a cliff in an insurance fraud scheme to buy a shortboard—fighting back tears as his prized possession plunged to a bitter, rocky end.

In theory the shortboard revolution was a pure technological shift. The invention of buoyant synthetic materials such as polyurethane foam enabled shapers to craft shorter and, thus, more maneuverable boards. Professional surfers could then use shortboards to more easily perform dramatic stunts like tube riding. But shortboards were never complete substitutes for longboards: they have a steeper learning curve and perform poorly on smaller waves. This explains the longboard revival of the 1990s, and the acceptance of both sizes today. (The Steve Bigler that Finnegan's friend trashed in 1968 would fetch high prices.) Compare surfboard sizes with the change in skateboard wheels from clay to urethane that occurred in the same era. No one would wish a return to the dreaded clay wheels, which flung skaters off the board upon contact with the tiniest pebble.

The shortboard revolution illustrates the great difficulty in identifying the exact causes of cultural change among economic, technological, and psychological factors. Do we switch to new behaviors in pursuit of improved efficiencies? Greater pleasures? Alternative ways of thinking? Curiosity for the new and boredom with the old? The idea of progress is always the most compelling: we replaced our impractical iceboxes with sensible electric refrigerators and primitive rotary landline phones with wireless mobile handsets. And we're also familiar with the downstream effects of changes to material conditions. Suburbs and supermarkets followed the rise of automobile ownership, and fifties youth culture arose when teens could listen to rock 'n' roll in their rooms on cheap transistor radios. When we find no obvious links between culture and material conditions, we assume ideological and spiritual realignments. Hippie men grew out their hair, we believe, in the principled rejection of oppressive middle-class manners and morality.

These arguments, however, are better for explaining slow-paced cultural change over decades and centuries than fast-paced cultural change exhibited in crazes for things like moptops, pop art, and shortboards. The famed linguist Edward Sapir spoke of "drift" in language to explain how words take on new meanings over decades, and eventually break off into dialects and other tongues. We can apply this concept to culture, as well. Learning Greek and Latin was once a core part of liberal arts education but faded out of the curriculum over

time. But the most notable cultural changes of the modern era share little resemblance to organic drift. Cultural inventions arise and rapidly diffuse across
society. Most surfers moved to shortboards within a year—despite many pre-
ferring not to make the switch.

Human behavior certainly adapts to shifts in the material environment, but
to understand cultural change, we must think of it as *cultural* change. For the
anthropologist Leslie White, "Culture determines and causes culture; culture
is to be explained in terms of culture." All cultural change ultimately describes
groups of individuals abandoning one convention for another. Tiny radios
didn't directly create youth culture; teenagers with tiny radios did. To explain
cultural change, we must look at why individuals make the switch. And as we
already know, conventions have their own gravity: rewarding conformity with
social approval and punishing dissent with social disapproval.

Like all human activities, surfing is based in conventions. The use of boards
may not be arbitrary—standing up on waves requires them—but history reveals that the sport of surfing can exist and prosper with both longboards and
shortboards. Both have advantages and disadvantages, but the ability to switch
means surfboard size is ultimately an arbitrary choice. Pro surfers in the late
1960s chose shortboards believing they were superior tools. From Finnegan's
story, however, we know that practicality alone didn't move the *entire* population of surfers to shortboards in such a short time.

As we've learned, we know that all public behaviors, including the use of
technologies and products, become signals in status appraisals. A surfboard is
never a mere tool but also a status symbol. Finnegan's story reveals that surfers
were highly sensitive to the judgment of their peers, and they considered the
status value of their board size alongside any promises of increased efficiencies
or greater pleasures. Pro surfers, who have the status to use any board they
please (world champion Kelly Slater has surfed on a door and a table), pounced
on shortboards for their specific practical advantages. But the shortboard revolution required the masses of amateur surfers like Finnegan, many of whom
preferred longboards, to also switch.

What best explains these swift changes—which can be broadly described
as *fashions*—is status seeking. If we return to Finnegan's story, he testifies that
longboards remained functional and even "beautiful," but they became worthless as their status value soured. In these conspicuous cases of fast cultural

change, status best explains the rise and fall of a convention. This then brings us to solving the final part of the Grand Mystery of Culture: *Why do we change behaviors over time, and why do some behaviors stick around?* This chapter will lay out the specific mechanics of how status motivates individuals and groups to change their behavior. And as we'll see, the modern status structure itself makes fashion an inevitable and perpetual process.

Fashion cycles are clearest in behaviors that offer no practical improvements and that arise within ornamental areas of life: slang, fonts, coffee preparation styles, landscaping, modes of painting, and particular citrus flavorings. For all its ubiquity and universality in human life, fashion has long raised the ire of serious thinkers. Fashion, writes the philosopher George Santayana, is the "barbarous" variety of cultural change that "produces innovation without reason and imitation without benefit." This becomes more pronounced when old-fashioned trends appear ludicrous in hindsight. The philosopher Montesquieu observed in the eighteenth century, "Women's hairstyles gradually go up and up, until a revolution brings them down again. There was a time when because of their enormous height a woman's face was in the middle of her body. At another time her feet occupied the same position." With no clear rationales to why hair goes up or down, we attribute these oscillations to "the madness of crowds"—collective delusions and temporary flights from rationality. This is especially true when trends push us toward inefficient, burdensome, or even harmful practices. The nineteenth-century Empress Elisabeth of Austria's extravagant coiffure gave her frequent headaches. Economist Thorstein Veblen believed these inherent malignancies explained the whole of fashion change: "The substantial futility" of a certain trend eventually becomes "unbearable," at which point "we take refuge in a new style." Or, as Oscar Wilde put it: fashion is "a form of ugliness so intolerable that we have to alter it every six months."

These antifashion attitudes originate in the moral expectations that individuals should act rationally, choose for themselves, and be detached from status concerns. Again, this is why we use alibis to explain our personal behavior. Likewise society shies away from awkward discussions of status seeking's role in cultural change. In early-twentieth-century France, the famed Parisian dancer Caryathis chopped her hair off in a fit, which then launched a fashion trend for short hair. When a reporter later asked the poet Jean Cocteau to explain Coco Chanel's cropped locks, he invented an implausible story that the women were simply acting "for charitable purposes," donating the cuttings to victims of World War I. Marketing campaigns help us in finding credible denials. The tagline on a 1980s Nike ad for a gray tennis sneaker with a flash of bold red stated, "Irreverence. Justified. See that color? It's not just there to make noise. It's where we put Durathane, a revolutionary new material that doubles the toe piece life." Why did the Durathane have to come in shocking scarlet? Unclear. But alibis work well because even *we* can't understand the source of our own desires. Our hearts draw no clear lines between functionality, pleasure, and status seeking.

In our preference for rational decision making, fashion becomes, in the words of the anthropologist Michael Thompson, "frivolous, ephemeral, transient, and irrational," and this has made it "not a fit subject for scholarly attention." This is unfortunate: fashion, in its broadest sense, explains the most frequent forms of cultural change in the modern world. Not all human behavior changes for status reasons, and not every instance of cultural change begins *as* fashion, but most behaviors we perceive as "culture" arrive through a fashion cycle where individuals adopt new conventions in a pursuit of status value. Conventions form around all behaviors—even the use of practical technologies. The umbrella is an obvious convenience to deploy in times of inclement weather and yet, at a certain time in the United Kingdom, men who dared use umbrellas "were so ill thought of that they were persecuted in the streets."

The role of status seeking in cultural change is well attested in sociologist Everett Rogers's authoritative theory on the diffusions of innovations. ("Invention" is a new idea; "innovation" describes the invention's use and widespread adoption.) In principle, rational humans will embrace technologies with greater efficiencies as soon as they become aware of them and can afford them. But Rogers had firsthand experience of the contrary. In 1936, a terrible drought decimated the family farm, and the Rogerses couldn't afford Christmas presents. Their neighbors, on the other hand, weathered the crisis just fine thanks to the newly developed farming technology hybrid seed corn. Rogers's father knew the benefits of hybrid seed corn and could afford to use it, but he stuck to open-pollinated seed corn, worried that the local old-timer farmers he most admired would look down on him for switching over to newfangled methods. Hoping to avoid another devastating crop failure, Rogers's father finally made the switch to the hybrid seed corn—after eight years of holding out.

Rogers thus knew to examine the diffusion of innovations as a *social* process. Individuals make adoption decisions within the framework of human interaction. They consider how, when, and from whom they receive information, how they view uncertainties about switching, and how they'll be judged in their community for making the switch. Rogers noticed that adoptions progressed in sequence through five distinct groups, which he called *innovators, early adopters, early majority, late majority,* and *laggards.* Individuals fall into these groups based on a trait Rogers calls *innovativeness,* "the degree to which an individual . . . is relatively earlier in adopting new ideas than other members of a social system." The distribution of this innovativeness is uneven: there are very few innovators, a small cadre of early adopters, most people in the majority groups, and a small batch of laggards. Rogers's research implies that most people *aren't* particularly excited to take up innovations at the time of their introduction.

What slows down adoption by majorities? They often have unequal access to information and different levels of trust in technology. But status also plays a major role. By definition, innovations pose a challenge to established conventions—to use hybrid seed corn is a distinctive act when everyone uses open-pollinated seed corn. Thus individuals may worry that switching will lead to social disapproval, even when there are clear practical benefits to doing so. Change causes anxiety. The philosopher Eric Hoffer notes, "Even in slight things the experience of the new is rarely without some stirring of foreboding." As seen in the American public's response to the moptop, the common majority response to innovations isn't quiet curiosity but "shock, astonishment, ridicule or disgust." Widespread change takes place only once conservative majorities feel secure that switching won't damage their status. And since status position impacts our quality of life as much as the benefits of practical technologies, we would be reasonable to consider the status implications of these adoption decisions.

It is also reasonable for us to consider status in explaining the common patterns of cultural change. Yet a particular stream in social science has attempted to show that trends can also arise in what's called the "neutral" model, where individuals glom onto the same practices through randomly copying one another with no regard for social position. Trends arise from unconscious imitation, they claim, not from emulation. But other researchers have shown that when status is added as a factor in these models—i.e., humans become more likely to imitate behaviors with cachet—the resulting adoption curves even better resemble the ups and downs we observe in real life.

Fashion cycles are thus a critical way to understand the whole of contemporary cultural change. But how exactly does this work? The sociologist Albert K. Cohen wonders, "How is it possible for cultural innovations to emerge while each of the participants in the culture is so powerfully motivated to conform to what is already established?" In *Hit Makers*, author Derek Thompson frames this question as a paradox: "Most consumers are simultaneously *neophilic*—curious to discover new things—and deeply *neophobic*—afraid of anything that's too new." As we'll see, there is no paradox: most people seek to participate publicly in new trends only where status value becomes obviously positive.

To understand this process, we'll examine each stage of the fashion cycle: elites' need for distinctive practices, mass media broadcasting, early adopters' emulation, mass producers' simplification, and the eventual achievement of critical mass. Cycles arise in the cultural ecosystem due to the interaction of the particular individuals and institutions: style icons, artists, status groups, critics, media outlets, manufacturers, distributors, retailers, out-of-touch laggards. And in contrast to popular theories of "viral contagion," this analysis of fashion cycles demonstrates how each stage *changes* the nature of the initial innovation. Where does a fashion cycle begin? It kicks off exactly where the principles of status suggest it would: among the highest-status individuals.

HIGH-STATUS EXCLUSIVITY

The most prized purple dye in the ancient world came from Phoenicia, where craftsmen worked to extract the milky secretions from marine molluscs of the Muricidae family. Producing a few drops of dye required crushing thousands of tiny sea snails in giant vats, and these limited quantities made garments fully dyed in "Tyrian purple" a treasure as desirable as gold. Upon his invasion of Persia, Alexander the Great plundered purple cloth of the modern equivalent of $68 million. In *The Natural History*, Pliny the Elder wondered why Rome in the first century AD was under such a "frantic passion for purple," given this particular dye's "offensive" rotting-sea-snail smell and its color, "harsh, of a greenish hue, and strongly resembling that of the sea when in a tempestuous state." Nero so loved Tyrian purple that upon ascending to power in AD 54, he outlawed anyone other than royalty wearing garments in the color.

In today's world overflowing with an abundance of synthetic dyestuffs, humans no longer give purple a privileged place in the visible spectrum of color. "Royal Purple" is nothing more than an automotive lubricant. The ancient fashion trend for Tyrian purple, then, had less to do with an intrinsic human preference for those particular wavelengths of light and more about cachet. The emperor desired purple, because the bold color served as an exclusive marker.

Elites' need for exclusive practices marks the beginning of the fashion cycle. As we learned in chapter 2, the logic of status hierarchies leads to the top status tiers desiring distinctive goods and practices. As sociologist Gabriel Tarde writes, "The supposedly superior individual is copied in all respects" but "he appears to copy no one below himself." Elites must be *arbiter elegantiarum*— tastemakers, not taste-followers.

Invention may arise anywhere in society, but its broader diffusion requires a boost of cachet. In needing exclusive goods and practices, high-status individuals are attracted to stylistic or technological innovations, precisely because they emerge, by definition, among a small number of adopters. This is where status seeking first intertwines with the diffusion of innovations. Innovativeness— the willingness to try out new things—increases as one moves up the status hierarchy from the middle tiers. Elites have a *need* to engage in exclusive behaviors, and the *privilege* to do so. In late-nineteenth-century France, police arrested middle-class women wearing trousers; the famed writer George Sand and the actress Sarah Bernhardt, by contrast, strolled down Parisian boulevards in pants with impunity.

Status also explains why innovativeness is found at the bottom of society as well. Outsiders, exiles, and misfits don't worry about the social risks of trying new things, because they have little status to lose. The principle of cachet, however, means that low-status convention-breaking is viewed as "deviance" and may not inspire any immediate imitation. High-status convention-breaking, on the other hand, kicks off emulation and becomes understood as a noble act of innovation.

Economists describe the inherent demand for exclusive goods as the *snob effect*: "the search for exclusiveness by individuals through the purchase of distinctive clothing, foods, automobiles, houses, or anything else that individuals

may believe will in some way set them off from the mass of mankind." Snobbish consumerism is not limited to nobles and billionaires but exists at the top
of all status groups at every level of society. In mid-1980s New York, hard-core
sneakerheads desired the Nike Air Force 1, simply because they could be purchased only at a single Bronx store. Snobs are often disparaged for valuing signaling costs over intrinsic qualities. Literary scholar Barbara H. Smith recalls,
"As a discriminating young snob, I was predisposed to find the value of any
poem inversely proportional to the frequency of its appearance in anthologies."

Since the very top elites are rarely craftspeople themselves, they must
procure their status symbols from elsewhere. Elites flock to three particular
categories of items that fulfill their needs: *rarities*, *novelties*, and *technological
innovations*.

Rarities are difficult-to-acquire objects, ranging from one-of-a-kind antiques
and heirlooms unavailable in the open market to brand-new luxuries requiring
vast fortunes to afford. Nobles of the ancient world collected bronze as a precious metal for distinctive decoration long before they knew how to employ it
in weaponry. Modern elites' preferences for rarities map to their class strategies: New Money desires obvious luxury goods with high financial costs, while
Old Money desires hard-to-obtain and subtle patinated antiques with high
time-based signaling costs. The Rockefellers owned brass candlesticks and
andirons dating from the American Revolution, as well as a French walnut side
table from the reign of Louis XIV. This desire for rarities also increases demand
for authenticity. Products with a verified provenance—Persian rugs, works of
art—are hard to obtain and assumed to be made with higher quality. The emphasis on authenticity also works to devalue any kitsch imitations that may
arise.

Status symbols such as these don't need to be rare in an absolute sense.
They only need to be perceived as rare within the community. This allows elites
to acquire rarities through the act of arbitrage—using their privileges to easily
procure goods from one domain and deploy them back home. In the Soviet
Union, modest foreign goods such as nylon stockings, imported cigarettes, and
Parker pens took on cachet, since only the top bureaucrats could travel abroad
or secure enough foreign currency to purchase them.

Rarities tend to be expensive, so elites with less economic capital may seek
distinction in novelties instead. New fashion styles, recording artists, musical

genres, or films use information as the primary signaling cost, and the creative classes are always the most in the know. Only informed elites know to eat at the French Laundry in Napa Valley or travel to Marfa, Texas. Arbitrage also works for novelties. Very few people remembered the Mountie-like Arby's logo hat from designer Vivienne Westwood's 1982–1983 collection, so when Pharrell Williams wore it to the 2014 Grammy Awards, it became known as the "Pharrell hat." For creative-class elites, one effective technique for novelties is to embrace aesthetically displeasing content—strange art, unusual styles, or shocking innovations—which will alienate conservative majorities.

Finally, technological innovations are also a form of rare goods, which happen to offer a strong alibi of practical advantage. The iPhone was new, expensive, and exclusive at its debut in 2007 but also provided clear benefits compared with previous mobile phones. New technologies work well for distinction, since they hit the market at high prices and signal other status criteria, such as rationality, hipness, and exacting standards for product excellence. People at the top of their professional fields seek out new tools that can further boost their performance. Hard-core New York street basketball players in the 1970s started a new shoelacing style where the lace went over the first eyelet and then under the others. Other players saw it as a "more vicious style" because they trusted better players' need for greater functionality.

While technological innovation implies the creation of brand-new gadgets and methods, cultural innovation can also be used to describe elite groups imbuing mundane or old things with cachet. Elites look for "blank slates" upon which to project their own high-status associations. Chelsea became a hip London neighborhood in the mid-1960s, precisely because it was "uncharted territory." Elite distinction can even elevate the plebeian. John Lennon made industrially produced, steel-rimmed "granny glasses" from National Health into a chic accessory, because he was John Lennon. In Argentina the tango arose as the dance of lower classes but received a status boost after gaining popularity in Paris, London, and New York. Suntans were long associated with the peasantry who worked outside all day, but as the work of European day laborers moved inside factories, the poor became paler. This created an opening for wealthy French elites such as Coco Chanel to redefine bronzed skin as evidence of time spent "sunbathing" at chic Mediterranean resorts. In these cases, there tends to be refinement of the original convention. As wine was elevated from a vulgar beverage to a tasteful hobby, out went demijohns, flasks, and large bottles, and in came delicate wineglasses, decanters, and narrow Bordeaux bottles.

The opposite of this phenomenon is also true. Rarities, novelties, and technological innovations fail to take on status value when overly associated with low-status groups. Upon its debut, the Segway scooter was novel and expensive, but it quickly took on an anticachet, as parodied by *Arrested Development*'s Gob Bluth and *Paul Blart: Mall Cop*.

Elite adoption imbues innovations with status value, which makes them attractive to individuals in lower tiers. High signaling costs are meant to serve as barriers, but as we'll see, the fashion cycle progresses as these costs decrease. The first defense to fail is the cost of information.

MASS MEDIA

After hours and hours of listening to the banter on prime-time TV shows like *What's My Line* and *I've Got a Secret*, eleven-year-old fifth-grader Glenn O'Brien of Cleveland, Ohio, became well versed in the basics of celebrity nightlife. He knew, for example, that after work they all haunted a swank, exclusive Manhattan spot called the Stork Club. So during a vacation to New York, O'Brien had his parents take him there and ditched them at the door. The Stork Club's maître d' was impressed with this precocious preteen in a bright red blazer and took O'Brien around to greet the high rollers sitting at the tables, including the famed actress Kitty Carlisle.

O'Brien's prodigious stockpile of cultural capital only snowballed over the years and, as an adult, he embarked upon a successful career in the media. His Beat column in Andy Warhol's *Interview* magazine became record labels' cheat sheet for signing new bands. In the late 1970s O'Brien ran a public-access program called *TV Party*, putting underground legends Iggy Pop, Jean-Michel Basquiat, and Robert Mapplethorpe on suburban television sets. And for most of the last two decades of his life, O'Brien wrote the Style Guy advice column at *GQ*, bequeathing his authoritative wisdom on dressing and manners to the next generation of dapper youth. Glenn O'Brien was never a household name, but just as game shows taught him about celebrity lifestyles as a preteen, his essays and reporting provided aspiring young creatives with rare and privileged information direct from the high-status downtown New York art scene. O'Brien's reporting on this closed milieu acted, in the words of his protégé the novelist Christopher Bollen, as "a lodestar" for teenagers bored in their "bland American towns."

The career of Glenn O'Brien demonstrates the crucial role of the mass media in moving trends through the cultural ecosystem. Elite conventions stay exclusive unless the media expands the common knowledge to people of lower status tiers. The Condé Nast empire of magazines, from *The New Yorker* to *Vogue*, ascended in global culture by serving this very function: providing how-to guides for the upper middle classes outside of New York, London, and Paris to keep up with the latest urban trends. And by indicating which new conventions have cachet, the mass media triggers emulation from the heaviest consumers of media—namely, the professional and creative classes. "When the movies came," writes the media theorist Marshall McLuhan, "the entire pattern of American life went on the screen as a nonstop ad. Whatever any actor or actress wore or used or ate was such an ad as had never been dreamed of." Mass media, then, isn't a neutral pipe that simply relays information, but a transformative tool that strengthens conventions by broadening common knowledge and adding status value.

The media supports the diffusion of innovations through four key functions: *selecting* the most appealing conventions, *broadcasting* them to a large audience, *explaining* why individuals should adopt, and explicitly *evaluating* quality. All four actions work to make elite conventions more attractive to media-savvy early adopters. And then, later in the fashion cycle, broadsheets, mainstream news shows, and other mass media introduce the early majority to conventions that meet their particular requirements for adoption—i.e., well-known (broadcasted), legitimate (well selected, evaluated), and nonarbitrary (explained).

Starting with selection, editors and producers must choose what to cover based on the particular standards of the outlet. Editors serve as gatekeepers, applying strict criteria to select what's newsworthy, and whatever makes the cut has implied importance, innovativeness, high quality, and is in good taste.

The media then broadcasts these selections to large audiences, expanding common knowledge of conventions to those unable to observe them firsthand. This increase in knowledge is necessary for widespread imitation. In the mid-1980s, hip-hop achieved only a handful of hits from novelty acts (the Fat Boys) and rock crossovers (Run-DMC collaborating with Aerosmith). The genre's takeover of American music began with the 1988 debut of the weekly television program *Yo! MTV Raps*, which quickly became the network's most watched show.

Broadcasting is powerful as a form of *meta-communication*: not only delivering messages but implying that many, many other individuals are seeing the same message. For high-end magazines with limited circulation, readers imagine the content will be read only by other high-status people, thus boosting a sense of cachet. Inclusion in the broadest mass media, like *USA Today* or *People*, by contrast, suggests conventions known to all, which may diminish status value for early adopters. American electronic music fans were horrified in 1991 when the main characters in the teen drama *Beverly Hills 90210* attended a rave: "It's dead! It's over! It's done! It's mainstream!"

Because innovations can often be obscure, abstract, or seemingly arbitrary, explanation plays a critical role in providing context to why elites have adopted an exclusive practice. This can take the form of written narrative, but in many cases, visual media like TV and films "explain" conventions without the need for direct explication. Footage of British girls in convulsive fits at the sight of the Beatles modeled how young American women should also behave.

The most important aspect of explanation is naming—identifying new conventions as distinct semantic entities. A name turns vague impressions and feelings into "things" up for discussion. In the late 1960s, the British casually called teens with shaved heads smithies, skulls, and peanuts. But the look didn't become a true style movement until the media agreed on its permanent designation: skinheads. "There are no unlabeled fads or fashions," write the sociologists Rolf Meyerson and Elihu Katz. Organizations are aware of this power and deploy new names for alienating phenomena to improve perceptions. "Punk" scared away radio stations, so an executive at Sire Records asked radio stations to call aggressive young bands New Wave instead. Americans in the 1990s loathed European "techno," so *Spin* magazine rechristened it "electronica."

Critics assist in explaining why artists' radical innovations are significant and not just arbitrary idiosyncrasies. (The dada poet Tristan Tzara resented this

fact: "Any work of art that can be understood is the product of a journalist.")
The mass media's "ideal reader" determines the complexity of explanations. To
ensure wide understanding, the linguist Terence Hawkes writes, there will be
"reducing or 'trimming' all experience to make it fit the categories we have
ready for it." Fashion magazines encourage participation in a fashion trend by
providing recipes for easy imitation. "For the perfect duchess-off-duty moment," suggests *Vogue*, "look no further than [Kate] Middleton's herringbone
blazer. The tailored jacket from Storets will evoke a similar feel—and at $228,
consider it a royally chic steal."

Media explanation can be so authoritative that even the subjects of the reporting often seek to conform to its exaggerations—a process Tom Wolfe called
"media ricochet." The 1953 film *The Wild One* dramatized the rise of outlaw
biker gangs, which provided the Hells Angels with their stylistic template. In
Hell's Angels, Hunter S. Thompson writes that *The Wild One* "gave the outlaws
a lasting romance-glazed image of themselves, a coherent reflection that only
a few had been able to find in a mirror." Writer John Seabrook points out that
the American aristocracy's idea of itself was "based on fiction created by wannabe elites themselves." Jay Gatsby was both a satire of New Money and its
aspirational idol.

Finally, the media can boost the value of certain conventions with explicit
evaluations of quality. Critics don't just introduce new products and artworks
but state if they're great, good, mediocre, bad, or horrible. In the late twentieth
century, the American upper middle class relied on *Consumer Reports* to vouch
for automobiles and appliances. Millennials in the 2000s read *Pitchfork Media*
to understand whether new music releases were masterpieces (10.0) or shameful bombs (0.0). Among professional and creative classes, familiarity with
these reviews serves as cultural capital in its own right. For the early majority,
on the other hand, entertainment reviews have little influence on their consumption. Critics pounded the 2018 film *Venom* (30% score on Rotten Tomatoes), which went on to make $210 million in the United States alone.

Since the arts are ultimately a private taste, even the most cultured individuals feel confident in ignoring the opinions of critics. For status-conscious
middle-class individuals, however, the *public* taste manifested in dress, manners, and home furnishing has serious implications for status position. The
fear of mistakes creates a robust market for etiquette books, manners guides,

and how-to manuals. Readers tend to strongly conform to the advice. After Charles Eastlake's *Hints on Household Taste* was published in 1868, Russell Lynes writes, "All its dicta were accepted as gospel truth. [The British people] hung their pictures and curtains just as Mr. Eastlake said they should; laid their carpets, colored their walls, hinged their doors, arranged their china, bought their candlesticks, insisted on their andirons, procured solid wood, abjured veneering, and eschewed curves, all after Mr. Eastlake's own heart." In the mid-twentieth century, millions of American women received an Amy Vanderbilt or Emily Post etiquette guide as a coming-of-age gift. When a small cult of stylish young men in the early 2000s sought guidance on how to dress up—e.g., whether to match sock color to pants or shoes—they looked to Glenn O'Brien to provide the canonical answers.

Another important form of evaluation is disparaging conventions of suspect quality and low status value. But there is truth to the old adage "All publicity is good publicity": broadcasting deplorable acts boosts their status value and creates an allure in infamy. The *Daily Mirror* railed against teddy boys to stoke the flames of moral panic, but the photos encouraged many working-class teens to buy their own drape coats and brothel creepers.

Taken together, the four acts of selection, broadcasting, explanation, and evaluation all strengthen, stabilize, and legitimize conventions. These services are critical for individuals living in fast-moving societies who are required to keep up with social norms. "We assume things will change," writes the sociologist Joel Best, "and this assumption, in turn, creates its own demands for media that can tell us what's happening." But this is a reflexive act: in the course of reporting on conventions and setting the direction of emulation, the media turns them into fashions and assists in their diffusion.

This discussion of mass media implies the existence of disembodied broadcast automatons at faceless organizations. But at every desk sits someone like Glenn O'Brien, whose decisions become part of their personal identities. They must consider the status implications of their selections, explanations, and evaluations. This acts as a filter on what gets reported, thus creating a difference between what is happening in the world and what is reported to be happening in the world. Most notably, the majority of media industry workers were born into a higher-status habitus or gained ample cultural capital during education. This results in a shared sensibility, one skeptical of brash New Money conspicuous consumption, middle-class parochialism, and lower-class "bad taste." For a long time, the media's selections leaned toward (1) new conventions in the milieu of the professional classes; (2) classic conventions of the tasteful wealthy; and (3) exciting conventions from radical artists, oppositional subcultures, and minorities. Music publications never took Celine Dion seriously, because, as music critic Carl Wilson notes, "Her voice itself is *nouveau riche*. It's a volume business."

The personal status concerns of media publications result in an underreporting of popular conventions within lower-status circles. Larry the Cable Guy's albums have gone platinum, but his popularity with rural, blue-collar audiences seems to be inversely correlated to his representation in the mass media's depiction of stand-up comedy. The mass media may also reshape jagged subcultural conventions to fit a more refined professional-class aesthetic. Punk developed from art school wrath and working-class dissent, and yet *GQ* assured readers in 1977 that "punk, if treated with extreme delicacy and sensibility, can be made to work with the season's overall fashion direction. Take the torn T-shirt. Carefully slashed to ribbons, it can work perfectly with freshly minted blue jeans and a wool overshirt."

Status competition within the media world also incentivizes reporters to hunt for the most distinctive evaluations—i.e., the "hottest takes." Scoops, exclusives, and early discoveries are necessary to stand out. The sociologist of art Jean Duvignaud writes, "No editor, no gallery director dare admit today to having 'let slip' a talented painter or poet, as much for reasons of the prestige which comes with the venture of 'launching' as for the immense material benefits which accompany success." This sometimes results in the creation of *false trends*—excitement about marginal or imaginary social movements. In 2009 *The New York Times* reported that the "burgeoning potbelly" had emerged as a stylish look for hipster men. *Slate*'s Jack Shafer lambasted the article, observing that the reporter "names no leader of potbelly hipness and uncovers no evidence of hip potbellies in the cinema, the stage, the concert hall, the night club, or elsewhere. It's just these random guts strolling around New York."

Does the high-status control of the media create significant bias in our culture? Judging by sales numbers, critics rarely prevent masses from flocking to their favorite entertainments. For all the invective against mystery writer Dan Brown, he has sold more than 200 million books. Critical opinion tends to kill the prospects only of films targeting educated elites. In 1994, the film critic Roger Ebert murdered the now forgotten $40 million budget Rob Reiner film *North* in his review: "I hated this movie. Hated, hated, hated, hated, hated this movie. Hated it." This is all to say that kitsch may better reflect the average taste of culture at any time, but the media, in controlling the narrative of the zeitgeist, can redirect attention to nonpopular things. In theory, critics provide a countervailing force against mass-marketed artworks with huge promotional budgets—at least with the professional and creative classes for whom critical opinion matters.

Mass media, then, speeds up cultural change by priming elite conventions for broader adoption—a process that tends to overindex high-status behaviors as "what is happening in the culture." Regardless, once information about innovations passes through broadcasting channels, early adopters are ready to join in.

EMULATION AND HIGH-STATUS ABANDONMENT

Magnolia Bakery opened on a corner of New York City's posh West Village in 1996, and within a few years its brightly colored cupcakes became a beloved late-night snack for the wealthy professionals who lived nearby. The TV show *Sex and the City* placed its protagonist, Carrie Bradshaw, in front of Magnolia during a 2000 episode, where she confesses a crush while eating the bakery's signature offering. Soon there was glowing coverage in *British Vogue*, and the hip fashion boutique Marc Jacobs opened down the block. By 2001 Magnolia cupcakes were a proud part of the New York professional-class identity. The fashion designer Jenna Lyons—who later became known as "the Woman Who Dresses America" at J.Crew—served cupcakes at her 2002 wedding, in remembrance of "many nights standing on the corner of Bleecker and West 11th."

By 2003, however, a new wave of New Yorkers started to show up at Magnolia Bakery—younger, less affluent, and residing far from the West Village. Next came the out-of-towners on *Sex and the City* tours. Magnolia began to sell three thousand cupcakes a day, and garbage cans in the nearby park overflowed with frosting-encrusted boxes. The insatiable hunger for gourmet cupcakes in New York spurred entrepreneurial bakers to start rival bakeries: Crumbs opened uptown, and then Sprinkles brought the treats to Los Angeles. By 2004 the initial buzz around Magnolia snowballed into a nationwide craze for fancy cupcakes.

There have been a near infinite number of delicacies in New York City—Glaser's Bake Shop's black-and-white cookie, Russ & Daughters' rugelach, Krispy Kreme's Original Glazed dougnut—but for a brief moment, investment bankers and fashion stylists gave their time, money, and blood sugar to fancy cupcakes instead. Was it because these cupcakes were particularly delicious? *The New York Times* concluded that Magnolia cupcakes "had no discernible flavor beyond the cocoa in the chocolate icing." Tourists were likewise confused: "You could never sell these in Michigan. People would just look at them and say, 'I could make those at home!'" For whatever deficiency in flavor, though, Magnolia cupcakes had cachet.

But this cachet crashed in the following decade's cupcake backlash. In 2013 Jen Doll of *The Atlantic* wrote, "Is there a more widely, vocally despised food than the prissy, expensive, full-of-itself gourmet cupcake?" Much could be blamed on overexposure: most major cities had their own cupcake spots. And cupcakes took over mass media: they were a key plot point in the film *Bridesmaids* and the TV show *2 Broke Girls*, the subject of countless blogs, and the anchor of a reality show, *Cupcake Wars*. The excitement began to wane. Crumbs had planned to open 150 additional stores within five years; by 2014, they ceased operations.

After media broadcasting, trends reach a new stage of the fashion cycle: the mid-status *emulation* of high-status behaviors, and subsequent high-status *abandonment*. *Sex and the City* turned Magnolia cupcakes into a fashion trend, and the oversaturation a decade later cemented its decline.

In Everett Rogers's diffusion model, semi-high-status individuals are known as early adopters. They tend to be members of the professional and creative classes, as these groups are heavy media consumers and learn about elite conventions before other groups. They're also well paid (economic capital), well connected (social capital), and well educated (educational and cultural capital). Moreover, they're cosmopolitan—aware of many alternative conventions and comfortable with breaking traditions. Most important, they signal through taste, which creates a responsibility to keep up with trends. In their semi-high status position, they are allowed some individual distinctiveness as long as they don't stray too far from group norms.

Early adopters' pursuit of the status value embodied in elite conventions thus creates a trickle-down flow of cultural practices. Nineteenth-century sociologist Gabriel Tarde saw cultural flows as a "kind of social *water-tower*, whence a continuous water-fall of imitation may descend." This trickle-down was unambiguous during feudal times. The king set stylistic conventions, which aristocrats followed, only to be copied by the bourgeoisie. With the emergence of democracy and capitalism, professionals could ape styles of the superrich, and even the poor found their own ways to emulate. In nineteenth-century Europe, the fashion for crinoline began among duchesses and ladies and ended up on East Prussian farming women working in the fields. Today elite conventions easily diffuse all the way across society. Wealthy yuppies were among the first Americans to drink the French sparkling mineral water brand Perrier; by 1988, it was America's bestselling bottled water. Perrier is now widely available in multiple flavors in nearly every supermarket.

Trickle-down patterns are very common for technological innovations, especially when new gadgets come to market with high price tags. The first black-and-white televisions cost more than some automobiles. Diffusion speeds up as costs come down, but the lingering cachet of ownership, not just practical benefits, is what excites many adopters. The American lower middle class bought TVs not just to be entertained but to signal economic success, which seems to explain why so many families placed their first TV sets on pedestals in their living rooms.

Fashion trends after World War II, however, strained the trickle-down metaphor. As the scholar Barbara Vinken notes, "Fashion is now made, worn and displayed, not by the bourgeoisie or the aristocracy, but on the street." As subcultural capital grew in importance for creative-class signaling, high-status groups began to embrace formerly low-status conventions. By the mid-1970s, journalist Tom Wolfe observed, "If you walk down the street in New York, you may see a couple emerging from a co-op wearing tie-dyed pre-faded bell-bottomed Levi's with aluminum studs up the outseam who happen to be the owners of a $175,000 apartment upstairs" (around $900,000 today). With the rich dressing like the poor, have we come to the end of trickle-down? Have we entered a new world of "trickle-up" or "trickle-across"?

Not quite. The fundamental human desire for status continues to direct imitation upward. All that has changed is that the cultural capital of urban, cosmopolitan groups includes knowledge of lower-status lifestyles. A conspicuous example is that middle-class white Americans must prove familiarity with Black culture, a phenomenon that drives multiple sectors of the creative economy. When Tommy Hilfiger wanted to sell his brand's preppy clothing in the early 1990s, he took the advice of the rap impresario Russell Simmons and first targeted African Americans rather than the preppies themselves.

But we shouldn't confuse the diversification of cultural capital as true trickle-up cultural flows. Elite tastemakers have always stolen ideas from tiers far below, because they can "slum it" without being mistaken for people living in slums. Lederhosen took its exalted place in German culture after elites wore farmer clothing as a joke. In the late nineteenth century, Gabriel Tarde noted, "Invention can start from the lowest ranks of the people, but its extension depends upon the existence of some lofty social elevation." Once these plundered practices take on cachet at the top, they can even influence the original communities. The historian Kobena Mercer notes that the white actress Bo Derek copied cornrows from the Black community, and "her success validated the style and encouraged more Black people to corn-row their hair." True trickle-up would involve the poor influencing the lower middle classes, who in turn influence the middle class and then elites—an unlikely chain of groups seeking to associate themselves with the tier beneath them. Perhaps the closest example of trickle-up would be Kim Kardashian, whose career progressed from a leaked sex tape to tabloids to reality shows to the cover of *Vogue*. But Kardashian is a wealthy celebrity, and her growing assets explain her rise more than individuals imitating the Kardashian worship beneath them.

Regardless of a cultural innovation's particular origin, the injection of status value encourages early adopters to emulate. But this inflow of lower-status individuals into the convention diminishes the cachet for the initial adopters. Imitation is annoying. Elites must now spend time and money looking for replacements, and to quickly adopt new conventions would undermine the stability and authenticity of their identities. The Duke of Bedford once mumbled that the upper classes "do not want anything from the Common Man except that he should remain common." This is precisely why elites choose things with high signaling costs in the first place.

There may be moments when high-status and low-status members of a population participate in the same trend, but they tend to be brief. Elites can't risk associations with contaminated styles. No matter how long they've enjoyed certain customs, they will abandon the practices once they no longer assist in demarcation from lower tiers. "Snobbism is a race, a competition," wrote Glenn O'Brien. "It's about getting there first and leaving first." As the flapper dress spread to the masses in the 1920s, Zelda Fitzgerald noted that the original flapper had "to move on to something else, parading her precious distinction for a while before once again passing it on to the less adventuresome." For centuries the wealthy took pride in their plumpness, as it signaled easy access to large quantities of food. When this bodily distinction disappeared with the expansion of potato farming and industrial food production, the rich abandoned rounder body types and became obsessed with exercise and nutrition.

For trends that spread across the entirety of society, adoption itself is less effective as a high-status signal than the *timing* of adoption. Elites adopt early, non-elites adopt later. As the indie rock cliché goes, "I *used* to like that band." The early adoption of a popular trend suggests many virtues—individualism, bravery, being an exemplar. In the long run, elites make the same choices as the masses, but they make them much faster.

Abandonment is thus as important as adoption in fashion cycles. But abandonment requires another round of adoption. To disavow cupcakes means taking up a new exclusive sweet (or giving up all sweets). When Perrier became too common, jet-setters signaled more sophisticated tastes by name-checking rival brand Badoit instead. The once rebellious long hair and beards of hippies eventually became, in the words of the writers Dick Pountain and David Robins, "the house style of urban lumpenproletariat and criminal underworlds across the globe, the uniform of every pimp, prostitute, dope dealer and television wrestler from Liverpool to Prague and Caracas to Manila." So by the late 1970s, the experimental filmmaker Wakefield Poole and his boyfriend shaved off their long locks for crew cuts.

When early adopters rush in to emulate elite conventions, elites abandon. But with the new wave of adopters creating so much excitement in the commercial marketplace, there arises an obvious economic incentive to further commercialize the trend.

MASS PRODUCTION

In 1988 two British men calling themselves the Timelords cobbled together a jock-jammy, *Doctor-Who*-and-Gary Glitter-sampling dance track called "Doctorin' the Tardis." *Melody Maker* pronounced it "excruciating," but the song hit number one on the British pop charts. The producers, who later emerged as the bestselling techno-pop act the KLF, followed "Doctorin' the Tardis" with a tongue-in-cheek book explaining their achievement called *The Manual (How to Have a Number One the Easy Way)*. The book promises, "By following the clear and concise instructions contained in this book . . . you can realise your childish fantasies of having a Number One hit single in the official U.K. Top 40 thus guaranteeing you a place forever in the sacred annals of Pop History." *The Manual* may be petulant satire, but it provides imitable and practical steps for producing a hit song: how to find the right grooves to sample, how to book cheap studio time, how to win over skeptical bank employees, and when to stop and enjoy a cup of tea.

Manuals are anathema to art in societies where creativity is based in the radical negation of established conventions. But that's *The Manual*'s point: pop songs aren't works of art. They are formulaic kitsch conforming to a preestablished set of "golden rules." These include a "dance groove," a run-time of less than 3:30, a structure based on "an intro, a verse, a chorus, second verse, a second chorus, a breakdown section, back into a double length chorus and outro," and lyrics that touch only the "most basic of human emotions." The entire enterprise of pop music, claims *The Manual*, is rewriting the same song over and over with slightly different sounds: "All records in the Top Ten (especially those that get to Number One) have far more in common with each other than with whatever genre they have developed from or sprung out of."

In Everett Rogers's theory of innovations, hits require products to go beyond early adopters and reach into early majorities. "The part of the diffusion curve from about 10 percent adoption to 20 percent adoption," he writes, "is the heart of the diffusion process." But this is a challenge: these two groups may sit next to each other in Rogers's diffusion curve, but there is an enormous gulf between them in terms of taste. As predicted by their status positions, early adopters have sophisticated and cosmopolitan tastes, and they have more confidence to try new things. Low-status early majorities are conservative and wary of breaking conventions in public. *The Manual* demonstrates there is a strategy that cultural industries use to cross the chasm—to locate high-status innovations with cachet and adapt their content to the existing tastes of mass audiences. Commercialization, then, is a process of lowering signaling costs, not just of money and availability, but also of difficult taste.

Mass production is where status logic collides with raw economic logic. Companies find it difficult to profit in unstable and unpredictable cultural markets and, as a way to minimize risk, they converge upon a *production logic*—tacit rules that shape the content and form of artworks, styles, and products in order to increase chances of mainstream consumer adoption. Production logic infects not only the form and content of mass-market films, songs, and TV shows, but the design of products, the specific marketing techniques used to sell them, and the tenor of advertising messages. *The Manual* outlines the production logic behind pop music and, in doing so, implies the actual song behind a hit is arbitrary—it can even be "excruciating"—as long as it conforms to the audience's desired forms.

While production logic is often understood as a consequence of capitalism, status directs how it plays out—namely, the fact that early majority consumers seek products that won't upset established conventions. Status also explains why manufacturers tend to copy innovations with cachet rather than create new conventions from scratch. Many gloss the term "marketing" to mean selling what a company already makes, but marketers see their own work as understanding what the public wants and producing goods that match to consumer desires. Companies thus use media reports, market buzz, and consumer research to identify conventions on the rise. Where they discover acts of emulation, they see dollar signs. If fancy cupcakes are selling well for high profit margins, rational entrepreneurs would take advantage of latent demand to open a rival cupcake shop.

Some companies have enough cachet to start their own trends from scratch, but, on the whole, borrowed innovations are more desirable than homegrown ideas. The twist succeeded as a popular dance because it tapped into a grassroots fad within both Black and youth cultures. When the East German authorities attempted to create a dance called the lipsi, everyone ignored it. Companies thus look at innovators and early adopters as an R&D lab, sweeping in to imitate whatever appears to be gaining momentum. As *The Manual* explains, young musicians create new sounds on their own—like "young, waving fields of corn"—and then "a very strange combined harvester will come along and pick the few lucky ears of corn while the rest of the field cheer, wither and die."

The most daring cultural innovations tend to come from subcultures and artists, who use high symbolic complexity to keep intruders out. Overly exclusionary tastes, however, are bad for business. Everett Rogers concluded, "The complexity of an innovation, as perceived by members of a social system, is negatively related to its rate of adoption." In order to expand beyond the original groups, manufacturers must *simplify* the ideas. By creating a simplified version of a hot new style or trendy product, companies retain the sense of novelty while reducing the need for consumers to break established norms.

In many cases the mass media will have already presimplified the innovation. The performance artist Allan Kaprow first coined the term "happening" at the end of the 1950s to describe esoteric theatrical artworks that play out in a specific time and space. By the time the Supremes sang "The Happening" in 1967, the media had already commandeered the term to describe lesser events, such as chaotic parties, promotional gimmicks, and fashion shows in swimming pools. The first major hip-hop single to break into the mainstream, "Rapper's Delight," was not a product of the Black underground, but an intentional effort by an upstart record label, Sugar Hill Records, whose managers cobbled together a group of neighborhood kids and had them rap another artist's rhymes over the bass line from Chic's hit song "Good Times."

When innovations are retooled to cross the early adopter/early majority divide, they may retain only a passing resemblance to the original. But it is important that manufacturers sell it as the *same* entity. Electronic music began as an avant-garde techno-futurism but blossomed in the United States decades later as electronic dance music (EDM)—a Las Vegas megaclub-ready genre of spine-tingling sonic thrills and DJs who throw sheet cakes at the audience. Once these simplified innovations are established as moneymakers, even less reputable manufacturers appear to make cheaper and lower-quality versions. Synthetic rayon copies of Hollywood silk dresses appeared in the 1940s so more could dress like the stars. English elites loved the imported Dutch liquor genever at the turn of the eighteenth century; local distillers mass-manufactured a dirt-cheap rotgut version that came to be known as "gin." Today the enormous industry of fast fashion operates under the same principle: quickly bringing runway collection knockoffs to market as cheap and disposable garments.

Mass-market consumers may have some threshold for quality, but it is often lower than that of elites. There is a more critical ingredient for hits, then. As Derek Thompson concludes in his study *Hit Makers*, "Content might be king, but distribution is the kingdom." The number of audience-friendly songs that *could* be hits is nearly infinite, but only a few will achieve the broad distribution required for success. To help consumers choose among infinite options, manufacturers must position their candidates as valuable, legitimate, and easily available. This begins with *physical distribution*—getting the actual goods into stores or otherwise ready for purchase. Companies must win over distribution gatekeepers, who are even more conservative and risk-averse. As low-margin businesses with limited shelf space, grocery stores, movie theaters, and drugstores will stock only products with a potential for high sales. There is also the distribution of information—i.e., *publicity*. As we saw with mass media, potential adopters need to know something exists. The importance of publicity is borne out by the questionable efforts companies take to capture the distribution channels. Music industry players, for example, have a long history of engaging in payola to bribe radio DJs to play their songs. Billy Joel's manager, Artie Ripp, admitted, "I was the guy who would fill up a hotel floor and put chicks in every room for the disk jockeys."

Advertising is a key form of publicity, especially for winning over early adopters. Ads employ seductive imagery and language in an attempt to imbue goods with higher status value. This is not always subtle: in 1927 Kotex sanitary pads assured potential consumers that they had been adopted by "8 in 10 better-class women." When advertising to the early majority, companies must suggest that their products are in line with social norms—or create the suggestion of new norms. Hoping to nudge middle-class consumers to buy additional cars, the American auto industry ran campaigns in the 1950s proposing the idea of "two-car families." A 1956 Chevrolet ad ran with the tagline "Going Our Separate Ways We've Never Been So Close" next to a photo of a middle-class family snuggling over the barbecue with a pair of automobiles behind them. Soon these imaginary standards became real: by 1960, 21.53 percent of American families owned two or more cars; a decade later, the number was 34.83 percent.

Commercial markets are critical for the cultural ecosystem because most conventions play out in material goods for sale. So, if production logic shapes the nature of goods, companies change our tastes—and, by extension, the broader culture. Pierre Bourdieu concludes, "The universe of products offered by each field of production tends in fact to limit the universe of the forms of experience (aesthetic, ethical, political etc.) that are objectively possible at any given moment." But this isn't a one-way system: to be successful in the first place, companies must make goods that cater to the status needs of customers. Production logic simplifies innovations not just to reduce manufacturing costs but also to better match existing conventions. The overall effect of commercialization is conservative: removing radical ideas and providing mass audiences with simplified versions claimed to be equal to the original. And with all the signaling costs—prices, information costs, barriers to access, and difficult tastes—reduced to nearly nothing, a onetime innovation is ready to be "for everyone."

MASS CULTURE

Chocolate has found a home in Western civilization. What would our holidays be without heart-shaped boxes of Russell Stover bonbons, Cadbury Creme Eggs, fun-size Baby Ruths, and advent calendars? Chocolate is *mass culture*. Nearly everyone eats it. But just like with shortboards, purple garments, and cupcakes, chocolate first emerged as an elite custom. In pre-Columbian Mexico, drinking chocolate was an exclusive privilege of royals and the bravest Aztec warriors. European conquistadores learned the practice and brought it home, and soon their aristocratic employers indulged in the daily habit of drinking hot chocolate prepared in silver pots. By the mid-seventeenth century, chocolate was a clear "marker of opulence." A 1640 Spanish "Panegyric to Chocolate" exclaimed, "Lettered men are those who drink it; rich men are those who eat it; the ignorant and poor do not dare to allow these greatnesses to enter through their door; it is brought to kings in golden jícaras; princes consume it; noble courtiers also participate; it is denied to the wretched and commoners." As part of knighthood in eighteenth-century England, men received a pound of chocolate.

As cocoa production expanded in Africa and Asia, hot cocoa finally came within reach of the middle class—at least for anyone willing to pay four times the price of coffee. An even bigger expansion came with the development of solid milk chocolate, which allowed the delicacy to be mass-produced and packaged for wide distribution. With the establishment of the Nestlé, Cadbury, and Hershey empires in the nineteenth century, millions across the globe began to eat chocolate on a frequent basis. But it long remained a clear symbol for prosperity. In *Charlie and the Chocolate Factory*, the impoverished young protagonist, Charlie Bucket, who subsists on cabbage soup, drools over the "great slabs of chocolate piled up" in shop windows and laments the other children "taking creamy candy bars out of their pockets and munching them greedily." In the ruins of postwar Japan, most children's first experience of American largesse was the chocolate thrown from military Jeeps; their first English phrase learned was "Give me chocolate!"

How exactly does an elite convention like chocolate eventually become mass culture? Bestsellers such as Malcolm Gladwell's *The Tipping Point* and Jonah Berger's *Contagious* have suggested that cultural trends play out like "social contagions"—with ideas spreading from person to person in an exponential pattern until the entire population is "infected." This framing, however, tends to disregard human agency. *We* choose to adopt and abandon, and make these decisions based on status value. But there is a bigger issue with the viral metaphor: the measles remains the measles as it spreads through a population, but cultural innovations change significantly on their path to becoming mass culture. Chocolate could not become ubiquitous until it took the form of massmanufactured, easily packaged, and affordable solid milk chocolate. The simplification arising from the participation of mass media and mass production changes the nature of all conventions over time.

These changes are necessary for any costly or symbolically difficult convention to win over less affluent and more conservative early majorities. For widespread diffusion, signaling costs need to be very low—especially social risks. So far we've seen how this happens over time: the mass media reduces information costs, mass manufacturers lower prices and expand access, and the initial adoption by high-status people suggests adoption won't break social norms.

Publicity and physical distribution also help achieve the *repetition* required to build common knowledge. Repeated observations are powerful for inducing new behaviors—what psychologists call the *mere exposure effect*. An enormous body of research has shown that repeated exposure makes us like things more. This analysis, however, often misses an important factor. Exposure works best for *legitimized* innovations. Despite a widespread and striking purple-colored ad blitz for the religious group Falun Gong's Shen Yun dance performances, the show has made no significant impact on American culture. Top 40 radio, by contrast, can tap the mere exposure effect because listeners already trust Top 40 radio as a musical authority.

After a significant number of people in a population embrace a new convention, it takes on its own gravity—pulling along further adopters like a planet attracts smaller objects. At this point in the diffusion process, the primary motivation for adoption flips from distinction for high status to imitation for normal status. People adopt because others adopt—i.e., the *bandwagon effect*. Widespread adoption, however, depletes any lingering cachet. Mass-culture conventions signal normal status and nothing more. But the shedding of distinctiveness brings new advantages. All popular trends have a guarantee of low risk thanks to *social proof*. Fifty million Elvis fans can't be wrong. Social proof even provides a guarantee for the future. Sociologist George Homans explains, "If [the imitator] conforms and the group is wrong, he does not lose anything: he has only been a boob with the rest, who are in no condition to turn on him."

Mass culture also gains new strength through *network effects*. The more people participate in a convention, the more useful it will be for interacting and communicating with others. Watching caber toss tournaments may afford individual distinction, but the previous night's Patriots game works better for office small talk. Mass culture offers the gratification of solidarity—as Baudelaire mused, "The pleasure of being in a crowd is a mysterious expression of delight in the multiplication of number." There was a special power in 72,000 people singing Queen songs in unison at Wembley Stadium during the 1985 Live Aid concert. And importantly, once an entire community takes up a convention, it transforms into a powerful symbol of the group's identity.

When innovations attain normalization, they reach *critical mass*, which Everett Rogers describes as "the point at which enough individuals in a system have adopted an innovation so that the innovation's further rate of adoption becomes self-sustaining." This means not only that a onetime innovation is the new standard, but also that the previous convention will be devalued and delegitimized. At this point imitation is required to maintain normal status. Critical mass brings in the very conservative late majority. When the Egyptian antiquities of King Tutankhamen traveled across the United States in the late 1970s, there may have been cachet in early attendance. But after a while, as attested by the sociologist Orrin Klapp, "*Not* having seen Tut, one had to admit one was 'out of it,' not up with what was going on." With the role of the most conservative majorities at the critical mass stage, Gladwell's tipping point appears to be a status threshold.

Is critical mass a requirement to be mass culture? There is no exact measure for "mass culture" based on a certain percentage of adopters in the population. In 1960 around 20 percent of all Americans watched the top TV show, *Gunsmoke*, whereas in 2020, only 3.8 percent of Americans watched the number one TV show, *NCIS*. Rather than raw numbers or proportions, conventions need to achieve near universal common recognition, even among nonadopters. Not everyone watches *NCIS*, but the majority are aware that it's an extremely popular program. Also, these conventions must be so well established that nonadoption would risk normal status. We know chocolate is mass culture because it's become a social norm to consume it.

Much of mass culture involves *partial adoption*, where majorities take up only a portion of the original innovation. Stephen Hawking's *A Brief History of Time* sold enough copies to be a hit without difficult physics concepts like "color confinement" and "eternal inflation hypothesis" ever becoming common knowledge. In the cases where majority adopters decide to directly engage with elitist conventions, especially artworks, they are often dissatisfied. On the book review site Goodreads, scores tend to go down over time for prize-winning books, as the bandwagon effect brings in readers who may have less patience for literary complexity.

Once an innovation becomes dominant in society, Rogers's final group, laggards, also adopt—but they do so passively. At some point in the early twentieth century, chocolate became so ubiquitous that it was impossible to avoid eating it. This kind of passive consumption is critical for mega-hits. The cultural critic Chuck Klosterman writes, "You don't create a phenomenon like *E.T.* by appealing to people who love movies. You create a phenomenon like *E.T.* by appealing to people who see one movie a year."

Late adopters often are unaware of their own conventions' origin stories. Many tourists eating cupcakes may have found Magnolia Bakery in a guidebook without ever seeing an episode of *Sex and the City*. In the 1960s, surfer Phil Edwards special-ordered pairs of quick-dry Hawaiian nylon swim trunks. This spurred imitation among early adopter surfers who wanted to look like their hero. Mass manufacturers then produced millions of these nylon trunks and distributed them far beyond surf communities. "Pretty soon every kid in Utica, N.Y.," writes Tom Wolfe, was "buying a pair of them, with the competition stripe and the whole thing, and they have never heard of Phil Edwards." In this trickle-down, everyone ultimately imitated Edwards, but only the high-status imitators knew they were doing so.

Laggards tend to have very low status. (Even the designation "laggard" is pejorative.) As individuals they are always out of sync with culture, which suggests a lack of social capital, a meager media diet, and, in some cases, a disregard for basic social norms. Therefore, any convention associated with this group has a negative status value. We have seen how elites abandon their conventions after early adopters join in, but an embrace by undesirable lower-status groups creates a full-on panic. Negative cachet is particularly unappealing to early adopters, who care about distinctiveness and are afraid of being lumped in with non-elite groups. When British working-class youth incorporated luxury-brand Burberry beige check into their outfits in the 1990s, the middle class grew weary. Justine Picardie, the editor in chief of *Harper's Bazaar* in the United Kingdom, noted at the time, "Burberry had become so associated with a downmarket image . . . that incredible legacy had become associated with the cheapest form of disposable rip-off fashion."

The embrace of laggards kills trends dead, and this marks the end of the diffusion process. Looking back at what was required for innovations to spread, we don't see an exponential "viral" expansion but a sequence of five social phenomena:

1. High-status adoption of a new convention—for distinction
2. Early adopters' embrace of that convention—as emulation of their status superiors
3. Early majority reinvention and simplification—to follow an emerging social norm
4. Late majority imitation—to avoid losing normal status
5. Laggards' passive adoption—without intention.

While most conventions rely on cachet as a fuel to reach escape velocity in the diffusion process, not all elite behaviors influence mass culture, and not all mass culture starts as elite conventions. New products targeting conservative majorities start the diffusion process in the middle of the status ladder without marketing to elites. And for every hit, there are thousands of failures that get stuck somewhere along the diffusion curve. Even trends with the right ingredients and industrial support still must beat out rivals. Just as hip-hop was taking hold in New York, an alternative Black musical genre, go-go, was becoming popular in Washington, D.C. Despite backing from the record label behind Bob Marley, go-go never went very far.

Most important, trends are always more than a critical mass of adopters. We *interpret* the outcomes of diffusion based on status logic. A high-status convention that never diffuses to other groups—usually due to prohibitively high signaling costs—is viewed as a desirable luxury. Artists take pride in their "voluntary unpopularity" when refusing to compromise with mass tastes. High-status conventions that appeal only to early adopters remain part of elitist culture, often resented by majorities toward the bottom of the socioeconomic ladder. In 1984 fashion designer Jean Paul Gaultier introduced "pants-skirts" for men; they never trickled down to Target, but were pants-skirts a failure if they still resonate today with fashion-forward men? At the same time, conventions that start among low-status audiences and stay there—the long-running and popular TV show *Hee Haw*, for example—achieve the scale of mass culture, but are often ignored within the public dialogue.

All taken together, the fashion cycle from elite distinction to laggard passive adoption demonstrates exactly how individuals' pursuit of status on a micro level leads to cultural change on a macro level. And as long as non-elites are able to imitate elite conventions, status seeking will *always* change culture.

PERPETUAL MOTION

Forget trickle-down, says anthropologist Grant McCracken. Fashion is a never-ending process of "chase and flight." Low-status individuals *chase* high-status individuals by imitating their conventions, which forces elites to *flee* to new ones. Since this fleeing will lead to another round of chasing and then fleeing, fashion creates perpetual cultural change, with status serving as the motor.

Fashion, then, is akin to a never-ending footrace. Runners on the cultural track all run in the same direction—toward elites. Like a race, there are no sudden moves backward, or zigzags. But unlike a racetrack, fashion has no finish line or ultimate destination. We can always give up, but to compete requires continual running. This is why fashion is so often cast as the opposite—or even the enemy—of progress. Thorstein Veblen notes, "After all the ingenuity and effort which have been spent on dress these many years, the fashions should have achieved a relative perfection and a relative stability, closely approximating to a permanently tenable artistic ideal." They haven't, and they won't, because the existence of fashion cycles is tied to the need to mark difference.

On the cultural racetrack, lower-status groups *never* catch up to their superiors through conventions alone. As soon as masses draw near, elites flee and deploy new means of creating social distance. This is the nefarious side of fashion: a race implies a competition, where winning tastes could potentially bring a meritocratic victory. There can be occasional dark-horse upsets, but lower-status groups will never win the fashion race as a collective. Fashion, writes Jean Baudrillard, "restores cultural inequality and social discrimination, establishing it under the pretense of abolishing it." The constant movement of cultural change masks profound "social inertia." In medieval societies with ascribed status, the static power structure made no false promises about social mobility. In dynamic capitalist societies, fashion sells itself as a potential means for status improvement when, in fact, it works to just legitimize the current structure.

The term "flight" suggests resentment at being imitated and, certainly, elites would save money, time, and energy if they could more easily keep their conventions exclusive. But they establish their superiority through repeatedly demonstrating that their embrace of uncertain innovations turned out to be "correct." In her research on British dance music, the anthropologist Sarah Thornton found that "nothing proves the originality and inventiveness of subcultural music and style more than its eventual 'mainstreaming.'" For all the elite complaints about fashion, it justifies their exalted position.

Does this mean emulation is a futile and irrational gesture for nonelites? Humans spend a significant portion of their incomes each year chasing cachet without making real status gains. And conventions change so much that many will have to adopt new practices just to continue receiving normal status. The more rational means of improving status would be to reinvest money and time into building more stable forms of capital. The acquisition of status symbols may fool others in the short term, but constant consumption resembles a form of addiction: we believe luxury goods are a cure for our status desires, only to realize we must buy ever more.

Whether or not fashion is regrettable, it's an inevitable by-product of status structures in liberal societies, where high-status conventions are, as Baudrillard explains, in "psychological circulation." When Nero can seize the property of anyone who dares wear Tyrian purple, elite conventions remain only with elites. Democratic ideals have done away with the idea that certain goods are off-limits for the public, and capitalism promises us there is nothing money can't buy. Large-scale manufacturers, in reproducing and distributing onetime luxury products, make emulation as simple as visiting a retail store or clicking Buy Now. Meanwhile, the modern mindset seeks to devalue traditions, thereby encouraging us to replace every customary behavior with a fashionable alternative. Every garden can be torn up and planted anew.

Despite these clear structural origins of fashion cycles, many blame them on capitalist conspiracies, in which malicious companies engage in a planned obsolescence of taste to make us keep buying things. Even Coco Chanel declared, "Fashion is made to be unfashionable." Yet the fashion industry is not necessary for fashion cycles. Isolated tribes change their hairstyles over the years without subscriptions to *GQ*. The sociologist Stanley Lieberson found clear fashion patterns in the popularity of first names—choices that require no money, with no commercial entities attempting to influence parents' choices. His broader conclusion was "Even though there are organizations with an economic interest in getting us to change—designers, manufacturers, retailers, and advertisers—it is a big mistake to assume that these entities are responsible for the *existence* of fashion."

Mass media and mass manufacturers, however, do speed up fashion cycles by ensuring we become aware of trends beyond what we can directly observe and by removing the obstacles to participation. This quickly turns little-known conventions into broad social norms. Companies are able to make this happen because they understand the fundamental human desire for status markers.

Marxists complain that capitalism creates "false needs," as capitalists chase "exchange value" over earnest "use value." The flaw in this analysis is that a primary use for goods is marking social distinction.

These inherent problems in perpetual fashion cycles have spurred many modern thinkers to find a remedy in goods designed according to universal principles of functionality. Form should follow function, not fashion. But this didn't work as a solution, either. Functionalism itself became a fashion trend, often resulting in artifacts as arbitrary as what preceded them. The flat roofs of modernist buildings can suffer bad leaks and, in winter, collect perilous amounts of snow. Likewise, we hope to identify "permanent style" in garments, but these standards, too, ebb and flow in the cultural drift. As much as we seek optimally efficient lives, status value will always make some conventions more attractive than others. And as long as elites don't want to share their conventions, we can expect fashion cycles to persist.

There are a few upsides to fashion, however. Status seeking often speeds up the adoption of useful technologies, whether electric cars or smartphones. The fashion process has also democratized culture over time. When companies sell kitsch versions of art and elite goods as the same entity, mass audiences come to believe their adoption makes them equally sophisticated. This creates a widespread confidence in the aesthetic value of kitsch. For Alexis de Tocqueville this power of mass culture was an obvious consequence of democracy: "As citizens become more equal and more alike the tendency of each to blindly believe in a given man or class diminishes. *The disposition to believe the masses increases* and public opinion guides society more and more." When asked to respond to elitist criticism of her schmaltzy music, Celine Dion proudly proclaimed, "[Our concerts have] been sold out for four years. *The audience is my answer.*" This solidarity has even shamed critics into a more serious consideration of mass culture as art, and this capitulation further bolstered pride among the majorities.

From the perspective of the cultural ecosystem, kitsch can be very important. The French information scientist Abraham Moles points out, "In a bourgeois society, and generally in a meritocratic one, the passage through kitsch is the normal passage in order to reach the genuine." And while most mass culture is stripped of its more ideological complexities, Umberto Eco argues, one can still "find elements of revolution and contestation in works that lend themselves to facile consumption." The blockbuster superhero movie *Black Panther* was, in the eyes of the BBC, "revolutionary" for its triumphant "representation of Black people in cinema." Perhaps more counterintuitively, the worst parts of mass culture are important for motivating invention. Overexposed and cliché conventions justify the stylistic rebellions that eventually lead to cultural refresh.

What we shouldn't do, however, is to look at mass culture and declare it a perfect expression of the *vox populi*. The culture industry certainly promotes the idea of a meritocratic market: good things rise, bad ones fall. But so many consumers adopt based on status value rather than any intrinsic qualities. Majorities seem to be *satisficing* when it comes to their consumer choices—settling on things they find satisfactory but not ideal. And if individuals are consuming simply because others are consuming, this so-called cumulative advantage enables random things of suspect quality to rise as smash hits. Mass culture may only be a "mirror" of consumer sentiment in that it illustrates the principle that most people prefer to consume the same things as others.

That being said, these social pressures can often work in the direction of complexity. For decades pundits pilloried the American taste for beers based on the ubiquity of bland pilsners. There was no room to explore deep aromatic hop in a Bud Light nation. But in the 2000s indie breweries created a robust market for bitter, flavorful IPAs, and these flavors have trickled down to the mainstream. Once it secured distribution from mega-corporation Constellation Brands, the onetime "elite" beer Ballast Point's Sculpin IPA became available in supermarket chains across the United States. What does this say about the underlying tastes of American beer drinkers if their palettes ultimately follow status value? Fashion reveals that tastes will always be very flexible, because conventions are arbitrary, and status can easily make them change.

⊷⊛⊷

Fashion cycles appear to be a waste of time and energy, moving the population from one arbitrary practice to another for no reason other than elitist distinction and social conformity. Emulation is a delusional lunge at status improvement that only bolsters the existing social hierarchy. Meanwhile, the diffusion process strips genius inventions of their complexity for mass production as kitsch.

All these criticisms aside, fashion, powered by status, has been a reliable engine for change. After centuries of numerous speedy fads and fashion cycles, humans have invented and enjoyed a monumental variety of material objects, styles, and new behaviors—many of which we still enjoy today. This includes much great art, but also interesting and skillful examples of kitsch. As individuals we have then been able to deploy this infinite variety of conventions in crafting unique personas. Artists can draw from this ever-expanding cornucopia of symbols to offer new ideas. And the ever-growing diversity also leads to greater tolerance toward difference itself.

Fashion reveals how status best explains the most conspicuous cultural changes of the last century. But movement isn't the only effect of status. It also creates pockets of stasis by allowing certain conventions to lodge within a society.

Chapter Nine

HISTORY AND CONTINUITY

⊰✕⊱

Button-down collars never went away, while fifties doo-wop died and
returned from the grave.

⊰✕⊱

HISTORICAL VALUE

During the 1950s, Virginia Packard of New Canaan, Connecticut, enjoyed steady
commissions from the town's wealthy families to paint portraits of their children. Parents tended to be the final arbiters of the work, but once, when painting a seventeen-year-old boarding school student, Packard suffered a harsh
rebuke from the subject himself. Upon seeing his likeness on canvas, standing
in a white dress shirt with no necktie, the boy became visibly aggravated. After
some back and forth, he finally divulged the source of his apprehension: there
were no buttons on his shirt collar. New England prep schoolers of the era all
wore oxford-cloth dress shirts with button-down collars, and he was mortified
that this townie artist was moments away from sealing an unspeakable sarto-
rial faux pas into his permanent portrait.

In the ensuing seven decades, teens may have lost their passion for shirt
ornamentation, but to understand this anecdote from bygone days, we don't
need to research the history of button-down collars, as we would for powdered
wigs, breeches, and dickies. Men and women still wear these shirts in the
twenty-first century. In fact, the button-down collar shirt, as *GQ* wrote in 2013,
"is one of those all-important pieces that remains a cornerstone of American
style . . . right up there with the navy blazer, blue jeans, and penny loafers."

Button-down collars aren't even a mark of "1950s style"—they're a *classic* that transcends a specific time period. The button-down collar can be found everywhere, from high-end fashion boutiques to the dorm room floors of frat guys and closets of their schlubby suburban fathers.

The previous chapter laid out how status seeking can move new conventions through a population. At any particular moment, however, culture is more than an accumulation of the latest fashions: it's a complex sediment of new and old, dynamic and static, superficial and deep, unconscious and conscious. While jumping on the bandwagon for the latest fads, we speak the language of our forebears, live and work in centuries-old buildings, and quote the wisdom of long-buried sages. We don't, however, respect all of these conventions equally. Customs and traditions possess more gravitas than fashions and fads. Button-down-collar oxford shirts have been reliable signals longer than Hard Rock Cafe T-shirts. Even in a hyperglobalized world where we can freely choose our lifestyles, we remain fond of culture associated with our heritage. However popular French bread is across East Asia, rice remains the main dietary staple.

If conventions gain eminence in survival, time must work to bolster cultural value. This principle becomes clearer once we recognize that most classic styles, such as the button-down collar shirt, first emerged in standard fashion cycles. The famed New York menswear store Brooks Brothers sold button-down shirts in the 1890s in imitation of English polo players, who sewed buttons on their soft collars to prevent the fabric from flailing around during matches. The look caught on with elite American university students, but buttons on collars eventually fizzled; *Men's Wear* noted in 1928 they were "almost entirely out of the picture." In the post–World War II return to collegiate life, however, the button-down collar popped back up. From there the convention experienced more ups and downs: a bust during the peacock days of the late 1960s, and another boom during the early 1980s preppy moment. When American traditional style became a global trend in the aughts, the button-down collar emerged as its cornerstone item. By the late 2010s, Shanghai overflowed with aspiring young capitalists wearing stiff oxford-cloth button-down collar shirts from designer Thom Browne.

The button-down's moments of popularity can be explained as fashion trends: consumers chasing the cachet of various elites, from British polo players to American Old Money to globally feted New York fashion designers. But the garment's entrenchment within American culture relies on an additional attribute: *historical value*. Similar to how status value derives from its symbolic associations with high-status individuals and groups, historical value is derived from positive symbolic associations with the past. Not everything old has historical value. Anthropologist Michael Thompson notes a difference between "transient" goods that never take on historical value and "durable" goods that do. In this chapter we'll investigate the sources of historical value and see how it makes certain conventions endure beyond their initial fashion cycle. More important, we'll learn that historical value isn't independent from status value: status guides how communities construct their histories and determine what is remembered and celebrated.

To better understand historical value, we first acknowledge that the "past," as the historian Eric Hobsbawm explains, is "a particular selection from the infinity of what is remembered or capable of being remembered." This means history, in its broadest sense, is a "formalized social past" that can never be an exact mirror of previous experiences. History is constructed, and the authority to construct is not equally distributed. Our collective memories are shallow, and we rely on a particular set of high-status historians, archivists, journalists, politicians, and religious leaders to lay out the most important moments of the past by means of compelling narratives. History is, thus, not the stories we tell about ourselves, but a connection of moments that specific well-positioned, high-status individuals choose to highlight and perpetuate.

History plays a major role in all civilizations, especially traditional societies. "For the greater part of history," writes Hobsbawm, "we deal with societies and communities for which the past is essentially the pattern for the present." The devout Hasidim or Amish still live lifestyles moored to centuries-old traditions. Individuals in cosmopolitan societies, by contrast, pick and choose from the past, replacing biased and harmful customs with ostensibly more practical alternatives.

But even for the most rational reformers, history serves as a useful storehouse of wisdom. The "good old days" can be observed like a human laboratory to test the plausibility of social proposals. When planning out the constitutional system, America's Founding Fathers studied failure points in Greek

democracy and the Roman republic. Of course, the appeal of history goes beyond pure function—former times offer magic and mythos. In 2020, a year
when thousands of clothing brands enticed consumers with inventive garments in shocking colors and surprising designs, a perfect replica of Princess
Diana's infamous "sheep sweater" from the early 1980s sold out in twenty-four
hours.

What is the appeal of historical value? First, there is a survivorship bias:
anything that remains with us today is assumed to have greater intrinsic value.
Humans are more likely to preserve high-quality luxury goods than cheap
kitsch. This certainly applies to artworks. Philosopher David Hume muses, "A
real genius, the longer his works endure, and the more wide they are spread,
the more sincere is the admiration which he meets with." This explains why
"the same Homer, who pleased at Athens and Rome two thousand years ago,
is still admired at Paris and at London." We also extend this principle to everyday behaviors. An arbitrary practice must be worth continuing if generation
after generation has decided to choose it over alternatives.

As we saw with Old Money in chapter 5, endurance is a powerful signaling
cost. A lottery winner can buy an old Rolls-Royce but can't immediately acquire
the prestige of *having long owned one*. And since Old Money's preference for
patina can provide cachet, older items also gain status value through historical
associations, real and imagined. A Louis XIV writing desk is valuable for its
royal associations—and is deemed even more valuable if purchased from the
Rockefellers' estate. Historical value also suggests authenticity: a closer connection to the artifact's origin. Contemporary recordings of baroque music
performed on period instruments in archaic 415 Hz tunings tend to be more
popular than arrangements in modern 440 Hz.

But historical value is more than just a matter of patina, Old Money cachet,
and rarity. Conventions with historical value are more likely to be repeated,
which assists in creating widespread common knowledge. Historical value is a
hedge against social risk: long-standing conventions are more well-known, ad-
hered to, and likely to be followed in the future. Rational humans, especially
conservative ones toward the middle of the status hierarchy, will choose older
forms over newer ones when signaling, and this keeps older conventions in
circulation.

Conventions with historical value become "durable" in different ways—specifically, customs, traditions, classics, and canonized works.

Customs and habits are internalized within a community's unconscious behavior. From everything we know about status, we see how elite conventions are more likely to become mass culture, and this primes them to become customary. When we drink hot cocoa, we keep alive the preferences and practices of Aztecs and French kings. Traditions are conscious acts of solidarity that let us spiritually commune with our ancestors. Conservative communities draw upon tradition to guide their decision making. Cosmopolitans dabble in tradition through intermittent participation: a few minutes of daily prayer, weekly attendance at services, celebration of yearly holidays. Or they can incorporate traditional elements into lifestyle choices: fashionable shirts in colorful African patterns, Star of David medallions on gold chains, Friday nights at Irish step-dancing class.

High-status individuals and groups may have an implicit influence on our habits and customs, but they wield explicit influence on traditions. The rituals at the heart of traditions are formalized and based on strict rules. We rely on community leaders to teach, preserve, and enforce the "proper" practices. Where groups lack traditions, leaders often create or revive them. Eric Hobsbawm and Terence Ranger coined the term "invented tradition" to explain the common practice of using history "as a legitimator of action and cement of group cohesion." Today each Scottish clan has a tartan, a practice that originated in the late eighteenth century when commercial weavers named each of their different patterns after a Highland clan or town; descendants of those clans then began to use them as unique markers of ancestry and identity despite no historical relationship. Companies use similar techniques to create consumer trends. In the 1970s, Kentucky Fried Chicken ran an advertising campaign in Japan making the dubious claim that Americans ate fried chicken on Christmas Day. Since that time, eating a Christmas bucket of KFC has become a Japanese holiday tradition.

Innovators can always lend legitimacy to their radical acts through past precedence. For all their literary innovations, twentieth-century authors often pulled their book titles from the Bible—*East of Eden* (Genesis 4:16), *The Sun Also Rises* (Ecclesiastes 1:5), and *Absalom, Absalom!* (2 Samuel 19:4)—or from

Shakespeare—*Pale Fire* (*Timons of Athens*), *Brave New World* (*The Tempest*), and *Infinite Jest* (*Hamlet*). The dada art movement named their performance event Cabaret Voltaire after the French philosopher Voltaire, and then in the 1970s, a group of post-punk musicians used Cabaret Voltaire as their band name.

Meanwhile, *classics* are "timeless" choices with historical associations stronger than contemporary associations. The little black dress, the Chuck Taylor sneaker, and blue jeans have achieved a "permanent value"—"you can't go wrong"—despite the fact that many people with lower status have adopted these same items. Button-down shirts endure because memories of Miles Davis and JFK wearing them override the negative status value of modern-day suburbanites in identical garments. Most classic clothing comes to us from hobbies of the affluent: boater hats, deerstalker caps, Norfolk jackets, and rugby shirts all link to sporting traditions of the wealthy. (The opposite is also true: the American football jersey and nylon boxing shorts are *not* part of a "classic" wardrobe.) Older functional goods used by the rich (e.g., a waxed cotton rain jacket in faded olive) are "classier" than practical innovations (e.g., Gore-Tex in bright red). Historical value enables classics to always be in good taste and rise above fashion, making them logical choices for risk-averse, middle-status individuals.

All of these durable artifacts, artworks, and styles constitute a *cultural canon* from the past that remains valuable in the present thanks to historical importance and long-term perceptions of high quality. The term "canon" was first used in literature to describe books that critics and academics recommended for use in instruction. A canon is necessary, scholars believed, because future generations can never consume all works from the past. Of the tens of thousands of novels written in the nineteenth century, we only still read about two hundred. The canon thus promises guidance toward the highest-quality and most influential works. *Rolling Stone*'s "500 Greatest Albums of All Time" and *Pitchfork Media*'s Pitchfork 500 perform this role for pop music. In fact, canon building could be considered the primary role of criticism. Film critic A. O. Scott writes, "Criticism has, since roughly the day after the beginning of time, consecrated itself to the veneration and preservation of masterpieces and traditions."

To create a canon, academics and critics curate explicit lists or keep certain works in circulation through repeated mention and reference. Art surveys maintain the canon by selecting certain artists and works to tell the narrative of art. Fauvism is far from a living and breathing artistic movement, but its importance in the story of modern art results in the continued enjoyment, study, and endorsement of Henri Matisse's paintings. Placement in the canon assures enough repetition and common knowledge to compete against newer alternatives—and makes them seem more important. Literary critic Barbara H. Smith writes that the inclusion of a poem in anthologies "not only promotes but goes some distance toward creating the value of that work, as does its repeated appearance on reading lists or its frequent citation or quotation by professors, scholars, critics, poets, and other elders of the tribe." David Hume could gush about Homer because academics and historians kept *The Iliad* and *The Odyssey* central in their teaching over the generations.

Canons are not decided in democratic forums. The builders, writes literary critic Harold Bloom, are "dominant social groups, institutions of education, traditions of criticism." How do they choose what qualifies? Artworks must possess artistic value, serving as a link in the unbroken chain of narrative events. Aesthetic value—a mastery of form—is also critical. The best candidates, in Bloom's view, possess "a mode of originality that either cannot be assimilated, or that so assimilates us that we cease to see it as strange." In both cases artworks must transcend the basic conventions of their era, so that future audiences will still be able to take unique value from the work. Shakespeare is the canonical example of a canonical writer: one who, to Bloom, "will not allow you to bury him, or escape him, or replace him." The canon may also contain a few *relics*—works that may not appeal to contemporary audiences on an aesthetic level yet mark an important moment in the historical narrative. Upton Sinclair's *The Jungle*, despite its melodramatic plot, strange pacing, and propagandistic prose, is still read and discussed, because the novel's role in influencing Congress to pass the Pure Food and Drug Act illustrates how art can directly affect politics.

Popularity can keep works in the collective dialogue, but critical appraisal is more important for long-term survival. This moves the canon toward elite tastes and away from kitsch. Chuck Klosterman writes, "We don't reinvestigate low culture with the expectation that it will entertain us a second time." Romance novelist Danielle Steel has sold enough paperbacks of her 190 books to heat a large city through winter, but unlike the major canonized works of our era, many of her titles lack Wikipedia pages.

Over time, the canon so directs our focus toward certain artworks of previous eras that it is easy to forget that alternatives ever existed. Documentary filmmaker Emile de Antonio complained, "Go back as far as the time before Giotto, the time of Cimabue, there were hundreds and hundreds of Italian painters around, but today most of us only recognize the names of a handful. People who care about painting may be able to name five, and scholars may know as many as fifteen, but the rest are all painters whose paintings are as dead as they are." For whatever memories do endure of an era, they will be subject to a competitive whittling as time goes on. Klosterman notes we can remember only a single composer of nineteenth-century marches, which is bad news for everyone other than John Philip Sousa.

While canon builders believe they are working toward a "higher individual, social, or transcendent good," they can be biased toward works matching their own high-status taste world. Styles overassociated with lower-middle-class majority consumers, no matter how important, rarely become classics. Double-knit polyester leisure suits dominated the lived experience of the 1970s but today live on only as a famed fashion misstep. The Canadian progressive rock band Rush achieved great fame in that era but lost its place in the pop music canon, especially when compared with punk contemporaries such as the Ramones. The journalist and rock historian David Weigel explains, "The fans showing up to hear Rush were the wrong kind of fans—the mockable ones, with mockable taste in music." Taste matters in canon building because critics and editors form their reputations when choosing works. They don't want to be on the record for embracing things with anticachet.

But there is always hope for the forgotten. The canon shifts each year to accommodate the latest changes in contemporary culture. When the Beatles best set the paradigm for pop music, *Rolling Stone* named their landmark 1967 album *Sgt. Pepper's Lonely Hearts Club Band* as the greatest of all time. But in 2020 *Rolling Stone* revised its Top 500 Albums list to better recognize the musical contributions of artists beyond the white male rock oeuvre. The new list dropped *Sgt. Pepper* to number 24 and put Marvin Gaye's seminal soul record *What's Going On*—arguably a more influential work on the direction of contemporary music—in the top spot.

In the last few decades there has been a vigorous debate about the ethics of the canon—in particular, whether it overrepresents dead white men. Previous biases in high culture against women and nonwhite artists not only stunted their careers at the time but dampened later critical interest in their work. The debate is far from pedantic: canonical works embody the values of a society, identifying certain conventions as permanently valuable while letting others wither away. Canons act as a "horizon" for all subsequent artistic judgment. We measure everything new—and old—against the touchstone of the canon. We end up in a situation, as Chuck Klosterman lays out, where "Shakespeare is better than Marlowe and Jonson because Shakespeare is more like Shakespeare, which is how we delineate greatness within playwriting." Until recently the sixties set the pop culture horizon. Our reverence for the particular works of those years lives on in classic rock radio stations, nostalgic TV shows, and endless news documentaries on the era's traumas and triumphs. By adding past-excluded artists—women composers, Black avant-garde artists, Native American novelists—into the canon, we can't right past wrongs, but we can change the contemporary standards for judgment and reassure contemporary creators from disadvantaged groups that their work will be properly valued.

The origins of customs, traditions, classics, and the canon demonstrate anthropologist Michael Thompson's idea that "lastingness is imposed not by intrinsic physical properties but by the social system." And in our social system, high-status groups have considerably more influence on history than low-status groups. This results in conventions of high-status taste being more durable than conventions of low-status origin. Those with status decide what is history, and what takes on historical value gets a status value boost, which then in turn justifies the high status of the elite groups. "Our experiences of the present," writes the anthropologist Paul Connerton, "largely depend upon our knowledge of the past, and . . . our images of the past commonly serve to legitimate a present social order."

For many, including Karl Marx, "the tradition of all dead generations weighs like a nightmare on the brain of the living." Modern thinkers have proposed many escapes from the bonds of the past, attempting to replace all customs and traditions with fairer, more rational behaviors. Dada and futurism demanded total liberation from the canon. Pop—"the exhortation to 'be here now'"—places the most valuable currency in the current.

But history stays alive, because even the fiercer modernists need it as a cautionary tale. Antitraditionalism can promise an auspicious future only by pointing to the vile past. Rationality is more persuasive when we can cite silly or harmful customs. Moreover, deep historical knowledge is necessary to demonstrate the fundamental conventionality of human behavior, as illustrated in the novelist L. P. Hartley's famed quotation "The past is a foreign country; they do things differently there."

For the most part, the modernists have succeeded, and today we live relatively rationalized lives. But historical value lives on, because it serves as a stable anchor in a turbulent globalized marketplace. As more and more new products are offered, many consumers will seek refuge in customs, traditions, classics, and canon. We prefer the durable treasures of the past over transient garbage. Hootie and the Blowfish sold 21 million copies of their album *Cracked Rear View*, but lacking cachet and critical support, they've faded from our collective musical history. At the same time, there appears to be ever greater potential for a "people's history," where popular demand keeps certain kitsch in circulation despite critical disfavor. The English band Queen never impressed music snobs, but "We Will Rock You" and "We Are the Champions" took on a second life as the soundtrack to athletic matches. And recently the band's biopic, *Bohemian Rhapsody*, a film with mixed reviews, carved out its own legacy through another wave of staggering popularity. Without high-status support, however, popular artworks and behaviors typically go down with their fans. In 1925 Americans consumed Gene Stratton-Porter's novel *The Keeper of the Bees* in much greater numbers than F. Scott Fitzgerald's *The Great Gatsby*; today on Goodreads, *Gatsby* has 1703 times more ratings.

And yet not all transient culture is lost forever. Modernity opens up another path for forgotten kitsch to rise from obsolescence into near canonical importance: the retro revival.

RETRO

The spring 1968 battles between protesters and police turned Columbia University into a war zone. Students awoke to the "morning sounds of glass being chipped from last night's broken windows onto the sidewalk, the tinkling mixing with the drone of a bullhorn echoing off Low Library's steps." At the end of April, police violently extracted hundreds of student protesters occupying administration buildings. The university canceled the last month of classes; graduation ceremonies became another tense moment with law enforcement on campus and students walking out in protest. Everyone was bitter: progressive students were disheartened, while conservatives and athletes blamed the longhairs for ruining their semester.

The bloody conclusion of the Columbia protests foreshadowed the violent turn of the hippie movement in 1969, as evidenced by Altamont and the Manson murders. But the Columbia debacle also gave birth to a key aesthetic sensibility that would define the next decade. During the unrest, the graduate student and singer George Leonard realized he could help unify the divided student body through a revival of past musical styles. In an era of earnest folk rock, he persuaded his student a cappella group, the Columbia Kingsmen, to hold a performance of the most outmoded artistic genre possible: bright-eyed vocal pop songs of the 1950s. This was an era before oldies radio; everyone remembered the fifties, writes Leonard, as "the Bomb-fearing, Commie-hunting, money grubbing era they were." Inspired by camp aesthetics, Andy Warhol's pop art, and the S. E. Hinton young adult novel *The Outsiders*, Leonard organized a musical revue called *The Glory That Was Grease* ("grease" being the oily hair products used to slick back duck's-ass pompadours). Flyers for the event read "Jocks! Freaks! ROTC! SDS! Let there be a truce! Bury the hatchet (not in each other)! Remember when we were all little greaseballs together watching the eighth-grade girls for pick-ups?" Students across New York gathered at Columbia to hear the Kingsmen's doo-wop, a success that encouraged Leonard to found a 1950s-inspired vocal group called Sha Na Na to take the glory nationwide.

Jimi Hendrix was an early fan, and Sha Na Na ended up as his opening act at Woodstock. The documentary film of the festival spread the group's gold-satin performance of the 1957 hit "At the Hop" to audiences across the world. Leonard and his brother ended up not just instigating a doo-wop revival but may have even invented what we know as "the fifties." In 1972, a like-minded musical called *Grease* made its Broadway debut, and *Life* magazine dedicated its June 16 issue to the newfound interest in that "happier" decade. A year later George Lucas evoked similar feelings of teenage nostalgia into box-office success with his film *American Graffiti*, which in turn inspired the long-running TV show *Happy Days*. In England this fifties boom materialized as a teddy boy revival. A Japanese visitor to London took ted style back to Tokyo and ushered in a fifties Americana craze there as well. And with the hit film adaptation of *Grease* starring John Travolta and Olivia Newton-John in 1978 (as well as Sha Na Na's syndicated variety show), much of the seventies ended up being about the fifties.

The fifties boom is a clear example of the cultural phenomenon we call retro, defined by the music critic and historian Simon Reynolds as "a self-conscious fetish for period stylisation (in music, clothes, design) expressed creatively through pastiche and citation." Where customs, traditions, classics, and canonized works involve a continuity of historical survival, retro describes a historical *revival*—a sudden reevaluation of transient artifacts and conventions. Unlike the high-culture rediscovery of forgotten genius or Renaissance obsessions with mythical golden ages, retro is the *ironic* use of kitsch from the recent past as novelties. "The retro sensibility," writes Reynolds, "tends neither to idealise nor sentimentalise the past, but seeks to be amused and charmed by it." While classics possess a near permanent cachet, retro grants new status value to discarded conventions. Before Sha Na Na, youth viewed 1950s vocal pop as goofy and embarrassing—silly songs with nonsense lyrics and simple chord changes that predated the rise of *real* music like the Beatles and Bob Dylan. But Sha Na Na's ironic appropriation made doo-wop desirable again. Retro established an additional way for the past to take on new value in the present: nostalgia masquerading as innovation for use in the fashion cycle.

No pop culture history of the twentieth century is possible without a consideration of retro revivals. The 1960s counterculture embraced a wide range of antiquated styles, from 1930s *Bonnie and Clyde* gangster fashion to ornate Napoleonic military uniforms. In the 1970s kids took up the aforementioned fifties sock hop look, while in the late 1980s college students stoked a psychedelic revival with neo-hippie bands like Edie Brickell & New Bohemians. Grunge of the 1990s updated the raw seventies rock of the Stooges. And in the early 2000s New York's electroclash scene, as well as bands like LCD Soundsystem and the Rapture, drew their sound from late 1970s disco, post-punk, and No Wave, as well as 1980s synthpop.

Retro is inevitable in fashion cycles. As poet and playwright Jean Cocteau observes: "Art produces ugly things which frequently become more beautiful with time. Fashion, on the other hand, produces beautiful things which always become ugly with time." Fashion cycles conclude with once coveted innovations ceded to laggards, and our brains interpret the resulting anticachet as "ugliness." Philosopher Walter Benjamin writes, "Each generation experiences the fashion of the one immediately preceding it as the most radical antiaphrodisiac imaginable." This is particularly true of kitsch, as it has few redeeming qualities to cushion its fall from grace.

After contaminated trends are fully abandoned, they may be forgotten. And as negative symbolic associations fade, the trends are primed for a comeback. Once a convention is removed from "circulation and consideration"—and no longer associated with present-day adopters—innovators can resurrect it as a new means of distinction. The Adidas Country sneaker debuted in 1971 as a suburban cross-country shoe popular with "corny preppy kids." But by 1987 it had disappeared from suburban culture, allowing New York's hip-hop elites to embrace it as their own.

The most iconic examples of retro, however, don't revive old styles as an empty vessel: they play with them as an *intentional* "antiaphrodisiac." As we've seen before, ugliness builds fences. "Where retro truly reigns as the dominant sensibility and creative paradigm," writes Simon Reynolds, "is in hipster land, pop's equivalent to highbrow." Youth raise their cultural fences on a budget— digging through bargain bins, thrift shops, garage sales, and Goodwill stores for ugly old things that will horrify adults. Youth love old kitsch because they'll never be confused for the original adopters. A nineteen-year-old pink-haired art school student in a hideous nylon bowling jacket is unlikely to be an actual member of the Old Baldy Shrine Club.

This subversive appreciation of past banality arguably began with the camp aesthetics of the gay community. Camp reveled in dated kitsch *for being dated kitsch*. Andy Warhol and pop art then brought this sensibility into "serious" galleries, museums, and academies. The *New York Times* art critic Hilton Kramer noted that pop art opened an era in which "there are now no pockets of bad taste or vulgar display buried in the past that are not ready for exhumation." After ironic appreciation of kitsch became part of high culture, these ideas trickled down to Sha Na Na and other experimenters. From there ironic revivals hit the commercial market, and retro became a common sensibility around the globe.

Retro provided an excellent source of innovations because the development costs are so low. Inventing from scratch is difficult and time-consuming. Retro offers something that feels "new" in the moment without the need of explanation and persuasion. Youth weaned on 1950s radio got the joke of Sha Na Na immediately. On a personal level we also feel excited to see a forgotten part of our heritage unearthed and reclaimed—old emotions pulled out of our brains in a gush of gleeful nostalgia.

Now that the past lives on in the form of highly durable material goods, there is a near infinite reservoir of objects to rediscover. For every canonized work that survives in memories and university syllabi, there are at least one hundred forgotten failures crumbled up in the wastebasket of history. Retro has appeared most often in the fields of music and fashion, because both industries churn out piles of new products that fall out of circulation within a short time.

The use of sampling in early hip-hop promised something even more romantic: the possibility of turning the musical phrases in crates of "worthless" LPs into the elements of exciting new songs. Warren G and Nate Dogg built their hip-hop hit "Regulate" from the groove of a forgotten Michael McDonald yacht rock single. Whether sampling for cleverness or retro homeliness, embarrassing artifacts are better to use than lost treasures. "The wiser historians and critics know," writes art scholar Renato Poggioli, "that unoriginal work, the mediocre or *manqué*, reveals the spirit of its own times in a sharp and direct way precisely because it remains a document and not a monument." Retro is not about honoring lost genius but celebrating the rote executions of dated conventions to convey a feeling of the past.

As we saw with subcultural styles and art, the creative class has enough status to imbue their retro trends with society-wide cachet. Glenn O'Brien explains, "Things come back into fashion after they have hit the bottom of the vintage barrel and are adopted by poor but stylish youth, who are then noticed and imitated by fashion designers." Retro is now built into the fashion process. Apparel designers plan each collection with a "mood board" filled with old photos of style icons and past design elements. In any field where individuals must produce a constant stream of novelties, there will be temptations to revive forgotten ideas.

The ubiquity of retro culture in the twentieth century—and the reliable rhythm of styles returning after twenty to twenty-five years—bolsters the old idea that history is fundamentally cyclical. In the case of retro, these repetitions are the product of predictable and logical forces. The timing of retro cycles relates to the number of years required for a population to fully abandon a certain trend during its initial diffusion. Retro also suggests, however, that "relatively cyclical" is a more accurate descriptor. The second wave of a trend is always more exaggerated and less radical. Retro trends can never be as dangerous as the original. A true radical innovation triggers a fear of the unknown; its retro revival is ugly in a very familiar way. Teddy boys were violent working-class delinquents in a conservative postwar Britain; teddy boy revivalists of the 1970s were harmless music fans and weekend hobbyists. Parody and camp prefer mannerist interpretations over accurate reproductions.

Whatever the banalities of retro, it offers a useful counterbalance to high-status biases in customs, traditions, classics, and canons. Stodgy British elites surely had no interest in reviving the teddy boys. And yet, with the national celebration of teds in the 1970s, drape coats and brothel creepers entered into the canon of permanent English style. "It was the young Teds of the seventies," write the teddy boy historians Ray Ferris and Julian Lord, "who firmly established the Teddy Boys as an enduring feature of the British social landscape and not just a passing fad." In fact the teddy boy version of Edwardian style is perhaps more memorable today than the actual dress of the Edwardian age. This reveals, however, how retro can be distorting in its own way. Our memory of certain looks tends to reflect the revival over the original. Later teddy boys looked not to yellowing tabloid photographs of fifties teds for style guidance but to Ringo Starr's outfits in his 1973 retro fifties film, *That'll Be the Day*.

While there are complaints that retro distracts us from inventing the future, the fifties, teds, folk, psychedelic, punk, and eighties revivals have succeeded in diversifying culture. These movements enabled us to inhabit past sensibilities, which transformed many transient relics into valuable artifacts for sincere enjoyment. "Only when a psychedelic revival occurred in pop culture during the late Eighties," writes music critic Ian MacDonald, "did The Beatles' records start to make emotional sense to their young descendants." Despite the irony and cynicism at the heart of retro, our revisiting of past styles allows a greater diversity of human understanding and experiences in the present. If the past is a foreign country, retro has been a useful passport.

-◦{≡}◦-

In 1937, the art historian James Laver published a now famous chart outlining how evaluations of a certain fashion trend change over time:

Indecent	10 years before its time
Shameless	5 years before its time
Outré	1 year before its time
Smart	. . . . .
Dowdy	1 year after its time
Hideous	10 years after its time
Ridiculous	20 years after its time
Amusing	30 years after its time
Quaint	50 years after its time
Charming	70 years after its time
Romantic	100 years after its time
Beautiful	150 years after its time

Laver's analysis may be more tongue-in-cheek than exact science, but it illustrates that our aesthetic judgments are always made in a temporal context. The eerie accuracy of Laver's time intervals can be attributed to how they match particular moments in the diffusion process—when innovation angers the mainstream, when cachet is injected, when status value decreases, when historical value emerges. The sequence of events may be nearly universal, but the length of each stage depends on the particular fashion cycle. For all the conventional wisdom that styles return after twenty to twenty-five years, a mere decade passed between fifties doo-wop and Sha Na Na's retro parody. The timing is always contingent upon how quickly we consume and forget. In the 1960s, rising incomes, the diffusion of new technologies like TV and radio, and a youth generation striving for difference from their parents created conditions for extremely rapid change, which then in turn shortened the time required for full abandonment. By 1968 the fifties felt like the distant past. As we'll see in the next chapter, the lack of major stylistic changes makes time feel slower today.

If we accept the logic behind Laver's chart, we solve the final part of the Grand Mystery of Culture: *Why do we change behaviors over time, and why do some behaviors persist?* Individual status seeking explains how rapid change occurs in the form of fashion. For status reasons, the Beatles changed from pompadours to moptops, and young Beatles fans followed them in tow. Status also determines how society remembers—through the slow uptake of once privileged habits as customs, authorized symbols of heritage as traditions, iconic looks of past heroes as classics, and critically lionized artworks as the canon. The Beatles' cachet in the 1960s helped the moptop not only diffuse in that decade but become classic over time. Status, then, plays a role in who creates history, and history plays a role in who gets status.

In the modern age, however, history is never fixed. Permanent value is never permanent. Customs are more reliable than fads, yet paradigms shift enough to devalue many customs. Each generation overvalues the art popular during their youth, and their hunger for nostalgia as wealthy adults pushes pop culture toward their particular sensibilities.

Despite the many controversies surrounding it, the canon does offer opportunities to experience the cultural excellence of the past. The best artworks possess a depth and "strangeness" that delight and resonate, no matter the generation. "A work is eternal," writes the literary theorist Roland Barthes, "not because it imposes a single meaning on different men, but because it suggests different meanings to a single man, speaking the same symbolic language in all ages: the work proposes, man disposes." This is only possible, however, because cultural innovation is not the same as technological innovation. Science may twist and turn but marches forward over time. The arbitrariness of culture means we can always hop from one convention to another, and this includes returning to what came before. We can rediscover the joys of a failed German disco pop single from the 1970s or turn its hook into a new composition. By comparison, superseded scientific knowledge, such as the "four humours" of the body or "luminiferous aether," is useless as practical instruction. Historical value exists precisely because the past can be a viable cultural guide for the present. When we seek an escape from stale, boring, corrupt, or decadent times, we can always delve back into history for inspiration. And as we'll see, many in the twenty-first century did just that: fleeing to the culture of the past as relief from the unmoored chaos of our internet lives.

Part Four

STATUS AND CULTURE IN THE TWENTY-FIRST CENTURY

Chapter Ten

THE INTERNET AGE

⊰✕⊱

Viral failures, Louis Vuitton–Supreme Ferraris, the Instagrammers of
Tuva, remorseful critics, battles for old and new, and other moments
from status signaling and cultural innovation in the digital realm

⊰✕⊱

THE INTERNET, VIRALITY, AND
THE DECLINE OF STATUS VALUE

In August 2013 I went viral. Kanye West had just released his album *Yeezus*,
and on the humbly titled third track, "I Am a God," he vented his deep frustra-
tion with lassitude at Paris boulangeries: "In a French-ass restaurant / Hurry
up with my damn croissants." On the website *Medium* I posted "An Open Letter to Kanye West from the Association of French Bakers"—a humor piece
imagining the French bakers' public explanation for the time required to make
croissants: "Bakers must carefully layer the dough, paint on perfect proportions of butter, and then roll and fold this trembling croissant embryo with the
precision of a Japanese origami master." Is there an Association of French
Bakers? I don't know. I invented it as a comic device, and signed my real name
to the resulting piece to ensure the letter would be read as satire, rather than
as an actual open letter from a real Association of French Bakers.

A few weeks later *Consumerist* fact-checked my piece and decided it was an
actual open letter from the real Association of French Bakers. *The Hollywood
Reporter* then ran a story under the headline FRENCH BAKERS CHIDE KANYE
WEST IN HILARIOUS LETTER, after which followed a flood: *USA Today, Time, Fox*

News, Billboard, and *Today.* A month later *The New Yorker* emailed, and I had
to convince the writer of my authorship by explaining how I invented the association's address. The resulting article on *newyorker.com* judged the case as
a true instance of fake news, and my brief moment of virality came to an end.

My eighteen-year-old self would have been elated that I had somehow pranked
the American mass media, had an audience of millions reading my work (or at
least the headlines), and gotten a write-up in *The New Yorker* (okay, *newyorker.com*).
But the impact of this viral success on my actual life was trivial. For all the attention and excitement, I received around *five* additional Twitter followers. And
no one—not even my closest friends and family—remembers, references, or
cares much about the entire episode. My self-published humor piece was randomly and mistakenly swept up into that day's news tornado, alongside many
other now forgotten, semitrue clickbait stories.

Most viral content follows this same pattern of fevered groundswell and
quick collapse. Celebrities can spin their viral moments into further celebrity,
but when normal people get thousands of shares on a post, there are few rewards or benefits. The journalist Peter Hamby notes, "Every hilarious viral
tweet is paired with a depressing reply tweet from the author saying 'wow
this blew up please buy my thing' and that one only has 12 likes." (Some companies now offer viral tweeters cash for placing ads for scammy services in the
thread.)

Ephemerality is not new to pop culture. Between 1955 and 2005, almost half
of all charting musicians were one-hit wonders. But in slower-moving, less
crowded marketplaces, hits secured enough repetition to help us *remember*
them later, even if in embarrassment. We can sing "My Sharona" at karaoke
and probably dance the "Macarena" at a wedding after a few flutes of champagne. The Pet Rock was a fad, but it's now a *legendary* fad. Viral content, on
the other hand, rarely becomes culture with any sense of permanence. It entertains us for a few seconds and then, like a freak snowstorm on a warm day,
immediately melts.

This transitoriness perhaps makes viral content the most representative form
of culture in the twenty-first century: an era of vast quantities, deep specificity,
and breakneck speed, where few individual artifacts, artworks, or conventions
leave a dent in society or bend the curve of history. Viral culture lacks depth

and weight, and it creates few new sensibilities or styles. And yet viral content resembles "real" culture: we consume silly videos just as we watched videos on MTV, read Twitter as we read newspaper articles, pin aspirational visuals to Pinterest boards like posters on a dorm room wall. We had high hopes for the internet: an infinite reservoir of content, free distribution, a broader canon, and a more diverse creator base, which would inspire more people to make more amazing things. But this "deluge" of digital culture, writes film critic A. O. Scott, "is often perceived as a drought."

Declinists speak of a "culture crash." Many hoped 9/11, the Iraq war, and the Great Recession would inspire wild and oppositional art, but instead we got emo and screamo, *American Idol*, junky Myspace pages, and a twenty-four-hour news cycle of TMZ celebrity gossip. The top-grossing film of the 2000s, *Avatar*, remains in our memory solely for being a hit film no one remembers much about. In 2011, Glenn O'Brien wrote, "There's something about our time that makes you wish that you lived in another one." For cultural cognoscenti like O'Brien, who had lived through the slow and steady infiltration of underground culture into the mainstream during the twentieth century, the aughts failed to entertain. Much of the cultural discourse of the early 2010s ended up fretting over cultural stasis—a feeling of stagnancy in the zeitgeist. Grammy-winning producer Ian Brennan quipped, "It's possible that lovestruck teens even lose their virginity listening to the same tune that their parents' conceived them to." The "general law of the world," wrote the philosopher Paul Virilio in the 1970s, was "stasis is death." With culture not seeming to move, did the twenty-first century begin as a funeral?

This negativity is unfortunate, because the internet does offer many advantages. We can enjoy more varieties of more content from a greater diversity of voices at greater convenience. In fact, the level of creativity and innovation in contemporary artworks may not actually have changed; the problem, rather, is in our *perception* of the output. The move from analog to digital has altered the nature of social interaction, consumerism, signaling, and taste. And all of these structural changes hinder the creation of a critical ingredient underlying our appreciation of culture—status value.

To understand how the internet affects status structures and status value, this chapter examines four related phenomena:

- the explosion of content
- the clash of maximalist and minimalist sensibilities accompanying the rise in global wealth
- the rejection of "taste" as a legitimate means of distinction
- the overvaluation of the past in Gen X "retromania," and the abandoning of the past in Gen Z "neomania."

All of these factors have reduced the status value of our contemporary cultural output. They also debase cultural capital as an asset, which makes popularity and economic capital even more central in marking status. The end result, at least so far, has been less incentive for individuals to both create and celebrate culture with high symbolic complexity.

-◦⟨⊛⟩◦-

Before we explore the internet's impact on culture, we must first heed the sociologist Duncan Watts's warning: "The Internet isn't really a thing at all. Rather, it's shorthand for an entire period of history, and all the interlocking technological, economic, and social changes that happened therein." As we know, technology doesn't automatically change culture. People using that technology must move from old conventions to new ones. So we must look at both how the technological, economic, and social changes of the internet age set new parameters for our actions, and how we have adjusted our status strategies accordingly.

While the internet became mass culture in the 1990s, its true global ubiquity began in the past two decades with the diffusion of smartphones and high-speed mobile connections. The number of internet users grew from one billion in 2005 to over five billion in 2021—but more important, the usage deepened. The web isn't just a place to check the occasional email from friends or do research for term papers. We *live* on the internet.

The influx of users has changed the nature of internet content. During the early days of the World Wide Web, online life gravitated toward the niche tastes of college students and tech geeks, like a virtual extension of campus life: liberal politics, rogue mp3 trading, FAQs about obscure Japanese animations, and expert guitar tabs for They Might Be Giants songs. During the rise of blogs in the early 2000s, top sites like Boing Boing and kottke.org continued this tradition of catering to nerd curiosity. By the 2010s, however, the internet became true mass culture—a democratization by both class and geography. A fifth of internet users now use it in Chinese. And with the appearance of visual apps like YouTube, Instagram, Twitch, and TikTok, being "extremely online" no longer even required literacy. People everywhere could participate through consuming visuals and music, speaking, singing, lip-syncing, or dancing. And so, over just three decades, the internet became the primary site where we interact with others and create personas. As the economist-blogger Noah Smith quipped, "Fifteen years ago, the internet was an escape from the real world. Now, the real world is an escape from the internet."

A ubiquitous visual internet has obvious implications for signaling. Our status claims are no longer limited to real-life interactions or mass media reports of our real-life interactions. With the rise of social media, signaling now happens 24/7, and status claims can potentially reach a global audience at no cost. The critic Jia Tolentino writes, "You can't just walk around and be visible on the internet—for anyone to see you, you have to *act*." And the "main purpose of this communication" is "to make yourself look good." Opting out of social media, observes the millennial writer Malcolm Harris, "is a deviant lifestyle choice." Only 5 to 15 percent of American teens are social media refuseniks.

Social media also enables us to *quantify* our status like never before: in likes, retweets, comments, and followers, and, for those at the top, in the number of brands reaching out with free products and promotional opportunities. In the internet age, we've applied quantification to almost everything. The early-2000s blogs *Socialite Rank* and *Park Avenue Peerage* provided weekly rankings for hopeful debutantes in New York high society—a system defended as "extremely fair" and "extremely mathematical." The failed start-up Klout attempted to extend these principles to everyone's social influence—assigning a "Klout score" to individuals on a one-hundred-point scale.

In this increase of signaling frequency, we have been numbed to many traditional status symbols. Vacation photos of a radiant beach sunset in a faraway land are no longer impressive when they're every other image on the feed. Moreover, cheating has never been easier. First came face-smoothing filters and devious cropping, and soon we'll have to be wary of deepfakes. We assume any photo of a young person drinking champagne in a private jet was taken inside a parked plane rented for that purpose. (There are Instagram accounts, like BallerBusters, that offer exposés of social media fraud *as* social media content.)

Beyond signals being devalued in toto, the internet has also debased two critical signaling costs: *barriers to information* and *barriers to acquisition*. Elites could once easily signal status through knowing certain facts about French cheese or owning a frayed Persian rug. The democratization of information on the internet and the globalization of supply chains have lowered the signaling costs for uncommon goods. Wikipedia can make us faux experts on anything within an hour, and we can acquire antique or rare goods with a few clicks. Information can't be a strong signaling cost when "information wants to be free." In the early 1960s, Bob Dylan had to literally steal folk records from an acquaintance in order to achieve his impressive mastery of the genre. YouTube allows anyone to learn almost any song without committing any misdemeanors—but will audiences be as impressed?

The internet also kills off arbitrage as a reliable source of status symbols. Hours after *The New York Times* wrote about Taliban soldiers in Afghanistan wearing a white Pakistani high-top sneaker called the Cheetah, a *GQ* editor looked to buy them but failed to find an online seller. A month later Pakistani e-tailers appeared to ship the shoes worldwide. With obscurity itself a fleeting state, *price* reemerges as the most reliable signaling cost. Le Creuset cookware can appeal to professional classes—and be *their* culture—because lower-income people are unlikely to pay that much for a stockpot. As elite groups fail to imbue their cachet upon products and knowledge relying only on obscurity as a signaling cost, entire swaths of "pure" indie culture lose status value.

The second factor draining status value is the explosion of content and goods. The internet makes creation and distribution easier, resulting in more artworks, more products, and more exposition. In the twentieth century, finite limits on pages and broadcast time restricted our knowledge of goods, artists, artworks, and styles. The internet is infinite: there are millions of websites and video channels reporting on millions of cultural artifacts—and search sites serve up whatever we want in microseconds. Once you're bored with the 70-million-plus tracks on Spotify, there are now more than two hundred digital files of rare Sudanese cassettes for free listening on archive.org. Meanwhile, mass customization enables consumers to tweak existing products into any number of personalized versions. Digitization equalizes all culture, whether past, present, or future, professional, amateur, or "prosumer." In the twentieth century, the content industry enjoyed a monopoly on creating audiovisual content of superior quality, but youth born and raised online have become comfortable watching footage from low-grade consumer cameras, listening to tinny compressed sound from their laptop speakers, and laughing at the hammy acting of social media superstars.

In 2004, Chris Anderson, the editor in chief of *Wired*, celebrated the possibilities of infinite cultural choice as "the long tail": "Our culture and economy are increasingly shifting away from a focus on a relatively small number of hits (mainstream products and markets) at the head of the demand curve, and moving toward a huge number of niches in the tail. In an era without the constraints of physical shelf space and other bottlenecks of distribution, narrowly targeted goods and services can be as economically attractive as mainstream fare." In Anderson's lingo, the "head" described mass culture, whereas the "long tail" culture was niche fare. And the emergence of a long-tail-dominated culture meant corporate overlords no longer could force us into cookie-cutter conformity. The internet unfurled a parsec-long cultural buffet from which we could pick and choose the most distinctive pieces to best reflect our true selves as part of our personas. After the dreaded straitjacket of mass culture, the internet would let us be authentically weird.

The long-tail hypothesis, however, ignores much of what we've learned in this book about status and taste. Pursuit of originality is correlated to top and bottom positions in a hierarchy. Most people *don't want* extreme uniqueness. Mass culture can be highly appealing in its low complexity and low social risk. The long-tail theory posits that we all want to sing our own individual songs, when there remains an obvious allure to singing "99 Luftballons" in unison at Oktoberfest. The long tail is a dream come true for a minority of ever curious oddballs, but most people seek conventions with broad common knowledge. Listening to Sudanese cassettes is isolating; listening to Cardi B's "WAP feat. Megan Thee Stallion" is taking part in a national conversation.

The resulting *information overload* of the long tail further complicates signaling. We see this play out in the "paradox of choice"—analysis paralysis, when there are too many options. In the twentieth century, the number of luxury goods expanded to match the growing number of status groups. But there is a limit to how many signals, status groups, and positions we can track.

Appraisers can interpret only those signals they can perceive. Signals pulled from long-tail culture don't serve as classifiers, other than perhaps classifying someone as a long-tail consumer—a category not currently sitting at the highest rungs of the status ladder. In the past, the difficulty of acquiring long-tail content suggested that a person had many underlying status assets, such as intelligence, curiosity, and deep knowledge. When anyone can find anything obscure on the internet within minutes, acquisition alone reveals no virtues or skills.

The explosion of media outlets also leads to lower status values. Mediation itself no longer suggests cachet, because there is now a website for almost everything. Yes, appearing on *vogue.com* suggests higher status than making an appearance on a third-rate content farm, but being on the internet alone doesn't bespeak influence. The ubiquity of virality also means we have come to expect random things of dubious quality to attract attention. "Winning the internet" for a day is less valuable than getting a number one on the music charts, because it demonstrates very little consumer commitment. A Gold record in 1970 required separating teenagers from their meager allowances; today, a meme goes viral because someone spent ten seconds laughing and one second hitting the share button. Ironic hate-watching often drives up the numbers. After it was dubbed "the worst video ever made," the wealthy teenager Rebecca Black's vanity single "Friday" drew 156 million views on YouTube.

Chris Anderson predicted, early in the 2000s, that "when mass culture breaks apart, it doesn't re-form into a different mass. Instead it turns into millions of microcultures, which coexist and interact in a baffling array of ways." What happened instead was something like the Revenge of the Head—the return of cultural influence to mass hits at the expense of the niches. Culture is collapsing around a small number of massive mainstream artists, athletes, and celebrities with enough industrial support to have staying power. In *Hit Makers* Derek Thompson augured, "The future of hits will be democratic, chaotic, and unequal. Millions will compete for attention, a happy few will go big, and a microscopic minority will get fantastically rich." Americans can seek refuge from the chaos of the long tail in the mass-culture pleasures of LeBron James, Beyoncé, superhero movies, premium cable, *The Office* reruns, *Pokémon Go*, and *Fortnite*. Athletic heroics, glossy pop songs, and too-big-to-fail cinema offer ample entertainment and reliable vehicles for positive social interactions.

The few "viral" moments that manage to become mass culture—like Carly Rae Jepsen's "Call Me Maybe"—are often "head" moments in disguise. Jepsen's surprise hit didn't spread from her native Canada to the United States through organic word-of-mouth; Justin Bieber heard the song, signed Jepsen to his manager's Schoolboy Records, and then promoted the track through his own social media channels. The head may not provide much status value, but at least our appraisers will know we're in sync with the times and not outcasts languishing in an obscure niche.

But the head is always relative, and much of mass culture claims victory with a mere plurality share. As the long tail spreads the population into thin niches, a "hit" describes only the largest niche. *Game of Thrones* was one of the "biggest" TV shows of the 2010s—but only around 5 to 6 percent of Americans ever watched it. Many things we call hits only track the aggressive overconsumption of superfans. The Korean pop group BTS has racked up number ones on the Billboard charts, but how many Americans can hum a BTS tune? If the long tail makes different branches of culture mutually incomprehensible and the common language centers around middle-of-the-road mega-hits, the internet further reduces the cachet of obscure culture.

The final factor behind a reduction in status value is the inherent high speed of the internet, which disrupts traditional fashion cycles. Elite groups need time to be the sole adopters of an innovation for it to gain cachet. For most of the twentieth century, slow fashion cycles meant high-status innovations could elude media discovery for at least a few months, if not years. Early adopters took a while to figure out how to emulate, and manufacturers needed time to make copies for mass consumption. Fashion relied on social friction to slow down the diffusion process, which allowed elites to look sincere and authentic in adoption—a gradual lifestyle upgrade rather than a flashy attempt at status distinction.

This entire system is upturned by light-speed information flows on the internet. Between the paparazzi industrial complex, social media, and fast fashion, an elite convention can spread to the masses in a matter of weeks, days, or even hours. Knowing this, elites may abstain from adopting new styles and goods that could be easily copied. Even rare Pakistani high-tops offer no guarantee to be the exclusive privilege of a small group. In fact, the very assumption of rapid diffusion alone may be enough to prevent adoption. The Taliban's

Cheetah sneakers would be distinctive for a few weeks in New York, but once fashion fans from lower status tiers pop up with the same pairs, the shoes would need to be abandoned.

The frenzied pace of internet culture thus pushes humans far beyond the acceptable rate of changes to our personas. Where elites are better off not investing in new trends, the culture becomes conservative. The quantity and velocity of information also robs us of the time to form emotional and sentimental bonds with artworks. Viral content—like my forgotten Kanye piece—helps us kill time but inspires little of the long-term devotion crucial for shaping identities. The *Kony 2012* video exploded on YouTube—over 70 million views within five days—and then most everyone forgot who Kony was.

For much of the twentieth century, we had to infer status symbols' cachet from advertising, media mentions, and rare observations on the street, and these imprecise calculations often led to overvaluations. Today the internet reveals to us exactly who has already adopted a new product. The ability to search past content also raises the bar for what's considered "original." On Twitter, there are always receipts for who came up with a style, joke, or meme first.

This all works toward a depletion of status value, which, I would argue, has a negative effect on the entirety of cultural value. In the twentieth century the use of culture in status struggles resulted in a constant stream of new artifacts, styles, and sensibilities—all injected with cachet, which allowed them to influence mass culture. On the internet there are more *things*, but fewer arrive with clear and stable status value. At an unconscious level, this affects our judgments of intrinsic quality: films, songs, and books without status value just aren't as rewarding as their predecessors. As part of our desire for status, we chase status value. And so if niche culture lacks status value, many have fled the long tail to return to the head.

To be very clear, this doom and gloom is not about the *artistic quality* of internet-era content. We live in a paradise of options, and the diminished power of gatekeepers has allowed more voices to flourish. The question is simply whether internet content can fulfill our basic human needs for status distinction. Many will be jubilant at this development, but reduced status value has negative downstream effects. Elites are less likely to adopt as many cultural innovations, which means fewer fashion trends to be diffused. When a trend evaporates as a superficial fad, there may not be enough collective memory for it to take on historical value, either. We'll never equate the half-baked electro-clash genre of 2001 with the four-year-long grunge movement that transformed the nineties.

Overall, the very medium of the internet changes how we signal and how status value is created, and these changes are playing out in how we feel about culture overall. Cultural capital is less valuable in a world of free information, and this raises the relative value of economic capital. This has major implications for the status struggles between classes, and we are watching it play out with new kinds of wealth in both advanced and emerging economies.

THE NEW NOUVEAU RICHE AND ITS BACKLASH

In early August 2017, Rashed Belhasa, a fifteen-year-old Emirati—still three years shy of Dubai's legal driving age—revealed his latest automotive acquisition on YouTube. Dipping into his father's vast construction fortune, Belhasa purchased a banana-yellow Ferrari F12berlinetta and asked a local body shop to wrap the car in the Louis Vuitton monogram print and the box logo from streetwear label Supreme. Upon seeing the final result, Belhasa exclaimed through orthodontic braces, "The best car in Dubai! The best car in the world!" Belhasa's video racked up ten-million-plus views and bolstered his career as a burgeoning social media influencer. Belhasa was no longer an unknown, medium-height rich kid with braces living on the Arabian Peninsula. The *Daily Mail* wrote up his possessions and friendships with celebrities. He had achieved global status.

Sports cars wrapped in luxury logos may be new, but the strategy behind Belhasa's brazen expenditure is extremely old. The young Belhasa's conspicuous consumption parallels the extravagance of bygone sultans and robber barons. Yet, somewhere in the combination of Middle Eastern fortunes, Supreme, YouTube, Instagram follower counts, and supercars, it is clear that globalization and technology are changing the composition of the status ladder.

As the internet further connects the world's inhabitants into Marshall McLuhan's "global village," status competition has only intensified. Belhasa represents the latest contenders: a new nouveau riche. The scions of petrostate fortunes, corrupt oligarchs, and construction monopolies are using Instagram and Weibo to reveal their lifestyle exploits—with tastes aligning around an amped-up, prefab bling. The emerging world has embraced bombastic conspicuous consumption as a rational status strategy, as demonstrated by the explosion of luxury sales in China, Russia, and India.

In less advanced economies, excess luxury works better than subtle and learned sophistication. And thanks to the internet, global status signaling is no longer limited to the G20 nations. In Tuva—a landlocked region of Central Asia in Russia, which the physicist Richard Feynman made famous as the most obscure place on earth—teenagers post on Instagram and TikTok in ways identical to their first-world peers. Women strike sultry poses with AirPods and filtered faces, young guys mug in angular jackets and shades. There are workout routines and yoga positions, creative makeup tutorials, Land Cruisers, pastry-making classes, and singing pop songs in parked cars. People in places as remote as Tuva are going online not just to access information but to join the global status hierarchy. If we can see Tuva on Instagram, it means Tuva can see us right back. The emerging universal grammar of signaling, based on Western conventions, has ushered in a global monoculture. Perhaps Mark Zuckerberg really did "bring the world closer together"—at least in an assimilation of flexes.

Individuals always signal with their most valuable assets, and when local Dubaian or Tuvan customs mean nothing to global audiences, the most obvious approach is to emphasize economic capital. Conspicuous consumption requires few secret codes, just the brute force of large expenditure. Milan Kundera was prescient when he wrote, "The brotherhood of man on earth will be possible only on a base of kitsch." He was off by one word: unity requires *luxury* kitsch. And so as the new nouveau riche emerges, so begins the Big Bling.

The primary proponents and benefactors of the Big Bling are minor royal families, corrupt politicians, monopolists in extractive industries, and organized crime leaders from formerly third-world countries—and critically, their children. The Rich Kids of Instagram may have begun with photos of American billionaire sons and daughters, but soon spawned imitators like Rich Russian Kids and Rich Kids of Turkey. The Center for Advanced Defense Studies tracked the importation of at least eight hundred luxury autos into North Korea. The sociologist Ashley Mears, who researched the top echelons of the global party circuit in New York, Miami, Ibiza, and Saint-Tropez, found that "the most dubious of big spenders were non-Westerners, like Russian, Arab, and 'crazy rich Asian' spenders" or guys who "own all the water in Serbia." The most notorious "whale" of the club scene was Jho Low, a Malaysian-Chinese investor who dropped millions on champagne, using wealth he allegedly siphoned from a government development fund.

While globalization has created many millionaires and billionaires outside of the West, they must show their faces abroad to gain global status. The internet, at least, provides a temporary solution for when private jets are grounded. *The New York Times'* Iva Dixit writes of the Indian stars of the reality series *Fabulous Lives of Bollywood Wives*, "What use is a Rolls-Royce if no one sees you getting out of it? The affliction of this class is a deep thirst to be witnessed, the same thirst that turns tech billionaires into Twitter obsessives and once respectable actresses into lifestyle bloggers." When the new nouveau riche travel, their extreme conspicuous consumption makes primo online content. Billionaire Saudi prince Turki Bin Abdullah brings his fleet of golden cars to London, and then YouTube automotive channels rush to broadcast the footage far beyond the pedestrians of Mayfair.

In countries with high income inequality, elites have long indulged in extreme conspicuous consumption, which becomes "good taste" in that community. Dictators proclaim their superiority through fleets of supercars and closets of Savile Row suits. The West, as real wages stagnate and middle-class jobs disappear, has also become a fertile ground for such autocratic and oligarchic sensibilities. The traditional Puritan disgust for ostentation is antiquated. Large evangelist Christian audiences flock to the "prosperity theology" of Joel Osteen and Creflo Dollar. Luminaries in the broader pop culture preach their own Gospel of Wealth. DJ Khaled, the successful music producer born to Palestinian immigrants, defended his spending to Larry King: "Of course I'm a hustler, you know what I'm sayin', I'm gonna always think nonstop how to get this money to take care of my mother and my father, my team. Now is that to live good? I want the house on the water. I want the nice car. I want the nice watch. I wanna stay fresh. I wanna stay clean. You know what I'm sayin'? Nothing wrong with that. You should strive for greatness."

These ballooning fortunes make Old Money barely money at all. What good is a no-frills trust fund when IPOs and crypto holdings turn former classmates into multimillionaires overnight? The flight from Old Money culture arguably began a long time ago anyway. Edie Sedgwick wasn't satisfied being a direct descendant of the early colonizers of Massachusetts; she preferred to be an infamous Warhol girl. Several decades later, Paris Hilton spun her family's hotel fortune into a New Money lifestyle of reality shows, paparazzi peekaboo, and Las Vegas DJ gigs. Henri Matisse painted his way into museums; his great-great-granddaughter Gaïa Jacquet-Matisse gets ink for her glossy Instagram account and dresses her emotional support Chihuahua, Bambi, in custom Ralph Lauren.

The collective lack of interest in quiet, stable wealth provides the tension in the 2010 film *The Social Network*—a battle at Harvard University over the founding of Facebook. The warring parties are Mark Zuckerberg, a nerdy, champion fencer graduate of top prep school Phillips Exeter, and the Winklevoss twins, a Wharton professor's six-foot-five rower sons who attended Connecticut's Brunswick School. Neither Zuckerberg nor the Winklevoss twins were content with the upper-upper-middle-class professional life, so they spent their years in higher education scheming toward tech fortunes. Zuck got there first, and the twins crossed ten digits with the rise of bitcoin. Traditional Old Money can't compete with these sums, but more important, tech wealth and television programs like *Shark Tank* frame giant fortunes as the righteous gains of shrewd entrepreneurialism and technical prowess. Hereditary wealth is shameful if not used as a pool of capital for further—and ethical—investments. This explains why in 2021 *Harper's Bazaar* reported that the "new rules of Old Money" involve giving much of it away to charity.

Despite a brief revival of Old Money taste in men's fashion from around 2008 to 2015, the antiquated, musty sensibility has lost its allure. This reached a symbolic peak with the 2020 bankruptcy of Brooks Brothers—a company that made millions over the decades selling Old Money charm to the middle class. For Gen Z, Old Money aesthetics aren't about detachment and subtlety but the glossy #oldmoneyaesthetic hashtag on TikTok. This isn't a surprise when our aesthetics are simply status strategies. The Old Money sensibility works best when signaling within a closed society; tiny details and obscure forms of patina wink at intimate contacts with the same stockpiles of cultural capital. On a global internet, these details shrink to pixel-size invisibility. Photos of vintage Rolexes and "M"-sized follower counts are much clearer signals. This is yet another strike against more complex forms of cultural capital.

The disappearance of true Old Money has only further emboldened the new nouveau riche. But another elite group has stepped in to countersignal gauche extravagance: the professional-class tech billionaires, who are forming their own taste culture. Growing up in well-educated, upper-middle-class households, the Gates, Bezos, Brin/Page, Zuckerberg types created wealth without shedding their professional-class habitus. In these circles there is a skepticism of glamour and a respect for thoughtful thrift. Like any good professional-class members, they make their choices based on functional rationales rather than the open pursuit of status symbols. Founder-CEOs would never send a fleet of golden cars to London, even though they could. Instead, they use the great deference afforded them to debase formality itself. Just 150 years ago, fashion historian James Laver notes, "to walk down Bond Street in mid-morning or stroll in the Park on Sunday in anything but frock coat and top-hat would have been unthinkable." An appropriate look for roaming downtown Palo Alto in the 2010s was Lululemon with the logo etched off. Social standing no longer requires putting on cummerbunds, struggling to stay awake during Mahler's Ninth, and learning the correct fork for the salad course. Suits and ties are necessary only when testifying in front of Congress.

Naturally, professional-class billionaires flex in their own way. Snug-fit athleisure shows off chiseled bodies and good health, achievable only through strict discipline, personal trainers, and staff nutritionists. Rather than spending money on looking "fresh" like DJ Khaled, tech billionaires work with charitable endeavors and invest in leapfrog technologies such as flying cars and spaceships. Conspicuous leisure is used to "recharge" for later work: surfing, flying, kiteboarding (surfing + flying), micro-dosing and macro-dosing psilocybin, "fancy camps" at Burning Man. The CEO of Goldman Sachs spins EDM as DJ D-Sol.

Rank-and-file members of tech companies share similar sensibilities with their billionaire executives: same habitus and black North Face down vest, but very different stock packages. They both prefer functional, authentic goods made with artisanal craftsmanship. There is goodness and beauty in sourdough rye, third-wave hand-drip single-origin coffee, apricot sour beers and session IPAs—all procured from shops with the highest crowdsourced ratings. The stripped-down "normcore" look of gray athleticwear that dominated in the early 2010s was based on the belief that the greatest lifestyle ornament is to not care about ornamentation at all. In 2016 the writer Kyle Chayka memorably revealed how this minimalist aesthetic took over interior design—the "Air-Space" look of austerity and texture-obsession. Airbnb rentals, writes Chayka, all have "white or bright accent walls, raw wood, Nespresso machines, Eames chairs, patterned rugs on bare floors, open shelving, the neutered Scandinavi-anism of HGTV."

For a long time the professional classes had a dominating impact on the aesthetics of the online space. Tech-savvy early adopters were the earliest users of new mobile apps, and the initial design and first wave of content reflected creative-class taste. But apps need "scale" to monetize, which creates the same trickle-down status dynamics we see in the life cycle of dance clubs. Facebook started as a playground for twentysomething elite college students and, through the years, morphed into a retirement community for elderly laggards to trade photos of grandchildren and right-wing conspiracy theories. To flee these in-coming hordes, the creative class migrated to Instagram in the early 2010s. For a brief moment that app was the "Happiest Place in the (Internet) World": a land of sunny and often abstract photos of daily life that avoided the intense status competition of Facebook's Potemkin-perfect lives. Then the strivers joined Instagram, with the most ambitious emerging as "social media influ-encers" known for their irony-free braggadocio and undying commitment to the hustle. The photos became glossier, and, judging by follower counts, this is exactly what audiences wanted.

The days may be numbered where tech elites and the creative class exclu-sively determine the basic taste on the main platforms of the internet. TikTok arrived from China rather than California—and with teens as the core user base, the app established its taste world in the middle of the global status lad-der. As a result, the most popular accounts' aesthetic is suburban high school pranksterism without any pretense of hipster snobbery. If every app is just a vessel for the collective taste of its median users, a future seven-billion-user internet will be an internet of kitsch, bling, and flash. As a site for creative-class couch-surfers, Airbnb generated AirSpace; but we should expect bungalows full of tchotchkes and "more is more" once the masses become the primary cus-tomer. The conventions guiding social media apps will grow more "basic" over time. In his newsletter *Garbage Day*, the journalist Ryan Broderick writes, "The ugly American weirdness of Facebook—the casual racism, the petty small town drama, the nameless grifters, the weird old people, the Minion memes, the public meltdowns at fast food restaurants, the goths, the bored nurses, the men in their trucks talking on their phones, the extremely basic backyard viral challenges—it will all come to TikTok." And if status must be procured by signaling *within* these apps, no one can flee the virtual town square. Social media apps are more likely to splinter into separate platforms for each status tier, just as there were different General Motors cars for every salary band. The members-only social networking app Raya sets a model for this approach, limiting its user base to a small group of celebrities and certified attractive people.

There is, of course, another class-based sensibility of the era, albeit without much influence on the wider culture: the often ignored, increasingly bitter provincial lower-middle-class sensibility of white majorities. In the mid-twentieth century, this group enjoyed its own respectable taste world of *Reader's Digest*, bowling clubs, and Lawrence Welk. They disliked highbrow eggheads but felt represented in the "average families" of prime-time TV comedies. The twenty-first-century economy has skewed media and consumption so decisively toward coastal elites as to be perceived among the lower middle class as a demeaning erasure. In fact, it's hardly accurate to use the designation "middle class" anymore: there's a massive cultural gulf between those soaring at the upper bands and those struggling at the bottom.

As the lower middle class falls in status, the "conservative" majority appears to have found respect for the Trump version of bling, especially when opulence and excess humiliate the professional classes. In the Red State status group, the top echelons are filled with the "American gentry" of chain restaurant franchisees and construction company owners, whom the historian Patrick Wyman describes as "the salt-of-the-earth millionaires who see themselves as local leaders in business and politics, the unappreciated backbone of a once-great nation." An important counterimitation for the entire group is to "own the libs" by reveling in whatever the professional class abhors: guns, coal, bleak suburban restaurant chains, giant pickup trucks. This open antagonism against liberal "decency"—and proximity to vindictive politics and outright bigotry—only makes the professional classes feel even more righteous about their own cosmopolitan tastes.

In any era, the class system provides the basic taste worlds undergirding culture. And in a globalized capitalist economy, the competition between sensibilities is not the West vs. the Rest but the latest chapter in an age-old struggle between global New Money conspicuous consumption and the Already Rich counterimitation. The main weapon against extravagance in the twentieth century was symbolically complex cultural capital, but we've already seen how the internet conspires against it. And that's not to mention another major cause of its downfall: the professional class itself has rejected the legitimacy of taste.

OMNIVORE TASTE

In 2003 the *Pitchfork* music critic Matt LeMay reviewed the indie rock singer-songwriter Liz Phair's pop-makeover album *Liz Phair* and gave it a 0.0 out of 10. LeMay found it an album full of "utterly generic" songs "that could have just as easily been made by anybody else." Sixteen years later LeMay recanted, apologizing on Twitter to Phair for his "condescending and cringey" review, which further propagated the snobbish ethos that "indie rock good / pop music bad." Phair celebrated LeMay's mea culpa in good spirits, and in 2021 *Pitchfork* updated its official review score to 6.0.

Did LeMay disown his review because he came to enjoy the album *Liz Phair?* No, that was beside the point. His original complaint was not about the music itself but that an indie darling would dare aim for mainstream success. A decade later this position would seem absurd, even to its author. The *Liz Phair* affair embodied the central conflict raised in the music critic Kelefa Sanneh's seminal 2004 essay "The Rap Against Rockism." *Rockist* critics wielded "imperial" taste to disparage nonrock music as inferior and, by doing so, propagated white, male, and straight values. Sanneh writes, "Rockism means idolizing the authentic old legend (or underground hero) while mocking the latest pop star; lionizing punk while barely tolerating disco; loving the live show and hating the music video; extolling the growling performer while hating the lip-syncher." An alternative approach, which later became known as *poptimism*, would provide a healthier form of critique—an openness to the creative possibilities of *all* culture, even the songs of teen idols produced by formula in profit-driven sonic laboratories. To Sanneh, "The shape-shifting feminist hip-pop of [Christina] Aguilera is every bit as radical as the punk rock of the 1970's." Poptimism didn't just assert a higher moral authority than rockism but better reflected the reality of artistic innovation. In 2016 critic Chuck Klosterman observed, "It's almost impossible to create a new rock song that doesn't vaguely resemble an old rock song." For decades the most innovative music production had been appearing in chart-topping hip-hop and R&B instead.

Rockism lost, and poptimism won. All cultural snootiness is now tedious. The digital publication *The Pudding* trained an AI on "a corpus of over two million indicators of objectively good music, including *Pitchfork* reviews, record store recommendations, and subreddits you've never heard of" to judge "How bad is your Spotify?" The entire point was not to help you find better music but to poke fun at the mechanical counterimitations inherent in indie snobbery. The zeitgeist proclaims: "Let people enjoy things." The critic B. D. McClay writes about this phrase, which has been exalted from the punch line in a web comic into dogma, "It is a pathological aversion, on a wide cultural level, to disagreement, discomfort, or being judged by others." In sum, *distaste has become distasteful.*

Both poptimism and "let people enjoy things" are part of the meta-sensibility behind postmodern culture: *omnivore taste.* The virtuous "cultured" individual should consume and like *everything*—not just high culture, but pop and indie, niche and mass, new and old, domestic and foreign, primitive and sophisticated. Where cultural capital exists, it is now "multicultural capital." The most masterly wardrobes mix vintage Givenchy with Uniqlo. True gourmands appreciate the finest French haute cuisine, seek out the artery-blocking buttery dishes of neighborhood Parisian bistros, and wait in line for cronuts. In 1999 the writer John Seabrook labeled this omnivore culture "nobrow," framing these changes as a logical extension of late-stage capitalism. In the old "townhouse" of *New Yorker*–era taste, "you got points for consistency in cultural preferences," whereas in the "mega store" of MTV, "you got status for preferences that cut across the old hierarchical lines."

The professional-class suspicion of highbrow intellectualism, however, has much earlier roots. The historian Louis Menand writes, "*The New Yorker* made it possible to feel that being an anti-sophisticate was the mark of true sophistication, and that any culture worth having could be had without special aesthetic equipment or intellectual gymnastics." Gen X fused this middlebrow ethos with a predilection for cultural diversity, all under their baby boomer parents' beliefs that pop culture could and *should* be transcendental. This resulted in a militant and somewhat elitist version of omnivorism obsessed with artistry and indie ethics. Millennials, whose post-1960s parents grew up on arena rock, disco, and MTV, embraced the full poptimist ethos, which also worked as a counterimitation of Gen X pretension. Nothing raised fences with indie nerds more than ditching Pavement for Britney Spears.

Omnivorism has had major effects on culture over the last few decades. In the past, taste worked as a social classifier by drawing clear lines between social groups; omnivorism drains this power by declaring nearly everything suitable for consumption. In an omnivore world, there is only one fence: Are you an omnivore or not? Once inside, further gradations are nearly taboo. Espresso martinis, noted the critic Hanson O'Haver in 2021, were "embraced by the chic and the normal and the embarrassingly uncool all at once, with equal enthusiasm, totally eschewing the standard cool-common-passé sequence."

In many ways omnivorism is the only possible taste left. A singular notion of good taste is unjustifiable in a cosmopolitan world. The scholar Kwame Anthony Appiah defines "cosmopolitanism" as "a recognition and celebration of the fact that our fellow world citizens, in their different places, with their different languages, cultures, and traditions, merit not just our moral concern but also our interest and curiosity." Cosmopolitanism is not just a superficial embrace of cultural diversity but a conscious rejection of the is-ought fallacy. Our enthusiasm for other communities' conventions supports our effort to *overcome conventionality itself.* For the early-twentieth-century philosopher Alfred North Whitehead, "Other nations of different habits are not enemies: they are godsends."

By collectively reaching this stage of meta-knowledge, we come to understand the arbitrariness of our own preferences, tastes, and culture. To proclaim superiority of preferred styles over others is accordingly an arrogant and bigoted act. A harpsichord concerto can't be judged to be "better" than an Indian rāga. The cultural studies scholar Fred Inglis explains, "To declare difference as a value is to refuse, according to liberalism's first protocol, to tell others how to live." Omnivore taste is also a precursor to ultraindividualism: for everyone to follow their hearts, *all* idiosyncratic choices must be tolerated.

Meanwhile, we've also become aware of the inherent class and demographic biases in previous notions of taste. In his landmark 1979 work *Distinction,* sociologist Pierre Bourdieu deconstructed the Kantian notion of detached, contemplative taste, revealing it to be a silent but powerful weapon of elite dominance.

Any notions of "correct" cultural choice worked to bolster the class structure. In the words of philosopher Charles Wegener, taste was "a bourgeois invention, an arbitrary standard reflecting only a class detachment from life and labor." For liberals and socialists, preferences for abstract art and uncomfortable sofas were no longer enlightened aesthetics, but subversive class warfare against the poor and powerless. In tandem, anti-imperialist ideology challenged the privileging of Western high culture—the literary canon, classical music, ballet, academic art—over Indigenous works from less prosperous countries. And how can we complain about kitsch when so many status-disadvantaged individuals rise up the social ladder through their market success in the culture industry? Omnivorism and poptimism would be a way to show contrition for past sins.

Outside of politics, taste has also come to seem absurd in a world of hyperspeed fashion cycles. Writing about the twentieth century, fashion scholar Quentin Bell notes, "The pace of fashion has become noticeable, so noticeable that the fashions of a man's youth could look dowdy by the time that he was middle-aged." Today a look can become dowdy within weeks. Righteousness about any particular trend, then, is foolish when we may soon be equally righteous about its opposite. And once we have lived through enough fads, we suspect that every new trend will end up a fad. Conventions function best when the population is ignorant of their existence. We have been cursed to understand the mechanisms of culture too well, making earnest taste nearly impossible.

Omnivorism, for all of its rejections of "taste," still presupposes that cultural choice can change society. Consumerism can support allies, shame enemies, and deny prestige and financial support to oppressors. The French theorist Gilles Lipovetsky writes that our "hypermodern" era involves "a broadening of the ideal of equal respect, a desire for *hyper-recognition* which, rejecting every form of the contempt, depreciation or sense of inferiority under which one might suffer, demands the recognition of the other as equal in his or her difference." Omnivore taste can then be used to dismantle the status structures that prevent the equitable distribution of respect. From this perspective, the problem with capital-T Taste is that it disenfranchises huge swaths of the population and overallocates money and status to established elites. And any distaste for the preferred culture of status-disadvantaged groups could be interpreted as a form of discrimination. Distaste can be noble, on the other hand, when wielded against the power structure, unrepentant snobs, and unreformed bigots. In omnivorism the angry passion of the avant-garde against established conventions is channeled into a clear-cut political battle against revanchist enemies. To give Liz Phair a 0.0 is a hostile act, but to denounce the role of "Manic Pixie Dream Girls" in the films *500 Days of Summer* and *Garden State* is virtuous. If the old taste was a quiet tool of elite power, omnivore taste can be a loud cry of insurgency.

There are few manifestos outlining the specific aims of contemporary "cultural politics," but there do seem to be implicit rules behind the most militant mode of omnivore taste:

1. *Artists* should create content that promotes progressive political views and reveals unconscious biases against oppressed groups.
2. *Gatekeepers* should work to represent minority voices by elevating minority artists.
3. *Consumers* should only buy artworks and goods with progressive values that are created by upright individuals.
4. *Majority groups* should never profit on styles or stories that originate within minority groups.
5. *Critics* should decanonize antiprogressive artists and their works, and question aesthetics associated with high-status distinction.

The most vocal complaint against "the culture wars" is that it channels political energy to changing superficial symbols rather than working toward structural changes to the economy and the law. But everything in this book points to the fact that *culture matters* for status equality. Status criteria live inside of our conventions, and history has shown us that altering those criteria opens up social mobility for disadvantaged groups. Culture sets what is permissible and what is possible. As Black culture attracted huge audiences among white youth in the twentieth century, cultural flows became more complicated than upper-class trickle-down. The appreciation of minority culture within elite cultural capital didn't overturn the status structure or eradicate racism, but it has arguably better distributed money and status to disadvantaged communities. Hip-hop started on the streets of the South Bronx and is now a multibillion-dollar global industry. And unlike mainstream rock cashing in on the innovations of rhythm 'n' blues, hip-hop's icons are overwhelmingly Black artists rather than white imitators.

Hypermodern liberalism and cosmopolitanism thus lead to omnivorism and poptimism—and even a detente with capitalism, as long as the spoils flow to the right people. By seeking a fairer distribution of money to disadvantaged groups and the dissemination of antiracist messages through mainstream media channels, cultural politics works *within* the mass market. In its wake, any negative notions of selling out must go. And art should avoid being for *art's* sake when social equity is at stake. Hustling is a virtuous necessity for those without capital; detachment is a privilege. Rappers are right to demand "money, power, and respect" because they grew up without them.

In the active embrace of the cultural industry as a means to an end, we must also dismantle Kant's division between the simple pleasures of bodily sensation and the true beauty observed in detached contemplation. The philosopher Markus Gabriel writes, "Nowadays there is the tendency to misjudge the aesthetic experience as mere entertainment"—but this is not a mistake. Aesthetic experiences, believe omnivores, should have no moral superiority over fun. Art is no better than kitsch, because kitsch is exciting, social, and delivers what it promises. The dubstep "wobble" bass is beautiful *because* it rattles the dance floor. The concept of guilty pleasures is a relic of old-timey snobbery. If there is no intrinsic superiority of high culture over low culture, there's no longer any need to suffer through long, difficult books or boring black-and-white Swedish movies. *New York Times* film critic A. O. Scott writes about our era, "No one will tell you that you have a duty to like, or even to look at, certain things, and anyone who tries to guilt-trip you in that way can be dismissed as a snob or a scold."

As with any value system, omnivorism contains inconsistencies. First, the refusal to erect fences veers toward monoculture. As we've seen, strong labels and classifications provide cultural goods with meaning and value; lumping a vast diversity of artifacts under a single permissive sensibility impedes the development of both. Second, omnivorism has an inherent hypocrisy. There is no way to accept *all* conventions, because of their inevitably contradictory nature. Musician David Byrne, famed for his great admiration of global rhythms and instruments, questions those who claim they love all kinds of music: "Some forms of music are diametrically opposed to one another! You can't love them all." Fences do exist—they are just openly political ones.

Omnivorism also may have a dampening effect on the cultural ecosystem. If the "friction" of status struggles is an important creative force, omnivorism defuses tensions within the social groups most likely to create new conventions: namely, artists, the creative class, the media, and subcultures. Much great art and culture arose from righteous indignation toward bad taste, commercialist kitsch, and the conservative establishment. By eliminating these as legitimate targets for criticism we create much weaker, less meaningful conventions. T. S. Eliot warned in the 1940s, "A world culture which was simply a *uniform* culture would be no culture at all." The idea of omnivorism is to support demographically marginalized creators in the short run, but these groups' previous use of radical taste in erecting their own tall fences often created great cultural value for the community in the long run.

Artist status remains a solid means to move up the social hierarchy, but in a tolerant, omnivore world, "outcasts" no longer need to become artists to find social acceptance. The art critic Jerry Saltz writes, "The imperative to ecstatic and eccentric self-expression—to be yourself, and to not let anyone make you pretend to be otherwise—is no longer just a niche value, cherished by a band of weirdos. It is the overwhelming message of American culture today." Radical innovations once caused social angst and then, eventually, delivered glory. Today most inventions are accepted without noise or struggle—and take their place among thousands of other inventions accepted without any noise or struggle.

With the Revenge of the Head in a long-tail world, cultural literacy for the last few decades requires reading a few serious books every year but also consuming products from the largest conglomerates: Marvel superhero movies (Walt Disney), Beyoncé (Columbia/Sony), *Keeping Up with the Kardashians* (Ryan Seacrest Productions backed by iHeartMedia, Inc., the new corporate name for the widely loathed Clear Channel). Poptimism means that elites should commune with these works, as they're "what the people want." But money can always fake the veneer of popularity. The cultural industry will always have the means and might to dominate our mind-space, and a major point of "indie snobbery" was to provide counterbalance. The music producer and writer Nick Sylvester worries, "By embracing the project of pop music, we might be complicit in letting our underground ecosystems dry up and making pop become the only game in town." By denying taste as a tool and hesitating to criticize popular works, outsider groups and critics have surrendered their primary way of pushing back. We now risk living in the world that essayist George W. S. Trow predicted in the 1980s: "Nothing was judged—only counted."

For all the worries about stasis in pop culture, the art world has also become seemingly subsumed under capitalist logic. This began as an enlightened hope for democratization. Sociologist Jean Duvignaud wrote in the late 1960s, "Art, as a charismatic and exclusive activity carried out in the nucleus of privileged groups and by an elite, has in effect disappeared. Instead, it has become the aspiration of all kinds of audiences, readers, enthusiasts and public groups which form momentary and changing pseudo-societies." Today the art market is thriving as an auxiliary to the Big Bling. Contemporary art provides both conspicuous consumption and great financial assets. The most representative artist of our era may be Jeff Koons—a former commodities trader whose pop-spectacles-as-artistic-statements have turned impish Duchampian and Warholian ideas into piles of cash. Like any good shaman, Koons predicted our future where avant-garde notions of voluntary unpopularity would just appear to be pathetic unpopularity. He once told art critic Calvin Tomkins, "I'm always very upset if somebody doesn't like my work, because I never want to lose anyone. I feel like I've failed if I do that." Under the Koonsian sensibility, his balloon dog sculpture is a masterpiece because everyone knows it, even children can enjoy it, and it sold for $58 million. Now, in the 2020s, nonfungible tokens (NFTs) open a new path for art to be an unambiguous means of financial speculation.

If the original goal of avant-garde art was to provide new frameworks for valuing the world, the pseudo-irony of embracing financial success as artistic achievement only duplicates the capitalist maxims already guiding our perception. But perhaps pure market logic has seemed like the only possible next step. The twentieth century burned too bright, exhausting most of the obvious challenges to existing conventions. And now, in an age of omnivorism, why strive for a radical destruction of convention when contemporary critics are obliged to give their attention to popular kitsch and immediate aesthetic experiences?

With artists less reliable to rip up convention, the responsibility for creativity may now fall to youth subcultures. But we seem to be in a "post-subculture" world. The sociologist David Muggleton writes, "Perhaps the very concept of subculture is becoming less applicable in postmodernity, for the breakdown of mass society has ensured that there is no longer a coherent dominant culture against which a subculture can express its resistance." Under the banner of cosmopolitanism, demographically disadvantaged groups no longer have to seek shelter in walled-off mini-societies. In 1995, MTV's comedy show *The State* ran a satirical sketch called "Dan, the Very Popular Openly Gay High School Student," imagining an alternate universe in which a gay teenager wins prom king. In 2011 an openly gay track star in Pennsylvania won prom king, and in 2021, a lesbian couple won both king and queen. The term "subculture" best resonates with youth today only in the realm of "style surfing." Middle-class teens jump from one look to another as "cosplay." The teen-oriented website Aesthetics Wiki offers hundreds of crowdsourced style formulas for teens to dabble in, starting with Bubblegum Bitch and Girl-Next-Door, extending into Beatnik, Skinheads, Mod, Teddies, Chav, and Avant-garde.

The internet has meanwhile raised up former nerd hobbies like gaming, comic book collecting, and sci-fi into mainstream culture. Subcultures may be waning but hard-core fan cultures are stronger than ever. Fierce, cultlike advocates focus their online activity into boosting the profiles of stars they "stan." This often translates into bulk buying of new products and repeated digital streaming to jack up play counts. A high school student named Benjamin Cordero told *The New York Times*, "A person on Stan Twitter probably bought [a] record 10 times, streamed a song on three separate playlists and racked up hundreds and hundreds of plays." Another duty is skirmishing with rivals; Lady Gaga's Little Monsters and Ariana Grande's Arianators are often at war. Taylor Swift stans sent death threats to a *Pitchfork* music critic for giving her 2020 album *Folklore* a good but not great review.

Hobbyist culture has always had two approaches: the highly analytical *nerds* who use high-culture techniques of textual analysis on low culture, and the *otaku* (a term first appearing in Japan during the 1980s) who focus on completist ownership of products and unquestioning faith in the creators. The otaku model is now dominant globally, with youth finding a means of "self-expression" in enlisting into a global "army." Avi, a twenty-six-year-old Indonesian fan of the Korean boy band BTS, told *The New York Times*, "It feels like we're promoting BTS, but we are also promoting our own voices, our own struggles, our own hope for a better world." Fan groups have channeled this intensity toward real outcomes in the cultural marketplace. Thanks to the BTS Army, the group can reach number one on Billboard before reaching the passive consumption that once marked the meaning of "mainstream" success.

Declarations of a post-subculture world are too hasty; there is plenty of subcultural behavior—just not where we used to seek it. In the past, creative-class youth admired working-class and minority subcultures as a joint struggle against the mainstream. The most potent subcultures of this new century, by contrast, have formed as a *reaction* to liberal omnivorism—appearing on the right flank of the political spectrum. In believing their social position is crumbling, many young American men have found a solution to their status anxiety by banding online together with black-pilled incels, right-wing trolls, and unrepentant Nazis. Right-wing youth form status groups with their own conventions, slang, and styles, and they reward one another for the most outrageous lib-owning. (We often overlook the precedents for this in the teddy boy violence against immigrant communities in the 1950s, and British skinhead culture's merger with the Far Right.)

The part that is post-subcultural, perhaps, is that the cultural industry no longer looks to these groups for innovations to pilfer. While a few memes like Pepe the Frog have bounced between pop culture and right-wing fever swamps, "incel chic" is unlikely to guide the next fashion season's ready-to-wear collections. Rightist subcultures revel in the "bad taste" of guns, fast food, and un-PC jokes—a counterimitation of effete cosmopolitans that effete cosmopolitans are unlikely to embrace.

A major media channel for the antiomnivore subcultural sensibility has been gaming, where a loud faction of male gamers has pushed back against the industry's growing diversity. Gaming has arguably replaced music and fashion as the most important medium for youth culture. The video game industry is now larger than sports or films, and a 2020 study found that 68 percent of male Gen Zers considered gaming a key ingredient of their identity. At present only one out of every seven hard-core gamers is a woman. But the transition away from male-dominated gaming has irked what the writer Vicky Osterweil calls "fashoid white boy" gamers. In analyzing the Gamergate controversy in 2014, *Deadspin's* Kyle Wagner came to see antifeminist gamers as "a mutant variant of the traditional American grievance movement." This may have limited hard-core gaming's appeal to the fashion industry. Marc Jacobs created virtual outfits for characters in *Animal Crossing*, not *Call of Duty*.

At first glance, online youth culture can look dark, illiberal, and nihilistic: e.g., online video creators' casual conspiracy mongering, the hacking and dissemination of private celebrity nudes on 4chan, and the menacing face tattoos and Trump support of SoundCloud rappers. But this isn't to overlook the positive developments. Youth culture has undermined the most oppressive aspects of the "cool" aesthetic. There is less snobbery, more inclusion, and more freedom to construct personas without having to hide actual desires. Avant-garde artists "killed their idols" by debasing the reigning artistic conventions; omnivore youth thin out the veteran ranks by canceling racists, sexists, and abusers. Freed from a knee-jerk hatred of kitsch, culture overflows with an endless stream of new content: highbrow, middlebrow, and lowbrow.

Yet in the past we did rely on stauncher notions of taste to encourage the very radical innovations idolized today. Taste was a powerful signaling cost—a *nonmonetary* way to keep certain styles and artifacts within the confines of certain communities. By rejecting taste, omnivorism weakens cultural and subcultural capital to the point of nonexistence. As a result, raw wealth becomes a more obvious criterion for status distinction.

If the internet, the new nouveau riche, and omnivorism all drain the status value of new culture, what do we use as a guide for lifestyle choices? Two approaches have emerged: the embrace of historical value, or a gleeful detachment from the past.

RETROMANIA VS. NEOMANIA

"The avant-garde is now an arrière-garde," concluded Simon Reynolds in his 2011 book, *Retromania*. Thanks to digitization, consumers in the twenty-first century could "access the immediate past so easily and so copiously" that they became more interested in the "cultural artifacts of [the] immediate past" than those of the immediate future. The "pioneers and innovators" of the creative class took up new roles as "curators and archivists." Creators applied the cut-and-paste of hip-hop sampling to nearly every art form. Bloggers acted as cultural grave robbers, digging up indulgent clickbait nostalgia each day to satiate readers' endless demand for new content. For all his prescience about the future of art, Marcel Duchamp got one thing extremely wrong: "I'm afraid that our dear century will not be very much remembered." We moved into the twenty-first century deep under the shadow of the last one.

The theorist Gilles Lipovetsky seemingly predicted retromania in his 2005 work *Hypermodern Times*—time would no longer be "structured by an absolute present" but "structured by a *paradoxical* present, a present that ceaselessly exhumes and 'rediscovers' the past." Glenn O'Brien confirmed it in 2011: "The funny thing about our time is that it is all times, all eras at once." In combination with omnivorism, retromania was fun at first, providing us more options to craft our personas thanks to an infinite reserve of older cultural artifacts and styles. We could embrace bohemian chic one day, eighties collegiate the next.

But where the avant-garde aimed to be seminal, retromania was a cultural vasectomy. With so much time, energy, and attention channeled into excavation, fewer seemed to be working toward the radically new. Rather than pose unfamiliar threats to mainstream culture, many artists, youth, subcultures, and minority groups chose to relive the glory days on loop—a "slow cancellation of the future." In a "head"-heavy market where consumer awareness is half the battle, Hollywood studios reduced risk by rebooting beloved franchises from the past. Between 2002 and 2019, there were eight live-action Spider-Man films—based on a comic book character who debuted in 1962. Pop finally ate itself: past classics towered in importance over contemporary inventions.

Improved digital technologies have also enabled creators' pastiche of the past to sound, look, and feel eerily similar to the originals. Literary critic Harold Bloom believed that "strong poets keep returning from the dead. . . . *How* they return is the decisive matter, for if they return intact, then the return impoverishes the later poets, dooming them to be remembered—if at all—as having ended in poverty, in an imaginative need they could not themselves gratify." Contemporary retro-inflected creations didn't seem to be using "strong poets" as a launching pad but as an easy way to tap into historical value through borrowing a classic vibe. Fifties retro inspired more than just revival acts; its sound quickly evolved into two distinctive new musical genres, glam rock and punk, both of which went on to define the seventies. The popular aughts act Franz Ferdinand, by contrast, very closely re-created the sound of post-punk bands such as Gang of Four. Listeners today hoping to inhabit this sonic world may be more inclined to return to the original than listen to the copy.

In looking backward, we violated the pop ethos that *now* would always be more interesting than *then*, only further adding to the sense of cultural stasis. For the composer Leonard Meyer, stasis doesn't entail "an absence of novelty and change" but just "the absence of ordered sequential change." This narrative chaos began with the style simultaneity of postmodernism, and then retromania further hindered the creation of tentpole moments that once marked each era as distinct. In 2011 the writer Kurt Andersen noted in *Vanity Fair*, "The recent past—the 00s, the 90s, even a lot of the 80s—looks almost identical to the present." *Back to the Future* provides a film's worth of gags based on the significant cultural changes between 1955 and 1985: Chuck Berry vs. heavy metal, ornate Cadillacs vs. sleek DeLoreans, minimalist greasers vs. overly layered preppies. A similar movie today looking back at the nineties would have characters looking vaguely outmoded but not unrecognizable. We don't watch *Friends* as a period piece.

Andersen attributed this cultural stasis to consumer exhaustion around change: "People have a limited capacity to embrace flux and strangeness and dissatisfaction, and right now we're maxed out." But is this principle always true? In the sixties, youth *demanded* flux and strangeness as proof of their desired social changes, and we're most certainly not lacking social changes to convert into new styles. Andersen also assumed retromania was a corporate conspiracy: monopolies have slowed down fashion changes to stabilize their businesses. Old Navy and the other Big Chino firms refuse to let us abandon twill pants in khaki tones. And yet the internet and its long tail have never made it easier to maneuver around monopoly. Retromania happened only because consumers—especially elite ones—found *more* value in old styles than in new ones.

In hindsight, retromania appears to have been a response to the plummeting cachet of contemporary culture. Between virality, a destruction of barriers to information and access, the celebration of simple nouveau riche aesthetics, and a rejection of taste, inventions haven't taken on as much status value as in the past. Meanwhile, we feel more pressure to be "authentic," which raises the bar for switching to new things. Before we consider adoption, new styles must prove they aren't fads—and they're mostly fads. With contemporary status value on the wane, historical value rises to the fore. The reliable past is more useful for crafting personas than an ephemeral present.

Retromania was a particularly Gen X approach to negotiating the internet age, since its members grew up in an era greatly respectful of historical value. The subsequent two generations, millennials and Gen Z, are "digital natives" and have very little firsthand knowledge of the analog age's slower fashion cycles. In fact, the most vibrant parts of their pop culture appear to be completely unmoored from the past. Youth relish in the extremely online, weightless culture of current times—a *neomania*. If the internet provides an infinite number of new things to be enjoyed, why not let ourselves enjoy them? Every minute of the day, social media apps feed us more and more relatable content. Affordable prosumer hardware and software enable creators to make videos, songs, and digital images at a minimal cost, and then distribute them to millions for free. There is warmth and friendship awaiting anyone who enlists in the BTS Army. Neomania does indulge in nostalgia—but as ironic, superficial fun, not the reverence of a golden age.

Worries about cultural stasis may have partly been about the poverty of new sensibilities—and yet neomania provides a new and very distinct aesthetic. The aughts lacked a "look" because culture was stuck in the migration from the iconic visuals of MTV and *Ray Gun* to a still text-heavy World Wide Web. (The blinking text of GeoCities may be a vibe now, but it looked pathetic in real time.) By contrast, the visual internet of the 2010s offered a specific style: amateurism glossed up in hi-fi digital sheen, sincere tears in confessional videos, goofy Vine loops, bitcrushed memes, cheesy dance fads, and blown-out SoundCloud rap recorded with the built-in MacBook microphone.

For much of human history, storytelling was the exclusive privilege of designated elders, bookish scholars, and ambitious artists. To create motion pictures, aspiring filmmakers had to pay their dues at schools and in the industry before getting their hands on a camera. The internet opened storytelling to everyone, a development long beheld as a great democratic revolution. But this also has robbed nerds of their longtime monopoly on content creation and gatekeeping. When everyone is making content, teens have extended the high school hierarchy into their viewing habits: Why watch the weirdos when the cool girls are showing off their shopping hauls and class clowns are embarrassing their bros in epic pranks? Thus the very appeal of TikTok is its "mediocrity," writes *Vox*'s Rebecca Jennings: "No one follows you because they expect you to be talented. They follow you because they like you." Previous generations of lowbrow Americans may have enjoyed passive consumption of *Candid Camera* and *America's Funniest Home Videos*, but Gen Z's analogous content is defining their generation the way the Beatles defined the baby boomers and MTV defined Gen X.

With popular-kid creators shooting their real lives, the resulting content is unsurprisingly low on obscure historical references or artistic pretensions. Few youth drop oblique allusions to Jean Genet novels in their prank videos. This focus on a limited cultural vocabulary makes neomania more inclusive, but the effect is to disconnect it from the twentieth-century paradigm of cool. Graying hipsters were primed for their successors to invent even angrier forms of rebellion and detachment, but youth rebelled through *abandoning* artistic radicalism and detachment (or at least focusing their radicalism on more pressing issues of social justice). There may be an "elite TikTok" of odd videos and "BookTok" of literary suggestions, but the more representational and seemingly beloved video content is kids simply being kids. If coolness was about donning a mask, the neomania mask is pretending to have no mask at all. Makeup gurus revel in the exaggerated homeliness of their plain faces before demonstrating their magic powers of cosmetic transformation. Goofy randomness is a key virtue. Defying any easy explanation, the most watched TikTok video of 2020 was the young woman Bella Poarch lip-syncing, head-bobbing, and crossing her eyes in rhythm—to a relatively obscure Blackpool grime track from four years prior.

If these attributes make neomania alienating for adults, that is perhaps the point. Just as MTV provided a hiding place for Gen X, TikTok offers a completely walled-off world where kids can escape the cultural dominance of adults and reveal themselves. "Sharing, and sometimes oversharing," writes Sejla Rizvic in *The Walrus*, "seems to be second nature to Gen Zers, which translates into their digital fluency and sense of openness online." The norm for oversharing builds further fences with older adults, whose social responsibilities of work and family prevent them from exposing their private lives and innermost feelings. Moreover, few adults would enjoy Gen Z antitaste as it manifests in dance routines channeling the communal spirit of church camp sing-alongs, the lo-fi production values of suburban audiovisual clubs, and meme-conforming short videos much like inside jokes in high school year-books.

Certainly the previous generations didn't always explore history as a virtuous preservation of human knowledge. When culture centered around canons, radical artists learned history in order to know the enemy. In the 1990s, familiarity with old records and films became cultural capital. With the world's knowledge always retrievable from an infinite expanse of free Wikipedia pages, digital natives have little incentive to memorize and analyze the past. After selling an NFT of his work for $69 million, the forty-year-old digital artist Beeple proudly told *The New Yorker*, "When you say, 'Abstract Expressionism,' literally, I have no idea what the hell that is." Familiarity with the canon is what allowed radical artists to gauge the innovation of their own works. And innovations more quickly became influential when they appeared to be principled rejections of established convention. Like many YouTubers, Marcel Duchamp engaged in juvenile pranks, but they're written up in history today as deep comments on the ontology of art. If we return to the maxim that "what doesn't grow out of tradition is plagiarism," inventions are unlikely to be influential when they're shallow re-creations of recent hits. With so little new art being canonized, perhaps the goal of permanence no longer provides motivation to creators anyway. Cashing in as a "creator" is a higher path to status than being honored as an "artist" in obscure circles.

There are signs, however, that righteous indignation toward the past remains a strong creative engine, even if the historical specifics are unknown. In 2021's *Neon Screams: How Drill, Trap and Bashment Made Music New Again*, the twentysomething critic Kit Mackintosh argues that the greater democratization of digital musical technology has led to a fecundity of neomaniacal Black genres around the globe. Almost as if he were picking up from F. T. Marinetti's 1909 "The Manifesto of Futurism," Mackintosh writes, "False prophets fearfully warned you that the twenty-first century hailed the end of innovation and the death of progress. . . . Come smash your old paradigms. Set them ablaze and be amazed by the sounds of the next century." Between ticky off-kilter rhythms and otherworldly digital voice processing, the experimental hip-hop genres trap and drill have delivered radical hymns from alien planets. Like all good futurists, Mackintosh hopes these genres mark a new musical paradigm, but, ironically, their alleged break from the past is precisely what will place them in the "unbroken chain." And with this new framing, the critical world is coming around to value trap and drill as radical invention rather than roughshod amateurism.

We shouldn't expect youth cultures to always be a fount of artistic value—that's hardly their intention—but their neomania innovations in 2022 perhaps feel the most different from those of 1965 because mainstream culture has been slow to embrace them. In the twentieth century, youth culture quickly took on cachet, infiltrated mainstream culture, and reshaped adults in their image. In the early 1960s, the twist dance fad went from Black youth to *American Bandstand* teenyboppers to wealthy Manhattanites at the upscale Peppermint Lounge. When it comes to drill, Kanye West and Drake quickly incorporated the genre's rappers and production into their own mass-market songs, but the breakthrough talent, like Fivio Foreign, have hardly become household names. Likewise suburban middle-class neomania has only made baby steps. When Addison Rae performed eight "TikTok dances" on *The Tonight Show with Jimmy Fallon,* many found it "cringey." For much of teenage online culture, diffusion has been stunted—like a trend for lanyard bracelets at summer camp that doesn't catch on back at school.

This is not to say social media apps are a digital backwater. Online stars are making millions a year without validation from established institutions. The question is whether these platforms inspire true artistic innovation. Every structural change we've noted in this chapter—pay-by-click internet platforms, the rise of a new nouveau riche, the death of cultural capital—incentivizes creators to aim for amassing economic capital rather than cultural capital. And the easier path toward reliable revenue-share agreements and commercial sponsorship is building "scale." Attracting large audiences is much easier with lowest-common-denominator content than with "art." The content follows the monetization.

In the past, creators had to hide their materialist dreams behind pronouncements of high-minded and transcendent goals. But in a world of celebrity wealth-gospel and millennial financial anxiety, young entertainers face little backlash for aggressively courting likes, subscribers, and advertisers. Follower counts and gross earnings appear to be the only relevant sign of cultural import. Starving artists simply starve. The comedian Brittany Mignanelli complained on Twitter, "Comedian in 1985: i made a joke about how women shop and now i am famous / Comedian in 2021: i do sketch, standup, improv, satire, i make dumb lil videos on tik tok, i have a podcast, a web series, 3 features, 5 pilots, i'm on twitter 22 hours per day & can't afford rent."

Within neomania, an open materialism bends the cultural ecosystem toward a full embodiment of capitalist logic. Tubercular bohemians died for their craft in squalid basements; creators live in multimillion-dollar "hype houses" to give their audiences the content they demand. Cash rules everything around youth. When a TikToker in 2020 interviewed her friends in L.A. about their outfits, each identified choices not by their color or style or even brand but by their prices.

Like the other changes caused by the internet, the forces of neomania conspire against increased symbolic complexity. But we should at least salute Gen Z for finding the means to reject their parents' canon and build their own. "TikTok," writes Sejla Rizvic, "has become a core way for Gen Z to express its own ethos, aesthetic, and attitudes—sometimes resulting in outright hostility toward millennials and boomers." As of 2022 culture is bifurcated between the big "head" of blockbuster movies and Super Bowl half-time concerts versus the Internet Famous. A full merger is inevitable at some point. SoundCloud rappers made inroads to commercial radio, although for many, their legal troubles and untimely deaths prevented full-scale celebrity. Our fears of cultural stasis, then, may be less about the creation of new artifacts, styles, and sensibilities than about their failure to *take over* mainstream culture. Within two years of forming, the Sex Pistols went from inhabiting a squalid London subculture to topping the British pop charts. TikTok and its ilk are chipping away at baby boomer and Gen X values, but the process is slow. Not that youth care: neomania culture raises fences with adults and builds bridges with other youth—and they get paid a lot for it.

-◈-

The technological, economic, and social structures of the internet have changed the rhythms of how creators pursue invention, how innovations take on value, and how radical ideas trickle down to mass culture. Today culture exists in infinite quantities, information barriers have been reduced to zero, and fashion cycles are fast and shallow—all of which work against the creation of status value. As this combines with a new nouveau riche emerging outside of the West and hungry to climb up the global status ladder, economic capital has reemerged as a clearer status criterion than cultural capital. The long tail predicted utopian cohabitation of tiny consumer subcultures but, instead, the professional classes have all coalesced into a world of omnivore taste where nothing is great because everything is good. The generations are split on how to proceed: either look back or don't look back at all.

At some point our expectations will adjust to these structural realities, but at the moment, we suffer from what Pierre Bourdieu calls *hysteresis*—the lingering values of a previous age continuing to guide our judgments. Take our feelings toward fame. In the past we assigned high status to anyone who could achieve celebrity. To be broadcasted required being on television, which was limited to very few. Today anyone with a smartphone and an internet connection can be broadcasted. Yet the sheer act of mediation still manages to make individuals seem more charismatic. But why should we still be enamored with fame at all when fame is so cheap? Maybe soon we won't be. And there are many other values we're likely to abandon as the internet age becomes the only age we know: historical value, artistic legacy, authenticity.

Kurt Andersen was confident that our cultural stasis was a temporary phase: "If this stylistic freeze is just a respite, a backward-looking counter-reaction to upheaval, then once we finally get accustomed to all the radical newness, things should return to normal." But we should consider the opposite: cultural change may follow a pattern of *punctuated equilibrium*, moments of dramatic transformation followed by long periods of stasis. Anthropologist A. L. Kroeber surveyed all civilizations and found that "aesthetic and intellectual endeavors resulting in higher values preponderantly realize themselves in temporary bursts, or growths, in all the higher civilizations examined." In other words, the breakneck cultural change of the sixties may have been the exception, not the norm. The August 1966 issue of *Esquire* complained that trends moved too fast and advocated "Let the next four years be a vacation." There will always be slow cultural drift, but the fast, hard, and exciting changes of the twentieth century relied on humans frequently switching to new conventions, which they did in pursuit of status value. We are still entertained today by novelties, but memes and viral videos are unlikely to define our personas.

Without individuals making changes, there will be no cultural movements either. Periods of stasis are more common in human history than moments of rapid change, but we're likely to feel disappointed about our own stasis as long as the previous century looms over our judgments.

The internet provides a new platform for human interaction, but it has not dissolved the link between status and culture. The final question should then be: If we now understand their interlocking principles, how should we use this knowledge to promote the best outcomes for both—equality *and* creativity?

STATUS EQUALITY AND CULTURAL CREATIVITY

Is show winner King's Royal Lassie a better dog than the farm-town pup Lassie? No, says the internet: "*All* dogs are good bois." This strain of canine egalitarianism powers the popular Twitter account WeRateDogs®, which rates everyday dogs on a strict 10-point scale—and always seems to reward them a 12, 13, or 14. Another goal of this unofficial movement is to eradicate the long-entrenched idea that purebred canines are superior to mutts. In contemporary society, "breed" is not only the way we classify dogs, but it unconsciously informs our value judgments as well. The world's most famous dogs are purebred: Lassie is a collie, Beethoven is a Saint Bernard, the Doge of Dogecoin is a Shiba Inu.

We began our exploration of status with collies, and we will conclude with dogs because they provide a clear example of how status changes our tastes, shapes our perception of nature, and influences the collective standards for beauty. The concept of breed steers our unconscious understanding of dogs today, and yet dog breeds, argue the scholars Michael Worboys, Julie-Marie Strange, and Neil Pemberton, are a "material and cultural invention" not even two hundred years old. In early-nineteenth-century England, wealthy women prized dogs for their emotional support, while aristocrats valued dogs for their usefulness as hunting companions. Everything changed with the midcentury arrival of dog shows—competitions among British aristocrats to determine who owned the best canines. To establish standards for objective judgment, show organizers settled upon a set of authoritative criteria for the correct shape, color, and size of previously general categories like terrier or retriever. Breeders then used these standards to select mating pairs, leading to today's panoply of distinct breeds.

As dog shows permeated English society, *Canis lupus familiaris* came to be valued in an entirely new way. An 1863 editorial in the magazine *The Field* stated, "A dog is a genuine Newfoundland, a retriever, a foxhound, pointer, a setter, a terrier, a spaniel, or a mastiff; a 'dawg' may be any of these or none of these, for he may be a monstrosity or a mongrel." From there the logic of human hierarchies seeped into canine hierarchies as well: English dogs were superior to foreign breeds, puppies of champions enjoyed great cachet. (Among the writer Dorothy Parker's final possessions was "a certificate of the aristocratic origins of a beloved poodle.") By the twentieth century, as historian Paul Fussell notes, the ownership of particular breeds served as class markers in the United States: Labradors and golden retrievers at the top, Scottish and Irish setters in the middle, and pit bulls at the bottom.

Our love for dogs may be genetic, but the way we perceive, classify, and value them can be traced to a specific status competition in the nineteenth century. Once dogs became status symbols rather than practical companions, the need for differentiation incentivized humans to transform them into dozens of distinct categories. This origin story has been lost to time, and breed-conforming dogs simply came to be perceived as more beautiful. Mutts are healthier than purebreds, yet the very designation "mutt" implies something is wrong with them. Research conducted in the Czech Republic demonstrated that people are twice as likely to reclaim their lost purebred dog from a pound than their runaway mutt.

We set out at the beginning of this book to solve the Grand Mystery of Culture—to determine why individuals cluster in their preferences for certain arbitrary practices and then switch to new ones over time. But in answering this question, we have arrived at a much deeper insight: Status structures provide the underlying conventions for each culture, which determine our behaviors, values, and perception of reality. Behaviors and objects with status value are good, beautiful, and desirable; those without are bad, ugly, and useless. The struggle for higher status—whether striving for basic equality or angling for the very top—shapes individual identities, spurs creativity and cultural change, and forms customs and traditions. Humans may possess an innate desire to create, but their inventions achieve broader diffusion when they fulfill others' status needs. These mechanisms often lead to structural biases against certain groups but, when given the right parameters, they can also open the path to social mobility and greater cultural diversity. The status upheavals of the twentieth century resulted in an explosion in new artifacts supporting a wide range of new sensibilities, as high-status groups used the conventions of less wealthy communities as cultural capital.

Is culture, then, a mere by-product of status? Certainly we'd rather believe that culture is a wondrous human invention that enables self-expression, group solidarity, emotional support, and the transmission of knowledge. Those are indeed beneficial functions, but they don't explain why culture arises and changes. The fundamental desire for status offers a clearer explanation in demonstrating why rational individuals end up forming the most commonly observed behavioral patterns. The "warm glow" we receive from cultural participation is another way of describing the benefits of normal status. Conventions tend to "express" something only when they classify us as members of certain groups. The unbridled human desire for individual distinction may derive from the need to mark super-high status positions. Culture enables us to transmit human knowledge, but the specific content—customs, traditions, classics, and the canon—tilts toward the preferences and behaviors of high-status individuals.

These are hardly heartwarming conclusions. Moreover, the deep influence of status on our individual choices challenges our very sense of free will. The sociologist Pitirim Sorokin writes, "When we ourselves determine something, we feel ourselves free; and especially when this self-determination flows spontaneously from us as something quite natural to us and emanating from our very nature." The regularity of mechanisms behind aesthetics, choice, taste, and identity all question where to draw the line between "*our* very nature" and our position within a particular hierarchy. Annoyed with Thorstein Veblen's theories, the famed American critic H. L. Mencken wrote, "Do I admire Beethoven's *Fifth Symphony* because it is incomprehensible to Congressmen and Methodists—or because I genuinely love music? Do I prefer terrapin à la Maryland to fried liver because plow-hands must put up with the liver—or because the terrapin is intrinsically a more charming dose?" Mencken correctly notes that status value isn't the only aspect of cultural value, but he's too

confident that he can separate the effects of status from his "pure" contemplation of beauty and pleasure. Over the course of history, humans repeatedly and
regularly changed their cultural preferences—almost always in the direction
of status. Our desire to adopt the norms of elites can seemingly override biological instinct, economic rationality, and personal psychology. Status concerns
nudged the Beatles to trade their proud rock 'n' roll pompadours for arty moptops and forced William Finnegan to abandon his beloved longboard.

Not every human choice is a direct result of status seeking, but when attempting to explain cultural change on a macro level, status value should be
considered as the primary factor. Taste is never only about the thing itself—
e.g., the flavor of a wine or the mechanical superiority of a car. Civilization is
fundamentally *symbolic,* and every choice communicates social position. This
suggests that evolutionary biology, neuroscience, and mathematical modeling,
taken in isolation, aren't sufficient for diagnosing cultural patterns. Questions
of aesthetics and taste are ultimately tied to status. For years, evolutionary biologists hoped to demonstrate an "innate" visual preference among humans
for savannah grasslands, theoretically developed during *Homo sapiens*'s many
years inhabiting sub-Saharan Africa. But even if this dubious theory were true,
status—not genetics—provides a much more direct explanation for the incredible diversity of artistic styles seen around the world. And status better ad-
dresses the aesthetic divisions that manifest in a single society—e.g., why the
upper classes like abstract painting and the lower classes don't. All analysis of
cultural trends should thus first work through an innovation's status implications. In 2019 *Vox* identified mini Australian shepherds as the "dog of the
moment," attributing their popularity to "portable, apartment-friendly size and
striking good looks." Many dog breeds are handsome and small enough for
apartment life; the article neglected to mention that mini Australian shepherds may also serve as status symbols. Just because no one who was interviewed for the article openly admitted their status seeking doesn't mean we
should take their alibis in good faith.

That being said, status isn't a crystal ball for how culture will change in the
future. Culture is capricious: status outlines the structure in which cultural
decisions take place, but the ultimate outcomes are stochastic. We can never
predict how interlopers will subvert the dominant conventions, nor which
groups will rise in stature over time. Identifying sources of cachet may help

lead us to the likely sources of innovation, and charting outmoded conventions can illuminate the candidates for retro. An item's or practice's initial status value may also have bearing on whether it becomes a custom or tradition. A major trend for women in 2004 was thong underwear "with straps worn high over the hips, exposed by fashionable low-rise jeans and Juicy Couture sweat pants." From what we've learned, is this look likely to be maintained as a long-term American tradition?

This also reminds us that we must be careful to distinguish culture and raw numerical measures. Based on his mathematical models, sociologist Duncan Watts has discounted the role of "influencers" in diffusion patterns and suggested that trends take off from "a complicated mix of individual choices, social constraints, and random chance." This may be objectively accurate, but fashions are never aggregations of all individual choices: they are specific narratives that specific high-status institutions introduce to the public. At any time the most common style in a population is, by fashion standards, "out of style." And every year the media ignores trends among huge swaths of low-status individuals because the mere discussion of them would be a low-status act. Twitterati discuss the Tesla Model 3 more than the bestselling Ford F-150 pickup truck. The status of adopters is a critical factor for not just understanding the cultural implications of any trend, but also forecasting its future prospects. By a purely mathematical measure, 1991 was a successful year for thermochromic shirt brand Hypercolor: $50 million in sales over just four months. But its hasty overexpansion tanked the cachet and, just a year later, the company filed for bankruptcy. In those same years, the streetwear brand Stüssy intentionally undersupplied the demand for its clothes—i.e., it *refused* to go viral. On the occasion of Stüssy's fortieth anniversary, *GQ* named it "streetwear's first heritage brand."

For many, "viral contagion" is an attractive metaphor for understanding culture precisely because it frames taste as an empirically observable phenomenon without any political implications. The "neutral" model of cultural diffusion is *neutral*: humans randomly imitate one another without any consideration of hierarchy or privilege. Status, by contrast, adds an uncomfortable political valence to every trend and custom. Despite ideals of equality, fraternity, and liberty, high-status groups wield greater influence on the public's choices, values, and perspectives. The lessons in this book lend credence to the Marxist idea of *hegemony*, which is defined by the Birmingham Centre for Contemporary Cultural Studies as "the shaping of the society's culture in the image of that of the dominant class." Through hegemony, the bottom of society comes to see self-interested bourgeois values as the natural order of the world. Status principles reveal that creating and maintaining hegemony requires no shadowy conspiracy—just individuals and institutions in capitalist economies gravitating toward behaviors that boost and protect their status.

But if all cultural forms are arbitrary, why should we be concerned that elites have more say in choosing the standards at any time? Again, we must clarify what is meant by "arbitrary." There is flexibility in the initial choice between practices but, once chosen, approved practices take on a differential value. Elites strategically form and maintain conventions for their own self-interest and, once these practices are established as legitimate, alternatives, even when equally effective, are "wrong." High-status individuals then point to their own effortless adherence as proof of their eminence.

For all of these worries about hegemony and power, however, culture never feels so sinister in everyday life. Is following a purebred Bernese mountain dog on Instagram a propagation of nineteenth-century aristocratic values? Is singing along to Taylor Swift's "Blank Space" in the car a capitulation to capitalist logic? To deny the influence of status on culture is naive, but to reduce culture to *only* a political tool denies us our humanity. "Culture is being threatened," writes Hannah Arendt, "when all worldly objects and things, produced by the present or the past, are treated as mere functions for the life process of society, as though they are there only to fulfill some need, and for this functionalization it is almost irrelevant whether the needs in question are of a high or a low order."

Instead of dismantling culture, we should deploy our enhanced knowledge about status and culture to simultaneously pursue two modest goals: (1) reduce the ills of social hierarchy, and (2) promote radical creativity. From what we've learned in this book, these two goals have often been contradictory. Intense status struggle and elitism have been a strong incentive for cultural invention, diffusion, valuation, and canonization. Jean-Jacques Rousseau believed inequality was responsible for "a multitude of bad things and very few good things"; Immanuel Kant countered that it was a "rich source of much that is evil, but also of everything that is good." No matter who is right in this centuries-old debate, both are correct that human equality and human creativity have long been interrelated variables, and not always positively correlated.

First off, what can we do toward reducing status inequity in contemporary society? The most substantial work remains in the legal and economic spheres: to dismantle biased laws and reduce bias in enforcement, and to provide more opportunities for individuals in disadvantaged groups to build capital. But status structures live within our minds and our conventions, and if status affects our daily well-being, we must also address the inequities inherent in cultural norms. Only political upheaval can alter the economic base of society; *we* can support the equitable distribution of status through taking better control of our personal social interactions and collective values.

There has been a long project in the last century to eradicate ascribed status structures that disadvantage certain races, ethnicities, gender expressions, and sexual orientations. A core tool in this mission is to reassess our status beliefs and, as sociologist Cecilia Ridgeway suggests, "to erode their appearance of consensuality." Conventions draw their power from broad acceptance as the natural state of the world, and so the exposure of inherent biases reduces their power. The long-standing beauty standard in Western culture for straight blond hair no longer feels preordained after we've deconstructed its origin. This is not to suggest that cultural change always leads to social change: men who grew out their hair in the sixties didn't all take on enlightened attitudes toward gender equality. And certainly culture should not be the only sphere where we work to promote equality. But over time, rebalancing the status value of majority and minority conventions would reduce dominant groups' self-propagating advantages.

Ascribed status categories aren't the only barriers against achieving equality. *All* social stratification produces a few winners and many losers. Bertrand Russell stated the obvious drawback of our current system: "The forms of happiness which consist of victory in a competition cannot be universal." In societies that frame social mobility as a personal responsibility, low status brings self-doubt and suffering. Knowing this, should we just rid ourselves of status completely? Cecilia Ridgeway concludes, "We will never actually eliminate status as a form of inequality." Hierarchy is inevitable as long as we continue to grant esteem to individuals who demonstrate impressive talents and feats. This is precisely why Rousseau blamed the downfall of humanity on esteem. In his imagining of the development of civilization, he observed, "He who sang or danced the best; he who was the most handsome, the strongest, the most adroit or the most eloquent became the most highly regarded, and this was the first step towards inequality and at the same time towards vice."

Radical political movements have attempted to rectify these status inequalities through fiat, only to witness elites quietly deploy new means of distinction. The Soviet Union abolished private property, flattened salaries, and downplayed consumerism, and yet status hierarchies popped up in bureaucratic micropositions, apartment sizes, and the procurement of foreign goods. Humans are adept at turning any small advantage into a status marker. In exploring the history of dental hygiene, the writer Molly Young notes, "As soon as it became possible for a slice of society to have good teeth, it became possible for them to humiliate the rest of society for having bad teeth. Smiling became a sole privilege of the rich: If the eyes were the window to a man's soul, his mouth was now the window to his bank account." Modernists believed banishing ornamentation would prevent art and design from use in conspicuous consumption, and then antiornamentation itself became a status symbol for the professional class.

Since the full eradication of status is unlikely, a more pragmatic approach would be to quell the collective craving for higher status. Allowing individuals to form their own alternative status groups is a good start, but this also requires equalizing the global distribution of status benefits among the groups. We can begin this process by providing more "free" benefits, such as basic courtesies, friendly greetings, and deference to people in lower status tiers—what the economist-writer Noah Smith calls the "redistribution of respect." Jesus took this to an extreme: forging brotherhood with lepers and turning the other cheek to blood rivals. This is not easy. Sigmund Freud believed this approach to be inherently contradictory: "A love that does not discriminate seems to me to forfeit a part of its own value . . . and secondly, not all men are worthy of love." And what may be even harder than showering enemies with love is treating superiors like peers. Sycophancy provides long-term rewards. Elites, then, would need to be a vanguard of status equality by refusing to accept special treatment.

Institutions could support status equality by increasing the duties required of high-status individuals in taking an exalted position. This would decrease the net benefits, thus ambiguating the advantages of higher status. Societies can also flatten their own hierarchies by raising the quality of standard benefits and reducing elite perks. In Japan high-speed rail has multiple classes of seating. But the basic seats are extremely pleasant and clean by American standards. Wealthier passengers can pay a bit more for a Green car upgrade, but it offers only marginal improvements. By contrast, economy class air travelers dream of upgrades to business class on international flights, because there is a huge gulf between sitting upright in cramped quarters for twelve hours and napping horizontally after a multicourse steak dinner.

While we can't outlaw signaling, we could attempt to reduce its frequency and effectiveness. This is the point of uniforms; unadorned culottes became standard during the French Revolution so that citizens were "free to deal with one another without the intrusion of differences in social status." But uniforms constrict personal expression. The better method would be to devalue status symbols by revealing them *as* status symbols. All luxuries should be seen as status markers, not superior conveniences. Exposing frauds and maintaining status integrity are also important, as cheaters make normal-status individuals feel that they're falling behind.

None of these ideas are new. In *Status Anxiety*, the writer Alain de Botton argues that the most notable radical ideologies, from democracy and Marxism to Christianity, are ultimately radical reassessments of status criteria. As de Botton explains, "Philosophy, art, politics, religion and bohemia have never sought to do away entirely with the status hierarchy; they have attempted, rather, to institute new kinds of hierarchies based on sets of values unrecognised by, and critical of, those of the majority." These visions often drift into utopianism, but again, we are not status monkeys, nor is there a primordial calculator in our genetic code that dooms us to dominance structures. Societies can—and do—take control of how esteem and benefits are allocated.

This then brings us to promoting cultural creativity. We must better guarantee that positive—and radical—contributions to the culture receive esteem and status benefits. But what is a "contribution" to culture? This question will always inspire debate, yet there may be a few areas of agreement. A robust, diverse, and complex cultural ecosystem is better than a bland, stagnant monoculture. Complexity doesn't have to involve impenetrable or esoteric art, just the skillful manipulation of higher-order symbols in new and surprising ways.

Complexity is good for our brains. The philosopher Nelson Goodman writes that the "exercise of the symbolizing faculties beyond immediate need has the more remote practical purpose of developing our abilities and techniques to cope with future contingencies."

One important aspect of complexity is ambiguity. Simple things have one interpretation; complex things have more. The neurobiologist Semir Zeki believes ambiguity is the secret of "great art," as it "corresponds to as many different concepts in as many different brains over as long a period of time as possible." At the same time, creativity tends to prosper with an increase in total artistic activity. Anthropologist A. L. Kroeber surveyed the world's civilizations and found that "a culture with a content several times as great as another—let us say with a total inventory of items several times larger—has more material to operate on, and ought therefore to be able to produce more combinations of items and richer or more intensive patterns." Symbols become more complex the more they refer to other symbols, and it helps when more people are involved in creating new ones.

Without any intervention, humans are well primed to create a culture of low symbolic complexity: simple melodies, figurative art, bawdy jokes. And capitalism ensures that established conventional art forms always find large audiences. While kitsch and extravagance have their charms, an ecosystem *solely* composed of low complexity culture quickly becomes stagnant. Even the most conservative humans seek some amount of surprise. Cultural ecosystems that encourage symbolic complexity solve this problem: innovations of high complexity trickle down and "refresh" mass culture. Contemporary country music would surely feel archaic in the twenty-first century without the influences of pop, rock, alternative, and hip-hop. When ecosystems push toward complexity at the margins, everyone wins. Smaller, erudite audiences enjoy difficult art, and simplified versions engage less knowledgeable audiences. Complex works endure longer, contributing to future generations' ecosystems and supporting the potential emergence of geniuses. Kroeber writes that as much as we attribute "great cultural products" to "great men," they're always "the composite product of personal superiority and cultural influence."

Rigid status systems lead to stagnancy in art. When economic capital is the exclusive means of distinction, elites are satisfied with simple symbols based on wealth. In systems where elite exclusion involves diversified forms of cultural capital, artists receive high status for their transgressions. In the twentieth century, the elite use of cultural capital opened the door for minorities and outcasts to forge new sensibilities in their rejection of the mainstream, resulting in avant-garde art, hip-hop, punk, camp, retro, etc. Elite adoption then helped these innovations trickle down to nearly everyone. As a result mass audiences have learned to see the world through multiple sensibilities. This arguably expanded the meta-knowledge of *conventionality* itself, which makes it easier to break the chains of oppressive customs.

The nefarious uses of cultural capital, however, have convinced many we should abolish the entire idea of taste. Complex art must be bad if it affords elite audiences any sense of superiority over mass audiences. And in democratic society, popularity appears to be a much fairer measure of quality than the opinions of an overeducated cabal. The people have spoken, and Drake, not John Cage, has amassed a fortune large enough to build a home of "overwhelming high luxury."

From what we've seen so far, the skepticism toward cultural capital has done little to flatten the status hierarchy; in fact, it has made economic capital a much more powerful asset in signaling. Meanwhile, the unbridled celebration of kitsch as folk culture has further directed consumer spending to the coffers of giant conglomerates. Humans can find community in any style of music, but rallying around Lady Gaga and the Black Eyed Peas was the best way to forge solidarity while enriching billionaire Jimmy Iovine at Interscope Records. Esteem is not infinite: every poptimist embrace of Lana Del Rey is *some* time, energy, enthusiasm—and status value—denied to a lesser-known creator pursuing less immediately comprehensible art. A marketing machine will ensure that Del Rey sells records whether critics pay attention or not; the path-breaking, mass-audience-alienating artist's best chance to build cachet has always been the attention and advocacy of critics.

Life is more interesting—and arguably better—when more people play in symbolic complexity and find surprising ways to break conventions. The best candidates are those with a deep and specialized knowledge of symbols. They don't have to be elites in the economic sense; radical invention is often a more natural exercise for those at the margins of society. Nor does artistic invention need to be a purely intellectual exercise, like the Glass Bead Game of Hermann Hesse's novel. There is creativity everywhere—some trained, some naive. But the most skilled practitioners should receive social rewards for their inventions—not just for the attraction of large audiences. Proponents of a universal basic income suggest that guaranteed wages will allow us to "all be artists." Perhaps we can all be *creators*; to be "artists," with all its associated high honors and esteem, we don't just need living expenses but a social system for doling out respect to the most genius negations of the dominant conventions.

The solution may not be a return of cultural *capital* but at least greater emphasis on cultural *competence*. Without artists receiving a status boost for their radical inventiveness and audiences receiving a boost for their understanding of radical inventiveness, culture falls prey to a pure economic logic. Cultural competence is not inherently evil if we feel in control of the values, behaviors, and artistic expressions embodied in the artworks and artifacts we celebrate. This, admittedly, is yet another recommendation of how to change the status criteria rather than completely flatten the social hierarchy. And it does engender some inequality: the sage would remain superior to the philistine. But this should be a distinction we can accept. For T. S. Eliot, "We should not consider the upper levels as possessing more culture than the lower, but as representing a *more* conscious culture and a greater specialisation of culture." Judging by the social origin of our artistic heroes and the most creative art forms, the ability to deeply understand culture is not classist. Creativity is more equally distributed across society than the ability to mint wealth.

Barring a drastic egalitarian revolution or technological changes that alter basic human motivations, status will remain an integral part of the human experience. There will still be status hierarchies in the "metaverse." We are resigned to a world with divisions, and the struggle between the divisions will shape culture. But we are never innocent bystanders in this process. Humans have agency to decide how we form our social hierarchies. Through taking control of our beliefs and conventions, we can promote a fairer, healthier hierarchy that better rewards collective contributions. And we have the agency to shape our culture. Past societies have endowed the honorific "artist" on different types of creators: conservative craftsmen, wily commercial entrepreneurs, and pioneers of symbolic manipulation. All three provide society with culture but only the last group has a strong track record of rapidly providing a wide range of new sensibilities with which to view the world. If society chooses to celebrate economic capital as the supreme virtue and to reject the celebration of any symbolic complexity as an oppressive tool, we should expect further creative stagnation.

Now that status and culture are no longer a mystery, we can be more conscious in our actions to improve them. If we do things right, there doesn't have to be a trade-off between social equality and cultural creativity. Why not both?

Acknowledgments

The idea to write about the fundamental laws of culture came to me during graduate school, and slowly took its current shape after fifteen years of reading large quantities of disintegrating secondhand English-language tomes from Tokyo's used-book stores (as well as the bulk purchases of deceased professors' libraries on Yahoo! Auctions). But not every idea for a book becomes a *book*, and for that I am grateful for the counsel, patience, and faith of my agent, Mollie Glick, at CAA, and the inspiring wisdom of my editor, Rick Kot, at Viking.

The fundamental solitude of writing makes it extremely meaningful when others provide their time, energy, and insight. First and foremost, I will forever be indebted to the grace of Roni Xu, who advised me throughout the project and lent her unparalleled brain to help me navigate the deepest paradoxes and philosophical dilemmas at the heart of status and cultural behavior.

I also extend my deepest gratitude to the expert fact-checking of Sejla Rizvic; Camille LeBlanc at Viking for the editorial assistance; Ruby Pseudo for the books and enthusiasm; Alex Smith for help with the Beatles anecdotes; my father, Morris Marx, for great edits and questioning the normal distribution of diffusion curves; Elvira Fischer for notes on neuroscience; Nick Sylvester, Matt Alt, Nathaniel Smith, Steve Hely, Tu Nguyen, and A. J. Lewen for reading rough drafts; Benjamin Novak, Josh Lambert, Gideon Lewis-Kraus, Craig Mod, Noah Smith, and Kyle Chayka for early encouragement; and my family for their support.

Notes

INTRODUCTION

xi **a chic "Caesar cut":** Mark Lewisohn, *The Beatles, All These Years*, 719.

xi **his "existentialist" German girlfriend:** Lewisohn, *The Beatles*, 730.

xi **"Bohemian beauties on the Left Bank":** Lewisohn, *The Beatles*, 974.

xi **With "near-baldness":** Nik Cohn, *Today There Are No Gentlemen*, 87.

xii **"One shake of the bushy fringe":** Frederick Lewis, "Britons Succumb to 'Beatlemania.'"

xii **"unsightly, unsafe, unruly, and unclean":** "Beatles Haircuts 'Unsightly, Unsafe, Unruly, and Unclean'—Fashion Archive, 1963," *Guardian*.

xii **Stamp Out the Beatles Society:** Rachel Emma Silverman, "It Was 35 Years Ago This Weekend That Haircuts Lost Their Luster."

xii **the Beatles' first U.S. press conference:** Quotations taken from the transcript at "Beatles Press Conference: American Arrival 2/7/1964."

xii **fifteen thousand Beatles wigs:** Martin Arnold, "Moneywise."

xii **a 1965 Gallup poll:** Betty Luther Hillman, *Dressing for the Culture Wars: Style and the Politics of Self-Presentation in the 1960s and 1970s*, which is also the source for other facets of the backlash against the Beatles.

xii **"no controversy, no protest":** Micky Dolenz and Mark Bego, *I'm a Believer: My Life of Monkees, Music, and Madness*, 82, citing Timothy Leary, *The Politics of Ecstasy*, 173–74.

xii **A moptop looked eminently respectable:** Mainly taken from Bob Spitz, *The Beatles*, 214, 222–25, 244–45. It is worth noting that discrepancies do exist among the major Beatles books on the origins of their moptops.

xiii **"looks just as good":** Faye Fearon, "The Enduring Appeal of the Beatles' Mop-Top Haircuts."

xiii **"Fashions are like human beings":** Charles Dickens, *David Copperfield*.

xiii **as a "random walk":** Tom Vanderbilt, *You May Also Like: Taste in an Age of Endless Choice*, 170.

xiv **cast it as "viral contagion":** Malcolm Gladwell, *The Tipping Point*, and Jonah Berger, *Contagious: Why Things Catch On*.

xiv **"A new fashion of dress":** William Graham Sumner, *Folkways*, 22.

xiv **an aggregation of individual:** Jon Elster, *Nuts and Bolts for the Social Sciences* ("The elementary unit of social life is the individual human action. To explain social institutions and social change is to show how they arise as the result of the action and interaction of individuals").

xiv **a "cultural gravity" nudging humans:** A. L. Kroeber, *Configurations of Culture Growth*, 3 ("There seem to lie certain forms of happenings which are more or less recurrent or generic, perhaps necessary and universal").

xv **considered a fundamental human desire:** C. Anderson, J. A. D. Hildreth, and L. Howland, "Is the Desire for Status a Fundamental Human Motive? A Review of the Empirical Literature."

xvi **Researchers recently concluded that the achievement:** C. Anderson, J. A. D. Hildreth, and D. L. Sharps, "The Possession of High Status Strengthens the Status Motive."

xvi **most people view stratification:** Robert H. Frank, *Choosing the Right Pond: Human Behavior and the Quest for Status*, 174.

xvi **"fundamental taboo, more so":** Dorothy M. Scura, ed., *Conversations with Tom Wolfe*, 44.

xvi **Open discussion of social hierarchy:** Frank, *Choosing the Right Pond*, 6, and Edward T. Hall, *Beyond Culture*, 61.

xvi **Nancy Mitford mused:** Evelyn Waugh, "An Open Letter," 93.

xvi **the modern word "villain":** Lionel Trilling, *Sincerity and Authenticity*, 16.

xvi **cultural change is much less mysterious:** The need to know the function of culture to understand its origin adapted from a similar insight in linguistics. Keller, *On Language Change*, 84: "If we knew what we use our language for, we would also know why it changes all the time through our acts of communication."

xvi **a similar "invisible-hand" mechanism:** Rudi Keller, *On Language Change: The Invisible Hand in Language*, 70, and Edna Ullmann-Margalit, *The Emergence of Norms*, 11.

xvii **how they manifest in cultural patterns:** That the origin of culture is related to its function is an idea adapted for linguistics: see Keller, *On Language Change*, 84 ("If we knew *what* we use our language *for*, we would also know *why* it changes all the time through our acts of communication").

xvii **Thorstein Veblen's writings:** Thorstein Veblen, *The Theory of the Leisure Class.*

xvii **seem *less cool* than before?:** Safy-Hallan Farah, "The Great American Cool."

xvii **media reporting of real-life appearances:** Marshall McLuhan, *Understanding Media: The Extensions of Man*, 218 ("'Conspicuous consumption' owed less to the phrase of Veblen than to the press photographer, who began to invade the entertainment spots of the very rich").

xx **"biggest thorn in all of social theory":** Russell Hardin, *One for All: The Logic of Group Conflict*, 11.

xx **not a "game":** See Will Storr, *The Status Game.*

xx **an invisible force undergirding:** Claude Lévi-Strauss, *Structural Anthropology*, 20 ("[Franz Boas] showed that the structure of a language remains unknown to the speaker until the introduction of a scientific grammar").

xxi **best parallel may be chemistry:** Clyde Kluckhohn, *Culture and Behavior*, 57.

CHAPTER ONE

3 **the ambiguities of the term "status":** My definition of this word is informed by many sources, but most notably, Cecilia L. Ridgeway, *Status: Why Is It Everywhere? Why Does It Matter?*, 1 ("Status is a comparative social ranking of people groups, or objects in terms of the social esteem, honor, and respect accorded to them").

3 **the young protagonist Timmy:** Will Gould and Hollingworth Morse, "Double Trouble."

5 **the exclusive New York nightclub Studio 54:** Kathy Benjamin, "What It Was Like Working at Studio 54."

5 **Lady Pink had to compete:** Jeff Chang, *Can't Stop, Won't Stop: A History of the Hip-Hop Generation*, 120.

5 **status is *bestowed by others*:** Ridgeway, *Status*, 97.

6 **"that movie made me feel":** Jeffrey Yorke, "Film Talk."

6 **"Any organized social group":** J. H. Abraham, *Origins and Growth of Sociology*, 419.

6 **"a human invention to manage":** Ridgeway, *Status*, 3.

6 **"The moment a digging stick":** Victor Turner, *The Ritual Process: Structure and Anti-Structure*, 140.

7 **"All human beings have":** Edmund Leach, *Culture and Communication: The Logic by Which Symbols Are Connected*, 54.

7 **"the smallest boy in his class":** James Baldwin, *Go Tell It on the Mountain*, 19.

7 **"Even if all actors":** Bertrand Russell, *Power*, 149.

7 **"All I care for":** Michael Thompson, *Rubbish Theory: The Creation and Destruction of Value*, 190.

7 **"in a hierarchical group":** Cameron Anderson and John Angus D. Hildreth, "Striving for Superiority: The Human Desire for Status."

8 **70 percent of research subjects:** C. Anderson, J. A. D. Hildreth, and L. Howland, "Is the Desire for Status a Fundamental Human Motive?"

8 **"individuals experience elevated social well-being":** Anderson, Hildreth, and Howland, "Is the Desire for Status a Fundamental Human Motive?"

8 **evolutionary "status instinct":** Steven Quartz and Annette Asp, *Cool: How the Brain's Hidden Quest for Cool Drives Our Economy and Shapes Our World*, 9.

8 **"In any organized group"**: Desmond Morris, *The Human Zoo*, 41.

8 **production of more serotonin**: Theodore Koutsobinas, *The Political Economy of Status: Superstars, Markets, and Culture Change*, 60–61.

8 **blood pressure**: Robert H. Frank, *Choosing the Right Pond: Human Behavior and the Quest for Status*, 23.

8 **"unspeakably primordial calculator"**: Bailey Steinworth, "Jordan Peterson Needs to Reconsider the Lobster."

8 **"a social form that is deeply cultural"**: Ridgeway, *Status*, 4.

8 **We are not "status monkeys"**: Eugene Wei, "Status as a Service (Staas)."

9 **"The desire of the esteem of others"**: John Adams, *The Works of John Adams*, 6:234.

9 **"The familiar yearning"**: Ridgeway, *Status*, 5.

9 **"an attitude, not an action"**: Geoffrey Brennan and Philip Pettit, *The Economy of Esteem: An Essay on Civil and Political Society*, 15.

9 **Firestone Tire and Rubber Company**: Vance Packard, *The Pyramid Climbers*, 29.

9 **"When I was a rookie"**: Joel M. Podolny, *Status Signals: A Sociological Study of Market Competition*, 10.

10 **"A man in a clean, well-pressed suit"**: Alison Lurie, *The Language of Clothes*, 14.

10 **"The man of rank and distinction"**: Adam Smith, *The Theory of Moral Sentiments*, 72.

10 **"Higher-status actors obtain"**: Podolny, *Status Signals*, 22.

10 **This attention also gives them more influence**: C. Anderson, O. P. John, D. Keltner, and A. M. Kring, "Who Attains Social Status? Effects of Personality and Physical Attractiveness in Social Groups."

10 **In Roman society, elites reclined**: Melitta Weiss Adamson and Francine Segan, *Entertaining from Ancient Rome to the Super Bowl: An Encyclopedia*, 20–21.

10 **Old Money American families**: Vance Packard, *The Status Seekers*, 125.

10 **literary critic Diana Trilling**: Paul Fussell, *Class: A Guide through the American Status System*, 185.

10 **the heavy metal singer Ozzy Osbourne**: Mötley Crüe and Neil Strauss, *The Dirt: Confessions of the World's Most Notorious Rock Band*.

11 **"You're coming on like you're Jimi Hendrix"**: Barry Miles, *The Zapple Diaries: The Rise and Fall of the Last Beatles Label*, 213.

11 **"low-status members are more likely"**: Ridgeway, *Status*, 57.

11 **the term "status syndrome"**: Quartz and Asp, *Cool*, 135.

11 **psychologist Dale T. Miller**: Anderson, Hildreth, and Howland, "Is the Desire for Status a Fundamental Human Motive?"

11 **can result in "psychological death"**: Bruce Hood, *The Self Illusion*, 188.

11 **40 percent of its engineers**: Seth Stephens-Davidowitz, *Everybody Lies: Big Lies, New Data, and What the Internet Can Tell Us about Who We Really Are*, 107.

11 **Pueblo society**: Ruth Benedict, *Patterns of Culture*, 99, and Elvin Hatch, *Theories of Man and Culture*, 80.

12 **"To live as one likes"**: José Ortega y Gasset, *The Revolt of the Masses*, 63.

12 **child's play in earlier ages**: Michelangelo Matos, *The Underground Is Massive*, 164.

12 **"You get to the point in life"**: Andy Warhol and Pat Hackett, *POPism: The Warhol Sixties*, 247.

12 **Michael Jordan swept the top NBA awards**: Michael Tollin et al., *The Last Dance*.

12 **electronic musician Moby**: Matos, *The Underground Is Massive*, 315.

13 **"It is through work"**: Lisa Chaney, *Coco Chanel*, 114.

13 **Chanel was certainly no heroine**: She said so herself: "I am not a heroine. But I have chosen the person I wanted to be" (Chaney, *Coco Chanel*, 392).

13 **certain *status criteria* at which**: See "status characteristic" in Joseph Berger, Susan J. Rosenholtz, and Morris Zelditch, Jr., "Status Organizing Processes."

13 **"People were often locked"**: Charles Taylor, *The Ethics of Authenticity*, 3.

13 **hierarchies around *ascribed status***: Ralph Linton, *The Study of Man: An Introduction*, 115.

13 **Pueblo tribes established**: Edward T. Hall, *The Silent Language*, 130.

13 **"The king, the peer, the knight"**: P. N. Furbank, *Unholy Pleasure: The Idea of Social Class*, 75, from Holdsworth's *History of English Law*.

14 **understood to be God's plan**: Werner Sombart, *Luxury and Capitalism*, 14.

14 **Marcel Proust wrote**: Marcel Proust, *Swann's Way*, 19.

14 **"respect, status, honor, attention, privileges"**: Isabel Wilkerson, *Caste: The Origins of Our Discontents*, 70.

14 **Basketball player LeBron James**: Wilkerson, *Caste*, 108.

15 *status advantaged*: Ridgeway, *Status*, 72.

15 **"the United States is unique"**: Packard, *The Status Seekers*, 251.

15 **"physical vigour and skill, physical bravery"**: Gabriel Tarde, *The Laws of Imitation*, 233.

16 *Occupational capital is*: Packard, *The Status Seekers*, 99.

16 **"Money is life in the sense"**: John Berger, *Ways of Seeing*, 143.

16 **Carolina Otero**: Chaney, *Coco Chanel*, 36.

17 *bodily capital*: Ashley Mears, *Very Important People: Status and Beauty in the Global Party Circuit*, 16.

17 **originate in aristocratic mores**: Maurice Halbwachs, *On Collective Memory*, 180 ("Magnificent deeds, exploits, or feats would not have sufficed to confer nobility had society not recognized in these deeds so many proofs that the one who accomplished them was worthy of occupying a noble position by right and as if in eternity. It is within the framework of the organization of the nobility and in conformity with the nobility's ideas and customs that the person aspiring to nobility behaved as a man of honor and courage").

17 **Models may socialize with billionaires**: Mears, *Very Important People*.

17 **"In order to know a man"**: Georg Simmel, *On Individuality and Social Forms*, 10.

17 **accumulating significant amounts of capital**: Packard, *The Status Seekers*, 57.

17 **called *status congruence***: George A. Theodorson and Achilles G. Theodorson, *Modern Dictionary of Sociology*.

18 **"inherited wealth, inherited beauty"**: Warhol and Hackett, *POPism*, 123.

18 **"Success should, as far as possible"**: Russell, *Power*, 149.

18 **universal emotion *envy***: Helmut Schoeck, *Envy: A Theory of Social Behavior*, 8.

19 **"The only people for me are the mad ones"**: Jack Kerouac, *On the Road*, 7.

19 **Living in a 1950s America**: Edward Halsey Foster, *Understanding the Beats*, 1–24.

19 **an example of a *status group***: Max Weber, *Selections in Translation*, 60 ("A 'status group' is a group of human beings who, in the context of some association, effectively claim a special evaluation of their status and possibly also certain special monopolies on the grounds of their status").

19 **share *status beliefs***: Ridgeway, *Status*, 69 ("Status beliefs are widely held cultural beliefs that link a recognized social difference among actors with greater or lesser status-worthiness and competence").

19 **"In a gang like ours"**: Michael Macilwee, *The Teddy Boy Wars*, 116.

20 **disparaged as "kooks"**: Ben Sobel, "Don't Be a Kook: The GQ Guide to Surf Etiquette."

20 **"When men willingly follow"**: Russell, *Power*, 12.

20 **Kerouac's status improved**: Foster, *Understanding the Beats*, 28–80.

20 **code switching between groups' competing demands**: Courtney McCluney, Kathrina Rohotham, Serenity Lee, Richard Smith, and Myles Durkee, "The Costs of Code-Switching."

20 **"whether they're intellectuals"**: Dorothy M. Scura, ed., *Conversations with Tom Wolfe*, 124.

20 **"all effort was uncool, a hassle"**: Nik Cohn, *Today There Are No Gentlemen*, 137.

21 **A surfer can be a great hero**: Diane Cardwell, "Black Surfers Reclaim Their Place on the Waves."

21 **the gap between the esteem**: C. Anderson, M. W. Kraus, A. D. Galinsky, and D. Keltner, "The Local-Ladder Effect: Social Status and Subjective Well-Being."

21 **anthropologist Daniel Miller explains**: Daniel Miller, *Material Culture and Mass Consumption*, 152.

21 **pioneering sociologist Max Weber**: Weber, *Selections in Translation*, 53.

21 **the Sinhalese rioted**: Russell Hardin, *One for All: The Logic of Group Conflict*, 57.

21 **"The interwar generation"**: Thomas B. Edsall, "The Resentment That Never Sleeps."

22 **The Trump voting bloc**: Marc Hooghe and Ruth Dassonneville, "Explaining the Trump Vote: The Effect of Racist Resentment and Anti-Immigrant Sentiments."

22 **"There is no respect"**: James Hohmann, "The Daily 202: Trump Voters Stay Loyal Because They Feel Disrespected."

22 **"a continual struggle over the hierarchy"**: Miller, *Material Culture and Mass Consumption*, 152.

22 **an overall increase in wealth**: Fred Hirsch, *Social Limits to Growth*, 102.

CHAPTER TWO

25 **Whit Stillman's 1990 film**: Whit Stillman, *Metropolitan*; further analysis in Christopher Beach, *Class, Language, and American Film Comedy*.

26 **Why "arbitrary"?**: Rudi Keller, *A Theory of Linguistic Signs*, 135 ("To say of a linguistic sign that it is arbitrary is to say that its suitability is not based on its makeup").

26 **the French communicate perfectly well:** Edmund Leach, *Culture and Communication: The Logic by Which Symbols Are Connected*, 20.

26 **"Men do not merely 'survive'":** Marshall Sahlins, *Culture and Practical Reason*, 168.

26 **"Human beings have a very":** Jon Elster, *Nuts and Bolts for the Social Sciences*, 36.

26 **"danger" suggested by the color red:** Leach, *Culture and Communication*, 58.

26 **During China's Cultural Revolution:** "Great Leap Forward at the Traffic Lights in China—Archive," *Guardian*.

27 **"though no doubt extremely agreeable":** Adam Smith, *The Theory of Moral Sentiments*, 284.

27 **"When you're in the beer tent":** Katrin Bennhold, "Bavarian Millennials Embrace Tradition (Dirndls, Lederhosen and All)."

27 **The answer is *conventions*:** David Lewis, *Convention*, with clarifications in Margaret Gilbert, *On Social Facts*, and Edna Ullmann-Margalit, *The Emergence of Norms*.

27 **"young men from Nevada":** Calvin Trillin, *American Fried: Adventures of a Happy Eater*, 130.

28 **nearly all Harvard Business School students:** Vance Packard, *The Pyramid Climbers*, 111.

28 **Hula-Hoops and the Atkins diet:** Joel Best, *Flavor of the Month: Why Smart People Fall for Fads*.

28 **"American writer's disease":** Phil Baker, *The Book of Absinthe*, 199.

28 **"oversized fits and long silhouettes":** Gregk Foley, "The Trends and Brands That Defined '90s Hip-Hop Fashion."

28 **"yellow filter":** Elisabeth Sherman, "Why Does 'Yellow Filter' Keep Popping Up in American Movies?"

29 **governments issue a *decree*:** Ullmann-Margalit, *The Emergence of Norms*, 76. Although Ullmann-Margalit sees decrees as distinct from conventions, I would argue that decrees become conventional over time.

29 **Tuxedo Proclamation:** Jamie Johnson, "Off with Their Coattails."

29 **part of *common knowledge*:** Lewis, *Convention*, 58.

29 **Men show up in tuxedos:** Lewis, *Convention*, 6.

29 **reversion of Okinawa:** Allen Richarz, "40 Years Ago, Okinawans Returned to Driving on the Left."

30 **"repays deprivation with hostility":** George Caspar Homans, *Social Behavior: Its Elementary Forms*, 146.

30 **"Status groups are specifically responsible":** Max Weber, *Selections in Translation*, 52.

31 **second power through *internalization*:** Ullmann-Margalit, *The Emergence of Norms*, 172 ("Once norms are internalized, one abides by them not out of fear of the pending sanctions associated with them, but out of some inner conviction").

31 **"The life-history":** Ruth Benedict, *Patterns of Culture*, 2.

31 **through the *chameleon effect*:** Bruce Hood, *The Self Illusion*, 206.

31 **the leaders of the French Revolution:** Michael Suk-Young Chwe, *Rational Ritual: Culture, Coordination, and Common Knowledge*, 23.

31 **"haughtiest country gentleman":** Gabriel Tarde, *The Laws of Imitation*, 215.

31 **"We dislike individuals":** Hood, *The Self Illusion*, 208.

32 **The Onion TV segment:** Geoff Haggerty, "Thousands of Girls Match Description of Missing Sorority Sister."

32 **"more makeup more expertly applied":** Stephanie Talmadge, "The Sisterhood of the Exact Same Pants."

32 **Internalization unlocks the final power:** Maurice Halbwachs, *On Collective Memory*, 168, and Nelson Goodman, *Languages of Art*, 7, citing Ernst Gombrich's idea of "There is no innocent eye."

32 **information is then interpreted through a screen:** Clyde Kluckhohn, *Culture and Behavior*, 39; see also Marshall H. Segall, Donald T. Campbel, and Melville J. Herskovit, "The Influence of Culture on Visual Perception."

32 **The perception of time:** Edward T. Hall, *Beyond Culture*, 44.

32 **Perception of color:** Umberto Eco, "How Culture Conditions the Colours We See."

32 **The Russian language divides:** Jonathan Winawer, Nathan Witthoft, Michael C. Frank, Lisa Wu, Alex R. Wade, and Lera Boroditskyl, "Russian Blues Reveal Effects of Language on Color Discrimination."

32 **"a subset of the theoretically infinite number":** Daniel J. Levitin, *This Is Your Brain on Music: The Science of a Human Obsession*, 29.

32 **major chords sound "happy":** Levitin, *This Is Your Brain on Music*, 38.

32 **Aldous Huxley confessed:** Goodman, *Languages of Art*, 89.

33 **"The schemes of the habitus":** Pierre Bourdieu, *Distinction*, 466.

33 **"Even such apparently biological processes":** Kluckhohn, *Culture and Behavior*, 22.

33 **health is critical for choosing:** Steven Pinker, *How the Mind Works*, 483 ("Symmetry, an absence of deformities, cleanliness, unblemished skin, clear eyes, and intact teeth[,] are attractive in all cultures").

33 **"heroin chic":** Edward Helmore, "'Heroin Chic' and the Tangled Legacy of Photographer Davide Sorrenti."

33 **preferred women with blackened teeth:** A. Venugopal and A. Marya, "Return of the Ohaguro."

33 **foot binding in China:** Fraser Newham, "The Ties That Bind."

33 **"a very nearly universal tendency":** Russell Hardin, *One for All: The Logic of Group Conflict*, 60. This is also explained in William Graham Sumner, *Folkways*, 13: "Each group nourishes its own pride and vanity, boasts itself superior, exalts its own divinities, and looks with contempt on outsiders. Each group thinks its own folkways the only right ones, and if it observes that other groups have other folkways, these excite its scorn."

33 **The Milanese adventurer Girolamo Benzoni:** Marcy Norton, *Sacred Gifts, Profane Pleasures: A History of Tobacco and Chocolate in the Atlantic World*, 8.

33 **"All their customs are upside-down":** Chinua Achebe, *Things Fall Apart*, 73.

33 **"meaningful orders of persons and things":** Sahlins, *Culture and Practical Reason*, x.

34 **part of the same "collectivity":** Gilbert, *On Social Facts*, 377.

34 **lifeblood of the nation:** Mark Lawrence Schrad, *Vodka Politics: Alcohol, Autocracy and the Secret History of the Russian State*, 320.

34 **acting as a "horizon":** Charles Taylor, *The Ethics of Authenticity*, 37.

34 ***Paradigm* describes these macro-conventions:** Young Back Choi, *Paradigms and Conventions*, 32.

34 **"The Beatles' way of doing things":** Ian MacDonald, *Revolution in the Head: The Beatles' Records and the Sixties*, xiii.

34 **"Norms of partiality":** Ullmann-Margalit, *The Emergence of Norms*.

34 **"the woman who strives to achieve":** Karen A. Callaghan, *Ideals of Feminine Beauty: Philosophical, Social, and Cultural Dimensions*, ix.

34 **stiff crinoline petticoats:** Russell Lynes, *The Tastemakers*, 76, and Rae Nudson, "A History of Women Who Burned to Death in Flammable Dresses."

35 **Emma Goldman lit up a cigarette:** Richard T. Drinnon, *Rebel in Paradise: A Biography of Emma Goldman*, 184.

35 **"The fact that there is a social norm":** Anthony Heath, *Rational Choice and Social Exchange*, 155.

35 **"best seen not as complexes of concrete":** Clifford Geertz, *The Interpretation of Cultures*, 44.

35 **"most complicated words in the English language":** Raymond Williams, *Keywords: A Vocabulary of Culture and Society*, 87.

35 **the 1952 book:** A. L. Kroeber and C. Kluckhohn, *Culture: A Critical Review of Concepts and Definitions*.

36 **"We have no record":** A. L. Kroeber, *Configurations of Culture Growth*, 818.

36 **"Nothing has spread socialistic feeling":** Lynes, *The Tastemakers*, 233.

36 **the cheapest cars started at $600:** David Gartman, *Auto-Opium: A Social History of American Automobile Design*, 33. See also Alfred Sloan Jr., *My Years with General Motors*, 20: "My first personal experience with automobiles was much like that of others at the time. I wanted one but couldn't afford it. Only about 4000 cars were made in the year 1900, and they were expensive."

36 **automobiles were exclusive to the rich:** Vance Packard, *The Status Seekers*, 274.

36 **By the 1950s, the lower middle class:** Marshall McLuhan, *Understanding Media: The Extensions of Man*, 243 ("The willingness to accept the car as a status symbol, restricting its more expansive form to the use of higher executives, is not a mark of the car and mechanical age, but of the electric forces that are now ending this mechanical age of uniformity and standardization, and recreating the norms of status and role").

36 **a special "Fleetwood" Cadillac:** Lynes, *The Tastemakers*, 308.

36 **"From reading the auto ads":** Packard, *The Status Seekers*, 274.

37 **Stratification determines the social space:** In *Class: A Guide through the American Status System*, Paul Fussell provides examples across all sectors of American life.

37 **"Social status is normally expressed":** Weber, *Selections in Translation*, 49.

37 **Aztec warriors marked their status:** Norton, *Sacred Gifts, Profane Pleasures*, 22.

37 **the Chevalier was so incensed:** Hardin, *One for All*, 91.

37 **Galician Jews of Ukraine:** Deenea Prichep, "The Gefilte Fish Line: A Sweet and Salty History of Jewish Identity."

37 **American-born Litvak grandmothers:** One of them was my own grandmother.

38 **At Los Angeles Airport, celebrities:** Adam Popescu, "Inside the Private, Celebrity-Friendly Terminal at LAX."

38 **differential *status value*:** See the discussion of "sign value" in Jean Baudrillard, *For a Critique of the Political Economy of the Sign*, 66. However, "sign value" is ambiguous as a term: Is it the value of its efficacy as a sign? Or its value as a sign of status?

39 **Papua New Guinea:** Glynn Cochrane, *Big Men and Cargo Cults*, 168.

40 **subjects preferred cheaper wines:** Liane Schmidt, Vasilisa Skvortsova, Claus Kullen, Bernd Weber, and Hilke Plassmann, "How Context Alters Value: The Brain's Valuation and Affective Regulation System Link Price Cues to Experienced Taste Pleasantness"; see also Hilke Plassmann et al., "Marketing Actions Can Modulate Neural Representations of Experienced Pleasantness."

40 **"What is rare and constitutes an inaccessible luxury":** Bourdieu, *Distinction*, 247.

40 **"going broke on a million dollars a year":** Tom Wolfe, *The Bonfire of the Vanities*, 142.

40 **"Having a million does not in itself":** Bourdieu, *Distinction*, 373.

40 **"One does not move up":** Lynes, *The Tastemakers*, 253.

40 **"the woman who doesn't have at least one Chanel":** Chaney, *Coco Chanel*, 111.

41 **"widely shared high status cultural signals":** Michèle Lamont and Annette Lareau, "Cultural Capital: Allusions, Gaps and Glissandos in Recent Theoretical Developments."

41 **"more important than belonging to the right club":** Packard, *The Pyramid Climbers*, 118.

41 **"The failure to consume":** Thorstein Veblen, *The Theory of the Leisure Class*, 74.

41 **"Once you had lived":** Wolfe, *The Bonfire of the Vanities*, 143.

41 **Nero faced an assassination attempt:** Joshua Levine, "The New, Nicer Nero."

41 **"Leave all this vanity":** Lynes, *The Tastemakers*, 26.

42 **"It's really hard to be roommates":** J. D. Salinger, *The Catcher in the Rye*, 98.

42 **neighbors of lottery winners:** Seth Stephens-Davidowitz, *Everybody Lies: Big Data, New Data, and What the Internet Can Tell Us about Who We Really Are*, 229.

42 **President Sukarno:** McLuhan, *Understanding Media*, 321.

42 **IMITATION AND DISTINCTION:** These are key terms from Georg Simmel's essay "Fashion," in *On Individuality and Social Forms*.

42 **The meme template for "Hipster Barista":** *Know Your Meme*.

43 **"primarily a pejorative":** Mark Greif, "What Was the Hipster?"

43 **Everyone hates hipsters:** In a 2013 PPP poll, only 16 percent of Americans had a favorable opinion of hipsters. See Tom Jensen, "Americans Not Hip to Hipsters."

43 **"Trying hard to be different":** Jeff Guo, "The Mathematician Who Proved Why Hipsters All Look Alike," quoting Jonathan Touboul.

43 **jewelry artist Keri Ataumbi:** Christian Allaire, "How This Indigenous Jeweler Is Embracing Tradition under Lockdown."

44 **"the way people dressed and acted":** Luis Buñuel, *My Last Breath*, 51.

44 **"Imitative behavior often occurs":** Robert H. Frank, *Choosing the Right Pond: Human Behavior and the Quest for Status*, 18.

44 **"One of the earliest of human distinctions":** Benedict, *Patterns of Culture*, 7.

44 **British upper-class terms:** Nancy Mitford, ed., *Noblesse Oblige*, 111.

44 **imitation creates "bridges":** Mary Douglas and Baron Isherwood, *The World of Goods*, 12.

44 **the girl gang the Pink Ladies:** Jim Jacobs and Warren Casey, *Grease*.

44 **"There's so much ritual":** Howard S. Becker, *Outsiders: Studies in the Sociology of Deviance*, 65.

45 **individual distinction is *emulation*:** Veblen, *The Theory of the Leisure Class*, 103.

45 **"Each class envies and emulates":** Veblen, *The Theory of the Leisure Class*, 103–4.

45 **built-in alibi:** Baudrillard, *For a Critique of the Political Economy of the Sign*, 32.

45 **When the robber barons:** Lynes, *The Tastemakers*, 138.

45 **"cult of the individual":** The term is from Émile Durkheim's *Suicide: A Study in Sociology*.

45 **"There is a certain way":** Taylor, *The Ethics of Authenticity*, 28.

45 **"We don't resign ourselves":** René Girard, *Evolution and Conversion: Dialogues on the Origins of Culture*, 43.

46 **"The woman who is chic":** "Fashion," *Lapham's Quarterly*.

46 **pinstripes that spelled out his name in Arabic:** Emine Saner, "Narendra Modi's Style Tip for World Leaders: Wear a Suit with Your Name Written on It."

46 **"To keep his high status":** Homans, *Social Behavior*, 339.

46 **"The living rooms":** Keller, *A Theory of Linguistic Signs*, 4.

47 **an additional challenge in** *pluralistic ignorance*: Chwe, *Rational Ritual*, 17.
47 **"I didn't want to see one other person":** Bobbito Garcia, *Where'd You Get Those? New York City's Sneaker Culture, 1960–1987*, 21.
47 **a strategy of "optimal distinctiveness":** Marilynn B. Brewer, "The Social Self: On Being the Same and Different at the Same Time."
47 **"You want to be perceived as original":** John Seabrook, *Nobrow: The Culture of Marketing, the Marketing of Culture*, 171.
47 **TV drama** *My So-Called Life*: Winnie Holzman and Scott Winant, "Pilot," *My So-Called Life*.
48 **available in Sri Lanka:** Alfred Gell, "Newcomers to the World of Goods: Consumption among the Murai Gonds," 113, quoting R. L. Stirratt.
48 **"most fantastic and":** Rudi Keller, *On Language Change: The Invisible Hand in Language*, 40.

CHAPTER THREE

51 **Moore had heard "Loser":** John Doran, "The Demolition Man: Thurston Moore Interviewed."
52 **the** *120 Minutes* **interview:** I watched Beck's appearance in real time, but it's also referenced in Joe Robinson, "TV's Most Surreal Music Performances: Beck, Thurston Moore and Mike D."
52 **flaunting gaudy plumage:** David Rothenberg, *Survival of the Beautiful: Art, Science, and Beauty*, 35.
52 **candidates signal their fitness:** Michael Spence, "Job Market Signaling."
52 **"Status enactment is always":** Hugh Dalziel Duncan, *Communication and Social Order*, xlvii.
53 **and becomes a sign:** Hugh Dalziel Duncan, *Symbols in Society*, 49 ("In personal relations, manners, customs, tradition, mores, and style are used to legitimize our right to purely social status. It is *how* we court, *how* we eat, *how* we rule and are ruled, *how* we worship, and even *how* we die, in short, the forms in which we act, that determine our feelings of propriety regarding our own actions and the actions of others").
53 **Beck produced Moore's solo album:** Doran, "The Demolition Man."
53 **"Symbols as seemingly insignificant":** C. Anderson, J. A. D. Hildreth, and L. Howland, "Is the Desire for Status a Fundamental Human Motive? A Review of the Empirical Literature."
53 **we judge wealth levels through individuals' clothing:** Princeton University, "In a Split Second, Clothes Make the Man More Competent in the Eyes of Others."
53 **"If you wish to do business":** Lisa Chaney, *Coco Chanel*, 203.
53 **"the condition of living among strangers":** Charles Lindholm, *Culture and Authenticity*, 3.
53 **"Nothing is so unimpressive":** Geoffrey Brennan and Philip Pettit, *The Economy of Esteem: An Essay on Civil and Political Society*, 36, quoting Jon Elster.
53 **We tend to discount information:** Jonah Berger, *Contagious: Why Things Catch On*, 8.
54 **"etiquette, dress, deportment, gesture, intonation":** Erving Goffman, "Symbols of Class Status."
54 **"observable characteristics attached to the individual":** Spence, "Job Market Signaling."
54 **Walt Frazier signaled his success:** Robert H. Frank, *Choosing the Right Pond: Human Behavior and the Quest for Status*, 149.
55 **"Her voice is full of money":** F. Scott Fitzgerald, *The Great Gatsby*, 115.
55 **also known as** *social shibboleths*: P. N. Furbank, *Unholy Pleasure: The Idea of Social Class*, 102.
55 **they put the** *h* **back in the wrong places:** John Edwards, *Sociolinguistics: A Very Short Introduction*.
55 **the son of David Campbell:** Nick Krewen, "Meet Beck's Dad, David Campbell, Who Has Helped Sell Nearly 1 Billion Records."
55 **"the woman who is deprived":** Simone de Beauvoir, *The Second Sex*, 528.
55 *significant absences*: Roland Barthes, *Elements of Semiology*, 77.
55 **businessmen wear neckties:** Rudi Keller, *A Theory of Linguistic Signs*, 1.
56 **the "Cadillac" of grain silos:** Bob Buyer, "Lawsuits Attack 'Cadillac' Silos," and Carl E. Feather, "Western Reserve Back Roads: Antiquated and Labor Intensive, Northeast Ohio Region's Farm Silos Face Bleak Future as Rural Skyscrapers." See also Everett M. Rogers, *Diffusion of Innovations*, 231.
56 **"When someone would ask where we lived":** Smoker 1, "Harvestore Silos."
56 **Mere interest in purchasing a Harvestore:** Mark Friedberger, *Shake-Out: Iowa Farm Families in the 1980s*, 38.
56 **"Wisconsin skyscrapers":** Lyn Allison Yeager, *The Icons of the Prairie: Stories of Real People, Real Places, and Real Silos*, 106.
56 **farmers claimed problems with mold:** Buyer, "Lawsuits Attack 'Cadillac' Silos."

56 **instances of spontaneous combustion:** Melissa Guay, "Spontaneous Combustion Likely Cause of Silo Fire."

56 **"The home is not merely":** De Beauvoir, *The Second Sex*, 528.

56 **"the signature of one's":** Thorstein Veblen, *The Theory of the Leisure Class*, 87.

57 **"symbol" is a technical term:** Keller, *A Theory of Linguistic Signs*, 148.

57 **camellias as a symbol to communicate:** Chaney, *Coco Chanel*, 208.

57 **known as the *sign-vehicle*:** Umberto Eco, *A Theory of Semiotics*, 23.

57 **iron could be evidence of wealth:** Keller, *A Theory of Linguistic Signs*, 148 ("There is a significant difference between 15 tons of copper and a Jaguar: a Jaguar counts as a status symbol, while 15 tons of copper do not. This is due to the fact that the Jaguar, unlike the copper, is often purchased for the express purpose of making its owner's prosperity visible").

57 **Blue Ivy Carter carried a Louis Vuitton Alma BB:** Carly Stern, "Battle of the Bags! Blue Ivy Carries a $1,800 Louis Vuitton Purse to the NBA All Star Game, while Beyonce Opts for a $1,400 Celine—but Neither Compares to Grandma Tina's $4,700 Gucci."

57 **"anti-dive control":** Marshall McLuhan, *Understanding Media: The Extensions of Man*, 243.

57 **ankle watches were popular:** J. H. Abraham, *Origins and Growth of Sociology*, 512.

57 **"The functionality of goods":** Marshall Sahlins, *Culture and Practical Reason*, 177, quoting Baudrillard.

57 **luxury goods that are initially exclusive:** For nutmeg, see Werner Sombart, *Luxury and Capitalism*, 120; for air-conditioning, see Vance Packard, *The Status Seekers*, 68.

58 **"There are just two classes":** Tom Wolfe, *The Kandy-Kolored Tangerine-Flake Streamline Baby*, 230.

58 **"individuals generally try to present":** Brennan and Pettit, *The Economy of Esteem*, 71, quoting Dale T. Miller and Deborah A. Prentice.

58 **"When two objects have frequently":** Adam Smith, *The Theory of Moral Sentiments*, 281.

58 **Cachet explains why a Jaguar:** In Mark Matousek's "These Are the 16 Most Unreliable Car Brands for 2020," the Jaguar was ranked as the third most unreliable.

59 **Gloria Vanderbilt's name on the tag:** Henrik Vejlgaard, *Anatomy of a Trend*, 126.

59 **the borzoi breed of dogs:** Michael Worboys, Julie-Marie Strange, and Neil Pemberton, *The Invention of the Modern Dog: Breed and Blood in Victorian Britain*, 13.

59 **"loses all the grace":** Smith, *The Theory of Moral Sentiments*, 282.

59 **Cliff Richard made black shirts:** Nik Cohn, *Today There Are No Gentlemen*, 48.

59 **these are called *signaling costs*:** Spence, "Job Market Signaling."

59 **The favorite fruit of aristocrats:** Molly Young, *The Things They Fancied*, 29.

60 **mint-blue Beefeater T-shirt:** My sister was a coxswain for the Cambridge University team and received an old shirt from a rower. She gave me the shirt to wear and, as a nonrower walking around the Head of the Charles Regatta, I got extremely angry looks from the Cambridge crew.

60 **relative merits of Harvard College's:** This is not an actual debate: Holworthy is clearly superior.

60 **"because it pleased him to give":** Chaney, *Coco Chanel*, 61.

60 **"absinthe had become a proletarian vice":** Phil Baker, *The Book of Absinthe*, 128.

61 **Chanel made fake costume jewelry:** Chaney, *Coco Chanel*, 226.

61 **"on coffee tables and as a source":** Gary S. Becker, *Accounting for Tastes*, 200.

61 **"carol a Mozart aria":** Herman Wouk, *The Caine Mutiny*, 16.

62 **proper classifications of status ranking:** Keller, *A Theory of Linguistic Signs*, 92.

62 **"secret society" of hard-core sneakerheads:** Bobbito Garcia, *Where'd You Get Those? New York City's Sneaker Culture, 1960–1987*, 73.

62 **Linguists speak of *semantic drift*:** Edward Sapir, *Language: An Introduction to the Study of Speech*, 155.

62 **Many Americans dress baby boys:** Jeanne Maglaty, "When Did Girls Start Wearing Pink?"

63 **"Don't walk down that way":** Jeff Chang, *Can't Stop, Won't Stop: A History of the Hip-Hop Generation*, 72.

63 **Richard Spencer adopted the same style:** Monica Hesse and Dan Zak, "Does This Haircut Make Me Look Like a Nazi?"

63 **Adidas signed the group:** Chang, *Can't Stop, Won't Stop*, 417.

63 **French youth wore stodgy tassel loafers:** Neil A. Lewis, "The Politicization of Tasseled Loafers."

63 **"RIP Clarks Desert Boots":** This tweet was taken down but it existed at https://twitter.com/dieworkwear/status/1118274805466222593?s=09.

64 **"it made me look mad":** Phil Knight, *Shoe Dog*, 60.

64 **engage in** *redundancy management*: Rudi Keller, *On Language Change: The Invisible Hand in Language*, 109. The term is Helmut Lüdtke's.

64 **"Every time there is signification"**: Eco, *A Theory of Semiotics*, 59.

64 **"Anna looked at the soul of New York"**: Jessica Pressler, "Maybe She Had So Much Money She Just Lost Track of It. Somebody Had to Foot the Bill for Anna Delvey's Fabulous New Life. The City Was Full of Marks."

65 **LVMH invested in the DFS network**: Dana Thomas, *Deluxe: How Luxury Lost Its Luster*.

65 **"To lay false claim"**: Ruth Benedict, *Patterns of Culture*, 260.

65 **"I don't think of this"**: Boon Jong Ho, *Parasite*.

66 **"elegant suit of clothing"**: Frank, *Choosing the Right Pond*, 153.

66 **And research shows**: Thor Berger and Per Engzell, "Trends and Disparities in Subjective Upward Mobility since 1940."

66 **"Objects don't make individual statements"**: Yiannis Gabriel and Tim Lang, *The Unmanageable Consumer*, 55.

66 **ownership of a Louis Vuitton bag**: W. David Marx, *Ametora: How Japan Saved American Style*, 151.

CHAPTER FOUR

69 **"one of the most important figures"**: Bénédicte de Montlaur, "France Honors Dennis Lim and John Waters."

69 **art museum named a rotunda**: Sloane Brown, "BMA John Waters Rotunda Dedication."

69 **"John Waters Baltimore tour"**: See https://baltimore.org/what-to-do/john-waters-baltimore/.

69 **Waters graced the cover of** *Town & Country*: Mike Albo, "The Marvelous Mr. John Waters."

69 **"If someone vomits watching"**: John Waters, *Shock Value: A Tasteful Book about Bad Taste*, 2.

69 **"One must remember"**: Waters, *Shock Value*, 2, which references Susan Sontag's essay "Notes on Camp."

70 **taste was "the faculty of estimating"**: Immanuel Kant, *The Critique of Judgement*, 41.

70 **complex pieces of classical music**: This era of authoritative good taste was embodied in Charles Batteux's writings, as explained in Luc Ferry, *Homo Aestheticus: The Invention of Taste in the Democratic Age*, 43.

70 **"sickness of the spirit"**: Luca Vercelloni, *The Invention of Taste: A Cultural Account of Desire, Delight and Disgust in Fashion, Food and Art*, 11, quoting Voltaire.

70 **the phrase has flipped to become**: Jukka Gronow, *The Sociology of Taste*, 9.

70 **Jony Ive wears Clarks Wallabees**: Sam Colt, "Apple Designer Jony Ive's Favorite Cars," and Stuart Dredge and Alex Hern, "Apple, Coffee and Techno: Jonathan Ive's Recipe for Success."

70 **Waters adores 1950s B movies**: Waters, *Shock Value*, 121.

71 **The philosopher Hannah Arendt called taste**: Hannah Arendt, "The Crisis in Culture."

71 **"Taste, like style, is"**: Roger Scruton, *Modern Culture*, 35.

71 **"brings together things" and also "people that go together"**: Pierre Bourdieu, *Distinction*, 241–43.

71 **Homer goes to war**: "Two Bad Neighbors," *The Simpsons*, season 7, episode 13.

71 **"We are apt to call barbarous"**: David Hume, "Of the Standard of Taste."

72 **We can call this a** *sensibility*: Susan Sontag, *Against Interpretation*, 276.

72 **"Camp asserts that good taste"**: Sontag, *Against Interpretation*, 291.

72 **pink turban over dyed green hair**: Phil Baker, *The Book of Absinthe*, 87–93.

72 **a defined number of** *taste worlds*: See "taste cultures" in Herbert Gans, *Popular Culture and High Culture: An Analysis and Evaluation of Taste*, 10.

72 **Episcopalians preferred more "literate" sermons**: Vance Packard, *The Status Seekers*, 179.

72 **taste a very useful classifier**: Bourdieu, *Distinction*, 6, 56, 173.

73 **"Jackie played a very active role"**: Oleg Cassini, *In My Own Fashion*, 334.

73 **"'different tastes' in musical instruments"**: David Berger, *Kant's Aesthetic Theory: The Beautiful and the Agreeable*, 16.

73 **"trust his own palate"**: David Lewis, *Convention*, 101.

73 **"To understand bad taste"**: Waters, *Shock Value*, 2.

74 **"one of refusal, a foregoing"**: Peter Corrigan, *The Sociology of Consumption*, 29, quoting Daniel Miller.

74 **There is also an anti-Kantian aesthetic**: The terms "contemplative" and "immediate" are mine, in order to avoid the jargon of Miller's "Kantian" and "anti-Kantian."

74 **Lifestyle choices also must reveal** *congruence*: Bourdieu, *Distinction*, 232.

74 **These established groupings of products:** Jean Baudrillard, *The Consumer Society: Myths and Structures*, 59.

75 **"To like what one 'ought'":** Berger, *Kant's Aesthetic Theory*, 123.

75 **"Outright biting [copying] someone's kicks":** Bobbito Garcia, *Where'd You Get Those? New York City's Sneaker Culture, 1960–1987*, 226.

75 **"Fashion belongs under":** Vercelloni, *The Invention of Taste*, 91, quoting Kant.

75 **"The faculty of taste":** Ludwig Wittgenstein, *Culture and Value*, 59.

76 **invented baby:** Seth Stephens-Davidowitz, *Everybody Lies: Big Data, New Data, and What the Internet Can Tell Us about Who We Really Are*, 37.

76 **harm children's future prospects:** William Kremer, "Does a Baby's Name Affect Its Chances in Life?"

76 **Japanese convenience store egg-salad:** Anthony Bourdain tweet, "The Unnatural, Inexplicable Deliciousness of the Lawson's egg salad sandwich," November 3, 2013, https://twitter.com/bourdain/status/397169495506448384.

76 **recognized "Tarantinoesque" as a term:** Nick Reilly, "'Lynchian,' 'Tarantinoesque,' and 'Kubrickian' Lead New Film Words Added to Oxford English Dictionary."

76 **"nice and fresh" clothes:** Jeff Chang, *Can't Stop, Won't Stop: A History of the Hip-Hop Generation*, 67.

77 **"pop's reigning sex symbol":** James Bernard, "Why the World Is After Vanilla Ice."

77 **dates Madonna:** Jeff Weiss, "The (Mostly) True Story of Vanilla Ice, Hip-Hop, and the American Dream."

77 **"Everyone seems to hate Vanilla Ice":** Bernard, "Why the World Is After Vanilla Ice."

77 **African American fraternity Alpha Phi Alpha:** Weiss, "The (Mostly) True Story of Vanilla Ice, Hip-Hop, and the American Dream."

77 **"closely guarded secret":** Stephen Holden, "The Pop Life," October 17, 1990.

77 **Ice was Robert Matthew Van Winkle:** Stephen Holden, "The Pop Life," December 19, 1990.

77 **an Eric B. & Rakim lyric:** Bernard, "Why the World Is After Vanilla Ice," quoting Eric B. & Rakim's "In the Ghetto."

77 **He may have even been sincere:** "The word [sincerity] as we now use it refers primarily to a congruence between avowal and actual feeling": Lionel Trilling, *Sincerity and Authenticity*, 2.

77 **"'Ice Ice Baby' remains a perfect debut":** Weiss, "The (Mostly) True Story of Vanilla Ice, Hip-Hop, and the American Dream."

77 **"A pine table is a proper thing":** Russell Lynes, *The Tastemakers*, 107.

78 **we believe it's "nature's handiwork":** Kant, *The Critique of Judgement*, 89.

78 **"promises a ticket":** Dan Fox, *Pretentiousness: Why It Matters*, 57.

78 **sells itself as "the real thing":** Thomas Frank, *The Conquest of Cool*, 142.

78 **the high-end chocolate brand:** Scott Craig, "What's Noka Worth? (Part 2)."

78 **discovering and realizing one's "originality":** Charles Taylor, *The Ethics of Authenticity*, 29.

78 **"marked by simplicity and naturalness":** S. I. Hayakawa, *Symbol, Status, and Personality*, 55, quoting Abraham Maslow.

78 **"The 'inauthentic' person":** René Girard, *Evolution and Conversion: Dialogues on the Origins of Culture*, 123.

78 **"phonies":** J. D. Salinger, *The Catcher in the Rye*.

78 **Vanilla Ice was always a "white poseur":** Chang, *Can't Stop, Won't Stop*, 425.

78 **"testimony to the history":** Walter Benjamin, *Illuminations*, 221.

79 **all signals should be *behavioral residue*:** Jonah Berger, *Contagious: Why Things Catch On*, 147.

79 **"You either have it, or you don't":** Charles Lindholm, *Culture and Authenticity*, 34.

79 **"An individual who implicitly":** Erving Goffman, *The Presentation of Self in Everyday Life*, 13.

79 **"the beauty of suitability":** Lynes, *The Tastemakers*, 185.

79 **"superficial application of ornament":** Edith Wharton and Ogden Codman Jr., *The Decoration of Houses*.

79 **she dishonestly claimed to have stumbled:** Lisa Chaney, *Coco Chanel*, 190.

80 **ultimate style move is *sprezzatura*:** G. Bruce Boyer, *True Style: The History and Principles of Classic Menswear*, 171–79.

80 **Gianni Agnelli:** Sid Mashburn, "The Most Stylish Men Ever to Wear a Watch."

80 **"achieved grace and charm":** Trilling, *Sincerity and Authenticity*, 22, quoting Castiglione.

80 **prohibited beat matching:** Michelangelo Matos, *The Underground Is Massive*, 324.

80 **"discover and articulate our own identity":** Taylor, *The Ethics of Authenticity*, 81.

80 **"Marginalized groups seeking to control":** Lindholm, *Culture and Authenticity*, 21.

81 **The most powerful form of authenticity:** Lindholm, *Culture and Authenticity*, 2.

81 **a Taiwanese whiskey, Kavalan:** Marian Liu, "How a Taiwanese Whisky Became a Global Favorite."

81 **Japanese textile mills have better preserved:** W. David Marx, *Ametora: How Japan Saved American Style*, 236.

81 **"Authenticity is our first priority":** James H. Gilmore and Joseph Pine, *Authenticity: What Consumers Really Want*, 54.

81 **marginalized communities can better protect:** Russell Hardin, *One for All: The Logic of Group Conflict*, 9.

81 **"can afford to relax and be a natural man":** George Caspar Homans, *Social Behavior: Its Elementary Forms*, 358.

82 **we build *personas*:** The terms "persona," "identity," and "self" are adapted from various sources; see the discussion of George Herbert Mead's "I" vs. "me" in Anthony Elliott, *Concepts of the Self*, 34.

82 **"the real me":** Dorothy M. Scura, ed., *Conversations with Tom Wolfe*, 19.

83 **"Man is nothing else":** Jean-Paul Sartre, *Existentialism and Human Emotions*, 15.

83 **"We have to create ourselves":** Hubert L. Dreyfus and Paul Rabinow, *Michel Foucault: Beyond Structuralism and Hermeneutics*, 351.

83 **the product of a teenage pregnancy:** Biographical details about Billie Holiday are drawn from Linda Dahl, *Stormy Weather: The Music and Lives of a Century of Jazz Women*, 136–40.

84 **"The ordinary man":** Friedrich Nietzsche, *Beyond Good and Evil*, 179.

84 **"each individual is different":** Charles Taylor, *Sources of Self: The Making of the Modern Identity*, 375.

85 **"Sk8er Boi":** "There is more than meets the eye / I see the soul that is inside."

85 **"was smarter than us":** Pierre Bourdieu, *The Field of Cultural Production*, 68.

85 **"The only time she's at ease":** Dahl, *Stormy Weather*, 139.

85 **the persona is simply the latest draft:** Adapted from Lacan's idea that the self "is a fiction" in Adam Roberts, *Frederic Jameson*, 64.

86 **no control over how they classify us:** Taylor, *The Ethics of Authenticity*, 40.

86 **two schlubs went around the United States:** Bob Balaban, *Spielberg, Truffaut and Me: An Actor's Diary*, 150.

86 **"live only in the opinion of others":** Jean-Jacques Rousseau, *A Discourse on Inequality*, 136.

86 **aristocratic principle:** Gronow, *The Sociology of Taste*, 41, and Arendt, "The Crisis in Culture."

87 **"I wanted what everyone wants":** Phil Knight, *Shoe Dog*, 117.

87 **"tend to think that we have selves":** Taylor, *Sources of Self*, 111.

87 **always engaged in *rationalization*:** Hayakawa, *Symbol, Status, and Personality*, 40.

87 **"Even if you deliberate":** Bruce Hood, *The Self Illusion*, 156–57.

88 **"respondents may be reluctant":** Everett M. Rogers, *Diffusion of Innovations*, 231.

88 **"utilitarian reasons, such as small size":** Sheena Iyengar, *The Art of Choosing*, 89.

88 **"more practical" than the iPod:** David Pogue, "Trying Out the Zune: IPod It's Not."

88 **"*consist* of interactions with others":** Georg Simmel, *On Individuality and Social Forms*, 16.

88 **"Today there are few things":** Frank, *The Conquest of Cool*, 227.

89 **elements of individual competence:** Rudi Keller, *On Language Change: The Invisible Hand in Language*, 92.

90 **"When people say that their relative standing":** Robert H. Frank, *Choosing the Right Pond: Human Behavior and the Quest for Status*, 38.

91 **"The hard way of doing better":** Jon Elster, *Nuts and Bolts for the Social Sciences*, 59.

CHAPTER FIVE

95 **"Whenever I need something incredible":** Stacie Stukin, "The Ice Age."

95 **he bought his mother a Rolex:** Ramses M, *How Kanye West Got Started: Lessons from a Legend (How It All Got Started)*.

95 **jewel-encrusted "Jesus piece":** Maureen O'Connor, "Kanye West Wore a WWJD Bracelet."

95 **nouveau riche, parvenus, and arrivistes:** Cf "acquisition classes" in Max Weber, *Selections in Translation*, 89.

96 **conspicuous consumption nearly universal:** Werner Sombart, *Luxury and Capitalism*, 81 ("The tendency of people to spend their quickly acquired wealth mostly on luxuries is an ever recurring

phenomenon in our civilization"). See also C. Anderson, J. A. D. Hildreth, and L. Howland, "Is the Desire for Status a Fundamental Human Motive? A Review of the Empirical Literature" ("Conspicuous consumption appears to occur across cultures").

96 **a palatial Miami home:** Laurence Bergreen, *Capone: The Man and the Era*, 283.

96 **the creativity that emerges:** T. S. Eliot, *Notes towards the Definition of Culture*, 24 ("Class distinction leads to conflict, so do religion, politics, science and art reach a point at which there is conscious struggle between them for autonomy or dominance. This friction is, at some stages and in some situations, highly creative").

97 **"look out into the same segment":** P. N. Furbank, *Unholy Pleasure: The Idea of Social Class*, 64, quoting Schumpeter.

97 **"the place you live":** Paul Fussell, *Class: A Guide through the American Status System*, 151.

97 **"A class itself":** Weber, *Selections in Translation*, 46.

97 **individuals in four groups:** Pierre Bourdieu, *Distinction*, 114, 258.

98 **converting their raw wealth:** Jean Baudrillard, *For a Critique of the Political Economy of the Sign*, 113–15.

98 **The titular character:** F. Scott Fitzgerald, *The Great Gatsby*.

98 **Bernard Docker:** Peter Lewis, *The Fifties*, 34.

98 **Drake built a 50,000-square-foot home:** Mayer Rus, "Inside Rapper Drake's Manor House in Hometown Toronto."

99 **Conspicuous consumption is a universal language:** Grant David McCracken, *Culture and Consumption: New Approaches to the Symbolic Character of Consumer Goods and Activities*, 36.

99 **"You can always tell how rich people are":** John Waters, *Shock Value: A Tasteful Book about Bad Taste*, 142 (quoting Divine), echoed in Michael Thompson, *Rubbish Theory: The Creation and Destruction of Value*, 19 ("The condition of richness or poorness is determined by the quantity of objects one possesses: a poor person possesses few objects, a rich person many objects").

99 **a fleet of luxury autos:** Sola, "Mugabe Amassed $1bn—Including a Rare Rolls-Royce Worth More Than Zimbabwe's Economy."

99 **known as Gucci Grace:** Jane Flanagan, "Grace Mugabe's Porsche, Rolls Royce and Range Rover Are Damaged When Cows Wander onto the Road as Motors Were Being Spirited Out of Zimbabwe under the Cover of Darkness."

99 **"third-world dictator" tastes:** Peter York, "Trump's Dictator Chic."

99 **"The rich were becoming fabulously rich":** Russell Lynes, *The Tastemakers*, 117.

99 *conspicuous waste*—**flamboyant expenditure:** Thorstein Veblen, *The Theory of the Leisure Class*, 96.

99 **Giacomo da Sant'Andrea:** Sombart, *Luxury and Capitalism*, 81.

99 **"humiliating, challenging and obligating":** Georges Bataille, *The Accursed Share: An Essay on the General Economy*, 1:67.

100 **"It's insulting to say":** Stephen Rodrick, "The Trouble with Johnny Depp."

100 **"Leisure works as a way":** Peter Corrigan, *The Sociology of Consumption*, 25.

100 **the ultrarich work even longer hours:** Vance Packard, *The Status Seekers*, 31; contemporary evidence in Elizabeth Currid-Halkett, *The Sum of Small Things: A Theory of the Aspirational Class*, 186.

100 **"carpets and tapestries, silver table service":** Veblen, *The Theory of the Leisure Class*, 99.

100 **"pecuniary canons of taste":** Veblen, *The Theory of the Leisure Class*, 115.

100 *vicarious consumption*: Veblen, *The Theory of the Leisure Class*, 68; also discussed in Baudrillard, *For a Critique of the Political Economy of the Sign*, 31.

100 **parvenus are often attracted to** *novelties*: Stephen Bayley, *Taste: The Secret Meaning of Things*, 157 ("Neomania assumes that purchasing the new is the same as acquiring value"). See also McCracken, *Culture and Consumption*, 42, which focuses on challenging Old Money symbols.

100 **1950s, Old Money women:** Packard, *The Status Seekers*, 121.

101 **drug dealer's pad:** Andy Warhol and Pat Hackett, *POPism: The Warhol Sixties*, 295.

101 **$6.9 million for a Jeff Koons:** Henri Neuendorf, "Here's What Japanese Billionaire Yusaku Maezawa Has Bought So Far at the Auctions."

101 **emphasis on communal sacrifice:** Andrew B. Trigg, "Veblen, Bourdieu, and Conspicuous Consumption," and Fussell, *Class*, 20.

101 **"was like a blinking neon sign":** Richard Conniff, *The Natural History of the Rich: A Field Guide*, 183, quoting Allen Grubman.

101 **Economists call this the "Veblen effect":** H. Leibenstein, "Bandwagon, Snob, and Veblen Effects in the Theory of Consumers' Demand."

102 **Johnnie Walker Black:** Aaron Goldfarb, "When Johnnie Walker Blue Was King."

102 **"gold-plated, fully armored":** Rylan Miller, "A Middle Eastern Businessman Just Paid $8 Million for a Gold-Plated Rolls Royce."

102 **insatiable hunger for imported luxury goods:** Sombart, *Luxury and Capitalism*, 168 ("The organization of industrial production is influenced to a far greater extent by increase in the consumption of luxury goods. In numerous cases [although not in all] increase in consumption opens the door to capitalism, permitting it to invade the sanctuary of trade").

102 **H. Jeremy Chisholm attended Le Rosey:** This and other biographical details are from the Chisholm Gallery website, https://chisholmgallery.com/hugh-jeremy-chisholm.

102 **Chisholm became annoyed:** Nelson W. Aldrich Jr., *Old Money: The Mythology of America's Upper Class*, 135.

102 **to wear Cartier Tank watches:** James Dowling, "100 Not Out: The Full History of the Cartier Tank."

103 **"casual, careless, nonchalant":** Aldrich, *Old Money*, 83.

103 **old jackets and shoes with visible patches:** Liz Jones, "The Patch-Up Prince: As He Is Pictured in a Jacket That's Been Repaired for Decades, How—from His Shoes Up—Prince Charles Has Always Made Do and Mended."

103 **beat-up station wagons:** Packard, *The Status Seekers*, 275.

103 **strived to be *iki*:** Shūzō Kuki, *Reflections on Japanese Taste: The Structure of Iki*, 93.

103 **"loud dress" would be deemed "offensive":** Veblen, *The Theory of the Leisure Class*, 187.

104 **To be granted an audience:** Paul Connerton, *How Societies Remember*, 85.

104 **"ancestral prestige still immensely outweighs":** Gabriel Tarde, *The Laws of Imitation*, 244.

104 **"the classes or persons":** Tarde, *The Laws of Imitation*, 233.

104 **"magic properties of chiefs":** Bertrand Russell, *Power*, 29.

104 **Old Money's multigenerational wealth:** Corrigan, *The Sociology of Consumption*, 5 ("New money, however, lacks a track record: it could be gone in six months or a year and could simply be a freakish occurrence").

104 **"High-status group members":** Cecilia L. Ridgeway, *Status: Why Is It Everywhere? Why Does It Matter?*, 106.

105 *petit goût*—**"trivial taste":** Bayley, *Taste*, 90.

105 **they pursue "Spartan wealth":** Baudrillard, *For a Critique of the Political Economy of the Sign*, 78.

105 **technique is called *countersignaling*:** Nick Feltovich, Rick Harbaugh, and Ted To, "Too Cool for School? Signalling and Countersignalling."

105 **pick up on their subtle cues:** Maurice Halbwachs, *On Collective Memory*, 128.

105 **"The growth of wealthy classes":** Corrigan, *The Sociology of Consumption*, 166.

105 **"In London, nobody knows":** Conniff, *The Natural History of the Rich*, 187.

105 **"a sign of high vulgarity":** Fussell, *Class*, 85, quoting Joseph Epstein.

105 **"slightly dirty" Chevys:** Fussell, *Class*, 85.

105 **"it is what a woman":** Lisa Chaney, *Coco Chanel*, 90, quoting Paul Poiret.

106 **"If John Bull turns round":** James Laver, *Dandies*, 21.

106 **"The good Savile Row tailor":** Quentin Bell, *On Human Finery*, 31.

106 **"the ultimate accolade":** Lisa Birnbach, *The Official Preppy Handbook*, 128.

106 **"it saves on breakages":** Mary Douglas and Baron Isherwood, *The World of Goods*, 118, quoting Prince Philip.

106 **"a thing beyond learning":** Aldrich, *Old Money*, 103.

106 **"One can almost hear the poor creature":** Aldrich, *Old Money*, 71, quoting Mark Hampton.

106 **"merely represent[s] a further degree of luxury":** Jean Baudrillard, *The Consumer Society: Myths and Structures*, 90.

106 **McCracken calls "patina":** McCracken, *Culture and Consumption*, 35.

107 **"I don't *buy* evening clothes":** G. Bruce Boyer, *True Style: The History and Principles of Classic Menswear*, 178.

107 **said to look "lived in":** Aldrich, *Old Money*, 76.

107 **"Orientals so old":** Fussell, *Class*, 88.

107 **Earl of Winchester:** As attested by Coco Chanel in Barbara Vinken, *Fashion Zeitgeist: Trends and Cycles in the Fashion System*, 69.

107 **"to save [them] the embarrassment":** Russell Lynes, "How Shoe Can You Get?"

107 **LL Bean boots:** Nelson W. Aldrich Jr., "Preppies: The Last Upper Class?"

108 *archaism*, **the preferences for antiquated styles:** Fussell, *Class*, 71.

108 **"Most Englishmen of a certain class"**: Bayley, *Taste*, 84.
108 **purple glass "Lavenders"**: Packard, *The Status Seekers*, 67, and Madeline Bilis, "Why Some Boston Brownstones Have Purple Windows."
108 **an Old Money "curriculum"**: Aldrich, *Old Money*, 39.
108 **"acquire the social, linguistic, and cultural"**: Michèle Lamont and Annette Lareau, "Cultural Capital: Allusions, Gaps and Glissandos in Recent Theoretical Developments," 155.
108 **to say "cheers"**: Nancy Mitford, ed., *Noblesse Oblige: An Enquiry into the Identifiable Characteristics of the English Aristocracy*, xi.
108 **"A small percentage of polyester"**: Birnbach, *The Official Preppy Handbook*, 121. For another example of detail orientation, see G. Bruce Boyer, "The Swelled Edge, a Quarter-Inch of Distinction."
108 **"In these matters, U-speakers"**: Mitford, ed., *Noblesse Oblige*, 85.
109 **"A work of art," writes Bourdieu**: Bourdieu, *Distinction*, 2.
109 **"unequal class distribution"**: Bourdieu, *Distinction*, 29.
109 **behaviors and norms we come to know as "virtues"**: Halbwachs, *On Collective Memory*, 151 ("The prestige that still today is linked to wealth can be explained at least in part by the feeling that the modern idea of virtue was elaborated in the wealthy class, and that the first and most memorable examples of it can be found in that class").
109 **"They model things for everyone else"**: Aldrich, *Old Money*, 79.
109 **"I can't buy imported cheese"**: Maureen Dowd, "Retreat of the Yuppies: The Tide Now Turns amid 'Guilt' and 'Denial.'"
110 **IBM once required**: Erynn Masi de Casanova, *Buttoned Up: Clothing, Conformity, and White-Collar Masculinity*, 227.
110 **They poured their earnings**: Marissa Piesman and Marilee Hartley, *The Yuppie Handbook: The State-of-the-Art Manual for Young Urban Professionals*, cover.
110 **"Taste is entirely a Middle Class concern"**: Peter Gammond, *The Bluffer's Guide to British Class*, 28.
111 **"I was taught by my parents"**: George W. S. Trow, *Within the Context of No Context*, 4.
111 **"all about Corvettes"**: Birnbach, *The Official Preppy Handbook*, 89.
111 **"Nonchalance sold along"**: Aldrich, *Old Money*, 142.
111 **Volvo automotive brand**: Thomas Frank, *The Conquest of Cool*, 145–46.
112 **Bobo tastes in these mock rules**: David Brooks, *Bobos in Paradise*.
112 **"[They] are at least as willing"**: Douglas B. Holt, "Distinction in America? Recovering Bourdieu's Theory of Taste from Its Critics."
112 **The vast majority of Whole Foods customers**: Currid-Halkett, *The Sum of Small Things*, 120, and Dominick Reuter, "Meet the Typical Whole Foods Shopper, a Highly Educated West Coast Millennial Woman Earning $80,000."
113 **the lower class was curling up**: Fussell, *Class*, 142, as echoed in Herbert Gans, *Popular Culture and High Culture: An Analysis and Evaluation of Taste*.
113 **piquant social satire and passing allusions**: References to Ludwig Wittgenstein are in the episode "The Springfield Files"; the Vassarbashing appears in "The PTA Disbands."
114 **other faction is the *creative class***: Richard Florida, *The Creative Class*.
114 **"[Horace] Liveright was possibly"**: Lillian Hellman, *An Unfinished Woman*, 36.
114 **Championship Vinyl**: Nick Hornby, *High Fidelity*.
115 **"I had Super PRO-Keds"**: Bobbito Garcia, *Where'd You Get Those? New York City's Sneaker Culture, 1960–1987*.
115 **"no class of society"**: Veblen, *The Theory of the Leisure Class*, 85.
115 **"long lines of Range Rovers"**: Misha Lanin, "Russia's Airbrushed Car Scene Is Out of Control."
115 **African American and Hispanic people spend 30 percent**: Kerwin Kofi Charles, Erik Hurst, and Nikolai Roussanov, "Conspicuous Consumption and Race."
116 **"There are no longer class differences"**: René Girard, *Evolution and Conversion: Dialogues on the Origins of Culture*, 45.
116 **generic "skippy" sneakers**: Garcia, *Where'd You Get Those?*, 14.
116 **"the notion of being accepted"**: Garcia, *Where'd You Get Those?*, 35.
116 **neighborhood had its own sneaker**: Garcia, *Where'd You Get Those?*, 151.
116 **"Biting was frowned upon"**: Garcia, *Where'd You Get Those?*, 12.
116 **"kitsch" is a pejorative term**: Matei Calinescu, *Five Faces of Modernity*, 235.
116 **a specific type of commercial product**: Tomáš Kulka, *Kitsch and Art*, 28; for additional thoughts on kitsch, see Clement Greenberg, *Art and Culture*, 10.

117 **"If formal explorations":** Bourdieu, *Distinction*, 43.

117 **"Consumers of kitsch":** Kulka, *Kitsch and Art*, 44.

117 **"After hearing them I would mark 'good'":** Norman Lebrecht, *The Book of Musical Anecdotes*, 233.

118 **a *flash* sensibility:** Paulo Hewitt, ed., *The Sharper Word: A Mod Anthology*, 74 ("They came from a post-war British working-class attitude to smartness, best described as 'flash'").

118 **"culture of transience":** Thompson, *Rubbish Theory*, 117.

118 **"easy come, easy go":** Thompson, *Rubbish Theory*, 63.

118 **Color Research Institute of Chicago:** Packard, *The Status Seekers*, 70.

118 **"rainbow mohair suits":** Dick Hebdidge, *Subculture: The Meaning of Style*, 41.

118 **airbrushed on their cars:** Lanin, "Russia's Airbrushed Car Scene Is Out of Control."

118 **The demonized "chav":** Owen Jones, *Chavs: The Demonization of the Working Class*, 121, and James Hall, "Burberry Brand Tarnished by 'Chavs.'"

118 **Porsches, Ferraris, and multiple Maybachs:** Jonathan Sawyer, "Jay-Z's Wild Car Collection Is Fitting for Hip-Hop's First Billionaire."

118 **Counterfeiters, who target:** Young Jee Han, Joseph C. Nunes, and Xavier Drèze, "Signaling Status with Luxury Goods: The Role of Brand Prominence."

118 **Vivian Nicholson:** Margalit Fox, "Vivian Nicholson, 79, Dies; A Rags-to-Riches Story Left in Tatters."

119 **Jennifer Southall:** Richard Pendlebury, "Spent, Spent, Spent—Pools Winner Now Living on £87 a Week."

119 **Sneaker brands develop new technologies:** Naomi Klein, *No Logo: Taking Aim at the Brand Bullies*.

120 **"pewter that the family":** Lynes, *The Tastemakers*, 239.

CHAPTER SIX

121 **George Hotel ballroom:** Image of this sign at https://www.messynessychic.com/2013/02/10/the-forgotten-1950s-girl-gang.

121 **This was a devastating reversal of fortune:** For the history of the Edwardian look and the teddy boys, see Nik Cohn, *Today There Are No Gentlemen*, and Ray Ferris and Julian Lord, *Teddy Boys: A Concise History*.

121 **long drape jackets:** Cohn, *Today There Are No Gentlemen*, 23.

121 **the Edwardian look attracted few:** Cohn, *Today There Are No Gentlemen*, 25–26.

122 **A moral panic ensued:** Michael Macilwee, *The Teddy Boy Wars*.

122 **animal torture:** Macilwee, *The Teddy Boy Wars*, 138, reports on how teds played "Throw the Cat."

122 **the diminutive form of Edward:** Ferris and Lord, *Teddy Boys*, 16, and Macilwee, *The Teddy Boy Wars*, 19–20.

122 **"Devil's garb":** Macilwee, *The Teddy Boy Wars*, 62.

122 **social workers proclaimed it:** Macilwee, *The Teddy Boy Wars*, 85, 230.

122 **"the whole of one's wardrobe":** Alan Sinfield, *Literature, Politics and Culture in Postwar Britain*, 174.

122 **a vivid example of a postwar *subculture*:** Cohn, *Today There Are No Gentlemen*, 28.

122 **The word first indicated:** Stuart Hall and Tony Jefferson, eds., *Resistance through Rituals*, 29; emphasis on working-class origins in ibid., 236.

122 **Subcultures are a clear example:** Albert K. Cohen, "A General Theory of Subcultures (1955)" ("One solution is for individuals who share such problems to gravitate towards one another and jointly to establish new norms, new criteria of status which define as meritorious the characteristics they do possess, the kinds of conduct of which they are capable").

122 **merely breaking milk bottles:** Macilwee, *The Teddy Boy Wars*, 115.

123 **"Members of established low status":** George Caspar Homans, *Social Behavior: Its Elementary Forms*, 341.

123 **"It took courage":** Macilwee, *The Teddy Boy Wars*, 132.

123 **"For the first time in the history":** Dorothy M. Scura, ed., *Conversations with Tom Wolfe*, 235.

123 **laborer-chic skinheads:** Dick Hebdidge, *Subculture: The Meaning of Style*, 55.

123 **Similar outcast groups:** Cohn, *Today There Are No Gentlemen*, and Macilwee, *The Teddy Boy Wars*, 295–300.

124 **yellow-suited dandies La Sape:** Daniele Tamangi, *Gentlemen of Bacongo*.

124 **"Black culture, and especially Black music":** Hall and Jefferson, eds., *Resistance through Rituals*, 161.

124 **flashy mohair suits and porkpie hats:** Hebdidge, *Subculture*, 64.

124 **Chicanos created their own culture:** Nili Blanck, "Inside L.A.'s Lowrider Car Clubs."

124 **African American teens bonded over rapping:** Jeff Chang, *Can't Stop, Won't Stop: A History of the Hip-Hop Generation.*

124 **In the 1960s, middle-class youth:** Phil Cohen, "Subcultural Conflict and Working-Class Community (1972)" ("I do not think the middle class produces subcultures, for subcultures are produced by a dominated culture, not by a dominant culture").

124 **abandoned their parents' staid customs:** Daniel Bell, *The Cultural Contradictions of Capitalism*, 190 ("[M]uch of the alienation of the young was a reaction to the social revolution that had taken place in their own status").

124 **countercultures tend to embrace explicit ideologies:** Hall and Jefferson, eds., *Resistance through Rituals*, 61; see also Roland Barthes and Andy Stafford, *The Language of Fashion*, 107 (hippies were an "inverted bourgeois").

124 *hobbyist group*: **pods of individuals:** Henry Jenkins, "Television Fans, Poachers, Nomads (1992)" ("These fans often draw strength and courage from their ability to identify themselves as members of a group of other fans who shared common interests and confronted common problems").

125 **"No one, not a soul":** Peter Lewis, *The Fifties*, 141.

125 **"As a former bullied kid":** Carl Wilson, *Let's Talk about Love: A Journey to the End of Taste*, 6.

125 **"nostalgia for the mud":** Scura, ed., *Conversations with Tom Wolfe*, 190.

125 **"For the first time, kids didn't want":** Cohn, *Today There Are No Gentlemen*, 33.

126 **Teddy boys retained the patriarchal gender values:** Hall and Jefferson, eds., *Resistance through Rituals*, 53, 102.

126 **Japanese blue-collar bikers:** Ikuya Satō, *Kamikaze Biker: Parody and Anomy in Affluent Japan.*

126 **Beat poets cribbed their deviant lifestyles:** Joel Dinerstein, *The Origins of Cool in Postwar America*, 230.

126 **"I went there expecting it":** *The Beatles Anthology*, 259.

127 **a fictional diary called *Go Ask Alice*:** Frankie Thomas, "A Queer Reading of *Go Ask Alice*"; see also https://www.snopes.com/fact-check/go-ask-alice.

127 **"We called ourselves Teddy Boys":** Ferris and Lord, *Teddy Boys*, 48.

127 **"normies":** David Muggleton, *Inside Subculture: The Postmodern Meaning of Style*, 85.

127 **"trendies":** Muggleton, *Inside Subculture*, 124.

127 **"smoothies," "casuals":** Muggleton, *Inside Subculture*, 67.

127 **"One is Hip":** Norman Mailer, "The White Negro," 339.

127 **"unemployment, educational disadvantage":** Hall and Jefferson, eds., *Resistance through Rituals*, 47.

128 *Bihaku* **("beautiful whiteness"):** Michelle H. S. Ho, "Consuming Women in Blackface: Racialized Affect and Transnational Femininity in Japanese Advertising."

128 **started to tan their skin:** For the history of *kogyaru* and *ganguro*, see W. David Marx, "The History of the Gyaru—Part One," "The History of the Gyaru—Part Two," and "The History of the Gyaru—Part Three."

128 **Men's tabloids lusted after the *kogyaru*:** Sharon Kinsella, "Black Faces, Witches, and Racism against Girls."

129 **"overtly close to the straight world":** Hall and Jefferson, eds., *Resistance through Rituals*, 93.

129 **"In the distance I heard":** Irish Jack quoted in Paolo Hewitt, ed., *The Sharper Word: A Mod Anthology*, 44.

130 *bricolage*—**the mixing and matching:** Hall and Jefferson, eds., *Resistance through Rituals*, 177.

130 *dokajan* **cold-weather jackets:** Kōji Nanba, *Yankii shinkaron*, 69.

130 *"obviously* **fabricated":** Hebdidge, *Subculture*, 101.

130 **a Nazi swastika T-shirt:** Hebdidge, *Subculture*, 116. For the symbol's use among Bronx gangs, see Chang, *Can't Stop, Won't Stop*, 42, 102; for actual Nazi affiliations among bikers, see Christopher Beam, "Highway to Heil."

131 **"hedonism, disdain for work":** Jack Young, "The Subterranean World of Play (1971)."

131 **"Punk's not a fashion":** Muggleton, *Inside Subculture*, 115.

131 **a punk "feeling" of combative disobedience:** Muggleton, *Inside Subculture*, 110.

131 **subcultures develop *subcultural capital*:** Sarah Thornton, "The Social Logic of Subcultural Capital (1995)."

131 **"I saw the Hatchetman":** Kent Russell, "American Juggalo."

131 **"They became clone-like":** Muggleton, *Inside Subculture*, 131, quoting Lydon.

132 **"punk is basically being yourself":** Muggleton, *Inside Subculture*, 57, 68.

132 **more complicated grammars and more difficult sounds:** John McWhorter, *The Language Hoax: Why the World Looks the Same in Any Language*, 67.

132 **This often spirals into further extremity:** Russell Hardin, *One for All: The Logic of Group Conflict*, 83, 101.

132 **high-status "total" members:** Herbert Gans, *Popular Culture and High Culture: An Analysis and Evaluation of Taste*, 13.

132 **Hard-core ravers hated "Techno Traceys":** Muggleton, *Inside Subculture*, 137.

132 **the Merry Pranksters detested:** Scura, ed., *Conversations with Tom Wolfe*, 149.

132 **"Plastic"—inauthentic, protean:** Ferris and Lord, *Teddy Boys*, 61, and Hedbidge, *Subculture*, 122.

132 **the "preppy punk" epithet:** Muggleton, *Inside Subculture*, 100.

132 **never owned an Edwardian suit:** Ferris and Lord, *Teddy Boys*, 11.

133 **a rural Jamaican commune:** The history of Pinnacle is drawn from Lucy McKeon, "The True Story of Rastafari," and Chris Salewicz, *Bob Marley*, 45–47.

133 **regarded as folk devils:** Salewicz, *Bob Marley*, 46.

133 **"These people—and I am glad":** Salewicz, *Bob Marley*, 47.

133 **He first absorbed the group's teachings:** Salewicz, *Bob Marley*, 118.

133 **a stigmatalike "nail-print":** Salewicz, *Bob Marley*, 112.

134 **at least one member of the Ku Klux Klan:** Sam Bright, "Klansman with Dreadlocks Astonishes Twitter."

134 **sales surpass $2 billion:** Boardriders, https://www.boardriders.com/history-inactive.

134 **Lydon to appear in television commercials:** David Teather, "Country Life Butter Soars after Johnny Rotten's Star Turn."

134 **"pure, simple, raging":** Hall and Jefferson, eds., *Resistance through Rituals*, 66.

134 **thirty thousand British teddy boys:** T. R. Fyvel, "Fashion and Revolt (1963)," 69.

135 **"the life of simple, rustic people":** Charles Taylor, *Sources of Self: The Making of the Modern Identity*, 297.

135 **"radical chic":** Tom Wolfe, *Radical Chic and Mau-Mauing the Flak Catchers*.

135 **Hippie ads thus preceded:** Thomas Frank, *The Conquest of Cool*, 173.

135 **students in art and fashion schools:** Simon Frith and Howard Horne, *Art into Pop*.

135 **punk's embrace of reggae:** Hebdidge, *Subculture*, 68–69.

135 **New York's downtown art scene:** Chang, *Can't Stop, Won't Stop*, 418.

135 **"What makes Hip":** Mailer, "The White Negro," 348.

136 **"carried the necessary conviction":** Hebdidge, *Subculture*, 63.

136 **to be in the know:** Thornton, "The Social Logic of Subcultural Capital (1995)."

136 **"being someone else was a way":** Dan Fox, *Pretentiousness: Why It Matters*, 63.

136 **off-the-rack mod garments:** Cohn, *Today There Are No Gentlemen*, 84.

136 **they are defused:** Hall and Jefferson, eds., *Resistance through Rituals*, 188.

137 **The vague "oppositional attitude":** Dick Pountain and David Robins, *Cool Rules: Anatomy of an Attitude*, 19.

137 **Velvet cuffs became a hallmark:** Ferris and Lord, *Teddy Boys*, 32.

137 **"deep social conviction" but "in homage":** John Waters, *Shock Value: A Tasteful Book about Bad Taste*, 36.

137 **second generation of teds:** Cohn, *Today There Are No Gentlemen*, 31.

137 **white suburban teens:** See John Seabrook, *Nobrow: The Culture of Marketing, the Marketing of Culture*, 76 ("By 1998, when hip-hop sold more than 81 million records, 70 percent to white fans, the genre had passed country as the most popular category in all pop music").

137 **"Death of the Hippie":** Andy Warhol and Pat Hackett, *POPism: The Warhol Sixties*, 293.

137 **"One by one, they would":** Cohn, *Today There Are No Gentlemen*, 31.

138 **"a tourist trap":** Cohn, *Today There Are No Gentlemen*, 112.

138 **the bikers switched to right-wing paramilitary uniforms:** W. David Marx, *Ametora: How Japan Saved American Style*, 143.

138 **"If you're working on a commercial band":** Howard S. Becker, *Outsiders: Studies in the Sociology of Deviance*, 60.

139 **confuse these later adherents:** Hebdidge, *Subculture*, 84.

139 **where the term "Edwardian" originated:** Ferris and Lord, *Teddy Boys*, 67.

139 **teddy-boy-themed collection in 2014:** David Bazner, "The Ted Trend Continues at Saint Laurent," and Steff Yotka and Amanda Brooks, "Watch: At Dior, Teddy Girls Take Center Stage."

139 **the worst artist in music history:** Russell, "American Juggalo."

139 **the fashion brand Extreme Christian Clothes:** Annette Lynch and Mitchell D. Strauss, *Changing Fashion: A Critical Introduction to Trend Analysis and Meaning*, 54.

140 **"resistance," trying to navigate the "contradictions":** Hall and Jefferson, eds., *Resistance through Rituals*, 32.

140 **"Studies carried out in Britain":** Muggleton, *Inside Subculture*, 126.

140 **groups' sense of "vague opposition":** Thornton, "The Social Logic of Subcultural Capital (1995)," 201 ("Vague opposition is certainly how many members of youth subcultures characterize their own activities").

140 **"love of the unnatural":** Susan Sontag, *Against Interpretation*, 275.

140 **"old-fashioned, out-of-date, démodé":** Sontag, *Against Interpretation*, 285.

140 **"supplementary" set of standards:** Sontag, *Against Interpretation*, 286.

141 **Zoot Suit Riots:** Ralph H. Turner and Samuel J. Surace, "Zoot-Suiters and Mexicans," 387.

141 **an invigorating "renewal":** Terence Hawkes, *Structuralism and Semiotics*, 72.

141 **to sell in the commercial marketplace:** Fred Davis, *Fashion, Culture, and Identity*, 162 ("The anti-fashion posture has become firmly, and perhaps irrevocably, incorporated into fashion's very own institutional apparatus").

CHAPTER SEVEN

143 **"Five francs. You can paint on the back":** Roger Shattuck, *The Banquet Years: The Origins of the Avant-Garde in France 1885 to World War I*, 66.

143 **"Monsieur Rousseau paints with his feet":** Shattuck, *The Banquet Years*, 52.

144 **an honorific title:** Howard S. Becker, *Art Worlds*, 14.

144 **"are you a real writer?":** Truman Capote, *Breakfast at Tiffany's*, 18.

144 **"priest or a sorcerer":** Jean Duvignaud, *The Sociology of Art*, 32.

144 **a "visionary genius":** Luca Vercelloni, *The Invention of Taste: A Cultural Account of Desire, Delight and Disgust in Fashion, Food and Art*, 117.

144 **with "extravagant individualism":** Duvignaud, *The Sociology of Art*, 24.

144 **who reaches "epiphanies":** Charles Taylor, *Sources of Self: The Making of the Modern Identity*, 419.

144 **a "magical process":** Duvignaud, *The Sociology of Art*, 24.

144 **"imagination to anticipate":** Duvignaud, *The Sociology of Art*, 42.

144 **"humanity face-to-face with a new event":** John D. Graham, *John Graham's System and Dialectics of Art*, 95.

144 **"to see and to make us see":** Henri Bergson, *The Creative Mind: An Introduction to Metaphysics*, 135.

145 **literally *alters our minds*:** Bergson, *The Creative Mind*, 157 ("Art enables us, no doubt, to discover in things more qualities and more shades than we naturally perceive").

145 **"the order which we find in nature":** Herschel Browing Chipp, Peter Selz, and Joshua C. Taylor, *Theories of Modern Art: A Source Book by Artists and Critics*, 224.

145 **As Oscar Wilde complained:** Matei Calinescu, *Five Faces of Modernity*, 229.

145 **Kant asserted three still authoritative criteria:** Immanuel Kant, *The Critique of Judgement*, 168–69.

145 **seemed to arise from his bizarre subconscious:** Rollo H. Myers, *Erik Satie*, 112 ("How else can one account for the emergence of the purest masterpieces from a brain which in other respects might well have belonged to the merest simpleton?").

145 **"last individual left in a mass society":** Hannah Arendt, "The Crisis in Culture," 200.

145 **"He was completely unmotivated":** B. H. Friedman, *Jackson Pollock: Energy Made Visible*, 181.

146 **the epithet "picture painter":** Becker, *Art Worlds*, 98.

146 **Glenn Gould got away with it:** Josh Jones, "How Glenn Gould's Eccentricities Became Essential to His Playing and Personal Style: From Humming Aloud While Playing to Performing with His Childhood Piano Chair."

146 **"attain honour, power, riches, fame":** Sigmund Freud, *Introductory Lectures on Psycho-Analysis*, 423.

146 **"Most of the artists were trying":** John Seabrook, *Nobrow: The Culture of Marketing, the Marketing of Culture*, 191.

146 **In the 1980s, "hair metal" bands:** Justin Quirk, *Nothin' but a Good Time*, 217.

146 **"When I am in my painting":** Friedman, *Jackson Pollock*, 100.

147 **"Only an artist can so represent":** Ludwig Wittgenstein, *Culture and Value*, 4.

147 **"primitive in performance":** Shattuck, *The Banquet Years*, 80.

147 **"There was nothing she could not draw":** Kathleen McKenna, "Edna Hibel, at 97; Versatile Creator of Many Works of Art."

147 **sold a Renoiresque painting:** This and additional details about Hibel from Kim Shippey, "Always Trying for the Best She Can Do."

148 **There are two definitions of art:** Noël Carroll, *Philosophy of Art*, 228, 253.

149 **The famed curator Roger Fry included him:** "Roger Eliot Fry (1866–1934)."

149 **"a sound draftsman":** McKenna, "Edna Hibel, at 97."

149 **Philosopher of art Tomáš Kulka explains:** Tomáš Kulka, *Kitsch and Art*, 55.

150 **"Composers can create and manipulate":** Becker, *Art Worlds*, 29–30.

150 **"The chief task of genius is precisely":** Stephen Bayley, *Taste: The Secret Meaning of Things*, 56.

150 **makes the creator an epigone:** Renato Poggioli, *The Theory of the Avant-Garde*, 179.

150 **their work is mere "taste":** Pierre Cabanne and Marcel Duchamp, *Dialogues with Marcel Duchamp*, 48.

150 **"A work of art is a problem":** Graham, *John Graham's System and Dialectics of Art*, 96.

151 **beloved maxim "What doesn't grow out":** From a Catalan philosopher named Eugenio d'Ors, as quoted in Luis Buñuel, *My Last Breath*, 69–70.

151 **"Not the dialectic between art and society":** Harold Bloom, *The Anxiety of Influence: A Theory of Poetry*, 99.

151 **"unbroken chain" of problems:** Graham, *John Graham's System and Dialectics of Art*, 177.

151 **the choreographer Trisha Brown forged:** Roland Aeschilmann et al., eds., *Trisha Brown: Dance and Art in Dialogue, 1961–2001*, and Trisha Brown, "Trisha Brown on Pure Movement."

152 **"misreading" poems:** Bloom, *The Anxiety of Influence*, 5.

152 **Cage obsessed over scribbles on Erik Satie scores:** Calvin Tomkins, *Ahead of the Game: Four Versions of the Avant-Garde*, 99.

152 **"one of the few accidents":** Tomkins, *Ahead of the Game*, 182.

152 **its artistic importance, not its aesthetic achievement:** Kulka, *Kitsch and Art*, 55.

152 **Picasso's art dealer believed this painting:** Christopher Green, "An Introduction to *Les Demoiselles d'Avignon*."

152 **"What a loss for French painting":** Kulka, *Kitsch and Art*, 53.

152 **"we become less and less":** Barbara Herrnstein Smith, *Contingencies of Value: Alternative Perspectives for Critical Theory*, 5.

152 **"possessing an ability to perform":** Graham, *John Graham's System and Dialectics of Art*, 99.

153 **"My three-year-old could do that":** Leonard B. Meyer, *Music, the Arts, and Ideas: Patterns and Predictions in Twentieth-Century Culture*, 71 ("It is easy, of course, to ridicule art created by accident—by asking 'what does it represent?' or asserting that 'my little child could have done that.' And perhaps the child could").

153 **all important art is "irritating":** Tomkins, *Ahead of the Game*, 104.

153 **"A painting that doesn't shock":** Cabanne and Duchamp, *Dialogues with Marcel Duchamp*, 69.

153 **"baffled and outraged so many visitors":** Tomkins, *Ahead of the Game*, 15.

153 **"Matisse and Picasso in 1900":** René Girard, *Evolution and Conversion: Dialogues on the Origins of Culture*, 18.

153 **"sheer egoism":** George Orwell, "Why I Write."

153 **"it's easy for a young person":** Andy Warhol and Pat Hackett, *POPism: The Warhol Sixties*, 20.

155 **leave the hall in a huff:** Tomkins, *Ahead of the Game*, 136.

155 **conspicuous acts of social disapproval:** Tomkins, *Ahead of the Game*, 70 ("The attitude of most New York subscription audiences, and most New York musicians for that matter, towards works by Cage is almost invariably hostile").

155 **"Even when *Atlas* is performed badly":** Tomkins, *Ahead of the Game*, 137.

155 **John Cage came out at number 31:** *BBC Music Magazine*, "The 50 Greatest Composers of All Time."

155 **"I threw the urinal into their faces":** Kulka, *Kitsch and Art*, 117.

156 **"The work of art":** Herbert Read, *Art and Society*, 85.

156 **"We surrender to music":** Daniel J. Levitin, *This Is Your Brain on Music: The Science of a Human Obsession*, 242.

156 **works begin as an esoteric *idiolect*:** Umberto Eco, *A Theory of Semiotics*, 272.

157 **"One of the phenomenal things":** Warhol and Hackett, *POPism*, 3.

157 **"Some of us eventually came":** David Byrne, *How Music Works*, 284.

157 **"every author, as far as he is great"**: Poggioli, *The Theory of the Avant-Garde*, 116, quoting Wordsworth.
157 **"A work of art *communicates*"**: Eco, *A Theory of Semiotics*, 270.
157 **Is John Cage's music**: Max Blau, "33 Musicians on What John Cage Communicates."
157 **initial supporters are drawn from**: Becker, *Art Worlds*, 115 ("Dealers, critics, and collectors develop a consensus about the worth of work and how it can be appreciated").
157 **"The characteristic of new art"**: Poggioli, *The Theory of the Avant-Garde*, 91, quoting Ortega y Gasset.
158 **Calvin Coolidge refused to accept**: Russell Lynes, *The Tastemakers*, 74.
158 **"If a work of art"**: Tom Wolfe, *The Painted Word*, 89.
158 **"fears to be taken for a bourgeois"**: Poggioli, *The Theory of the Avant-Garde*, 158.
158 **John Cage found his most avid supporters**: Alex Ross, "The John Cage Century," and Alex Ross, "Searching for Silence."
158 **"Whenever a truly innovative artist"**: Dan Ozzi, "Rock Is Dead, Thank God."
158 **fourteen million albums**: Combined sales for Bush and Stone Temple Pilots are from Wikipedia.
159 **"Aesthetic expression aims"**: Jonathan D. Culler, *Saussure*, 100.
159 **the successful artist is "condemned" to repetition**: Jean Baudrillard, *For a Critique of the Political Economy of the Sign*, 106.
159 **"spend the rest of their lives"**: Bill Drummond and Jimmy Cauty, *The Manual (How to Have a Number One the Easy Way)*.
159 **"the basic Pop statements"**: Warhol and Hackett, *POPism*, 145.
159 **"School of Satie"**: Myers, *Erik Satie*, 54.
159 **"Whenever I've found that what I'm doing"**: Tomkins, *Ahead of the Game*, 104.
159 **"They kept [their music] from becoming stale"**: Ian MacDonald, *Revolution in the Head: The Beatles' Records and the Sixties*, 11.
159 **"He called us to question"**: Blau, "33 Musicians on What John Cage Communicates," quoting Robert Spano.
160 **"vital importance for a society"**: T. S. Eliot, *Notes towards the Definition of Culture*, 58.
160 **struggles become "highly creative"**: Eliot, *Notes towards the Definition of Culture*, 24.
161 **artists received relatively high standing**: Raymond Williams, *The Sociology of Culture*, 57.
161 **form of change called *shu ha ri***: W. David Marx, *Ametora: How Japan Saved American Style*, 235.
161 **"I am made of literature"**: Adam Kirsch, "Kafka Wanted All His Work Destroyed after His Death. Or Did He?"
162 **"parody this world, illustrate it"**: Baudrillard, *For a Critique of the Political Economy of the Sign*, 110.
162 **Status-driven cultural invention tends to be *rebellious***: Daniel Bell, *The Cultural Contradictions of Capitalism*, 120.
162 **"Never has a more profound originality"**: Tomkins, *Ahead of the Game*, 22, quoting André Breton.
162 **"once you thought Pop"**: Warhol and Hackett, *POPism*, 50.
162 **radical negation tends to "exhaust"**: Baudrillard, *For a Critique of the Political Economy of the Sign*, 48.
162 **"Rebellion has turned into procedure"**: Bell, *The Cultural Contradictions of Capitalism*, 20, quoting Octavio Paz.
162 **"apparent conservatism" was now the "progressive" option**: Peter Fuller, *Aesthetics after Modernism*, 5.
163 **artworks never found large audiences**: Stephen Jay Gould, *Full House: The Spread of Excellence from Plato to Darwin*, 228 ("Perhaps we have already explored most of what even a highly sophisticated audience can deem accessible. Perhaps, in other words, we have reached the right wall of styles that a sympathetic, intelligent, but still nonprofessional audience can hope to grasp with understanding and compassion").

CHAPTER EIGHT

167 **The journalist William Finnegan**: For the story of the shortboard revolution, see William Finnegan, *Barbarian Days: A Surfing Life*, 78–90.
167 **"eagerly converted en masse"**: Finnegan, *Barbarian Days*, 87.
167 **"embarrassing, no longer presentable"**: Finnegan, *Barbarian Days*, 90.
168 **The invention of buoyant synthetic materials**: Davis Jones, "History of Surfing: The Great Plastics Race."

168 **the change in skateboard wheels:** Agi Orsi, Stacy Peralta, Craig Stecyk, and Sean Penn, *Dogtown and Z-Boys.*

168 **Edward Sapir spoke of "drift" in language:** Edward Sapir, *Language: An Introduction to the Study of Speech*, 155.

169 **to understand cultural change:** Leonard B. Meyer, *Music, the Arts, and Ideas: Patterns and Predictions in Twentieth-Century Culture*, 109 ("Extra-stylistic 'forces' do not in themselves appear to be either necessary or sufficient causes for style change").

169 **"Culture determines and causes culture":** Leslie A. White, *The Concept of Cultural Systems*, 6; see also Young Back Choi, *Paradigms and Conventions*, 106 ("[S]ocial change is the replacement of one set of conventions by another").

170 **"produces innovation without reason":** George Santayana, *The Life of Reason: Reason in Religion*, 113.

170 **"Women's hairstyles gradually go":** "Fashion," *Lapham's Quarterly*, quoting Montesquieu.

170 **"the madness of crowds":** A reference to the title of Charles Mackay's *Extraordinary Popular Delusions and the Madness of Crowds.*

170 **Empress Elisabeth of Austria:** Molly Young, *The Things They Fancied*, 23.

170 **"The substantial futility":** Thorstein Veblen, *The Theory of the Leisure Class*, 177.

170 **"a form of ugliness":** Oscar Wilde, "The Philosophy of Dress."

170 **Caryathis chopped her hair:** Lisa Chaney, *Coco Chanel*, 210.

171 **"frivolous, ephemeral, transient, and irrational":** Michael Thompson, *Rubbish Theory: The Creation and Destruction of Value*, 54.

171 **Not all human behavior changes:** Meyer, *Music, the Arts, and Ideas*, 101 ("Change, then, is not one thing. There are many different kinds of change and at least as many different causes as there are kinds").

171 **a fashion cycle where individuals adopt:** This framing of fashion cycles follows Simmel's classic theory of imitation and distinction in Georg Simmel, "Fashion," *On Individuality and Social Forms.*

171 **"were so ill thought of":** Nancy Mitford, ed., *Noblesse Oblige: An Enquiry into the Identifiable Characteristics of the English Aristocracy*, 143.

171 **the Rogerses couldn't afford Christmas presents:** Everett M. Rogers, *The Fourteenth Paw: Growing Up on an Iowa Farm in the 1930s*, 40.

172 **"the degree to which an individual":** Everett M. Rogers, *Diffusion of Innovations*, 267.

172 **"Even in slight things the experience":** Eric Hoffer, *The Ordeal of Change*, 1.

172 **"shock, astonishment, ridicule or disgust":** Quentin Bell, *On Human Finery*, 114.

173 **status is added as a factor in these models:** Alberto Acerbi et al., "The Logic of Fashion Cycles."

173 **the resulting adoption curves:** Paul Nystrom, *Economics of Fashion*, 23.

173 **"How is it possible for cultural innovations":** Albert K. Cohen, "A General Theory of Subcultures (1955)."

173 **"Most consumers are simultaneously *neophilic*":** Derek Thompson, *Hit Makers: The Science of Popularity in an Age of Distraction*, 7.

173 **Alexander the Great plundered purple cloth:** Ruth Kassinger, *Dyes: From Sea Snails to Synthetics*, 33.

173 **"frantic passion for purple":** Pliny (the Elder), *The Natural History of Pliny*, vol. 2.

174 **Nero so loved Tyrian purple:** Suetonius, "The Life of Nero."

174 **"The supposedly superior individual":** Gabriel Tarde, *The Laws of Imitation*, 232.

174 **Elites must be *arbiter elegantiarum*:** Pierre Bourdieu, *Distinction*, 255.

174 **strolled down Parisian boulevards in pants:** Chaney, *Coco Chanel*, 45.

174 **"the search for exclusiveness by individuals":** H. Leibenstein, "Bandwagon, Snob, and Veblen Effects in the Theory of Consumers' Demand."

175 **Nike Air Force 1:** Bobbito Garcia, *Where'd You Get Those? New York City's Sneaker Culture, 1960–1987*, 156.

175 **"As a discriminating young snob":** Howard S. Becker, *Art Worlds*, 215, quoting Barbara H. Smith.

175 **bronze as a precious metal for distinctive decoration:** Colin Renfrew, "Varna and the Emergence of Wealth in Prehistoric Europe," 144.

175 **The Rockefellers owned brass candlesticks:** Christie's, "The Collection of Peggy and David Rockefeller: Online Sale."

175 **In the Soviet Union, modest foreign goods:** Jukka Gronow, *The Sociology of Taste*, 50.

176 **known as the "Pharrell hat":** Allison P. Davis, "Pharrell's Grammys Hat Actually Not So Ridiculous."

176 **"more vicious style":** Garcia, *Where'd You Get Those?*, 188.

176 **Chelsea became a hip London neighborhood:** Nik Cohn, *Today There Are No Gentlemen*, 55.

176 **John Lennon made industrially produced:** Cohn, *Today There Are No Gentlemen*, 104.

176 **a status boost after gaining popularity:** Charles Lindholm, *Culture and Authenticity*, 95.

176 **redefine bronzed skin:** Chaney, *Coco Chanel*, 103, 209.

177 **elevated from a vulgar beverage:** Luca Vercelloni, *The Invention of Taste: A Cultural Account of Desire, Delight and Disgust in Fashion, Food and Art*, 145.

177 **Glenn O'Brien of Cleveland, Ohio:** Biographical details about Glenn O'Brien are drawn from Jesse Thorn, "An Interview with Glenn O'Brien," and Stephen Greco, "That Fast Thing: The Late Glenn O'Brien."

178 **"a lodestar" for teenagers:** Christopher Bollen, "Glenn O'Brien Saved My Life."

178 **"When the movies came":** Marshall McLuhan, *Understanding Media: The Extensions of Man*, 252.

178 **broadening common knowledge:** Michael Suk-Young Chwe, *Rational Ritual: Culture, Coordination, and Common Knowledge*, 92.

179 **The genre's takeover of American music began:** Jeff Chang, *Can't Stop, Won't Stop: A History of the Hip-Hop Generation*, 320, 419.

179 **"It's dead! It's over!":** Michelangelo Matos, *The Underground Is Massive*, 124.

179 **The most important aspect of explanation:** Francis Mulhern, *Culture/Metaculture*, 110, and Rogers, *Diffusion of Innovations*, 250.

179 **smithies, skulls, and peanuts:** Cohn, *Today There Are No Gentlemen*, 156.

179 **"There are no unlabeled fads":** Rolf Meyersohn and Elihu Kaz, "Notes on a Natural History of Fads," 600.

179 **an executive at Sire Records:** Iain Ellis, "New Wave: Turning Rebellion into Money."

179 *Spin* **magazine rechristened it "electronica":** Matos, *The Underground Is Massive*, 230.

180 **"Any work of art that can be understood":** Tom Wolfe, *The Painted Word*, 38, quoting Tristan Tzara.

180 **"reducing or 'trimming' all experience":** Terence Hawkes, *Structuralism and Semiotics*, 104.

180 **"For the perfect duchess-off-duty moment":** Maria Ward, "At 35, Kate Middleton Already Has an Archive of Memorable Fashion Moments."

180 **"media ricochet":** Dorothy M. Scura, ed., *Conversations with Tom Wolfe*, 189. For the Hells Angels, see ibid., 278.

180 *The Wild One* **"gave the outlaws":** Hunter S. Thompson, *Hell's Angels*, 74.

180 **"based on fiction created by wannabe elites":** John Seabrook, *Nobrow: The Culture of Marketing, the Marketing of Culture*, 50.

180 **30% score on Rotten Tomatoes:** rottentomatoes.com/m/venom_2018.

181 **"All its dicta were accepted":** Russell Lynes, *The Tastemakers*, 100.

181 **"We assume things will change":** Joel Best, *Flavor of the Month: Why Smart People Fall for Fads*, 60.

182 **"Her voice itself is** *nouveau riche*": Carl Wilson, *Let's Talk about Love: A Journey to the End of Taste*, 69.

182 **"punk, if treated with extreme delicacy":** Annette Lynch and Mitchell D. Strauss, *Changing Fashion: A Critical Introduction to Trend Analysis and Meaning*, 110.

182 **"No editor, no gallery director":** Jean Duvignaud, *The Sociology of Art*, 129.

182 **the creation of** *false trends*: See "pseudo-events" in Daniel J. Boorstin, *The Image*, 21.

182 **"names no leader of potbelly hipness":** Jack Shafer, "Bogus Trend Stories, Summer Edition."

183 **"I hated this movie":** Roger Ebert, "North."

183 **glowing coverage in** *British Vogue*: Bob Morris, "The Age of Dissonance: Babes in Adultland."

183 **"many nights standing on the corner":** "The Wedding Album: Jenna Lyons and Vincent Mazeau."

183 **three thousand cupcakes a day:** Julia Moskin, "Once Just a Cupcake, These Days a Swell."

183 **garbage cans in the nearby park:** Robert Sietsema, "Me and Magnolia: Life before and after the Cupcake Bomb Went Off."

183 **entrepreneurial bakers to start rival bakeries:** Elizabeth Nathanson, "Sweet Sisterhood: Cupcakes as Sites of Feminized Consumption and Production."

184 **"had no discernible flavor":** Eric Asimov, "One Critic's Delight . . ."

184 **"You could never sell these in Michigan":** Moskin, "Once Just a Cupcake, These Days a Swell."

184 **"Is there a more widely, vocally despised food":** Jen Doll, "The Icing Is off the Cupcake Craze."

184 **cupcakes took over mass media:** Nathanson, "Sweet Sisterhood."

184 **Crumbs had planned to open:** Leah Bourne, "The Cupcake Craze Is Officially Over: Crumbs Is Going Out of Business."

184 **Everett Rogers's diffusion model:** Rogers, *Diffusion of Innovations*, 288–91.

185 **"kind of social** *water-tower*": Tarde, *The Laws of Imitation*, 221.

185 **the fashion for crinoline:** Bell, *On Human Finery*, 109.

185 **the French sparkling mineral water brand Perrier:** Marissa Piesman and Marilee Hartley, *The Yuppie Handbook: The State-of-the-Art Manual for Young Urban Professionals.*

185 **The first black-and-white televisions:** Editors of Consumer Reports, *I'll Buy That: 50 Small Wonders and Big Deals That Revolutionized the Lives of Consumers,* 26.

185 **pedestals in their living rooms:** Paul Fussell, *Class: A Guide through the American Status System,* 92.

185 **"Fashion is now made":** Barbara Vinken, *Fashion Zeitgeist: Trends and Cycles in the Fashion System,* 41.

185 **"If you walk down the street":** Scura, ed., *Conversations with Tom Wolfe,* 97.

185 **"trickle-up" or "trickle-across"?:** Herbert Blumer, "Fashion: From Class Differentiation to Collective Selection."

186 **Tommy Hilfiger wanted to sell:** Seabrook, *Nobrow,* 170.

186 **"Invention can start from the lowest ranks":** Tarde, *The Laws of Imitation,* 221.

186 **"her success validated the style":** Kobena Mercer, "Black Hair/style Politics (1987)," 434.

186 **"do not want anything from the Common Man":** Richard Conniff, *The Natural History of the Rich: A Field Guide,* 172.

187 **"Snobbism is a race":** Glenn O'Brien and Jean-Philippe Delhomme, *How to Be a Man,* 215.

187 **"to move on to something else":** Nelson W. Aldrich Jr., *Old Money: The Mythology of America's Upper Class,* 79, quoting Zelda Fitzgerald.

187 **the rich abandoned rounder body types:** Alison Lurie, *The Language of Clothes,* 14, 73, and David J. Hutson, "Plump or Corpulent? Lean or Gaunt? Historical Categories of Bodily Health in Nineteenth-Century Thought."

187 **"I *used* to like that band":** Wilson, *Let's Talk about Love,* 93.

187 **name-checking rival brand Badoit:** "How Badoit Took on Perrier."

187 **"urban lumpenproletariat and criminal underworlds":** Dick Pountain and David Robins, *Cool Rules: Anatomy of an Attitude,* 97.

187 **the experimental filmmaker Wakefield Poole:** Henrik Vejlgaard, *Anatomy of a Trend,* 89.

188 **"By following the clear and concise instructions":** Richard T. Drummond and Jimmy Cauty, *The Manual (How to Have a Number One the Easy Way).*

188 **"The part of the diffusion curve":** Rogers, *Diffusion of Innovations,* 274.

189 **production logic—tacit rules that shape the content:** See Paul DiMaggio, "Market Structure, the Creative Process, and Popular Culture: Toward an Organizational Reinterpretation of Mass-Culture Theory," and Paul M. Hirsch, "Processing Fads and Fashions: An Organization-Set Analysis of Cultural Industry Systems."

189 **The twist succeeded as a popular:** Ron Mann, *Twist.*

189 **a dance called the lipsi:** David Byrne, *How Music Works,* 316.

190 **"The complexity of an innovation":** Rogers, *Diffusion of Innovations,* 257.

190 **manufacturers must *simplify* the ideas:** Rogers, *Diffusion of Innovations,* 186.

190 **commandeered the term to describe lesser events:** Andy Warhol and Pat Hackett, *POPism: The Warhol Sixties,* 65.

190 **"Rapper's Delight":** Chang, *Can't Stop, Won't Stop,* 132.

190 **blossomed in the United States decades later:** Matos, *The Underground Is Massive,* 356–57.

190 **Synthetic rayon copies:** Lynch and Strauss, *Changing Fashion,* 114.

190 **local distillers mass-manufactured:** Lesley Jacobs Solmonson, *Gin: A Global History,* 44.

191 **"Content might be king":** Thompson, *Hit Makers,* 8.

191 **The number of audience-friendly songs:** Thompson, *Hit Makers,* 37.

191 **gatekeepers, who are even more conservative:** Jonah Berger, *Contagious: Why Things Catch On,* 68.

191 **There is also the distribution of information:** John Berger, *Ways of Seeing,* 131.

191 **"I was the guy":** Fred Schruers, *Billy Joel,* 82.

191 **Ads employ seductive imagery:** Grant David McCracken, *Culture and Consumption: New Approaches to the Symbolic Character of Consumer Goods and Activities,* 77.

191 **"8 in 10 better-class women":** Chwe, *Rational Ritual,* 41.

191 **"two-car families":** Nancy McGuckin and Nanda Srinivasan, "Journey-to-Work Trends in the United States and Its Major Metropolitan Areas, 1960–2000," https://rosap.ntl.bts.gov/view/dot/5543.

191 **Soon these imaginary:** McGuckin and Srinivasan, "Journey-to-Work Trends in the United States and Its Major Metropolitan Areas, 1960–2000."

192 **"The universe of products":** Bourdieu, *Distinction,* 230.

192 **In pre-Columbian Mexico:** Marcy Norton, *Sacred Gifts, Profane Pleasures: A History of Tobacco and Chocolate in the Atlantic World,* 22.

192 **"marker of opulence"**: Norton, *Sacred Gifts, Profane Pleasures*, 180.

192 **"Panegyric to Chocolate"**: Norton, *Sacred Gifts, Profane Pleasures*, 180.

192 **As part of knighthood**: Norton, *Sacred Gifts, Profane Pleasures*, 180.

193 **four times the price of coffee**: Mort Rosenblum, *Chocolate: A Bittersweet Saga of Dark and Light*, 14.

193 **the Nestlé, Cadbury, and Hershey empires**: Sophie D. Coe and Michael D. Coe, *The True History of Chocolate*.

193 **"great slabs of chocolate"**: Roald Dahl, *Charlie and the Chocolate Factory*, 6.

193 **"Give me chocolate!"**: John Dower, *Embracing Defeat: Japan in the Wake of World War II*, 72.

193 **cultural trends play out like "social contagions"**: Malcolm Gladwell, *The Tipping Point*, 7, and Berger, *Contagious*, 4.

193 **the *mere exposure effect***: Thompson, *Hit Makers*, 29, and Sheena Iyengar, *The Art of Choosing*, 149.

194 **the *bandwagon effect***: Leibenstein, "Bandwagon, Snob, and Veblen Effects in the Theory of Consumers' Demand."

194 **thanks to *social proof***: Berger, *Contagious*, 128.

194 **strength through *network effects***: Rogers, *Diffusion of Innovations*, 350.

194 **"The pleasure of being in a crowd"**: McLuhan, *Understanding Media*, 119, quoting Baudelaire.

194 **"the point at which enough individuals"**: Rogers, *Diffusion of Innovations*, 343.

195 **"*Not* having seen Tut"**: Orrin E. Klapp, *The Inflation of Symbols*, 163.

195 **tipping point appears to be a status threshold**: See "taboo breaking point" in Leibenstein, "Bandwagon, Snob, and Veblen Effects in the Theory of Consumers' Demand."

195 **20 percent of all Americans**: David R. Greenland, *The Gunsmoke Chronicles: A New History of Television's Greatest Western*, 5.

195 **partial adoption, where majorities**: McCracken, *Culture and Consumption*, 97, and Rogers, *Diffusion of Innovations*, 177.

195 **A Brief History of Time sold enough**: Gary S. Becker, *Accounting for Tastes*, 200.

195 **On the book review site Goodreads**: Balázs Kovács and Amanda J. Sharkey, "The Paradox of Publicity: How Awards Can Negatively Affect the Evaluation of Quality."

195 **they do so passively**: Vance Packard, *The Status Seekers*, 136, citing an idea of Dwight Macdonald's; see also Rogers, *Diffusion of Innovations*, 180.

195 **"You don't create a phenomenon"**: Chuck Klosterman, *But What If We're Wrong?*, 182.

196 **"Pretty soon every kid in Utica"**: Tom Wolfe, *The Pump House Gang*, 33–34.

196 **"laggard" is pejorative**: Best, *Flavor of the Month*, 97.

196 **"Burberry had become so associated"**: Rupert Neate, "How an American Woman Rescued Burberry, a Classic British Label."

197 **go-go never went very far**: Chang, *Can't Stop, Won't Stop*, 408–9.

197 **their "voluntary unpopularity"**: Renato Poggioli, *The Theory of the Avant-Garde*, 45.

197 **Gaultier introduced "pants-skirts" for men**: Fred Davis, *Fashion, Culture, and Identity*, 34.

197 **process of "chase and flight"**: McCracken, *Culture and Consumption*, 94.

198 **never-ending footrace**: Jon Elster, *Nuts and Bolts for the Social Sciences*, 95 ("When all are motivated by the desire to earn a bit more than their neighbors, they end up running as fast as they can in order to remain in the same place").

198 **fashion has no finish line or ultimate destination**: Marshall Sahlins, *Culture and Practical Reason*, 184 ("Sapir's dictum that fashion is custom in the guise of a departure from custom").

198 **"After all the ingenuity"**: Veblen, *The Theory of the Leisure Class*, 174.

198 **"restores cultural inequality and social discrimination"**: Jean Baudrillard, *For a Critique of the Political Economy of the Sign*, 50–51.

198 **innovations turned out to be "correct"**: Peter Corrigan, *The Sociology of Consumption*, 9 ("If having the socially 'correct' goods would grant one social status, and if 'correctness' was still set by the upper classes, then classes lower in the hierarchy would imitate as best they could the consumption patterns of the higher classes who, of course, would then change just to make sure a difference was retained").

198 **"nothing proves the originality"**: David Muggleton, *Inside Subculture: The Postmodern Meaning of Style*, 143.

199 **"psychological circulation"**: Jean Baudrillard, *The System of Objects*, 149.

199 **"Fashion is made to be unfashionable"**: Davis, *Fashion, Culture, and Identity*, 162, quoting Coco Chanel.

199 **Isolated tribes change their hairstyles**: Ralph Linton gives an example from the Bara tribe in Madagascar, quoted in J. H. Abraham, *Origins and Growth of Sociology*, 513.

199 **"Even though there are organizations":** Stanley Lieberson, *A Matter of Taste: How Names, Fashions, and Culture Change*, 92.

200 **capitalism creates "false needs":** Herbert Marcuse, *One-Dimensional Man: Studies in the Ideology of Advanced Industrial Society*, 4–5.

200 **"exchange value" over earnest "use value":** Jon Elster, *Making Sense of Marx*, 311.

200 **flat roofs of modernist buildings:** Tom Wolfe, *From Bauhaus to Our House*, as well as Peter Lewis, *The Fifties*, 197.

200 **"As citizens become more equal":** Tarde, *The Laws of Imitation*, 229, quoting Alexis de Tocqueville.

200 **"[Our concerts have] been sold out":** Wilson, *Let's Talk about Love*, 16.

200 **"In a bourgeois society":** Matei Calinescu, *Five Faces of Modernity*, 258, quoting Abraham Moles.

200 **"find elements of revolution":** Calinescu, *Five Faces of Modernity*, 285, quoting Umberto Eco.

201 **"representation of Black people in cinema":** Nicholas Barber, *"Black Panther*: The Most Radical Hollywood Blockbuster Ever?"

201 **Majorities seem to be *satisficing*:** Anthony Heath, *Rational Choice and Social Exchange*, 87.

201 **this so-called cumulative advantage:** Duncan J. Watts, *Everything Is Obvious: How Common Sense Fails Us*, 172.

201 **Ballast Point's Sculpin IPA:** Peter Rowe, "Ballast Point's Rise, Fall and Sale: Inside Craft Beer's Most Baffling Deal." Constellation eventually sold Ballast Point at a massive loss, but craft beer is certainly more available in mainstream American supermarkets than ever before.

CHAPTER NINE

203 **Virginia Packard:** Vance Packard, *The Status Seekers*, 122.

203 **"is one of those all-important pieces":** Jake Gallagher, "Dropping Knowledge: The Button-Down Collar."

204 **a complex sediment of new and old:** Culture is "cumulative" in Clyde Kluckhohn, *Culture and Behavior*, 35, as well as Howard S. Becker, *Art Worlds*, 350 ("Each wave of innovation leaves behind a shelf of sediment made up of the art makers and art appreciators who can't or won't switch their allegiance to the new wave that has taken over their field").

204 **However popular French bread:** Gabriel Tarde, *The Laws of Imitation*, 340.

204 **the button-down collar shirt, first emerged:** O. E. Schoeffler and William Gale, *Esquire's Encyclopedia of 20th Century Men's Fashion*, 198–213.

204 **"almost entirely out of the picture":** Schoeffler and Gale, *Esquire's Encyclopedia of 20th Century Men's Fashion*, 202.

205 **"transient" goods that never take on historical value:** Michael Thompson, *Rubbish Theory: The Creation and Destruction of Value*, 4.

205 **"a particular selection":** Eric Hobsbawm, *On History*, 10–11.

205 **"formalized social past":** Hobsbawm, *On History*, 11.

205 **History is constructed:** Leonard B. Meyer, *Music, the Arts, and Ideas: Patterns and Predictions in Twentieth-Century Culture*, 92.

205 **"For the greater part of history":** Hobsbawm, *On History*, 10.

205 **The "good old days":** Hobsbawm, *On History*, 25.

205 **Founding Fathers studied failure points:** Paul Meany, "First Principles: What America's Founders Learned from the Greeks and Romans and How That Shaped Our Country."

206 **Diana's infamous "sheep sweater":** Rachel Syme, "The Second Life of Princess Diana's Most Notorious Sweater."

206 **"A real genius, the longer":** David Hume, "Of the Standard of Taste."

206 **archaic 415 Hz tunings:** Charles Lindholm, *Culture and Authenticity*, 26.

207 **Customs and habits are internalized:** Paul Connerton, *How Societies Remember*, 72.

207 **Traditions are conscious acts of solidarity:** Michael Suk-Young Chwe, *Rational Ritual: Culture, Coordination, and Common Knowledge*, 3.

207 **"a legitimator of action and cement":** Eric Hobsbawm and Terence Ranger, *The Invention of Tradition*, 12.

207 **each Scottish clan has a tartan:** "What Is Tartan?"

208 **Most classic clothing comes to us:** Quentin Bell, *On Human Finery*, 165.

208 **The term "canon" was first used:** Harold Bloom, *The Western Canon: The Books and School of the Ages*, 15.

208 **tens of thousands of novels:** Franco Moretti, *Graphs, Maps, Trees: Abstract Models for Literary History*, 4.

208 **"Criticism has, since roughly the day":** A. O. Scott, *Better Living through Criticism*, 184.

209 **"not only promotes but goes":** Barbara Herrnstein Smith, *Contingencies of Value: Alternative Perspectives for Critical Theory*, 10.

209 **"dominant social groups":** Bloom, *The Western Canon*, 19.

209 **"a mode of originality":** Bloom, *The Western Canon*, 3.

209 **"will not allow you to bury him":** Harold Bloom, *The Anxiety of Influence: A Theory of Poetry*, xviii.

209 *relics*—**works that may not appeal:** Smith, *Contingencies of Value*, 49.

209 **"We don't reinvestigate":** Chuck Klosterman, *But What If We're Wrong?*, 164.

209 **Romance novelist Danielle Steel:** Klosterman, *But What If We're Wrong?*, 53.

210 **"Go back as far as the time":** Andy Warhol and Pat Hackett, *POPism: The Warhol Sixties*, 26, quoting Emile de Antonio.

210 **John Philip Sousa:** Klosterman, *But What If We're Wrong?*, 64–65.

210 **"higher individual, social, or transcendent good":** Smith, *Contingencies of Value*, 42.

210 **Double-knit polyester leisure suits:** Barbara Vinken, *Fashion Zeitgeist: Trends and Cycles in the Fashion System*, 66; Deidre Clemente, *Dress Casual: How College Students Redefined American Style*, 142.

210 **a famed fashion misstep:** Glenn O'Brien and Jean-Philippe Delhomme, *How to Be a Man*, 134, 138.

210 **"The fans showing up":** Kelefa Sanneh, "The Persistence of Prog Rock," quoting David Weigel.

210 *Sgt. Pepper's Lonely Hearts Club Band:* "500 Greatest Albums List (2003)," *Rolling Stone*.

210 **revised its Top 500 Albums list:** "The 500 Greatest Albums of All Time," *Rolling Stone*; for commentary, see Sheldon Pearce, "The Futility of Rolling Stone's Best-Albums List."

211 **Canons act as a "horizon":** Adam Roberts, *Frederic Jameson*, 50.

211 **the touchstone of the canon:** Smith, *Contingencies of Value*, 50.

211 **"Shakespeare is better than Marlowe":** Klosterman, *But What If We're Wrong?*, 94.

211 **"lastingness is imposed":** Thompson, *Rubbish Theory*, 52.

211 **"Our experiences of the present":** Connerton, *How Societies Remember*, 3.

211 **"the tradition of all dead generations":** Karl Marx, "The Eighteenth Brumaire of Louis Bonaparte."

211 **"the exhortation to 'be here now'":** Simon Reynolds, *Retromania: Pop Culture's Addiction to Its Own Past*, xix.

212 **"The past is a foreign country":** Lisa Chaney, *Coco Chanel*, 242, reprinting the opening line of L. P. Hartley's novel *The Go-Between*.

212 *Bohemian Rhapsody,* **a film with mixed reviews:** See Metacritic, https://www.metacritic.com/movie/bohemian-rhapsody/critic-reviews

212 **In 1925 Americans consumed:** https://en.wikipedia.org/wiki/Publishers_Weekly_list_of_best selling_novels_in_the_United_States_in_the_1920s.

212 *Gatsby* **has 1703 times more ratings:** As of December 5, 2021, there are 4,224,328 ratings for Fitzgerald's novel versus 2480 ratings for Stratton Porter's.

212 **"morning sounds of glass being chipped":** George Leonard and Robert Leonard, "Sha Na Na and the Woodstock Generation."

214 **A Japanese visitor to London:** The visitor was Masayuki Yamazaki, founder of the store Cream Soda; see W. David Marx, *Ametora: How Japan Saved American Style*, 135.

214 **"a self-conscious fetish":** Reynolds, *Retromania*, xii.

214 **"The retro sensibility":** Reynolds, *Retromania*, xxx.

214 **gangster fashion to ornate Napoleonic military uniforms:** Nik Cohn, *Today There Are No Gentlemen*, 122, 127.

214 **"Art produces ugly things":** "Fashion," *Lapham's Quarterly*, 137, quoting Jean Cocteau.

215 **"Each generation experiences":** "Fashion," *Lapham's Quarterly*, 28, quoting Walter Benjamin.

215 **"circulation and consideration":** Joshua O. Reno, introduction to Thompson, *Rubbish Theory*, viii.

215 **"corny preppy kids":** Bobbito Garcia, *Where'd You Get Those? New York City's Sneaker Culture, 1960–1987*, 153.

215 **"Where retro truly reigns":** Reynolds, *Retromania*, xix.

215 **Old Baldy Shrine Club:** From a satin 1950s bowling jacket.

215 **"there are now no pockets":** Matei Calinescu, *Five Faces of Modernity*, 231, quoting Hilton Kramer.

216 **"The wiser historians and critics know":** Renato Poggioli, *The Theory of the Avant-Garde*, 216.

216 **"Things come back into fashion":** O'Brien and Delhomme, *How to Be a Man*, 84.

217 **"relatively cyclical":** Pitirim A. Sorokin, *Social and Cultural Dynamics*, 1:185.

217 **"It was the young Teds"**: Ray Ferris and Julian Lord, *Teddy Boys: A Concise History*, 81.

217 *That'll Be the Day*: Ferris and Lord, *Teddy Boys*, 110.

217 **"Only when a psychedelic revival"**: Ian MacDonald, *Revolution in the Head: The Beatles' Records and the Sixties*, 373.

218 **Laver published a now famous chart**: James Laver, *Taste and Fashion: From the French Revolution to the Present Day*.

219 **"A work is eternal"**: Terence Hawkes, *Structuralism and Semiotics*, 157, quoting Roland Barthes.

CHAPTER TEN

223 **"Bakers must carefully layer"**: W. David Marx, "An Open Letter to Kanye West from the Association of French Bakers." See also Emily Greenhouse, "About Kanye's Croissant."

224 **"Every hilarious viral tweet"**: Peter Hamby tweet, "Every hilarious viral tweet," March 15, 2021, https://twitter.com/PeterHamby/status/1371505865249992713.

224 **Some companies now offer viral tweeters**: Rebecca Jennings, "Your Tweet Goes Viral. Here Come the Companies Asking You to Sell Their Crap."

224 **one-hit wonders**: Paul Resnikoff, "Nearly Half of All Charting Songs Are One-Hit Wonders."

224 **The Pet Rock**: Gary R. Dahl, *Advertising for Dummies*.

225 **"is often perceived as a drought"**: A. O. Scott, *Better Living through Criticism*, 251.

225 **Declinists speak of a "culture crash"**: Scott Timberg, *Culture Crash: The Killing of the Creative Class*.

225 **inspire wild and oppositional art**: See, e.g., Steph Harmon, "Amanda Palmer: 'Donald Trump Is Going to Make Punk Rock Great Again.'"

225 **"There's something about our time"**: Glenn O'Brien and Jean-Philippe Delhomme, *How to Be a Man*, 187.

225 **a feeling of stagnancy in the zeitgeist**: Simon Doonan, "The End of Trends," and Cathy Horyn, "The Post-Trend Universe."

225 **"It's possible that lovestruck"**: Ian Brennan, "How Music Dies: Aristocracy Is Killing Artistry."

225 **"general law of the world"**: Paul Virilio, *Speed and Politics*, 38.

226 **"The Internet isn't really a thing"**: Duncan J. Watts, *Everything Is Obvious: How Common Sense Fails Us*, 154.

226 **the internet became mass culture**: Chuck Klosterman, *But What If We're Wrong?*, 231.

226 **The number of internet users grew**: See https://www.internetworldstats.com/stats.htm, as well as https://www.nngroup.com/articles/one-billion-internet-users/.

226 **expert guitar tabs**: I started using the internet in 1993—a time when lyrics and guitar tabs were the killer content of the proto-web. For some reason, most of the chord progressions were wrong, but whoever did all the They Might Be Giants ones had them all perfect, down to the major sevenths and ninths.

227 **A fifth of internet users**: Evelyn Cheng, "China Says It Now Has Nearly 1 Billion Internet Users."

227 **"Fifteen years ago"**: Noah Smith tweet, "15 years ago," August 28, 2017, https://twitter.com/noahpinion/status/902301308702515202.

227 **"You can't just walk around"**: Jia Tolentino, *Trick Mirror: Reflections on Self-Delusion*, 7.

227 **"deviant lifestyle choice"**: Malcolm Harris, *Kids These Days: The Making of Millennials*, 178.

227 **social media refuseniks**: Christine Rosen, "Teens Who Say No to Social Media."

227 *Socialite Rank* and *Park Avenue Peerage*: Isaiah Wilner, "The Number-One Girl."

227 **The failed start-up Klout**: *The Guardian*, "Klout Is Dead."

228 **BallerBusters**: Taylor Lorenz, "On the Internet, No One Knows You're Not Rich. Except This Account."

228 **Elites could once easily signal status**: Technology's negative effect on exclusivity was demonstrated as early as 1961 in Dwight E. Robinson, "The Economics of Fashion Demand," 390.

228 **"information wants to be free"**: Steven Levy, "'Hackers' and 'Information Wants to Be Free.'"

228 **Dylan had to literally steal folk records**: Bob Dylan et al., *No Direction Home: Bob Dylan*.

228 **a white Pakistani high-top sneaker**: Thomas Gibbons-Neff and Fahim Abed, "In Afghanistan, Follow the White High-Tops and You'll Find the Taliban."

228 *GQ* **editor looked to buy them**: Noah Johnson, Rachel Tashjian, and Samuel Hine, "The 10 Best Things We Saw at Fashion Week."

228 **Pakistani e-tailers**: See, e.g., www.shopnowpk.com.

228 **Le Creuset cookware**: Amanda Mull, "The New Trophies of Domesticity."

229 **"Our culture and economy":** Chris Anderson, *The Longer Long Tail*, 52.

229 **"paradox of choice":** Barry Schwartz, *The Paradox of Choice.*

230 **Rebecca Black's vanity single "Friday":** Willa Paskin, "An Oral History of 'Friday.'"

230 **"when mass culture breaks":** Anderson, *The Longer Long Tail*, 183.

230 **"The future of hits":** Derek Thompson, *Hit Makers: The Science of Popularity in an Age of Distraction*, 10.

231 **Jepsen's "Call Me Maybe":** Thompson, *Hit Makers*, 34; also see Thompson's theory of "dark broadcasters" (ibid., 194).

231 *Game of Thrones* **was one:** Joe Otterson, "'Game of Thrones' Season 8 Premiere Draws 17.4 Million Viewers, Sets Multi-Platform Record."

231 **how many Americans can hum:** cf. Anderson, *The Longer Long Tail*, 2 ("Number one is still number one, but the sales that go with that are not what they once were").

232 **The *Kony 2012* video:** Thompson, *Hit Makers*, 194.

233 **"The best car in Dubai!":** For the Belhasa quote, see https://www.youtube.com/watch?v=4TwTtH 4DCCc, posted August 4, 2017.

233 **The *Daily Mail* wrote up:** Natalie Corner, "At Home with a Teenage Billionaire: Dubai Instagram Star, 16, with a $1 Million Collection of Trainers Shows Off the Family Mansion—Including the Private Zoo."

234 **the most obscure place on earth:** Ralph Leighton, *Tuva or Bust!*

234 **teenagers post on Instagram:** Personal observation from watching in 2020 and 2021.

234 **"bring the world closer together":** Mark Zuckerberg, "Bringing the World Closer Together," Facebook, March 15, 2021, https://www.facebook.com/notes/393134628500376/.

234 **"The brotherhood of man":** Tomáš Kulka, *Kitsch and Art*, 16, quoting Milan Kundera.

234 **primary proponents and benefactors:** Rebecca Arnold, *Fashion: A Very Short Introduction*, 84 (Tom Ford: "It is the beginning of the reawakening of cultures that have historically worshipped luxury and haven't had it for so long").

234 **luxury autos into North Korea:** Lucas Kuo and Jason Arterburn, *Lux and Loaded: Exposing North Korea's Strategic Procurement Networks.*

234 **"the most dubious of big spenders":** Ashley Mears, *Very Important People: Status and Beauty in the Global Party Circuit*, 90.

235 **Jho Low:** Mears, *Very Important People*, 79.

235 **"What use is a Rolls-Royce":** Iva Dixit, "'Bollywood Wives' Is an Accidental Documentary about India's Gilded Class."

235 **Turki Bin Abdullah:** Keiligh Baker, "Best Friends with Dr Dre and an Entourage of Six 'Minders' Wherever He Goes: How Saudi Billionaire Playboy, 23, with a Fleet of Golden Cars Spends His Summer in London."

235 **"Of course I'm a hustler":** Larry King, "DJ Khaled's Illuminating Convo: Influence of Hip Hop, Jay Z's Genius & Young Rapper Mistakes."

235 **Edie Sedgwick wasn't satisfied:** Andy Warhol and Pat Hackett, *POPism: The Warhol Sixties*, 123.

236 **Gaïa Jacquet-Matisse:** Mara Siegler, "Gaïa Matisse Doesn't Care if You Think She's Just a 'Blond with Big Boobs.'"

236 **"new rules of Old Money":** Nancy Jo Sales, "The New Rules of Old Money."

236 **bankruptcy of Brooks Brothers:** Lisa Birnbach, "Save Brooks Brothers!"

236 **#oldmoneyaesthetic hashtag:** Rebecca Jennings, "Are You Ready for the Return of Prep?"

237 **"to walk down Bond Street":** James Laver, *Dandies*, 87.

237 **Snug-fit athleisure:** Elizabeth Currid-Halkett, *The Sum of Small Things: A Theory of the Aspirational Class*, 103–4.

237 **stripped-down "normcore" look:** K-HOLE, "Youth Mode: A Report on Freedom."

238 **"white or bright accent walls":** Kyle Chayka, "Welcome to AirSpace."

238 **"Happiest Place in the (Internet) World":** Allie Burke, "Instagram Is the Happiest Place in the (Internet) World."

238 **"The ugly American weirdness":** Ryan Broderick, "I'm Being Gaslit by the TikTok Lamborghini."

239 **social networking app Raya:** Kyle Chayka, "Raya and the Promise of Private Social Media."

239 **lower-middle-class sensibility:** Herbert Gans, *Popular Culture and High Culture: An Analysis and Evaluation of Taste*, 84–89.

239 **the designation "middle class":** Noah Smith, "For Corrosive Inequality, Look to the Upper Middle Class."

239 **"the salt-of-the-earth millionaires"**: Patrick Wyman, "American Gentry."

239 **giant pickup trucks**: Alex Lauer, "Why Pickup Trucks Keep Getting Bigger and Bigger."

240 **"utterly generic" songs**: Matt LeMay, "Liz Phair: *Liz Phair*."

240 **"condescending and cringey" review**: Matt LeMay tweet, "1 / I tremendously enjoyed this inter-view," September 5, 2019, https://twitter.com/mattlemay/status/1169739122451386371.

240 **Phair celebrated LeMay's mea culpa**: Liz Phair tweet, "I've always enjoyed criticism," September 5, 2019, https://twitter.com/PhizLair/status/1169800245133201408.

240 *Pitchfork* **updated its official review score**: *Pitchfork*, "Pitchfork Reviews: Rescored."

240 **"Rockism means idolizing"**: Kelefa Sanneh, "The Rap against Rockism."

240 **An alternative approach**: Jody Rosen, "The Perils of Poptimism," and Carl Wilson, *Let's Talk about Love: A Journey to the End of Taste*, 12.

240 **"The shape-shifting feminist hip-pop"**: Sanneh, "The Rap against Rockism."

240 **"It's almost impossible to create"**: Klosterman, *But What If We're Wrong?*, 63.

241 *The Pudding* **trained an AI**: "How Bad Is Your Spotify?," *The Pudding*.

241 **"It is a pathological aversion"**: B. D. McClay, "Let People Enjoy This Essay."

241 **behind postmodern culture: *omnivore taste***: The term entered the lexicon after R. A. Peterson, "Understanding Audience Segmentation: From Elite and Mass to Omnivore and Univore."

241 **"multicultural capital"**: Bethany Bryson, "'Anything but Heavy Metal': Symbolic Exclusion and Musical Dislikes."

241 **"you got points for consistency"**: John Seabrook, *Nobrow: The Culture of Marketing, the Marketing of Culture*, 65.

241 **"*The New Yorker* made it possible"**: Louis Menand, "Finding It at the Movies."

242 **"embraced by the chic"**: Hanson O'Haver, "The Great Irony-Level Collapse."

242 **"a recognition and celebration"**: Kwame Anthony Appiah, "The Importance of Elsewhere."

242 **"Other nations of different habits"**: T. S. Eliot, *Notes towards the Definition of Culture*, 50, quoting Alfred North Whitehead.

242 **"To declare difference"**: Fred Inglis, *Cultural Studies*, 244.

243 **"a bourgeois invention"**: Luca Vercelloni, *The Invention of Taste: A Cultural Account of Desire, Delight and Disgust in Fashion, Food and Art*, 66, quoting Charles Wegener.

243 **Omnivorism and poptimism would be**: Rosen, "The Perils of Poptimism," who calls poptimism "a kind of penance"; critiques include Saul Austerlitz, "The Pernicious Rise of Poptimism," and Rob Harvilla, "Have We Reached the End of Poptimism?"

243 **"The pace of fashion"**: Quentin Bell, *On Human Finery*, 76.

243 **"a broadening of the ideal"**: Gilles Lipovetsky, *Hypermodern Times*, 65.

244 **"Manic Pixie Dream Girls"**: Hugo Schwyzer, "The Real-World Consequences of the Manic Pixie Dream Girl Cliché."

244 **rules behind the most militant mode of omnivore taste**: I compiled these rules myself but am indebted to Glenn Jordan and Chris Weedon, *Cultural Politics: Class, Gender, Race and the Postmodern World*.

245 **a detente with capitalism**: Seabrook, *Nobrow*, 71 ("The mainstream market, once the enemy of the artist, even began to acquire a kind of integrity, insofar as it represented a genuinely populist ex-pression of the audience's preferences").

245 **"money, power, and respect"**: See the Lox's "Money, Power & Respect" (featuring DMX and Lil' Kim), as well as Pop Smoke's "MPR" and Travis Scott's "Money Power Respect."

245 **"Nowadays there is the tendency"**: Markus Gabriel, *Why the World Does Not Exist*, 197.

245 **"No one will tell you"**: Scott, *Better Living through Criticism*, 113.

246 **"Some forms of music"**: David Byrne, *How Music Works*, 354.

246 **"A world culture"**: Eliot, *Notes towards the Definition of Culture*, 62.

246 **"The imperative to ecstatic"**: Jerry Saltz, "Glenn O'Brien and the Avant-Garde That Lost."

247 **"By embracing the project"**: Nick Sylvester, "The Internet Doesn't Matter, You're Making Music in L.A."

247 **"Nothing was judged—only counted"**: George W. S. Trow, *Within the Context of No Context*, 44.

247 **"Art, as a charismatic and exclusive activity"**: Jean Duvignaud, *The Sociology of Art*, 128.

247 **"I'm always very upset"**: Calvin Tomkins, "The Turnaround Artist: Jeff Koons, Up from Banality."

247 **But we seem to be in a "post-subculture"**: cf. David Muggleton and Rupert Weinzierl, *The Post-Subcultures Reader*.

248 **"Perhaps the very concept"**: David Muggleton, *Inside Subculture: The Postmodern Meaning of Style*, 48.

248 **"Dan, the Very Popular":** *The State*, season 3, episode 4.

248 **an openly gay track star in Pennsylvania:** "Gay Track Star Voted Prom King."

248 **a lesbian couple:** Jo Yurcaba, "Ohio High School Elects a Lesbian Couple as Prom King and Queen."

248 **"style surfing":** Muggleton, *Inside Subculture*, 48.

248 **Aesthetics Wiki:** See https://aesthetics.fandom.com/wiki/List_of_Aesthetics.

248 **"A person on Stan Twitter":** Joe Coscarelli, "How Pop Music Fandom Became Sports, Politics, Religion and All-Out War," quoting Benjamin Cordero.

248 **Taylor Swift stans sent death threats:** Gita Jackson, "Taylor Swift Super Fans Are Furious about a Good Review."

248 **"It feels like we're promoting BTS":** Coscarelli, "How Pop Music Fandom Became Sports."

249 **black-pilled incels:** Discussion of the misogyny and bigotry of 4chan trolls in Tolentino, *Trick Mirror*, 24 ("Through identifying the effects of women's systemic objectification as some sort of vagina-supremacist witchcraft, the men that congregated on 4chan gained an identity, and a useful common enemy"). Also see Harris, *Kids These Days*, 208 ("I worry that misogyny will acquire a countercultural sheen. Hatred for women could replace hatred for Jews as what Ferdinand Kronawetter called the 'socialism of fools' and confound efforts to clarify what is really happening to American working people").

249 **68 percent of male Gen Zers:** Sean Monahan, "Video Games Have Replaced Music as the Most Important Aspect of Youth Culture."

249 **only one out of every seven hard-core gamers:** Kyle Wagner, "The Future of the Culture Wars Is Here, and It's Gamergate."

249 **"fashoid white boy" gamers:** Vicky Osterweil, "What Was the Nerd?"

249 **"a mutant variant":** Wagner, "The Future of the Culture Wars Is Here."

250 **Marc Jacobs created virtual outfits:** Jessica Heron-Langton, "Marc Jacobs Drops Six Cute Looks on Animal Crossing."

250 **online video creators' casual conspiracy mongering:** Kat Tenbarge, "The Era of A-list YouTube Celebrities Is Over. Now, the People Cancelling Them Are on Top."

250 **"The avant-garde is now":** Simon Reynolds, *Retromania: Pop Culture's Addiction to Its Own Past*, xx.

250 **"access the immediate past so easily and so copiously":** Reynolds, *Retromania*, xxi.

250 **"pioneers and innovators":** Reynolds, *Retromania*, xxi.

251 **"I'm afraid that our dear century":** Calvin Tomkins, *Ahead of the Game: Four Versions of the Avant-Garde*, 67, quoting Duchamp.

251 **"structured by an absolute present":** Lipovetsky, *Hypermodern Times*, 57.

251 **"The funny thing about our time":** O'Brien and Delhomme, *How to Be a Man*, 224.

251 **"slow cancellation of the future":** A line originally from Franco "Bifo" Berardi, made famous by Mark Fisher.

251 **"strong poets keep returning":** Harold Bloom, *The Anxiety of Influence: A Theory of Poetry*, 140.

252 **"an absence of novelty":** Leonard B. Meyer, *Music, the Arts, and Ideas: Patterns and Predictions in Twentieth-Century Culture*, 102.

252 **"The recent past—the oos":** Kurt Andersen, "You Say You Want a Devolution?"

252 **"People have a limited capacity":** Andersen, "You Say You Want a Devolution?"

254 **"No one follows you":** Rebecca Jennings, "The Blandness of TikTok's Biggest Stars."

254 **"Sharing, and sometimes oversharing":** Sejla Rizvic, "Everybody Hates Millennials: Gen Z and the TikTok Generation Wars."

255 **"When you say, 'Abstract Expressionism'":** Kyle Chayka, "How Beeple Crashed the Art World."

255 **"False prophets fearfully warned you":** Kit Mackintosh, *Neon Screams: How Drill, Trap and Bashment Made Music New Again*.

256 **the twist dance fad:** Ron Mann, *Twist*.

256 **Addison Rae performed eight "TikTok dances":** Rebecca Jennings, "A Super-Famous TikTok Star Appeared on Jimmy Fallon. It Didn't Go Great."

257 **"Comedian in 1985":** Brittany Mignanelli tweet, "Comedian in 1985," February 2, 2021, https://twitter.com/Brittymigs/status/1356687700225626112.

257 **A TikToker in 2020 interviewed her friends:** LBgotSOLE tweet, "Not one good fit here I'm cryinggggggg," November 4, 2020, https://twitter.com/LBgotSOLE/status/1324073257709031424; I discovered this through Rachel Seville Tashjian's Twitter account.

257 **"a core way for Gen Z":** Rizvic, "Everybody Hates Millennials."

258 **Pierre Bourdieu calls *hysteresis*:** Pierre Bourdieu, *Distinction*, 142.

258 **"If this stylistic freeze"**: Andersen, "You Say You Want a Devolution?"

258 **a pattern of *punctuated equilibrium***: Franco Moretti, *Graphs, Maps, Trees: Abstract Models for Literary History*, 18. See also Young Back Choi, *Paradigms and Conventions*, 111 ("Social change, the process of replacing one set of conventions with another, tends to occur intermittently and discontinuously").

258 **"aesthetic and intellectual endeavors"**: A. L. Kroeber, *Configurations of Culture Growth*, 838.

258 **"Let the next four years"**: Warhol and Hackett, *POPism*, 24.

CONCLUSION

261 **rates everyday dogs:** The WeRateDogs® Twitter account can be found at https://twitter.com /dog_rates.

261 **"material and cultural invention"**: Michael Worboys, Julie-Marie Strange, and Neil Pemberton, *The Invention of the Modern Dog: Breed and Blood in Victorian Britain*, 1.

262 **"A dog is a genuine Newfoundland"**: Worboys, Strange, and Pemberton, *The Invention of the Modern Dog*, 73.

262 **human hierarchies seeped into canine hierarchies**: Worboys, Strange, and Pemberton, *The Invention of the Modern Dog*, 224.

262 **"a certificate of the aristocratic origins"**: Lillian Hellman, *An Unfinished Woman*, 224.

262 **the ownership of particular breeds**: Paul Fussell, *Class: A Guide through the American Status System*, 95.

262 **Research conducted in the Czech Republic**: Eva Voslarova et al., "Breed Characteristics of Abandoned and Lost Dogs in the Czech Republic."

263 **The "warm glow" we receive**: Carl Wilson, *Let's Talk about Love: A Journey to the End of Taste*, 109, and Roger Scruton, *Modern Culture*, 155.

263 **"When we ourselves determine something"**: J. H. Abraham, *Origins and Growth of Sociology*, 425, quoting Pitirim Sorokin.

263 **"Do I admire Beethoven's"**: H. L. Mencken, "Professor Veblen."

264 **"innate" visual preference**: John H. Falk and John Balling, "Evolutionary Influence on Human Landscape Preference."

264 **mini Australian shepherds**: Eliza Brooke, "When a Dog Breed Becomes a Trend."

264 **the ultimate outcomes are stochastic**: Jon Elster, *Nuts and Bolts for the Social Sciences*, 169 ("Humphrey Lyttelton said about a similar problem, 'If I knew where jazz was going I'd be there already'").

265 **"with straps worn high"**: Alex Kuczynski, "Now You See It, Now You Don't."

265 **"a complicated mix of individual choices"**: Duncan J. Watts, *Everything Is Obvious: How Common Sense Fails Us*, 81, 262.

265 **Twitterati discuss the Tesla Model 3:** Based on hashtag usage analysis in late 2021, as well as Google Trends.

265 **the cultural implications of any trend**: Umberto Eco, *A Theory of Semiotics*, 22.

265 **shirt brand Hypercolor**: Emily Spivack, "Why Hypercolor T-shirts Were Just a One-Hit Wonder."

265 **"streetwear's first heritage brand"**: Rachel Tashjian, "How Stüssy Became the Chanel of Streetwear."

266 **"the shaping of the society's culture"**: Stuart Hall and Tony Jefferson, eds., *Resistance through Rituals: Youth Subcultures in Post-War Britain*, 189.

266 **creating and maintaining hegemony**: See Edna Ullmann-Margalit, *The Emergence of Norms*, 181 ("As Robert Nozick points out, conspiracy theories [or 'hidden hand explanations'] are, in an obvious sense, diametrically opposed to invisible hand explanations").

266 **"Culture is being threatened"**: Hannah Arendt, "The Crisis in Culture," 208.

266 **"a multitude of bad things"**: Jean-Jacques Rousseau, *A Discourse on Inequality*, 133.

266 **"rich source of much that is evil"**: Ralk Dahrendorf, "On the Origin of Inequality among Men," quoting Immanuel Kant.

267 **"to erode their appearance"**: Cecilia L. Ridgeway, *Status: Why Is It Everywhere? Why Does It Matter?*, 142. See also Robert Nozick, *The Nature of Rationality*, 32 ("the many Freudian symbolic meanings that, when they enter into conscious deliberation as symbolic, lose their power and impact").

267 **"The forms of happiness"**: Bertrand Russell, *Power*, 184.

267 **"We will never actually eliminate status"**: Ridgeway, *Status*, 162.

268 **"He who sang"**: Rousseau, *A Discourse on Inequality*, 114.

268 **"As soon as it became possible"**: Molly Young, *The Things They Fancied*.

268 **quell the collective craving for higher status:** Fred Hirsch, *Social Limits to Growth*, 183 ("If the extent of individual striving for position can be curtailed in such a way as to preserve the beneficial minimum of competition and choice, an unqualified benefit should ensue").

268 **"redistribution of respect":** Noah Smith, "Redistribute Wealth? No, Redistribute Respect."

268 **"A love that does not discriminate":** Sigmund Freud, *Civilization and Its Discontents*, 57.

269 **"free to deal with one another":** Paul Connerton, *How Societies Remember*, 10.

269 **"Philosophy, art, politics, religion":** Alain de Botton, *Status Anxiety*, 293.

270 **"exercise of the symbolizing faculties":** Nelson Goodman, *Languages of Art*, 256.

270 **"corresponds to as many different concepts":** Semir Zeki, "The Neurology of Ambiguity."

270 **"a culture with a content":** A. L. Kroeber, *Configurations of Culture Growth*, 795.

270 **Contemporary country music:** Shuja Haider, "The Invention of Twang: What Makes Country Music Sound like Country?"

270 **ecosystems push toward complexity:** Rollo H. Myers, *Eric Satie*, 116 ("Manet, Cézanne, Picasso, Derain, Braque and others broke away from these bad traditions and, risking everything, saved painting and artistic thinking generally from complete and absolute stultification").

270 **"the composite product of personal superiority":** Kroeber, *Configurations of Culture Growth*, 7.

271 **popularity appears to be a much fairer measure:** Derek Thompson, *Hit Makers: The Science of Popularity in an Age of Distraction*, 37 ("Critics and audiences might prefer to think that markets are perfectly meritocratic and the most popular products and ideas are self-evidently the best").

272 **allow us to "all be artists":** Samar Shams, "We Will All Be Artists in the Future."

272 **it does engender some inequality:** Luc Ferry, *Homo Aestheticus: The Invention of Taste in the Democratic Age*, 198.

272 **"We should not consider":** T. S. Eliot, *Notes towards the Definition of Culture*, 48.

272 **status will remain an integral part:** Roy Wagner, *The Invention of Culture*, 158 ("The future of Western society lies in its ability to create social forms that will make explicit distinctions between classes and segments of society, *so that these distinctions do not come of themselves as implicit racism, discrimination, corruption, crises, riots, necessary 'cheating' and 'finagling,' and so on*").

Bibliography

Abraham, J. H. *Origins and Growth of Sociology*. Harmondsworth, Eng.: Penguin, 1973.

Acerbi, Alberto, et al. "The Logic of Fashion Cycles." *PLOS One* 7, no. 3: e32541.

Achebe, Chinua. *Things Fall Apart*. New York: Anchor/Doubleday, 1959.

Adams, John. *The Works of John Adams*. Vol. 6, *Defence of the Constitution IV, Discourses on Davila*. Jazzybee Verlag, 2015.

Adamson, Melitta Weiss, and Francine Segan. *Entertaining from Ancient Rome to the Super Bowl: An Encyclopedia*. Santa Barbara, Calif.: ABC-CLIO, 2008.

Aeschlimann, Roland, et al., eds. *Trisha Brown: Dance and Art in Dialogue, 1961–2001*. Cambridge, Mass.: MIT Press, 2002.

Albo, Mike. "The Marvelous Mr. John Waters." *Town & Country*, September 20, 2021.

Aldrich, Nelson W., Jr. *Old Money: The Mythology of America's Upper Class*. New York: Vintage, 1989.

———. "Preppies: The Last Upper Class?" *The Atlantic*, January 1979.

Allaire, Christian. "How This Indigenous Jeweler Is Embracing Tradition under Lockdown." *Vogue*, April 26, 2020, https://www.vogue.com/slideshow/keri-ataumbi-indigenous-artist-photo-diary.

Andersen, Kurt. "You Say You Want a Devolution?" *Vanity Fair*, January 2012; posted online December 7, 2011, https://www.vanityfair.com/style/2012/01/prisoners-of-style-201201.

Anderson, Cameron, and John Angus D. Hildreth. "Striving for Superiority: The Human Desire for Status." IRLE Working Paper 115–16, October 2016.

Anderson, C., J. A. D. Hildreth, and L. Howland. "Is the Desire for Status a Fundamental Human Motive? A Review of the Empirical Literature." *Psychological Bulletin* 141, no. 3 (May 2015): 574–601, https://doi.org/10.1037/a0038781.

Anderson, C., J. A. D. Hildreth, and D. L. Sharps. "The Possession of High Status Strengthens the Status Motive." *Personality and Social Psychology Bulletin* 46, no. 12 (December 2020): 1712–23, https://doi.org/10.1177/0146167220937544.

Anderson, C., O. P. John, D. Keltner, and A. M. Kring. "Who Attains Social Status? Effects of Personality and Physical Attractiveness in Social Groups." *Journal of Personality and Social Psychology* 81, no. 1 (July 2001): 116–32, https://doi.org/10.1037//0022-3514.81.1.116.

Anderson, C., M. W. Kraus, A. D. Galinsky, and D. Keltner. "The Local-Ladder Effect: Social Status and Subjective Well-Being." *Psychological Science* 23, no. 7 (2012): 764–71, http://www.jstor.org/stable/23262493.

Anderson, C., R. Willer, G. J. Kilduff, and C. E. Brown. "The Origins of Deference: When Do People Prefer Lower Status?" *Journal of Personality and Social Psychology* 102, no. 5 (May 2012): 1077–88, https://doi.org/10.1037/a0027409.

Anderson, Chris. *The Longer Long Tail*. New York: Hyperion, 2008.

Appadurai, Arjun. "Introduction: Commodities and the Politics of Value." In *The Social Life of Things*, edited by Arjun Appadurai. Cambridge: Cambridge University Press, 1986.

Appiah, Kwame Anthony. "The Importance of Elsewhere." *Foreign Affairs*, March/April 2019, https://www.foreignaffairs.com/articles/2019-02-12/importance-elsewhere.

Arendt, Hannah. "The Crisis in Culture." In *Between Past and Future*. New York: Viking, 1961.

Arnold, Martin. "Moneywise." *New York Times*, February 17, 1964, https://www.nytimes.com/1964/02/17/archives/moneywise.html.

Arnold, Rebecca. *Fashion: A Very Short Introduction*. New York: Oxford University Press, 2009.

Asimov, Eric. "One Critic's Delight . . ." *New York Times*, November 5, 2003, https://www.nytimes.com/2003/11/05/dining/one-critic-s-delight.html.

Austerlitz, Saul. "The Pernicious Rise of Poptimism." *New York Times Magazine*, April 4, 2014, https://www.nytimes.com/2014/04/06/magazine/the-pernicious-rise-of-poptimism.html.

Baker, Keiligh. "Best Friends with Dr Dre and an Entourage of Six 'Minders' Wherever He Goes: How Saudi Billionaire Playboy, 23, with a Fleet of Golden Cars Spends His Summer in London." *Mail Online*, May 2, 2016, https://www.dailymail.co.uk/news/article-3567339/MailOnline-meets-billionaire-Saudi-playboy-owns-gold-supercars.html.

Baker, Phil. *The Book of Absinthe*. New York: Grove, 2001.

Balaban, Bob. *Spielberg, Truffaut and Me: An Actor's Diary*. Rev. ed. London: Titan Books, 2003.

Baldwin, James. *Go Tell It on the Mountain*. New York: Dell, 1985.

Barber, Nicholas. "*Black Panther*: The Most Radical Hollywood Blockbuster Ever?" *BBC*, February 6, 2018, https://www.bbc.com/culture/article/20180206-black-panther-the-most-radical-hollywood-blockbuster-ever.

Barthes, Roland. *Elements of Semiology*. Translated by Annette Lavers and Colin Smith. New York: Hill and Wang/Noonday Press, 1967.

Barthes, Roland, and Andy Stafford. *The Language of Fashion*. Oxford: Berg, 2006.

Bataille, Georges. *The Accursed Share: An Essay on the General Economy*. Vol. 1, *Consumption*. New York: Zone Books, 1991.

Baudrillard, Jean. *The Consumer Society: Myths and Structures*. London: Sage Publications, 1998.

———. *For a Critique of the Political Economy of the Sign*. Translated by Charles Levin. Candor, N.Y.: Telos Press, 1981.

———. *The System of Objects*. Translated by James Benedict. London: Verso, 1996.

Bayley, Stephen. *Taste: The Secret Meaning of Things*. New York: Pantheon, 1991.

Bazner, David. "The Ted Trend Continues at Saint Laurent." *GQ*, January 19, 2014, https://www.gq.com/story/ted-at-saint-laurent.

BBC Music Magazine. "The 50 Greatest Composers of All Time." *Classical Music*, January 30, 2020, https://www.classical-music.com/composers/50-greatest-composers-all-time/.

Beach, Christopher. *Class, Language, and American Film Comedy*. Cambridge: Cambridge University Press, 2001.

Beam, Christopher. "Highway to Heil." *Slate*, January 27, 2011, https://slate.com/culture/2011/01/jesse-james-nazi-photos-how-common-is-nazi-iconography-among-bikers.html.

The Beatles Anthology. San Francisco: Chronicle, 2000.

"Beatles Haircuts 'Unsightly, Unsafe, Unruly, and Unclean'—Fashion Archive, 1963." *Guardian*, December 6, 2017, https://www.theguardian.com/fashion/2017/dec/06/beatles-hair-cut-fashion-archive-1963.

"Beatles Press Conference: American Arrival 2/7/1964." http://www.beatlesinterviews.org/db1964.0207.beatles.html; accessed December 1, 2021.

Becker, Gary S. *Accounting for Tastes*. Cambridge, Mass.: Harvard University Press, 1996.

Becker, Howard S. *Art Worlds*. 2nd ed. Berkeley: University of California Press, 2008.

———. *Outsiders: Studies in the Sociology of Deviance*. 1963. Reprint, New York: Free Press, 1973.

Bell, Daniel. *The Cultural Contradictions of Capitalism*. New York: Basic Books, 1976.

Bell, Quentin. *On Human Finery*. 2nd ed. New York: Schocken, 1978.

Benedict, Ruth. *Patterns of Culture*. Boston: Mariner, 2005.

Benjamin, Kathy. "What It Was like Working at Studio 54." *Grunge*, January 12, 2021, https://www.grunge.com/311268/what-it-was-like-working-at-studio-54/.

Benjamin, Walter. *Illuminations*. Translated by Harry Zohn. New York: Schocken, 1968.

Bennhold, Katrin. "Bavarian Millennials Embrace Tradition (Dirndls, Lederhosen and All)." *New York Times*, October 10, 2018, https://www.nytimes.com/2018/10/10/world/europe/germany-bavaria-dirndl-lederhosen.html.

Berger, David. *Kant's Aesthetic Theory: The Beautiful and the Agreeable*. London: Continuum, 2009.

Berger, Jonah. *Contagious: Why Things Catch On*. New York: Simon and Schuster, 2013.

Berger, John. *Ways of Seeing*. London: British Broadcasting Corporation/Penguin, 1973.

Berger, Joseph, Susan J. Rosenholtz, and Morris Zelditch, Jr. "Status Organizing Processes." *Annual Review of Sociology* 6 (1980): 479–508.

Berger, Thor, and Per Engzell. "Trends and Disparities in Subjective Upward Mobility since 1940." *Socius* (January 2020).

Bergreen, Laurence. *Capone: The Man and the Era*. New York: Touchstone, 1994.

Bergson, Henri. *The Creative Mind: An Introduction to Metaphysics*. New York: Citadel, 1992.

Bernard, James. "Why the World Is after Vanilla Ice." *New York Times*, February 3, 1991, http://www.nytimes.com/1991/02/03/arts/why-the-world-is-after-vanilla-ice.html.

Best, Joel. *Flavor of the Month: Why Smart People Fall for Fads*. Berkeley: University of California Press, 2006.

Bilis, Madeline. "Why Some Boston Brownstones Have Purple Windows." *Boston Magazine*, September 23, 2015, https://www.bostonmagazine.com/property/2015/09/23/purple-windows-boston/.

Birnbach, Lisa. *The Official Preppy Handbook*. New York: Workman, 1980.

———. "Save Brooks Brothers!" *New York Times*, July 22, 2020, https://www.nytimes.com/2020/07/22/style/brooks-brothers-bankruptcy-lisa-birnbach-preppy-handbook.html.

Blanck, Nili. "Inside L.A.'s Lowrider Car Clubs." *Smithsonian Magazine*, May 5, 2021, https://www.smithsonianmag.com/travel/vibrant-history-lowrider-car-culture-in-la-180977652/.

Blau, Max. "33 Musicians on What John Cage Communicates." *NPR*, September 5, 2012, https://www.npr.org/2012/08/30/160327305/33-musicians-on-what-john-cage-communicates.

Bloom, Harold. *The Anxiety of Influence: A Theory of Poetry*. 2nd ed. New York: Oxford University Press, 1997.

———. *The Western Canon: The Books and School of the Ages*. New York: Harcourt Brace, 1994.

Blumer, Herbert. "Fashion: From Class Differentiation to Collective Selection." *Sociological Quarterly* 10, no. 3 (Summer 1969): 275–91.

Bollen, Christopher. "Glenn O'Brien Saved My Life." *The Cut*, April 7, 2017, https://www.thecut.com/2017/04/glenn-obrien-saved-my-life.html.

Bong Joon-ho (director). *Parasite*. Neon, 2019.

Boorstin, Daniel J. *The Image*. Harmondsworth, Eng.: Penguin, 1961.

Bourdieu, Pierre. *Distinction*. Cambridge, Mass.: Harvard University Press, 1984.

———. *The Field of Cultural Production*. New York: Columbia University Press, 1993.

Bourne, Leah. "The Cupcake Craze Is Officially Over: Crumbs Is Going Out of Business." *Stylecaster*, July 8, 2014, https://stylecaster.com/beauty/cupcake-craze-over-crumbs-going-out-of-business/.

Boyer, G. Bruce. "The Swelled Edge, a Quarter-Inch of Distinction." *Ivy Style*, October 29, 2013, http://www.ivy-style.com/the-swelled-edge-a-quarter-inch-of-distinction.html.

———. *True Style: The History and Principles of Classic Menswear*. New York: Basic Books, 2015.

Brennan, Geoffrey, and Philip Pettit. *The Economy of Esteem: An Essay on Civil and Political Society*. Oxford: Oxford University Press, 2004.

Brennan, Ian. "How Music Dies: Aristocracy Is Killing Artistry." *Huck*, May 11, 2016, https://www.huckmag.com/perspectives/how-music-dies/

Brewer, Marilynn B. "The Social Self: On Being the Same and Different at the Same Time." *Personality and Social Psychology Bulletin* 17, no. 5 (October 1, 1991): 475–82.

Bright, Sam. "Klansman with Dreadlocks Astonishes Twitter." *BBC*, July 10, 2017, https://www.bbc.com/news/blogs-trending-40559913.

Broderick, Ryan. "I'm Being Gaslit by the TikTok Lamborghini." *Garbage Day*, October 9, 2021, https://www.garbageday.email/p/im-being-gaslit-by-the-tiktok-lamborghini.

Brooke, Eliza. "When a Dog Breed Becomes a Trend." *Vox*, July 29, 2019, https://www.vox.com/the-goods/2019/7/29/8930131/mini-australian-shepherd-american-aussie.

Brooks, David. *Bobos in Paradise*. New York: Simon and Schuster, 2000.

Brown, Sloane. "BMA John Waters Rotunda Dedication." *Baltimore Snap*, May 20, 2021.

Brown, Trisha. "Trisha Brown on Pure Movement." *Dance Magazine*, May 1, 2013, https://www.dancemagazine.com/trisha_brown_on_pure_movement-2306909524.html.

Bryson, Bethany. "'Anything but Heavy Metal': Symbolic Exclusion and Musical Dislikes." *American Sociological Review* 61, no. 5 (October 1996): 884–99.

Buñuel, Luis. *My Last Breath*. Translated by Abigail Israel. London: Vintage, 1994.

Burke, Allie. "Instagram Is the Happiest Place in the (Internet) World." *Psychology Today*, January 24, 2016, https://www.psychologytoday.com/us/blog/paper-souls/201601/instagram-is-the-happiest-place -in-the-internet-world.

Buyer, Bob. "Lawsuits Attack 'Cadillac' Silos." *Buffalo News*, October 26, 1991.

Byrne, David. *How Music Works*. New York: Three Rivers Press, 2017.

Cabanne, Pierre, and Marcel Duchamp. *Dialogues with Marcel Duchamp*. New York: Viking, 1971.

Calinescu, Matei. *Five Faces of Modernity*. Durham, N.C.: Duke University Press, 1987.

Callaghan, Karen A. *Ideals of Feminine Beauty: Philosophical, Social, and Cultural Dimensions*. Westport, Conn.: Greenwood Press, 1994.

Capote, Truman. *Breakfast at Tiffany's*. New York: Penguin, 2011.

Cardwell, Diane. "Black Surfers Reclaim Their Place on the Waves." *New York Times*, August 31, 2021, https://www.nytimes.com/interactive/2021/08/31/sports/black-surfers.html.

Carroll, Noël. *Philosophy of Art*. London: Routledge, 1999.

Cassini, Oleg. *In My Own Fashion*. New York: Simon and Schuster, 1987.

Chaney, Lisa. *Coco Chanel*. New York: Viking, 2011.

Chang, Jeff. *Can't Stop, Won't Stop: A History of the Hip-Hop Generation*. London: Ebury, 2005.

Charles, Kerwin Kofi, Erik Hurst, and Nikolai Roussanov. "Conspicuous Consumption and Race." *Quarterly Journal of Economics* 124, no. 2 (May 2009): 425–67.

Chayka, Kyle. "How Beeple Crashed the Art World." *New Yorker*, March 22, 2021, https://www.newyorker .com/tech/annals-of-technology/how-beeple-crashed-the-art-world.

———. "Raya and the Promise of Private Social Media." *New Yorker*, October 15, 2021, https://www .newyorker.com/culture/infinite-scroll/raya-and-the-promise-of-private-social-media.

———. "Welcome to AirSpace." *The Verge*, August 3, 2016, https://www.theverge.com/2016/8/3/12325104 /airbnb-aesthetic-global-minimalism-startup-gentrification.

Cheng, Evelyn. "China Says It Now Has Nearly 1 Billion Internet Users." *CNBC*, February 4, 2021, https://www.cnbc.com/2021/02/04/china-says-it-now-has-nearly-1-billion-internet-users.html.

Chipp, Herschel Browning, Peter Selz, and Joshua C. Taylor. *Theories of Modern Art: A Source Book by Artists and Critics*. Berkeley: University of California Press, 1968.

Choi, Young Back. *Paradigms and Conventions*. Ann Arbor: University of Michigan Press, 1993.

Christie's. "The Collection of Peggy and David Rockefeller: Online Sale." May 1–11, 2018. https://onlineonly .christies.com/s/collection-peggy-david-rockefeller-online-sale/lots/466.

Chwe, Michael Suk-Young. *Rational Ritual: Culture, Coordination, and Common Knowledge*. Princeton, N.J.: Princeton University Press, 2013.

Clemente, Deidre. *Dress Casual: How College Students Redefined American Style*. Chapel Hill: University of North Carolina Press, 2014.

Cochrane, Glynn. *Big Men and Cargo Cults*. Oxford: Clarendon, 1970.

Coe, Sophie D., and Michael D. Coe. *The True History of Chocolate*. London: Thames and Hudson, 1996.

Cohen, Albert K. "A General Theory of Subcultures (1955)." In *The Subcultures Reader*, edited by Sarah Thornton and Ken Gelder. London: Routledge, 1997.

Cohen, Phil. "Subcultural Conflict and Working-Class Community (1972)." In *The Subcultures Reader*, edited by Sarah Thornton and Ken Gelder. London: Routledge, 1997.

Cohn, Nik. *Today There Are No Gentlemen*. London: Weidenfeld and Nicolson, 1971.

Colt, Sam. "Apple Designer Jony Ive's Favorite Cars." *Business Insider*, February 14, 2015, https://www .businessinsider.com/jony-ive-favorite-cars-2015-2.

Connerton, Paul. *How Societies Remember*. Cambridge: Cambridge University Press, 1989.

Conniff, Richard. *The Natural History of the Rich: A Field Guide*. New York: W. W. Norton, 2002.

Corner, Natalie. "At Home with a Teenage Billionaire: Dubai Instagram Star, 16, with a $1 Million Collection of Trainers Shows Off the Family Mansion—Including the Private Zoo." *Daily Mail*, December 6, 2018, https://www.dailymail.co.uk/femail/article-6463387/Inside-home-16-year-old-billionaire-rich -kid-Dubai-private-ZOO.html.

Corrigan, Peter. *The Sociology of Consumption*. London: Sage Publications, 1997.

Coscarelli, Joe. "How Pop Music Fandom Became Sports, Politics, Religion and All-Out War." *New York Times*, December 25, 2020, https://www.nytimes.com/2020/12/25/arts/music/pop-music-superfans -stans.html.

Craig, Scott. "What's Noka Worth? (Part 2)." *DallasFood*, December 11, 2006, https://dallasfood.org/2006 /12/noka-chocolate-part-2/.

Culler, Jonathan D. *Saussure*. Glasgow: Fontana/Collins, 1976.

Currid-Halkett, Elizabeth. *The Sum of Small Things: A Theory of the Aspirational Class*. Princeton, N.J.: Princeton University Press, 2017.

Dahl, Gary R. *Advertising for Dummies*. New York: Hungry Minds, 2001.

Dahl, Linda. *Stormy Weather: The Music and Lives of a Century of Jazz Women*. New York: Pantheon, 1984.

Dahl, Roald. *Charlie and the Chocolate Factory*. New York: Puffin Books, 2013.

Dahrendorf, Ralf. "On the Origin of Inequality among Men." In *Essays in the Theory of Society*. Palo Alto, Calif.: Stanford University Press, 1968.

Davis, Allison P. "Pharrell's Grammys Hat Actually Not So Ridiculous." *The Cut*, January 27, 2014, https://www.thecut.com./2014/01/pharrells-grammys-hat-not-so-ridiculous.html.

Davis, Fred. *Fashion, Culture, and Identity*. Chicago: University of Chicago Press, 1992.

Davis, Kingsley, and Wilbert E. Moore. "Some Principles of Stratification." *American Sociological Review* 10, no. 2 (1944): 242–49 (Annual Meeting Papers, April 1945).

De Beauvoir, Simone. *The Second Sex*. Translated by H. M. Parshley. New York: Vintage, 1989.

De Botton, Alain. *Status Anxiety*. Toronto: Viking Canada, 2004.

de Casanova, Erynn Masi. *Buttoned Up: Clothing, Conformity, and White-Collar Masculinity*. Ithaca, N.Y.: ILR Press, 2015.

de Montlaur, Bénédicte. "France Honors Dennis Lim and John Waters." Order of Arts and Letters Ceremony at the Cultural Services of the French Embassy in New York, May 7, 2018, https://frenchculture.org/awards/8088-france-honors-dennis-lim-and-john-waters.

Dickens, Charles. *David Copperfield*. https://www.gutenberg.org/files/766/766-h/766-h.htm.

DiMaggio, Paul. "Market Structure, the Creative Process, and Popular Culture: Toward an Organizational Reinterpretation of Mass-Culture Theory." *Journal of Popular Culture* 11, no. 2 (September 1977): 436–52, https://doi.org/10.1111/j.0033-2840.1977.00436.x.

Dinerstein, Joel. *The Origins of Cool in Postwar America*. Chicago: University of Chicago Press, 2017.

Dixit, Iva. "'Bollywood Wives' Is an Accidental Documentary about India's Gilded Class." *New York Times*, January 7, 2021, https://www.nytimes.com/2021/01/07/magazine/fabulous-lives-bollywood-wives-netflix.html.

Dolenz, Micky, and Mark Bego. *I'm a Believer: My Life of Monkees, Music, and Madness*. New York: Hyperion, 1993.

Doll, Jen. "The Icing Is off the Cupcake Craze." *The Atlantic*, April 17, 2013, https://www.theatlantic.com/business/archive/2013/04/icing-cupcake-craze/316195/.

Doonan, Simon. "The End of Trends." *New York Observer*, March 3, 2010, https://observer.com/2010/03/the-end-of-trends/.

Doran, John. "The Demolition Man: Thurston Moore Interviewed." *The Quietus*, July 5, 2011, https://thequietus.com/articles/06534-thurston-moore-interview.

Douglas, Mary, and Baron Isherwood. *The World of Goods*. New York: Basic Books, 1979.

Dowd, Maureen. "Retreat of the Yuppies: The Tide Now Turns amid 'Guilt' and 'Denial.'" *New York Times*, June 28, 1985, https://www.nytimes.com/1985/06/28/nyregion/retreat-of-the-yuppies-the-tide-now-turns-amid-guilt-and-denial.html.

Dower, John. *Embracing Defeat: Japan in the Wake of World War II*. New York: W. W. Norton, 1999.

Dowling, James. "100 Not Out: The Full History of the Cartier Tank." *Esquire*, May 1, 2018, https://www.esquire.com/uk/watches/a33818670/cartier-tank-history/.

Dredge, Stuart, and Alex Hern. "Apple, Coffee and Techno: Jonathan Ive's Recipe for Success." *Guardian*, December 8, 2013, https://www.theguardian.com/technology/2013/dec/08/jonathan-ive-apple-coffee-techno.

Dreyfus, Hubert L., and Paul Rabinow. *Michel Foucault: Beyond Structuralism and Hermeneutics*. Chicago: University of Chicago Press, 1983.

Drinnon, Richard T. *Rebel in Paradise: A Biography of Emma Goldman*. New York: Bantam, 1973.

Drummond, Bill, and Jimmy Cauty. *The Manual (How to Have a Number One the Easy Way)*. https://freshonthenet.co.uk/the-manual-by-the-klf/.

Duncan, Hugh Dalziel. *Communication and Social Order*. New Brunswick, N.J.: Transaction, 1985.

———. *Symbols in Society*. New York: Oxford University Press, 1968.

Durkheim, Émile. *Suicide: A Study in Sociology*. Trans. John A. Spaulding. New York: Free Press, 1997.

Duvignaud, Jean. *The Sociology of Art*. Translated by Timothy Wilson. London: Paladin, 1972.

Dylan, Bob. "Ballad of a Thin Man." *Highway 61 Revisited*. Columbia, 1965.

Dylan, Bob, Joan Baez, Allen Ginsberg, Maria Muldaur, and Pete Seeger. *No Direction Home: Bob Dylan*. 2005. Paramount Home Entertainment.

Eagleton, Terry. *Culture*. New Haven, Conn.: Yale University Press, 2016.

Ebert, Roger. "North." *RogerEbert.com*, July 22, 1994.

Eco, Umberto. "How Culture Conditions the Colours We See." In *On Signs*, edited by Marshall Blonsky. Baltimore: The Johns Hopkins University Press, 1985.

———. *A Theory of Semiotics*. Bloomington: Indiana University Press, 1976.

Editors of Consumer Reports. *I'll Buy That: 50 Small Wonders and Big Deals That Revolutionized the Lives of Consumers*. Mount Vernon, N.Y.: Consumers Union, 1986.

Edsall, Thomas B. "The Resentment That Never Sleeps." *New York Times*, December 9, 2020.

Edwards, John. *Sociolinguistics: A Very Short Introduction*. Oxford: Oxford University Press, 2013.

Ehrenreich, Barbara, Elizabeth Hess, and Gloria Jacobs. "Beatlemania: A Sexually Defiant Consumer Subculture? (1992)." In *The Subcultures Reader*, edited by Sarah Thornton and Ken Gelder. London: Routledge, 1997.

Eliot, T. S. *Notes towards the Definition of Culture*. London: Faber and Faber, 1962.

Elliott, Anthony. *Concepts of the Self*. 2nd ed. Cambridge: Polity, 2008.

Ellis, Iain. "New Wave: Turning Rebellion into Money." *Pop Matters*, February 14, 2019, https://www.popmatters.com/new-wave-rebellion-into-money-2628904704.html.

Elster, Jon. *Making Sense of Marx*. Cambridge: Cambridge University Press, 1985.

———. *Nuts and Bolts for the Social Sciences*. Cambridge: Cambridge University Press, 1989.

Falk, John H., and John Balling. "Evolutionary Influence on Human Landscape Preference." *Environment and Behavior* 42, no. 4 (July 2010): 479–93, https://www.researchgate.net/publication/249624620_Evolutionary_Influence_on_Human_Landscape_Preference.

Fanon, Frantz. *The Wretched of the Earth*. Translated by Richard Philcox. New York: Grove, 2004.

Farah, Safy-Hallan. "The Great American Cool." *The Goods by Vox*, July 14, 2021, https://www.vox.com/the-goods/22570006/cool-consumer-identity-gen-z-cheugy.

"Fashion." *Lapham's Quarterly*, Fall 2015.

Fearon, Faye. "The Enduring Appeal of the Beatles' Mop-Top Haircuts." *GQ UK*, December 6, 2019, https://www.gq-magazine.co.uk/grooming/article/the-beatles-haircut.

Feather, Carl E. "Western Reserve Back Roads: Antiquated and Labor Intensive, Northeast Ohio Region's Farm Silos Face Bleak Future as Rural Skyscrapers." *Star Beacon* (Ashtabula, Ohio), November 24, 2006, https://www.starbeacon.com/community/silos/article_cd242cd9-5c3b-5b4b-b3b5-8b11992a06c6.html.

Feltovich, Nick, Rick Harbaugh, and Ted To. "Too Cool for School? Signalling and Countersignalling." *RAND Journal of Economics* 33, no. 4 (Winter 2002): 630–49.

Ferris, Ray, and Julian Lord. *Teddy Boys: A Concise History*. Preston, Eng.: Milo Books, 2012.

Ferry, Luc. *Homo Aestheticus: The Invention of Taste in the Democratic Age*. Translated by Robert de Loaiza. Chicago: University of Chicago Press, 1994.

Finnegan, William. *Barbarian Days: A Surfing Life*. New York: Penguin, 2015.

Fisher, Mark. "The Slow Cancellation of the Future." *Ghosts of My Life: Writings on Depression, Hauntology and Lost Futures*. Winchester, U.K.: Zero Books, 2014.

Fitzgerald, F. Scott. *The Great Gatsby*. London: Penguin, 1950.

"The 500 Greatest Albums of All Time." *Rolling Stone*, September 22, 2020, https://www.rollingstone.com/music/music-lists/best-albums-of-all-time-1062063/.

"500 Greatest Albums List (2003)." *Rolling Stone*, May 31, 2009, https://www.rollingstone.com/music/music-lists/500-greatest-albums-of-all-time-156826/.

Flanagan, Jane. "Grace Mugabe's Porsche, Rolls Royce and Range Rover Are Damaged When Cows Wander onto the Road as Motors Were Being Spirited Out of Zimbabwe under the Cover of Darkness." *Daily Mail*, January 22, 2018, https://www.dailymail.co.uk/news/article-5297435/Grace-Mugabes-supercars-crashed-taken-Zimbabwe.html.

Florida, Richard. *The Creative Class*. New York: Basic Books, 2002.

Foley, Gregk. "The Trends and Brands That Defined '90s Hip-Hop Fashion." *High Snobiety*, 2020, https://www.highsnobiety.com/p/90s-hip-hop-fashion/.

Foster, Edward Halsey. *Understanding the Beats*. Columbia: University of South Carolina Press, 1992.

Fox, Dan. *Pretentiousness: Why It Matters*. Minneapolis: Coffee House Press, 2016.

Fox, Margalit. "Vivian Nicholson, 79, Dies; A Rags-to-Riches Story Left in Tatters." *New York Times*, April 17, 2015, https://www.nytimes.com/2015/04/19/world/europe/vivian-nicholson-rags-to-riches-to-rags-icon-dies-at-79.html.

Frank, Robert H. *Choosing the Right Pond: Human Behavior and the Quest for Status*. New York: Oxford University Press, 1985.

Frank, Thomas. *The Conquest of Cool*. Chicago: University of Chicago Press, 1997.

Freud, Sigmund. *Civilization and Its Discontents*. Translated by James Strachey. New York: W. W. Norton, 1961.

———. *Introductory Lectures on Psycho-Analysis*. Translated by James Strachey. New York: Penguin, 1966.

Friedberger, Mark. *Shake-Out: Iowa Farm Families in the 1980s*. Lexington: University Press of Kentucky, 1989.

Friedman, B. H. *Jackson Pollock: Energy Made Visible*. New York: McGraw-Hill, 1974.

Frith, Simon, and Howard Horne. *Art into Pop*. London: Methuen, 1989.

Fuller, Peter. *Aesthetics after Modernism*. London: Writers and Readers, 1983.

Furbank, P. N. *Unholy Pleasure: The Idea of Social Class*. Oxford: Oxford University Press, 1985.

Fussell, Paul. *Class: A Guide through the American Status System*. New York: Touchstone, 1983.

Fyvel, T. R. "Fashion and Revolt (1963)." In *The Subcultures Reader*, edited by Sarah Thornton and Ken Gelder. London: Routledge, 1997.

Gabriel, Markus. *The Power of Art*. Cambridge: Polity, 2020.

———. *Why the World Does Not Exist*. Cambridge: Polity, 2015.

Gabriel, Yiannis, and Tim Lang. *The Unmanageable Consumer*. 2nd ed. London: Sage Publications, 2006.

Gallagher, Jake. "Dropping Knowledge: The Button-Down Collar." *GQ*, March 6, 2013, https://www.gq.com/story/dropping-knowledge-the-button-down-collar.

Gammond, Peter. *The Bluffer's Guide to British Class*. West Sussex, Eng.: Ravette Books, 1986.

Gans, Herbert. *Popular Culture and High Culture: An Analysis and Evaluation of Taste*. New York: Basic Books, 1974.

Garcia, Bobbito (director). *Rock Rubber 45s*. 2018. Goldcrest/Saboteur FilmsDistributor.

———. *Where'd You Get Those? New York City's Sneaker Culture, 1960–1987*. New York: Testify Books, 2003.

Gartman, David. *Auto-Opium: A Social History of American Automobile Design*. London: Routledge, 1994.

"Gay Track Star Voted Prom King." *The Advocate*, May 10, 2011, https://www.advocate.com/news/daily-news/2011/05/10/gay-high-schooler-voted-prom-king.

Geertz, Clifford. *The Interpretation of Cultures*. New York: Basic Books, 1973.

Gell, Alfred. "Newcomers to the World of Goods: Consumption among the Murai Gonds." In *The Social Life of Things*, edited by Arjun Appadurai. Cambridge: Cambridge University Press, 1986.

Gibbons-Neff, Thomas, and Fahim Abed. "In Afghanistan, Follow the White High-Tops and You'll Find the Taliban." *New York Times*, January 28, 2021.

Giddens, Anthony. *Modernity and Self-Identity: Self and Society in the Late Modern Age*. Stanford, Calif.: Stanford University Press, 1991.

Gilbert, Margaret. "Notes on the Concept of a Social Convention." *New Literary History* 14, no. 2 (Winter 1983): 225–51.

———. *On Social Facts*. Princeton, N.J.: Princeton University Press, 1989.

Gilmore, James H., and Joseph Pine. *Authenticity: What Consumers Really Want*. Cambridge, Mass.: Harvard Business Press, 2007.

Girard, René. *Evolution and Conversion: Dialogues on the Origins of Culture*. London: Bloomsbury, 2008.

Gladwell, Malcolm. *The Tipping Point*. New York: Back Bay/Little, Brown, 2000.

Goffman, Erving. *Interaction Ritual: Essays on Face-to-Face Behavior*. New York: Anchor, 1967.

———. *The Presentation of Self in Everyday Life*. Garden City, N.Y.: Doubleday/Anchor, 1959.

———. *Relations in Public: Microstudies of the Public Order*. New York: Harper Torchbooks, 1971.

———. "Symbols of Class Status." *British Journal of Sociology* 2, no. 4 (December 1951): 294–304.

Goldfarb, Aaron. "When Johnnie Walker Blue Was King." *Punch*, May 6, 2020, https://punchdrink.com/articles/when-johnnie-walker-blue-label-whisky-was-king.

Goodman, Nelson. *Languages of Art*. Indianapolis: Hackett, 1976.

Gould, Stephen Jay. *Full House: The Spread of Excellence from Plato to Darwin*. New York: Harmony, 1996.

Gould, Will (writer), and Hollingsworth Morse (director). March 11, 1962. Episode #281, season 8, episode 7. "Double Trouble." In R. Golden (Producer), *Lassie*. CBS.

Graham, John D. *John Graham's System and Dialectics of Art*. Baltimore: The Johns Hopkins University Press, 1971.

"Great Leap Forward at the Traffic Lights in China—Archive." *Guardian*, August 25, 1966, https://www.theguardian.com/world/2016/aug/25/china-traffic-lights-red-guards-communism-great-leap.

Greco, Stephen. "That Fast Thing: The Late Glenn O'Brien." *Upstate Diary*, no. 4, 2017, https://www.upstatediary.com/glenn-obrien.

Green, Christopher. "An Introduction to *Les Demoiselles d'Avignon*." In *Picasso's Les Demoiselles d'Avignon*, edited by Christopher Green, 1–14. Cambridge: Cambridge University Press, 2001.

Greenberg, Clement. *Art and Culture*. Boston: Beacon, 1989.

Greenhouse, Emily. "About Kanye's Croissant." *New Yorker*, September 12, 2013, https://www.newyorker.com/culture/culture-desk/about-kanyes-croissant.

Greenland, David R. *The Gunsmoke Chronicles: A New History of Television's Greatest Western*. Duncan, Okla.: Bear Manor Media, 2013.

Greif, Mark. "What Was the Hipster?" *New York Magazine*, October 24, 2010.

Gronow, Jukka. *The Sociology of Taste*. London: Routledge, 1997.

Guay, Melissa. "Spontaneous Combustion Likely Cause of Silo Fire." *Post Star* (Glen Falls, N.Y.), May 7, 2007.

Guo, Jeff. "The Mathematician Who Proved Why Hipsters All Look Alike." *Washington Post*, November 11, 2014, https://www.washingtonpost.com/news/storyline/wp/2014/11/11/the-mathematician-who-proved-why-hipsters-all-look-alike/.

Haggerty, Geoff (director). "Thousands of Girls Match Description of Missing Sorority Sister." *The Onion*. 2010.

Haider, Shuja. "The Invention of Twang: What Makes Country Music Sound like Country?" *The Believer*, August 1, 2019, https://believermag.com/the-invention-of-twang/.

Halbwachs, Maurice. *On Collective Memory*. Translated by Lewis A. Coser. Chicago: University of Chicago Press, 1992.

Hall, Edward T. *Beyond Culture*. New York: Anchor, 1976.

———. *The Silent Language*. New York: Doubleday, 1981.

Hall, James. "Burberry Brand Tarnished by 'Chavs.'" *The Telegraph*, November 28, 2004, http://www.telegraph.co.uk/finance/2900572/Burberry-brand-tarnished-by-chavs.html.

Hall, Stuart, and Paul du Gay. *Questions of Cultural Identity*. London: Sage Publications, 1996.

Hall, Stuart, and Tony Jefferson, eds. *Resistance through Rituals: Youth Subcultures in Post-War Britain*. 2nd ed. London: Routledge, 1976.

Han, Young Jee, Joseph C. Nunes, and Xavier Drèze. "Signaling Status with Luxury Goods: The Role of Brand Prominence." *Journal of Marketing* 74, no. 4 (2010): 15–30, http://www.jstor.org/stable/27800823.

Hardin, Russell. *One for All: The Logic of Group Conflict*. Princeton, N.J.: Princeton University Press, 1995.

Harmon, Steph. "Amanda Palmer: 'Donald Trump Is Going to Make Punk Rock Great Again.'" *Guardian*, December 29, 2016.

Harris, Malcolm. *Kids These Days: The Making of Millennials*. New York: Back Bay, 2017.

Harvilla, Rob. "Have We Reached the End of Poptimism?" *The Ringer*, November 16, 2017, https://www.theringer.com/music/2017/11/16/16666306/taylor-swift-poptimism-2017.

Haskell, Caitlin Welsh. "Henri Rousseau, 1908 and After: The Corpus, Criticism, and History of a Painter without a Problem." PhD diss., University of Texas at Austin, 2012.

Hatch, Elvin. *Theories of Man and Culture*. New York: Columbia University Press, 1973.

Hawkes, Terence. *Structuralism and Semiotics*. Berkeley: University of California Press, 1977.

Hayakawa, S. I. *Symbol, Status, and Personality*. New York: Harcourt, Brace and World, 1953.

Heath, Anthony. *Rational Choice and Social Exchange*. Cambridge: Cambridge University Press, 1976.

Hebdidge, Dick. *Subculture: The Meaning of Style*. London: Methuen, 1979.

Hellman, Lillian. *An Unfinished Woman*. Boston: Little, Brown, 1969.

Helmore, Edward. "'Heroin Chic' and the Tangled Legacy of Photographer Davide Sorrenti." *Guardian*, May 23, 2019, https://www.theguardian.com/fashion/2019/may/23/heroin-chic-and-the-tangled-legacy-of-photographer-davide-sorrenti.

Heron-Langton, Jessica. "Marc Jacobs Drops Six Cute Looks on Animal Crossing." *Dazed Digital*, May 5, 2020, https://www.dazeddigital.com/fashion/article/49114/1/marc-jacobs-drops-six-cute-looks-animal-crossing-valentino-instagram.

Hesse, Monica, and Dan Zak. "Does This Haircut Make Me Look Like a Nazi?" *Washington Post*, November 30, 2016, https://www.washingtonpost.com/news/arts-and-entertainment/wp/2016/11/30/does-this-haircut-make-me-look-like-a-nazi/.

Hewitt, Paolo, ed. *The Sharper Word: A Mod Anthology*. Rev. ed. London: Helter Skelter, 2009.

Hillman, Betty Luther. *Dressing for the Culture Wars: Style and the Politics of Self-Presentation in the 1960s and 1970s*. Lincoln: University of Nebraska Press, 2015.

"Hipster Barista." *Know Your Meme*, https://knowyourmeme.com/memes/hipster-barista.

Hirsch, Fred. *Social Limits to Growth*. Cambridge, Mass.: Harvard University Press, 1976.

Hirsch, Paul M. "Processing Fads and Fashions: An Organization-Set Analysis of Cultural Industry Systems." *American Journal of Sociology* 77, no. 4 (1972): 639–59.

Ho, Michelle H. S. "Consuming Women in Blackface: Racialized Affect and Transnational Femininity in Japanese Advertising." *Japanese Studies* 37, no. 1 (2017): 49–69.

Hobsbawm, Eric. *On History*. London: Weidenfeld and Nicolson, 1997.

Hobsbawm, Eric, and Terence Ranger. *The Invention of Tradition*. Cambridge: Cambridge University Press, 1983.

Hoffer, Eric. *The Ordeal of Change*. New York: Harper and Row, 1963.

Hohmann, James. "The Daily 202: Trump Voters Stay Loyal Because They Feel Disrespected." *Washington Post*, May 14, 2018, https://www.washingtonpost.com/news/powerpost/paloma/daily-202/2018/05/14/daily-202-trump-voters-stay-loyal-because-they-feel-disrespected/5af8aac530fb0425887994cc/.

Holden, Stephen. "The Pop Life." *New York Times*, October 17, 1990, https://www.nytimes.com/1990/10/17/arts/the-pop-life-075590.html.

———. "The Pop Life." *New York Times*, December 19, 1990, https://www.nytimes.com/1990/12/19/arts/the-pop-life-161090.html.

Holt, Douglas B. "Distinction in America? Recovering Bourdieu's Theory of Taste from Its Critics." *Poetics* 25, no. 2–3 (November 1997): 93–120.

———. "Does Cultural Capital Structure American Consumption?" *Journal of Consumer Research* 25, no. 1 (June 1998): 1–25.

Holzman, Winnie (writer), and Scott Winant (director). August 25, 1994. "Pilot." In Marshall Herskovitz and Edward Zwick (producers), *My So-Called Life*. ABC.

Homans, George Caspar. *Social Behavior: Its Elementary Forms*. London: Routledge, 1973.

Hood, Bruce. *The Self Illusion*. Oxford: Oxford University Press, 2012.

Hooghe, Marc, and Ruth Dassonneville. "Explaining the Trump Vote: The Effect of Racist Resentment and Anti-Immigrant Sentiments." *PS: Political Science and Politics* 51, no. 3 (July 2018): 528–34, https://doi.org/10.1017/S1049096518000367.

Hornby, Nick. *High Fidelity*. New York: Riverhead, 2000.

Horyn, Cathy. "The Post-Trend Universe." *T Magazine*, February 15, 2015, https://www.nytimes.com/2015/02/15/t-magazine/post-trend-universe-cathy-horyn.html.

"How Bad Is Your Spotify?" *The Pudding*, https://pudding.cool/2020/12/judge-my-spotify/.

"How Badoit Took on Perrier." *New York Times*, October 30, 1988, https://www.nytimes.com/1988/10/30/business/how-badoit-took-on-perrier.html.

Hume, David. "Of the Standard of Taste." *Essays: Moral, Political, and Literary*. Carmel, Ind.: Liberty Fund, 1985.

Hutson, David J. "Plump or Corpulent? Lean or Gaunt? Historical Categories of Bodily Health in Nineteenth-Century Thought." *Social Science History* 41, no. 2 (Summer 2017): 283–303.

Inglis, Fred. *Cultural Studies*. Oxford: Blackwell, 1993.

Iyengar, Sheena. *The Art of Choosing*. New York: Twelve/Grand Central, 2011.

Jackson, Gita. "Taylor Swift Super Fans Are Furious about a Good Review." *Motherboard*, July 31, 2020, https://www.vice.com/en/article/v7gpx8/taylor-swift-super-fans-are-furious-about-a-good-review.

Jacobs, Jim, and Warren Casey. *Grease*. 1972.

Jenkins, Henry. "Television Fans, Poachers, Nomads (1992)." In *The Subcultures Reader*, edited by Sarah Thornton and Ken Gelder. London: Routledge, 1997.

Jennings, Rebecca. "Are You Ready for the Return of Prep?" *The Goods by Vox*, August 24, 2021, https://www.vox.com/the-goods/22638568/old-money-aesthetic-dark-academia-prep-tiktok-pinterest-instagram.

———. "The Blandness of TikTok's Biggest Stars." *The Goods by Vox*, May 18, 2021, https://www.vox.com/the-goods/2021/5/18/22440937/tiktok-addison-rae-bella-poarch-build-a-bitch-charli-damelio-mediocrity.

———. "A Super-Famous TikTok Star Appeared on Jimmy Fallon. It Didn't Go Great." *The Goods by Vox*, March 30, 2021, https://www.vox.com/the-goods/2021/3/30/22357132/addison-rae-jimmy-fallon-tonight-show-tiktok-dance.

———. "Your Tweet Goes Viral. Here Come the Companies Asking You to Sell Their Crap." *The Goods by Vox*, March 3, 2021, https://www.vox.com/the-goods/22309184/ocean-galaxy-light-twitter-clout-mining-viral.

Jensen, Tom. "Americans Not Hip to Hipsters." *Public Policy Polling*, May 13, 2013, https://www.public
  policypolling.com/polls/americans-not-hip-to-hipsters/.
Johnson, Jamie. "Off with Their Coattails." *Wall Street Journal*, April 30, 2011, https://www.wsj.com
  /articles/SB10001424052748704132204576285250103874450.
Johnson, Noah, Rachel Tashjian, and Samuel Hine. "The 10 Best Things We Saw at Fashion Week."
  Corporate Lunch, episode 120, February 1, 2021, https://open.spotify.com/episode/34b0Q11BwQG5uI27
  kWEsrA.
Jones, Davis. "History of Surfing: The Great Plastics Race." *Surfer*, June 28, 2017, https://www.surfer
  .com/features/history-surfing-pu-foam/.
Jones, Josh. "How Glenn Gould's Eccentricities Became Essential to His Playing and Personal Style:
  From Humming Aloud While Playing to Performing with His Childhood Piano Chair." *Open Culture*, November 14, 2018, https://www.openculture.com/2018/11/glenn-goulds-eccentricities.html.
Jones, Liz. "The Patch-Up Prince: As He Is Pictured in a Jacket That's Been Repaired for Decades, How—
  from His Shoes Up—Prince Charles Has Always Made Do and Mended." *Daily Mail*, May 25, 2021,
  https://www.dailymail.co.uk/femail/article-9618545/As-pictured-repaired-jacket-Prince-Charles-big
  -fan-recycled-outfits.html.
Jones, Owen. *Chavs: The Demonization of the Working Class*. 2nd ed. London: Verso, 2012.
Jordan, Glenn, and Chris Weedon. *Cultural Politics: Class, Gender, Race and the Postmodern World*. Oxford:
  Blackwell, 1995.
Kant, Immanuel. *The Critique of Judgement*. Translated by James Creed Meredith. Oxford: Clarendon,
  1952.
Kassinger, Ruth. *Dyes: From Sea Snails to Synthetics*. Brookfield, Minn.: Twenty-First Century Books, 2003.
Keller, Rudi. *On Language Change: The Invisible Hand in Language*. London: Routledge, 1994.
———. *A Theory of Linguistic Signs*. Oxford: Oxford University Press, 1995.
Kerouac, Jack. *On the Road*. London: Penguin Classics, 2000.
K-HOLE. "Youth Mode: A Report on Freedom." K-HOLE, October 2013, http://khole.net/issues/youth
  -mode/.
King, Larry. "DJ Khaled's Illuminating Convo: Influence of Hip Hop, Jay Z's Genius & Young Rapper
  Mistakes." *Larry King Now*. August 5, 2014. https://www.youtube.com/watch?v=M0be5674X9Y.
Kinsella, Sharon. "Black Faces, Witches, and Racism against Girls." In *Bad Girls of Japan*, edited by Laura
  Miller and Jan Bardsley, 143–58. New York: Palgrave Macmillan, 2005.
Kirsch, Adam. "Kafka Wanted All His Work Destroyed after His Death. Or Did He?" *Australian Finance
  Review Magazine*, September 6, 2018, https://www.afr.com/life-and-luxury/arts-and-culture/kafka
  -wanted-all-his-work-destroyed-after-his-death-or-did-he-20180906-h14zsd.
Klapp, Orrin E. *The Inflation of Symbols*. New Brunswick, N.J.: Transaction, 1991.
Klein, Naomi. *No Logo: Taking Aim at the Brand Bullies*. Toronto: Knopf Canada, 2000.
Klosterman, Chuck. *But What If We're Wrong?* New York: Blue Rider, 2016.
"Klout Is Dead—How Will People Continuously Rank Themselves Online Now?" *Guardian*, May 11,
  2018, https://www.theguardian.com/technology/shortcuts/2018/may/11/klout-is-dead-how-will-people
  -continously-rank-themselves-online-now.
Kluckhohn, Clyde. *Culture and Behavior*. Edited by Richard Kluckhohn. New York: Free Press, 1962.
Knight, Phil. *Shoe Dog*. London: Simon and Schuster, 2016.
Kopytoff, Igor. "The Cultural Biography of Things: Commoditization as Process." In *The Social Life of
  Things*, edited by Arjun Appadurai. Cambridge: Cambridge University Press, 1986.
Koutsobinas, Theodore. *The Political Economy of Status: Superstars, Markets, and Culture Change*. Chel-
  tenham, Eng.: Edward Elgar, 2014.
Kovács, Balázs, and Amanda J. Sharkey. "The Paradox of Publicity: How Awards Can Negatively Affect
  the Evaluation of Quality." *Administrative Science Quarterly* 59, no. 1 (March 2014): 1–33.
Kremer, William. "Does a Baby's Name Affect Its Chances in Life?" *BBC World Service*, April 11, 2014,
  https://www.bbc.com/news/magazine-26634477.
Krewen, Nick. "Meet Beck's Dad, David Campbell, Who Has Helped Sell Nearly 1 Billion Records." *Toronto
  Star*, June 14, 2014, https://www.thestar.com/entertainment/music/2014/06/14/meet_becks_dad
  _david_campbell_who_has_helped_sell_nearly_1_billion_records.html.
Kroeber, A. L. *Configurations of Culture Growth*. Berkeley: University of California Press, 1944.
Kroeber, A. L., and C. Kluckhohn. *Culture: A Critical Review of Concepts and Definitions*. Vol. 47, no. 1 of
  Papers of the Peabody Museum of Archaeology and Ethnology, Harvard University. Cambridge, Mass.:
  Peabody Museum, 1952.

Kuczynski, Alex. "Now You See It, Now You Don't." *New York Times*, September 12, 2004, https://www
    .nytimes.com/2004/09/12/fashion/now-you-see-it-now-you-dont.html.
Kuki, Shūzō. *Reflections on Japanese Taste: The Structure of Iki*. Translated by John Clark. Sydney: Power,
    1997.
Kulka, Tomáš. *Kitsch and Art*. University Park: Pennsylvania State University Press, 1996.
Kuo, Lucas, and Jason Arterburn. *Lux and Loaded: Exposing North Korea's Strategic Procurement Networks*.
    Center for Advanced Defense Studies, 2019, https://static1.squarespace.com/static/566ef8b4d8af107
    232d5358a/t/5d307a43bf42140001877def/1563458128965/Lux+%26+Loaded.pdf.
Lamont, Michèle, and Annette Lareau. "Cultural Capital: Allusions, Gaps and Glissandos in Recent
    Theoretical Developments." *Sociological Theory* 6 (1988): 153–68.
Lanin, Misha. "Russia's Airbrushed Car Scene Is Out of Control." *Jalopnik*, November 2, 2020, https://
    jalopnik.com/russias-airbrushed-car-scene-is-out-of-control-1843107995.
Lauer, Alex. "Why Pickup Trucks Keep Getting Bigger and Bigger." *Inside Hook*, September 6, 2019,
    https://www.insidehook.com/article/vehicles/why-pickup-trucks-keep-getting-bigger.
Laver, James. *Dandies*. Worcester, U.K.: Trinity Press, 1968.
———. *Taste and Fashion: From the French Revolution to the Present Day*. London: George G. Harrap, 1937.
Leach, Edmund. *Culture and Communication: The Logic by Which Symbols Are Connected*. Cambridge:
    Cambridge University Press, 1976.
Leary, Timothy. *The Politics of Ecstasy*. New York: Putnam, 1986.
Lebrecht, Norman. *The Book of Musical Anecdotes*. New York: Free Press, 1985.
Leibenstein, H. "Bandwagon, Snob, and Veblen Effects in the Theory of Consumers' Demand." *Quar-
    terly Journal of Economics* 64, no. 2 (May 1950): 183–207.
Leighton, Ralph. *Tuva or Bust!* New York: W. W. Norton, 1991.
LeMay, Matt. "Liz Phair: Liz Phair." *Pitchfork*, June 24, 2003, https://pitchfork.com/reviews/albums/6255
    -liz-phair/.
Leonard, George, and Robert Leonard. "Sha Na Na and the Woodstock Generation." *Columbia College
    Today*, Spring/Summer 1989, 28, http://www.georgeleonard.com/sha-na-na-and-the-woodstock
    -generation.htm.
Lévi-Strauss, Claude. *Structural Anthropology*. Translated by Claire Jacobson and Brooke Grundfest
    Schoepf. Garden City, N.Y.: Anchor, 1963.
Levine, Joshua. "The New, Nicer Nero." *Smithsonian Magazine*, October 2020.
Levitin, Daniel J. *This Is Your Brain on Music: The Science of a Human Obsession*. New York: Dutton, 2006.
Levy, Steven. "'Hackers' and 'Information Wants to Be Free.'" *Backchannel*, November 22, 2014, https://
    medium.com/backchannel/the-definitive-story-of-information-wants-to-be-free-a8d95427641c.
Lewis, David. *Convention*. Oxford: Blackwell, 2002.
Lewis, Frederick. "Britons Succumb to 'Beatlemania.'" *New York Times*, December 1, 1963, https://www
    .nytimes.com/1963/12/01/archives/britons-succumb-to-beatlemania.html.
Lewis, Neil A. "The Politicization of Tasseled Loafers." *New York Times*, November 3, 1993, https://www
    .nytimes.com/1993/11/03/garden/the-politicization-of-tasseled-loafers.html.
Lewis, Peter. *The Fifties*. London: Heinemann, 1978.
Lewisohn, Mark. *The Beatles, All These Years*. Vol. 1, *Tune In*. Extended spec. ed. London: Little, Brown, 2013.
Lieberson, Stanley. *A Matter of Taste: How Names, Fashions, and Culture Change*. New Haven, Conn.: Yale
    University Press, 2000.
Lindholm, Charles. *Culture and Authenticity*. Malden, Mass.: Blackwell, 2008.
Linton, Ralph. *The Study of Man: An Introduction*. New York: Appleton-Century-Crofts, 1936.
Lipovetsky, Gilles. *Hypermodern Times*. Translated by Andrew Brown. Cambridge: Polity, 2005.
Liu, Marian. "How a Taiwanese Whisky Became a Global Favorite." *CNN Travel*, September 15, 2017,
    https://edition.cnn.com/travel/article/taiwan-whisky-kavalan/index.html.
Lorenz, Taylor. "On the Internet, No One Knows You're Not Rich. Except This Account." *New York Times*,
    November 11, 2019.
Lurie, Alison. *The Language of Clothes*. New York: Henry Holt, 2000.
Lynch, Annette, and Mitchell D. Strauss. *Changing Fashion: A Critical Introduction to Trend Analysis and
    Meaning*. Oxford: Berg, 2007.
Lynes, Russell. "How Shoe Can You Get?" *Esquire*, September 1953.
———. *The Tastemakers*. New York: Dover, 1980.
M, Ramses. *How Kanye West Got Started: Lessons from a Legend (How It All Got Started)*. Purple Circus
    Productions, 2015.

MacDonald, Ian. *Revolution in the Head: The Beatles' Records and the Sixties.* 2nd rev. ed. London: Vintage, 2008.

Macilwee, Michael. *The Teddy Boy Wars.* Preston, Eng.: Milo Books, 2015.

Mackay, Charles. *Extraordinary Popular Delusions and the Madness of Crowds.* New York: Three Rivers Press, 1980.

Mackintosh, Kit. *Neon Screams: How Drill, Trap and Bashment Made Music New Again.* London: Repeater Books, 2021.

Maglaty, Jeanne. "When Did Girls Start Wearing Pink?" *Smithsonian Magazine,* April 7, 2011, https://www.smithsonianmag.com/arts-culture/when-did-girls-start-wearing-pink-1370097.

Mailer, Norman. "The White Negro." *Advertisements for Myself.* Cambridge, Mass.: Harvard University Press, 1959.

Mann, Ron (director). *Twist.* Alliance Entertainment, 1992.

Marcuse, Herbert. *One-Dimensional Man: Studies in the Ideology of Advanced Industrial Society.* Boston: Beacon, 1964.

Marx, Karl. "The Eighteenth Brumaire of Louis Bonaparte." In *The Marx-Engels Reader,* edited by Robert C. Tucker. New York: W. W. Norton, 1972.

Marx, W. David. *Ametora: How Japan Saved American Style.* New York: Basic Books, 2015.

———. "The History of the Gyaru—Part One." *Néojaponisme,* February 28, 2012, https://neojaponisme.com/2012/02/28/the-history-of-the-gyaru-part-one/.

———. "The History of the Gyaru—Part Two." *Néojaponisme,* May 8, 2012, https://neojaponisme.com/2012/05/08/the-history-of-the-gyaru-part-two/.

———. "The History of the Gyaru—Part Three." *Néojaponisme,* June 6, 2012, https://neojaponisme.com/2012/06/06/the-history-of-the-gyaru-part-three/.

———. "An Open Letter to Kanye West from the Association of French Bakers." *Medium.com,* August 13, 2013, https://medium.com/@wdavidmarx/an-open-letter-to-kanye-west-from-the-association-of-french-bakers-377952a582eb.

Mashburn, Sid. "The Most Stylish Men Ever to Wear a Watch." *Hodinkee,* April 28, 2021, https://www.hodinkee.com/articles/the-most-stylish-men-ever-to-wear-a-watch.

Matos, Michaelangelo. *The Underground Is Massive.* New York: Dey Street, 2015.

Matousek, Mark. "These Are the 16 Most Unreliable Car Brands for 2020." *Business Insider,* February 27, 2020, https://www.businessinsider.com/most-unreliable-car-brands-for-2020-jd-power-2020-2.

McClay, B. D. "Let People Enjoy This Essay." *Gawker,* August 19, 2021, https://www.gawker.com/culture/let-people-enjoy-this-essay.

McCluney, Courtney L., Kathrina Robotham, Serenity Lee, Richard Smith, and Myles Durkee. "The Costs of Code-Switching." *Harvard Business Review,* November 15, 2019, https://hbr.org/2019/11/the-costs-of-codeswitching.

McCracken, Grant David. *Culture and Consumption: New Approaches to the Symbolic Character of Consumer Goods and Activities.* Bloomington: Indiana University Press, 1988.

———. "Culture and Consumption: A Theoretical Account of the Structure and Movement of the Cultural Meaning of Consumer Goods." *Journal of Consumer Research* 13, no. 1 (1986): 71–84.

McGuckin, Nancy, and Nanda Srinivasan. "Journey-to-Work Trends in the United States and Its Major Metropolitan Areas, 1960–2000." United States Federal Highway Administration, June 30, 2003, https://rosap.ntl.bts.gov/view/dot/5543.

McKenna, Kathleen. "Edna Hibel, at 97; Versatile Creator of Many Works of Art." *Boston Globe,* December 24, 2014, https://www.bostonglobe.com/metro/obituaries/2014/12/24/edna-hibel-prolific-artist-created-thousands-works-many-forms/lEbyFWJyqftepXgVP5orlN/story.html.

McKeon, Lucy. "The True Story of Rastafari." *New York Review of Books,* January 6, 2017, https://www.nybooks.com/daily/2017/01/06/the-true-story-of-rastafari/.

McLuhan, Marshall. *Understanding Media: The Extensions of Man.* London: Routledge Classics, 1964.

McWhorter, John H. *The Language Hoax: Why the World Looks the Same in Any Language.* Oxford: Oxford University Press, 2014.

Meany, Paul. "First Principles: What America's Founders Learned from the Greeks and Romans and How That Shaped Our Country." *Cato Journal,* Spring/Summer 2021.

Mears, Ashley. *Very Important People: Status and Beauty in the Global Party Circuit.* Princeton, N.J.: Princeton University Press, 2020.

Menand, Louis. "Finding It at the Movies." *New York Review of Books,* March 23, 1995.

Mencken, H. L. "Professor Veblen." In *Prejudices, First Series.* New York: Alfred A. Knopf, 1919.

Mercer, Kobena. "Black Hair/Style Politics (1987)." In *The Subcultures Reader*, edited by Sarah Thornton and Ken Gelder. London: Routledge, 1997.

Meyer, Leonard B. *Music, the Arts, and Ideas: Patterns and Predictions in Twentieth-Century Culture*. Chicago: University of Chicago Press, 1967.

Meyersohn, Rolf, and Elihu Katz. "Notes on a Natural History of Fads." *American Journal of Sociology* 62, no. 6 (1957): 594–601.

Miles, Barry. *The Zapple Diaries: The Rise and Fall of the Last Beatles Label*. New York: Abrams Image, 2016.

Miller, Daniel. *Material Culture and Mass Consumption*. Oxford: Basil Blackwell, 1987.

Miller, Rylan. "A Middle Eastern Businessman Just Paid $8 Million for a Gold-Plated Rolls Royce." *Business Insider*, August 4, 2011, https://www.businessinsider.com/gold-plated-rolls-royce-2011-8.

Mitford, Nancy, ed. *Noblesse Oblige: An Enquiry into the Identifiable Characteristics of the English Aristocracy*. New York: Harper & Brothers, 1956.

Monahan, Sean. "Video Games Have Replaced Music as the Most Important Aspect of Youth Culture." *Guardian*, January 11, 2021.

Money Kicks. "My New LV Supreme Ferrari." *YouTube*, August 4, 2017. https://www.youtube.com/watch?v=4TwTtH4DCCc; accessed June 7, 2021.

Moretti, Franco. *Graphs, Maps, Trees: Abstract Models for Literary History*. London: Verso, 2005.

Morris, Bob. "The Age of Dissonance: Babes in Adultland." *New York Times*, June 3, 2001, https://www.nytimes.com/2001/06/03/style/the-age-of-dissonance-babes-in-adultland.html.

Morris, Desmond. *The Human Zoo*. New York: Dell, 1969.

Moskin, Julia. "Once Just a Cupcake, These Days a Swell." *New York Times*, November 5, 2003, https://www.nytimes.com/2003/11/05/dining/once-just-a-cupcake-these-days-a-swell.html.

Mötley Crüe and Neil Strauss. *The Dirt: Confessions of the World's Most Notorious Rock Band*. New York: Regan/HarperCollins, 2002.

Muggleton, David. *Inside Subculture: The Postmodern Meaning of Style*. Oxford: Berg, 2002.

Muggleton, David, and Rupert Weinzierl. *The Post-Subcultures Reader*. New York: Berg, 2003.

Mulhern, Francis. *Culture/Metaculture*. London: Routledge, 2000.

Mull, Amanda. "The New Trophies of Domesticity." *The Atlantic*, January 30, 2020, https://www.theatlantic.com/health/archive/2020/01/kitchenaid-le-creuset-peak-domesticity/605716/.

Myers, Rollo H. *Erik Satie*. New York: Dover, 1968.

Nanba, Kōji. *Yankii shinkaron* (The evolution of Yankii). Tokyo: Kōbunsha, 2009.

Nathanson, Elizabeth. "Sweet Sisterhood: Cupcakes as Sites of Feminized Consumption and Production." In *Cupcakes, Pinterest, and Ladyporn*, edited by Elana Levine. Urbana: University of Illinois Press, 2015.

Neate, Rupert. "How an American Woman Rescued Burberry, a Classic British Label." *Guardian*, June 15, 2013, https://www.theguardian.com/business/2013/jun/16/angela-ahrendts-burberry-chav-image.

Neuendorf, Henri. "Here's What Japanese Billionaire Yusaku Maezawa Has Bought So Far at the Auctions." *Artnet*, May 12, 2016, https://news.artnet.com/market/see-japanese-collector-yusaku-maezawa-bought-far-auction-495899.

Newham, Fraser. "The Ties That Bind." *Guardian*, March 21, 2005, https://www.theguardian.com/world/2005/mar/21/china.gender.

Nicolson, Benedict. "Post-Impressionism and Roger Fry." *Burlington Magazine* 93, no. 574 (1951): 11–15, http://www.jstor.org/stable/870622.

Nietzsche, Friedrich. *Beyond Good and Evil*. Harmondsworth, Eng.: Penguin, 1973.

Norton, Marcy. *Sacred Gifts, Profane Pleasures: A History of Tobacco and Chocolate in the Atlantic World*. Ithaca, N.Y.: Cornell University Press, 2008.

Nozick, Robert. *The Nature of Rationality*. Princeton, N.J.: Princeton University Press, 1993.

Nudson, Rae. "A History of Women Who Burned to Death in Flammable Dresses." *Racked*, December 19, 2017, https://www.racked.com/2017/12/19/16710276/burning-dresses-history.

Nystrom, Paul. *Economics of Fashion*. New York: Ronald Press, 1928.

O'Brien, Glenn, and Jean-Philippe Delhomme. *How to Be a Man*. New York: Rizzoli, 2011.

O'Connor, Maureen. "Kanye West Wore a WWJD Bracelet." *The Cut*, July 12, 2013, https://www.thecut.com/2013/07/kanye-west-wore-a-wwjd-bracelet.html.

O'Haver, Hanson. "The Great Irony-Level Collapse." *Gawker*, November 9, 2011, https://www.gawker.com/culture/the-great-irony-level-collapse.

Olson, Mancur. *The Logic of Collective Action: Public Goods and the Theory of Groups*. Cambridge, Mass.: Harvard University Press, 1971.

Orsi, Agi (producer), Stacy Peralta (director and writer), Craig Stecyk (writer), and Sean Penn (narrator). *Dogtown and Z-Boys*. 2002. Sony Pictures Classics.

Ortega y Gasset, José. *The Revolt of the Masses*. New York: W. W. Norton, 1932.

Orwell, George. "Why I Write." In *Essays*. New York: Penguin Modern Classics, 2000.

Osterweil, Vicky. "What Was the Nerd?" *Real Life*, November 16, 2016, https://reallifemag.com/what-was-the-nerd/.

Otterson, Joe. "'Game of Thrones' Season 8 Premiere Draws 17.4 Million Viewers, Sets Multi-Platform Record." *Variety*, April 15, 2019.

Ozzi, Dan. "Rock Is Dead, Thank God." *Noisey*, June 15, 2018, https://www.vice.com/en/article/a3aqkj/rock-is-dead-thank-god.

Packard, Vance. *The Pyramid Climbers*. Harmondsworth, Eng.: Pelican Books, 1962.

———. *The Status Seekers*. Harmondsworth, Eng.: Penguin, 1959.

Parkin, Frank. "Social Stratification." In *A History of Sociological Analysis*, edited by Tom Bottomore and Robert Nisbet. London: Heinemann, 1978.

Parsons, Talcott. *The Social System*. New York: Free Press, 1951.

Paskin, Willa. "An Oral History of 'Friday.'" *Slate*, May 22, 2020, https://slate.com/culture/2020/05/rebecca-black-friday-oral-history.html.

Pearce, Sheldon. "The Futility of Rolling Stone's Best-Albums List." *New Yorker*, October 2, 2020, https://www.newyorker.com./culture/cultural-comment/the-futility-of-rolling-stones-best-albums-list.

Pendlebury, Richard. "Spent, Spent, Spent—Pools Winner Now Living on £87 a Week." *Daily Mail*, April 22, 2007, http://www.dailymail.co.uk/femail/article-449820/Spent-spent-spent—pools-winner-living-87-week.html.

Peterson, R. A. "Understanding Audience Segmentation: From Elite and Mass to Omnivore and Univore." *Poetics* 21, no. 4 (1992): 243–58.

Piesman, Marissa, and Marilee Hartley. *The Yuppie Handbook: The State-of-the-Art Manual for Young Urban Professionals*. New York: Pocket, 1984.

Pinker, Steven. *How the Mind Works*. London: Penguin, 1997.

Pitchfork. "Pitchfork Reviews: Rescored." *Pitchfork*, October 5, 2021.

Plassmann, Hilke, et al. "Marketing Actions Can Modulate Neural Representations of Experienced Pleasantness." *Proceedings of the National Academy of Sciences* 105, no. 3 (January 2008): 1050–54.

Pliny (the Elder). *The Natural History of Pliny*. Vol. 2. London: H. G. Bohn, 1855.

Podolny, Joel M. *Status Signals: A Sociological Study of Market Competition*. Princeton, N.J.: Princeton University Press, 2005.

Poggioli, Renato. *The Theory of the Avant-Garde*. Cambridge, Mass.: Belknap/Harvard University Press, 1968.

Pogue, David. "Trying Out the Zune: IPod It's Not." *New York Times*, November 9, 2006, https://www.nytimes.com/2006/11/09/technology/09pogue.html.

Popescu, Adam. "Inside the Private, Celebrity-Friendly Terminal at LAX." *Vanity Fair*, August 16, 2017, https://www.vanityfair.com/style/2017/08/inside-the-private-celebrity-friendly-terminal-at-lax.

Pountain, Dick, and David Robins. *Cool Rules: Anatomy of an Attitude*. London: Reaktion, 2000.

Pressler, Jessica. "Maybe She Had So Much Money She Just Lost Track of It. Somebody Had to Foot the Bill for Anna Delvey's Fabulous New Life. The City Was Full of Marks." *The Cut*, May 28, 2018.

Prichep, Deena. "The Gefilte Fish Line: A Sweet and Salty History of Jewish Identity." *NPR: The Salt*, September 24, 2014, https://www.npr.org/sections/thesalt/2014/09/24/351185646/the-gefilte-fish-line-a-sweet-and-salty-history-of-jewish-identity.

Princeton University. "In a Split Second, Clothes Make the Man More Competent in the Eyes of Others." *Phys.org*, December 9, 2019, https://phys.org/news/2019-12-eyes.html.

Proust, Marcel. *In Search of Lost Time*. Vol. 1, *Swann's Way*. Translated by C. K. Scott Moncrieff, Terence Kilmartin, and D. J. Enright. New York: Modern Library, 2003.

Quartz, Steven, and Annette Asp. *Cool: How the Brain's Hidden Quest for Cool Drives Our Economy and Shapes Our World*. New York: Farrar Straus Giroux, 2015.

Quirk, Justin. *Nothin' but a Good Time*. London: Unbound, 2021.

Read, Herbert. *Art and Society*. New York: Schocken, 1966.

Reilly, Nick. "'Lynchian,' 'Tarantinoesque' and 'Kubrickian' Lead New Film Words Added to Oxford English Dictionary." *NME.com*, October 5, 2018, https://www.nme.com/news/lynchian-tarantinoesque-and-kubrickian-lead-new-film-words-added-to-oxford-english-dictionary-definition-2387041.

Renfrew, Colin. "Varna and the Emergence of Wealth in Prehistoric Europe." In *The Social Life of Things*, edited by Arjun Appadurai. Cambridge: Cambridge University Press, 1986.

Resnikoff, Paul. "Nearly Half of All Charting Songs Are One-Hit Wonders." *Digital Music News*, March 11, 2012, https://www.digitalmusicnews.com/2012/03/11/charting/.

Reuter, Dominick. "Meet the Typical Whole Foods Shopper, a Highly Educated West Coast Millennial Woman Earning $80,000." *Business Insider*, August 5, 2021, https://www.businessinsider.com/typical-whole-foods-shopper-demographic-millennial-woman-earning-middle-income-2021-8.

Reynolds, Simon. *Retromania: Pop Culture's Addiction to Its Own Past*. New York: Farrar Straus Giroux, 2011.

Richarz, Allan. "40 Years Ago, Okinawans Returned to Driving on the Left." *Atlas Obscura*, July 30, 2018, https://www.atlasobscura.com/articles/730-monument.

Ridgeway, Cecilia L. *Status: Why Is It Everywhere? Why Does It Matter?* New York: Russell Sage Foundation, 2019.

Rizvic, Sejla. "Everybody Hates Millennials: Gen Z and the TikTok Generation Wars." *The Walrus*, February 9, 2021, https://thewalrus.ca/everybody-hates-millennials-gen-z-and-the-tiktok-generation-wars/.

Roberts, Adam. *Frederic Jameson*. London: Routledge, 2000.

Robinson, Dwight E. "The Economics of Fashion Demand." *Quarterly Journal of Economics* 75, no. 3 (August 1961): 376–98.

Robinson, Joe. "TV's Most Surreal Music Performances: Beck, Thurston Moore and Mike D." *Diffuser*, March 13, 2014, https://diffuser.fm/beck-thurston-moore-mike-d-120-minutes.

Rodrick, Stephen. "The Trouble with Johnny Depp." *Rolling Stone*, June 21, 2018, https://www.rollingstone.com/feature/the-trouble-with-johnny-depp-666010/.

"Roger Eliot Fry (1866–1934)." King's College Cambridge. https://www.kings.cam.ac.uk/archive-centre/roger-eliot-fry-1866-1934.

Rogers, Everett M. *Diffusion of Innovations*. 5th ed. New York: Free Press, 2003.

———. *The Fourteenth Paw: Growing Up on an Iowa Farm in the 1930s*. Singapore: Asian Media Information and Communication Centre (AMIC), 2008.

Rosen, Christine. "Teens Who Say No to Social Media." *Wall Street Journal*, August 25, 2016.

Rosen, Jody. "The Perils of Poptimism." *Slate*, May 9, 2006, https://slate.com/culture/2006/05/does-hating-rock-make-you-a-music-critic.html.

Rosenberg, Harold. *The Tradition of the New*. New York: Da Capo, 1994.

Rosenblum, Mort. *Chocolate: A Bittersweet Saga of Dark and Light*. New York: North Point, 2005.

Ross, Alex. "The John Cage Century." *New Yorker*, September 4, 2012, https://www.newyorker.com/culture/culture-desk/the-john-cage-century.

———. "Searching for Silence." *New Yorker*, September 27, 2010, https://www.newyorker.com/magazine/2010/10/04/searching-for-silence.

Rothenberg, David. *Survival of the Beautiful: Art, Science, and Beauty*. New York: Bloomsbury, 2011.

Rousseau, Jean-Jacques. *A Discourse on Inequality*. Translated by Maurice Cranston. London: Penguin, 1984.

Rowe, Peter. "Ballast Point's Rise, Fall and Sale: Inside Craft Beer's Most Baffling Deal." *Los Angeles Times*, December 12, 2019.

Rus, Mayer. "Inside Rapper Drake's Manor House in Hometown Toronto." *Architectural Digest*, April 8, 2020, https://www.architecturaldigest.com/story/inside-rapper-drakes-hometown-manor-in-toronto.

Russell, Bertrand. *Power*. London: Unwin Paperbacks, 1975.

Russell, Kent. "American Juggalo." *n+1*, Fall 2011, https://nplusonemag.com/issue-12/essays/american-juggalo.

Sahlins, Marshall. *Culture and Practical Reason*. Chicago: University of Chicago Press, 1976.

Sales, Nancy Jo. "The New Rules of Old Money." *Harper's Bazaar*, October 7, 2021, https://www.harpersbazaar.com/culture/features/a37628920/radical-giving-october-2021/.

Salewicz, Chris. *Bob Marley: The Untold Story*. London: Harper, 2009.

Salinger, J. D. *The Catcher in the Rye*. New York: Little, Brown, 1991.

Saltz, Jerry. "Glenn O'Brien and the Avant-Garde That Lost." *Vulture*, April 25, 2017, https://www.vulture.com/2017/04/glenn-obrien-and-the-avant-garde-that-lost.html.

Saner, Emine. "Narendra Modi's Style Tip for World Leaders: Wear a Suit with Your Name Written on It." *Guardian*, January 26, 2015, https://www.theguardian.com/fashion/shortcuts/2015/jan/26/narendra-modi-personlised-pinstripe-suit-fashion-india-barack-obama.

Sanneh, Kelefa. "The Persistence of Prog Rock." *New Yorker*, June 19, 2017, https://www.newyorker.com/magazine/2017/06/19/the-persistence-of-prog-rock.

Sanneh, Kelefa. "The Rap against Rockism." *New York Times*, October 31, 2004, https://www.nytimes
.com/2004/10/31/arts/music/the-rap-against-rockism.html.

Santayana, George. *The Life of Reason: Reason in Religion*. New York: Charles Scribner's Sons, 1905.

Sapir, Edward. "Fashion." In *Encyclopaedia of the Social Sciences*, 139–44. Vol. 6. New York: Macmillan,
1931.

———. *Language: An Introduction to the Study of Speech*. New York: Harcourt, Brace, 1921.

Sartre, Jean-Paul. *Existentialism and Human Emotions*. New York: Carol Publishing Group, 1993.

Satō, Ikuya. *Kamikaze Biker: Parody and Anomy in Affluent Japan*. Chicago: University of Chicago Press,
1991.

Sawyer, Jonathan. "Jay-Z's Wild Car Collection Is Fitting for Hip-Hop's First Billionaire." *High Snobiety*,
September 11, 2020, https://www.highsnobiety.com/p/jay-z-car-collection/.

Schmidt, Liane, Vasilisa Skvortsova, Claus Kullen, Bernd Weber, and Hilke Plassmann. "How Context
Alters Value: The Brain's Valuation and Affective Regulation System Link Price Cues to Experienced
Taste Pleasantness." *Scientific Reports* 7, article 8098 (2017), https://www.nature.com/articles/s41598
-017-08080-0.

Schoeck, Helmut. *Envy: A Theory of Social Behavior*. Translated by Martin Secker. Indianapolis: Liberty
Fund, 1987.

Schoeffler, O. E., and William Gale. *Esquire's Encyclopedia of 20th Century Men's Fashion*. New York:
McGraw-Hill, 1973.

Schrad, Mark Lawrence. *Vodka Politics: Alcohol, Autocracy, and the Secret History of the Russian State*.
Oxford: Oxford University Press, 2014.

Schruers, Fred. *Billy Joel*. New York: Three Rivers Press, 2014.

Schwartz, Barry. *The Paradox of Choice*. New York: Harper Perennial, 2004.

Schwyzer, Hugo. "The Real-World Consequences of the Manic Pixie Dream Girl Cliché." *The Atlantic*,
July 10, 2013.

Scott, A. O. *Better Living through Criticism*. New York: Penguin Press, 2016.

Scruton, Roger. *Modern Culture*. London: Bloomsbury, 2000.

Scura, Dorothy M., ed. *Conversations with Tom Wolfe*. Jackson: University Press of Mississippi, 1990.

Seabrook, John. *Nobrow: The Culture of Marketing, the Marketing of Culture*. New York: Alfred A. Knopf,
2000.

Segall, Marshall H., Donald T. Campbell, and Melville J. Herskovit. "The Influence of Culture on Visual
Perception." In *Social Perception*, edited by Hans Toch and Clay Smith. Indianapolis: Bobbs-Merrill,
1968.

Shafer, Jack. "Bogus Trend Stories, Summer Edition." *Slate*, August 14, 2009, https://slate.com/news
-and-politics/2009/08/the-bogus-trend-stories-of-summer-chubby-is-hip-laptoppers-evicted-from
-coffee-shops-diy-burial.html.

Shams, Samar. "We Will All Be Artists in the Future." *Future of Work Hub*, March 19, 2018, https://www
.futureofworkhub.info/comment/2018/3/19/we-will-all-be-artists-in-the-future.

Shattuck, Roger. *The Banquet Years: The Origins of the Avant-Garde in France 1885 to World War I*. Rev. ed.
New York: Vintage, 1968.

Sherman, Elisabeth. "Why Does 'Yellow Filter' Keep Popping Up in American Movies?" *Matador Network*, April 27, 2020, https://matadornetwork.com/read/yellow-filter-american-movies/.

Shippey, Kim. "Always Trying for the Best She Can Do." *Christian Science Sentinel*, June 30, 2003,
https://sentinel.christianscience.com/shared/view/nq9yum1pxc.

Siegler, Mara. "Gaïa Matisse Doesn't Care if You Think She's Just a 'Blond with Big Boobs.'" *Page Six*,
March 29, 2016, https://pagesix.com/2016/03/29/gaia-matisse-doesnt-care-if-you-think-shes-just-a
-blond-with-big-boobs/.

Sietsema, Robert. "Me and Magnolia: Life before and after the Cupcake Bomb Went Off." *Eater*, July 14,
2016, https://ny.eater.com/2016/7/14/12189132/magnolia-and-me.

Silverman, Rachel Emma. "It Was 35 Years Ago This Weekend That Haircuts Lost Their Luster." *Wall
Street Journal*, February 5, 1999.

Simmel, Georg. *On Individuality and Social Forms*. Edited by Donald N. Levine. Chicago: University of
Chicago Press, 1971.

———. *Simmel on Culture: Selected Writings*. Edited by David Frisby and Mike Featherstone. London:
Sage Publications, 1998.

The Simpsons. Season 6, episode 21, "The PTA Disbands." Directed by Swinton O. Scott III. FOX, April
16, 1995.

———. Season 7, episode 13, "Two Bad Neighbors." Directed by Wes Archer. FOX, January 14, 1996.
———. Season 8, episode 10, "The Springfield Files." Directed by Steven Dean Moore. FOX, January 12, 1997.
Sinfield, Alan. *Literature, Politics and Culture in Postwar Britain*. London: Continuum, 2007.
Skyrms, Brian. *Signals: Evolution, Learning, and Information*. Oxford: Oxford University Press, 2010.
Sloan, Alfred P., Jr. *My Years with General Motors*. Edited by John McDonald with Catharine Stevens. New York: Macfadden-Bartell, 1965.
Smith, Adam. *The Theory of Moral Sentiments*. Amherst, N.Y.: Prometheus, 2000.
Smith, Barbara Herrnstein. *Contingencies of Value: Alternative Perspectives for Critical Theory*. Cambridge, Mass.: Harvard University Press, 1988.
Smith, Noah. "For Corrosive Inequality, Look to the Upper Middle Class." *Bloomberg*, December 24, 2020.
———. "Redistribute Wealth? No, Redistribute Respect." *Noahpinion*, December 27, 2013, http://noahpinionblog.blogspot.com/2013/12/redistribute-wealth-no-redistribute.html.
Smoker 1. "Harvestore Silos" in General Chat. *Red Power Magazine*, September 1, 2017, https://www.redpowermagazine.com/forums/topic/109603-harvestore-silos/; accessed December 7, 2021.
Sobel, Ben. "Don't Be a Kook: The GQ Guide to Surf Etiquette." *GQ*, July 8, 2013, https://www.gq.com/story/kook-surf-etiquette-guide-2013.
Sola. "Mugabe Amassed $1bn—Including a Rare Rolls-Royce Worth More Than Zimbabwe's Economy." *Punch*, November 23, 2017, https://punchng.com/mugabe-amassed-1bn-including-a-rare-rolls-royce-worth-more-than-zimbabwes-economy/.
Solmonson, Lesley Jacobs. *Gin: A Global History*. London: Reaction, 2012.
Sombart, Werner. *Luxury and Capitalism*. Translated by W. R. Dittmar. Ann Arbor: University of Michigan Press, 1967.
Sontag, Susan. *Against Interpretation*. New York: Delta, 1966.
Sorokin, Pitirim A. *Social and Cultural Dynamics*. Vol. 1, *Fluctuation of Forms of Art*. New York: Bedminster, 1962.
Spence, Michael. "Job Market Signaling." *Quarterly Journal of Economics* 87, no. 3 (August 1973): 355–74, https://doi.org/10.2307/1882010.
Spitz, Bob. *The Beatles*. New York: Back Bay, 2006.
Spivack, Emily. "Why Hypercolor T-shirts Were Just a One-Hit Wonder." *Smithsonian Magazine*, January 22, 2013, https://www.smithsonianmag.com/arts-culture/why-hypercolor-t-shirts-were-just-a-one-hit-wonder-3353436/.
The State. Season 3, episode 5, "Dan, the Very Popular Openly Gay High School Student." MTV, 1995.
Steinworth, Bailey. "Jordan Peterson Needs to Reconsider the Lobster." *Washington Post*, June 4, 2018, https://www.washingtonpost.com/news/posteverything/wp/2018/06/04/jordan-peterson-needs-to-reconsider-the-lobster/.
Stephens-Davidowitz, Seth. *Everybody Lies: Big Data, New Data, and What the Internet Can Tell Us about Who We Really Are*. New York: Dey Street, 2017.
Stern, Carly. "Battle of the Bags! Blue Ivy Carries a $1,800 Louis Vuitton Purse to the NBA All Star Game, while Beyonce Opts for a $1,400 Celine—but Neither Compares to Grandma Tina's $4,700 Gucci." *Daily Mail*, February 19, 2018.
Stillman, Whit (director and writer). *Metropolitan*. 1990. New Line Cinema.
Stukin, Stacie. "The Ice Age." *Vibe*, August 2004.
Suetonius. "The Life of Nero." In *The Lives of the Caesars*. Cambridge, Mass.: Loeb Classical Library, 1914.
Sumner, William Graham. *Folkways*. New York: Dover, 1959.
Sylvester, Nick. "The Internet Doesn't Matter, You're Making Music in L.A." *New York*, August 8, 2017, https://www.vulture.com/2017/08/why-is-los-angeles-a-great-place-to-make-pop-music.html.
Syme, Rachel. "The Second Life of Princess Diana's Most Notorious Sweater." *New Yorker*, November 20, 2020, https://www.newyorker.com/culture/on-and-off-the-avenue/the-second-life-of-princess-dianas-most-iconic-sweater.
Talmadge, Stephanie. "The Sisterhood of the Exact Same Pants." *Racked*, August 30, 2017, https://www.racked.com/2017/8/30/16218066/sorority-dress-code-rush-t-shirts.
Tamangi, Daniele. *Gentlemen of Bacongo*. London: Trolley, 2009.
Tarde, Gabriel. *The Laws of Imitation*. Translated by Elsie Clews Parsons. New York: Henry Holt, 1903.
Tashjian, Rachel. "How Stüssy Became the Chanel of Streetwear." *GQ*, May 10, 2021, https://www.gq.com/story/stussy-revival-2021.
Taylor, Charles. *The Ethics of Authenticity*. Cambridge, Mass.: Harvard University Press, 1991.

Taylor, Charles. *Sources of Self: The Making of the Modern Identity*. Cambridge, Mass.: Harvard University Press, 1989.

Teather, David. "Country Life Butter Soars after Johnny Rotten's Star Turn." *Guardian*, February 3, 2009, https://www.theguardian.com/business/2009/feb/03/dairycrestgroup-sexpistols.

Tenbarge, Kat. "The Era of A-list YouTube Celebrities Is Over. Now, the People Cancelling Them Are on Top." *Insider*, October 22, 2020, https://www.insider.com/dangelo-wallace-interview-youtube-shane-jeffree-tati-drama-channels-2020-9.

Theodorson, George A., and Achilles G. Theodorson. *Modern Dictionary of Sociology*. New York: Thomas Y. Crowell, 1969.

Thomas, Dana. *Deluxe: How Luxury Lost Its Luster*. New York: Penguin, 2008.

Thomas, Frankie. "A Queer Reading of *Go Ask Alice*." *Paris Review*, January 22, 2018, https://www.theparisreview.org/blog/2018/01/22/queer-reading-go-ask-alice/.

Thompson, Derek. *Hit Makers: The Science of Popularity in an Age of Distraction*. New York: Penguin Press, 2017.

Thompson, Hunter S. *Hell's Angels*. London: Penguin Books, 1966.

Thompson, Michael. *Rubbish Theory: The Creation and Destruction of Value*. 2nd ed. London: Pluto, 2017.

Thorn, Jesse. "An Interview with Glenn O'Brien." *Put This On*, April 7, 2017, https://putthison.com/an-interview-with-glenn-obrien-glenn-obrien-the/.

Thornton, Sarah. "The Social Logic of Subcultural Capital (1995)." In *The Subcultures Reader*, edited by Sarah Thornton and Ken Gelder. London: Routledge, 1997.

Thornton, Sarah, and Ken Gelder, eds. *The Subcultures Reader*. London: Routledge, 1997.

Timberg, Scott. *Culture Crash: The Killing of the Creative Class*. New Haven, Conn.: Yale University Press, 2015.

Tolentino, Jia. *Trick Mirror: Reflections on Self-Delusion*. London: Fourth Estate, 2019.

Tollin, Michael et al. (producers). *The Last Dance*. 2020. ESPN Films / Netflix.

Tomkins, Calvin. *Ahead of the Game: Four Versions of the Avant-Garde*. Middlesex, Eng.: Penguin, 1968.

———. "The Turnaround Artist: Jeff Koons, Up from Banality." *New Yorker*, April 16, 2007, https://www.newyorker.com/magazine/2007/04/23/the-turnaround-artist.

Trigg, Andrew B. "Veblen, Bourdieu, and Conspicuous Consumption." *Journal of Economic Issues* 35, no. 1 (March 2001): 99–115.

Trillin, Calvin. *American Fried: Adventures of a Happy Eater*. New York: Penguin, 1970.

Trilling, Lionel. *Sincerity and Authenticity*. Cambridge, Mass.: Harvard University Press, 1972.

Trow, George W. S. *Within the Context of No Context*. New York: Atlantic Monthly, 1997.

Turner, Bryan S. *Status*. Milton Keynes, Eng.: Open University Press, 1988.

Turner, Ralph H., and Samuel J. Surace. "Zoot-Suiters and Mexicans: Symbols in Crowd Behavior (1956)." In *The Subcultures Reader*, edited by Sarah Thornton and Ken Gelder. London: Routledge, 1997.

Turner, Victor. *The Ritual Process: Structure and Anti-Structure*. Ithaca, N.Y.: Cornell University Press, 1969.

Ullmann-Margalit, Edna. *The Emergence of Norms*. Oxford: Oxford University Press, 1977.

Vanderbilt, Tom. *You May Also Like: Taste in an Age of Endless Choice*. New York: Alfred A. Knopf, 2016.

Veblen, Thorstein. *The Theory of the Leisure Class*. New York: Penguin, 1994.

Vejlgaard, Henrik. *Anatomy of a Trend*. New York: McGraw-Hill, 2007.

Venugopal, A., and A. Marya. "Return of the Ohaguro." *British Dental Journal* 231, 69 (2021), https://doi.org/10.1038/s41415-021-3280-9.

Vercelloni, Luca. *The Invention of Taste: A Cultural Account of Desire, Delight and Disgust in Fashion, Food and Art*. Translated by Kate Singleton. London: Bloomsbury, 2016.

Vinken, Barbara. *Fashion Zeitgeist: Trends and Cycles in the Fashion System*. Oxford: Berg, 2005.

Virilio, Paul. *Speed and Politics*. Translated by Mark Polizzotti. South Pasadena, Calif.: Semiotext(e), 2006.

Voslarova, Eva, et al. "Breed Characteristics of Abandoned and Lost Dogs in the Czech Republic." *Journal of Applied Animal Welfare Science* 18, no. 4 (2015): 332–42.

Wagner, Kyle. "The Future of the Culture Wars Is Here, and It's Gamergate." *Deadspin*, October 14, 2014, https://deadspin.com/the-future-of-the-culture-wars-is-here-and-its-gamerga-1646145844/.

Wagner, Roy. *The Invention of Culture*. 2nd ed. Chicago: University of Chicago Press, 2016.

Ward, Maria. "At 35, Kate Middleton Already Has an Archive of Memorable Fashion Moments." *Vogue*, January 9, 2017, https://www.vogue.com/article/kate-middleton-birthday-best-looks-celebrity-style.

Warhol, Andy, and Pat Hackett. *POPism: The Warhol Sixties*. Boston: Mariner, 2006.

Waters, John. *Shock Value: A Tasteful Book about Bad Taste*. Philadelphia: Running Press, 2005.

Watts, Duncan J. *Everything Is Obvious: How Common Sense Fails Us*. New York: Crown Business, 2011.

Waugh, Evelyn. "An Open Letter." In *Noblesse Oblige: An Enquiry into the Identifiable Characteristics of the English Aristocracy*, edited by Nancy Mitford. New York: Harper & Brothers, 1956.

Weber, Max. *The Interpretation of Social Reality*. Edited by J. E. T. Eldridge. New York: Schocken, 1980.

———. *Selections in Translation*. Edited by W. G. Runciman, translated by Eric Matthews. Cambridge: Cambridge University Press, 1978.

"The Wedding Album: Jenna Lyons and Vincent Mazeau." *2003 New York Wedding Guide*, September 7, 2002, https://nymag.com/shopping/guides/weddings/album/jennavincent.htm.

Wei, Eugene. "Status as a Service (Staas)." *Remains of the Day*, February 26, 2019, https://www.eugenewei .com/blog/2019/2/19/status-as-a-service.

Weiss, Jeff. "The (Mostly) True Story of Vanilla Ice, Hip-Hop, and the American Dream." *The Ringer*, October 6, 2020, https://www.theringer.com/music/2020/10/6/21494291/vanilla-ice-to-the-extreme -ice-ice-baby-history-30th-anniversary.

Wharton, Edith, and Ogden Codman Jr. *The Decoration of Houses*. New York: Charles Scribner's Sons, 1914. https://www.gutenberg.org/cache/epub/40367/pg40367-images.html.

"What Is Tartan?" The Scottish Tartans Museum and Heritage Center, https://www.scottishtartans museum.org/content.aspx?page_id=22&club_id=170857&module_id=290899.

White, Leslie A. *The Concept of Cultural Systems*. New York: Columbia University Press, 1975.

Wilde, Oscar. "The Philosophy of Dress." *New York Tribune*, April 19, 1885.

Wilkerson, Isabel. *Caste: The Origins of Our Discontents*. New York: Random House, 2020.

Williams, Raymond. *Keywords: A Vocabulary of Culture and Society*. London: Fontana, 1976.

———. *The Sociology of Culture*. Chicago: University of Chicago Press, 1981.

Wilner, Isaiah. "The Number-One Girl." *Nymag.com*, May 4, 2007, https://nymag.com/news/people /31555/.

Wilson, Carl. *Let's Talk about Love: A Journey to the End of Taste*. New York: Bloomsbury, 2007.

Winawer, Jonathan, Nathan Witthoft, Michael C. Frank, Lisa Wu, Alex R. Wade, and Lera Boroditskyl. "Russian Blues Reveal Effects of Language on Color Discrimination." *Proceedings of the National Academy of Sciences* 104, no. 19 (May 2007): 7780–85, https://doi.org/10.1073/pnas.0701644104.

Wittgenstein, Ludwig. *Culture and Value*. Translated by Peter Winch. Chicago: University of Chicago Press, 1980.

———. *Lectures and Conversations: On Aesthetics, Psychology, and Religious Belief*. Edited by Cyril Barrett. Berkeley: University of California Press, 2007.

Wohlforth, William C., and David C. Kang. "Hypotheses on Status Competition (2009)." APSA 2009 Toronto Meeting Paper, https://ssrn.com/abstract=1450467.

Wolfe, Alan. "Taking the Starch Out of Status." *New York Times*, November 15, 1998, https://www.nytimes .com/1998/11/15/magazine/taking-the-starch-out-of-status-783773.html.

Wolfe, Tom. *The Bonfire of the Vanities*. New York: Bantam, 1987.

———. *The Electric Kool-Aid Acid Test*. New York: Bantam, 1968.

———. *From Bauhaus to Our House*. New York: Pocket, 1981.

———. *The Kandy-Kolored Tangerine-Flake Streamline Baby*. New York: Pocket, 1965.

———. *The Painted Word*. New York: Farrar Straus Giroux, 1975.

———. *The Pump House Gang*. New York: Farrar Straus Giroux, 1968.

———. *Radical Chic and Mau-Mauing the Flak Catchers*. New York: Bantam, 1999.

Worboys, Michael, Julie-Marie Strange, and Neil Pemberton. *The Invention of the Modern Dog: Breed and Blood in Victorian Britain*. Baltimore: The Johns Hopkins University Press, 2018.

Wouk, Herman. *The Caine Mutiny*. New York: Back Bay, 1992.

Wyman, Patrick. "American Gentry." *The Atlantic*, September 23, 2021, https://www.theatlantic.com /ideas/archive/2021/09/trump-american-gentry-wyman-elites/620151/.

Yeager, Lyn Allison. *The Icons of the Prairie: Stories of Real People, Real Places, and Real Silos*. Author-House, 2008.

York, Peter. "Trump's Dictator Chic." *Politico*, March/April 2017, https://www.politico.com/magazine /story/2017/03/trump-style-dictator-autocrats-design-214877/.

Yorke, Jeffrey. "Film Talk." *Washington Post*, July 18, 1986, https://www.washingtonpost.com/archive /lifestyle/1986/07/18/film-talk/f7fdaeeb-c96a-409c-82cc-9ebd25ae51ee/.

Yotka, Steff, and Amanda Brooks. "Watch: At Dior, Teddy Girls Take Center Stage." *Vogue*, March 5, 2019, https://www.vogue.com/article/dior-fall-2019-runway-show-video.

Young, Jock. "The Subterranean World of Play (1971)." In *The Subcultures Reader*, edited by Sarah Thornton
    and Ken Gelder. London: Routledge, 1997.
Young, Molly. *The Things They Fancied* (zine). 2020.
Yurcaba, Jo. "Ohio High School Elects a Lesbian Couple as Prom King and Queen." *NBC News*, May 1,
    2021.
Zeki, Semir. "The Neurology of Ambiguity." *Consciousness and Cognition* 13, no. 1 (March 2004): 173–96.
Zemeckis, Robert (director). *Back to the Future*. 1985. Universal Pictures and Amblin Entertainment.

Index

Italicized page numbers indicate material in photographs or illustrations.

trends (*cont.*)
  creative class and, 136
  elite abandonment of, 184, 187
  emulation of high-status behaviors in, 184
  false, 182
  fashion, *see* fashion cycles; fashions
  in internet age, xviii, 243
  laggards and, 196
  media and, 180, 184, 199
  professional class and, 120
  revived, *see* retro
  temporal context of, 218
Trevino, Lee, 9–10
triangulation, 66, 72
trickle-down flow of cultural practices, xix, 126, 141,
      185–86, 238, 244, 257, 270, 271
Trillin, Calvin, 27
Trilling, Diana, 10
Trow, George W. S., 111, 247
Trump, Donald, 22, 239, 250
Turki Bin Abdullah, Prince, 235
Turner, Victor, 6
TV Guide, 113
TV Party, 177
Twitch, 227
"Two Bad Neighbors" (*Simpsons* episode), 71
2 Broke Girls (TV show), 184
Tzara, Tristan, 179–80

Uncut Gems (film), 98
"Under Pressure" (Bowie), 77
upper class, *see* elites; Old Money
USA Today, 179, 223–24

Vanderbilt, Amy, 181
Vanderbilt, Gloria, 59
van Gogh, Vincent, 149
Vanilla Ice, 77, 136
  inauthenticity of, 77, 78, 79, 90–91, 138
Vanity Fair, 252
Van Winkle, Robert Matthew, *see* Vanilla Ice
Veblen, Thorstein, xvii, 41, 45, 56–57, 99, 100, 103,
      115, 170, 198, 263
Veblen effect, 101
Venom (film), 180
vicarious consumption, 100
Vinken, Barbara, 185
Virilio, Paul, 225
virtuosity, 146, 152, 161
Vogue, 113, 178, 180, 186
vogue.com, 230
Voltaire, 37, 70, 208
Volvo, 111–12
Vox, 264

Wagner, Kyle, 249
Walking on the Wall (Brown), 151
Walrus, The, 254
"WAP feat. Megan Thee Stallion" (Cardi B), 229

Warhol, Andy, 12, 153, 157, 159, 162, 177, 213, 215
Warren G, 216
Waters, John, 69, 70, 71, 72, 73, 76, 137, 140
Watts, Duncan, 226, 265
wealth, *see* economic capital
"We Are the Champions" (Queen), 212
Weber, Max, 21, 30, 37, 97
Wegener, Charles, 243
Weibo, 233
Weigel, David, 210
Weiss, Jeff, 77
West, Kanye, 95, 100, 223, 256
"We Will Rock You" (Queen), 212
Wharton, Edith, 79, 148
What's Going On (Gaye), 210
What's My Line (TV show), 177
"What Was the Hipster?" (Greif), 42–43
White, E. B., 36
White, Leslie, 169
Whitehead, Alfred North, 242
"White Negro, The" (Mailer), 127
white supremacy, 239
Wilde, Oscar, 145, 170
Wild One, The (film), 180
Wilkerson, Isabel, 14
Williams, Pharrell, 176
Williams, Raymond, 35
Wilson, Carl, 125, 182
Wilson, Woodrow, 36
Winchester, Earl of, 107
Wind River Reservation, 43
Winklevoss twins, 236
Wired, 229
Wittgenstein, Ludwig, 75, 147
Wolfe, Tom, xvi, 20, 40, 58, 123, 135, 158, 180,
      185, 196
Worboys, Michael, 261
Wordsworth, William, 157
Wouk, Herman, 61
Wyman, Patrick, 239
Wynn, May (char.), 61–62

Xanadu (Newton-John), 52

yamamba, 128
Yeezus (West), 223
Yo! MTV Raps (TV show), 179
Young, Molly, 268
youth, youth cultures, 125–26, 130, 134, 136,
      153, 250
YouTube, 227, 228
Yuppie Handbook, The, 109–10
yuppies, xviii, 95, 109–10, 185
  see also professional class

Zeki, Semir, 270
Zoot Suit Riots, 141
Zuckerberg, Mark, 234, 236, 237
Zune music players, 88